An OPUS book

The Foundations of Buddhism

Rupert Gethin is Lecturer in Indian Religions in the Department of Theology and Religious Studies, and co-director of the Centre for Buddhist Studies, at the University of Bristol. He is author of *The Buddhist Path to Awakening* (1992) and is a specialist in Theravāda Buddhism.

OPUS books provide concise, original, and authoritative introductions to a wide range of subjects in the humanities and social sciences. They are written by experts for the general reader as well as for students.

The Foundations of Buddhism

Rupert Gethin

Oxford New York
OXFORD UNIVERSITY PRESS

OXFORD
UNIVERSITY PRESS

Great Clarendon Street, Oxford OX2 6DP

Oxford University Press is a department of the University of Oxford.
It furthers the University's objective of excellence in research, scholarship,
and education by publishing worldwide in

Oxford New York

Auckland Bangkok Buenos Aires Cape Town Chennai
Dar es Salaam Delhi Hong Kong Istanbul Karachi Kolkata
Kuala Lumpur Madrid Melbourne Mexico City Mumbai Nairobi
São Paulo Shanghai Taipei Tokyo Toronto

First published as an Oxford University Press paperback 1998

British Library Cataloguing in Publication Data
Data available

Library of Congress Cataloging in Publication Data
Gethin, Rupert.
The foundations of Buddhism / Rupert Gethin.
Includes index.
1. Buddhism. I. Title.
BQ4012.G47 1998 294.3—dc21 98-12246

ISBN 0-19-289223-1

9

Typeset by Graphicraft Typesetters Ltd., Hong Kong
Printed in Great Britain by
Clays Ltd, St Ives plc

For my mother

Acknowledgements

My understanding of the Buddhist tradition owes much to many. Some of what is owed and to whom is apparent from the notes and bibliography of the present volume, but some deserve special mention. To Lance Cousins, who first introduced me to Buddhism, I owe a special debt. A number of people have read drafts of parts of this book during the course of its writing; to Lance Cousins, Hugh Gethin, Michael Houser, Rita Langer, Ken Robinson, Alexander von Rospatt, Ornan Rotem, Gregory Schopen, and Paul Williams I am especially grateful for their comments, criticisms, and encouragement. I am also grateful to my students and all those others whose questions and puzzled faces have prompted me to try to express what I understand of Buddhism more clearly. Finally a word of thanks to my editor at OUP, George Miller, for his patience and help.

siddhir astu
śubham astu

Contents

List of Tables and Figure

Tables

Figure

List of Maps

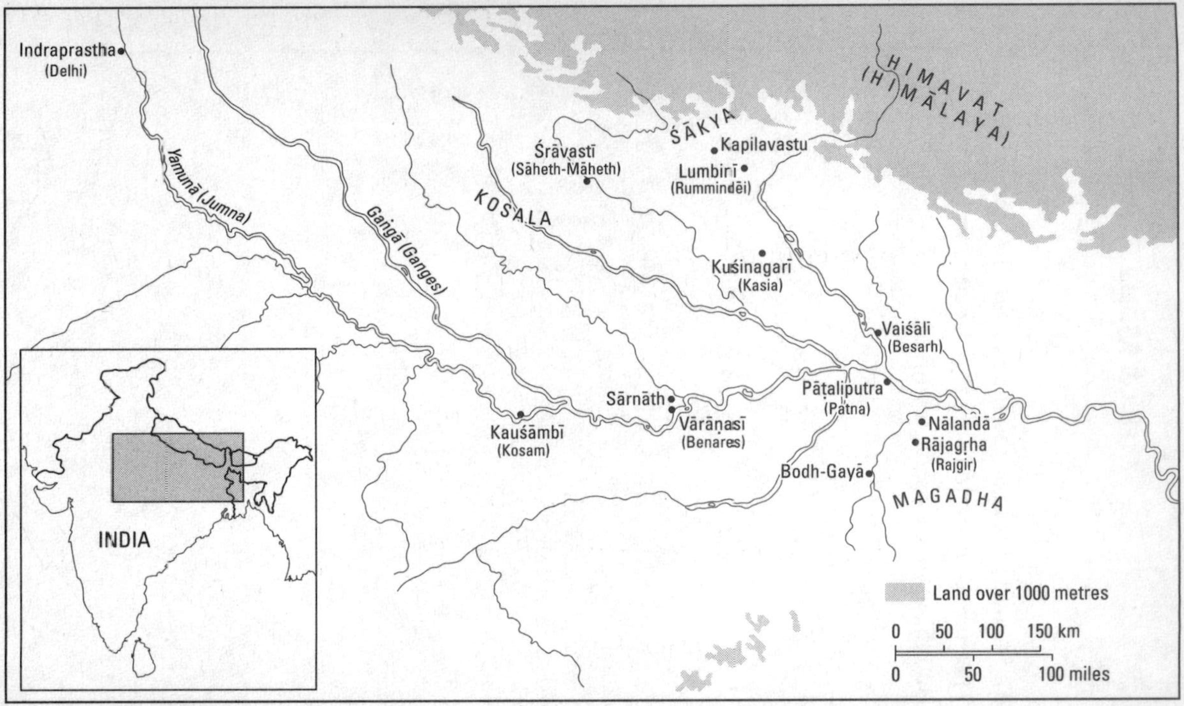

MAP I. *The Ganges basin at the time of the Buddha*

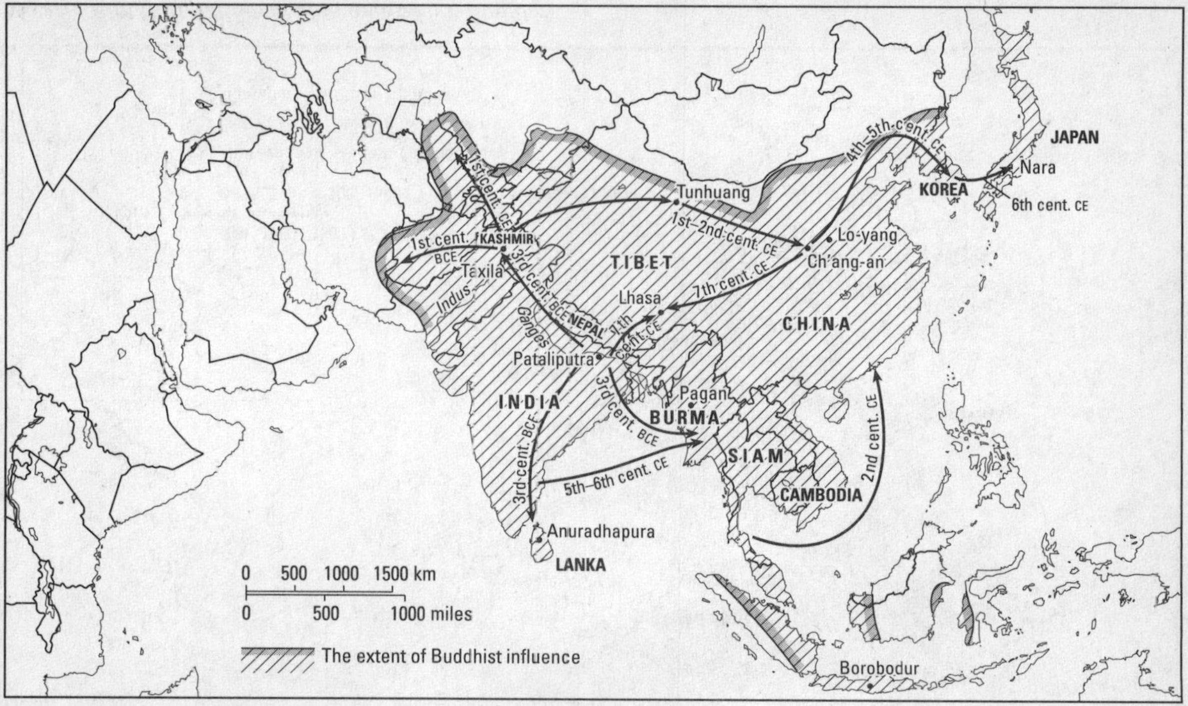

MAP 2. *The spread of Buddhism in the ancient world*

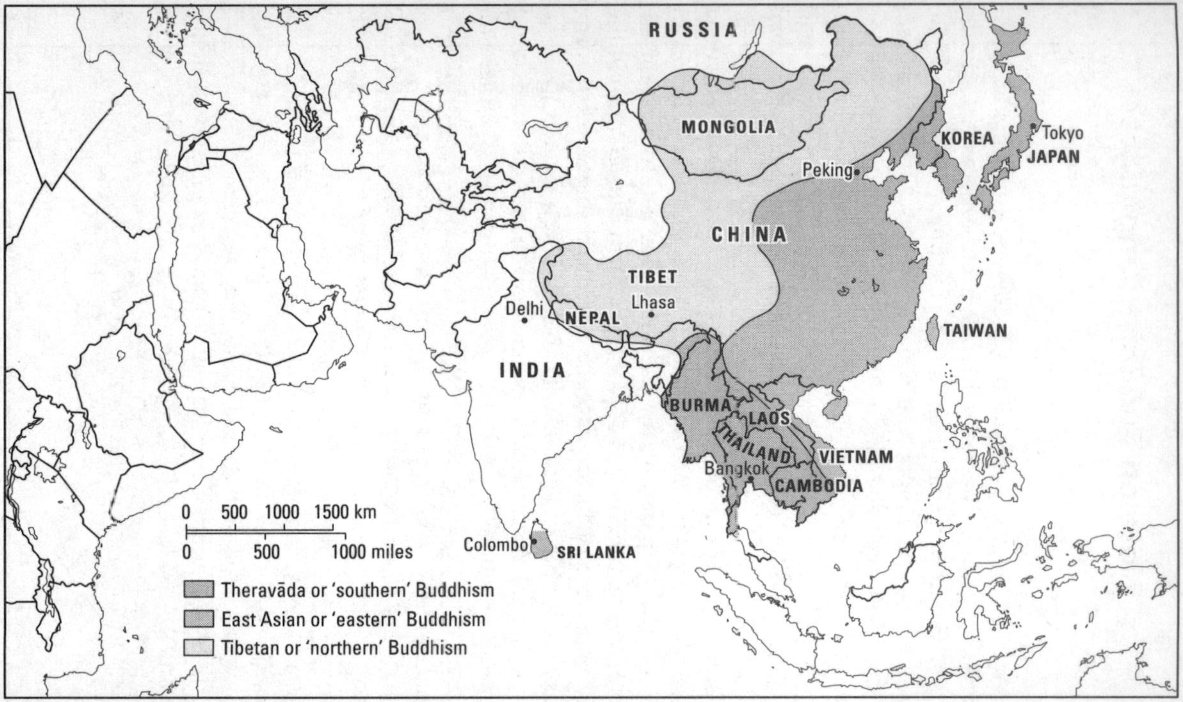

MAP 3. *Buddhism in the modern world*

A Note on Buddhist Languages

The original language of Buddhist thought is problematic. It was not Sanskrit (Old Indo-Aryan) but a closely related Middle Indo-Aryan dialect similar to Pali, the canonical language of the Buddhism of Sri Lanka and South-East Asia. As Buddhism developed in ancient India it tended increasingly to speak the universal language of ancient Indian culture, Sanskrit. Subsequently Buddhist texts were translated into Chinese and Tibetan which became major Buddhist languages in their own right.

The general principle I have adopted is to quote universal Buddhist terms in both Sanskrit and (when there is a difference) Pali, placed in parentheses after the English translation so: 'aggregates' (*skandha/khandha*). If the term is used again in the body of the text I have generally preferred the Sanskrit form, unless the context is exclusively that of Theravāda Buddhism. Terms that are specific or characteristic of a particular Buddhist tradition are quoted in the appropriate language(s), either Pali or Sanskrit with, where appropriate, their Chinese or Tibetan, or occasionally their Japanese or Korean translation.

The transliteration of Indian languages follows the standard transliteration scheme (see A. L. Basham, *The Wonder that Was India*, 506–8); Chinese is quoted according to the Wade–Giles system, rather than Pin-Yin, Tibetan according to the Wylie system. Words that have become part of the English language (i.e. would be found in an English dictionary) are left unitalicized but the appropriate diacritical marks have been added, hence 'nirvāṇa'.

Introduction

The term 'Buddhism' refers to a vast and complex religious and philosophical tradition with a history that stretches over some 2,500 years, taking in, at one time or another, the greater part of Asia, from Afghanistan and parts of Persia in the west to Japan in the east, from the great islands of Sumatra and Java in the south to Mongolia and parts of southern Russia in the north. As one writer reminds us, over half the world's population today lives in areas where Buddhism has at one time or another been the dominant religious influence.[1] Living Buddhism divides into three broad traditions:[2]

1. The Theravāda tradition of Sri Lanka and South-East Asia, also sometimes referred to as 'southern' Buddhism. Its canonical scriptures are preserved in Pali, an ancient Indian language closely related to Sanskrit. The school exemplifies a certain conservatism. Relative to the other two traditions, it can be regarded as *generally* closer in doctrine and practice to ancient Buddhism as it existed in the early centuries BCE in India. Today it is the religious tradition followed by a population of over 100 million in Sri Lanka, Burma, Thailand, Cambodia, and Laos.
2. The East Asian tradition of China, Korea, Japan, and Vietnam, also sometimes referred to as 'eastern' Buddhism. Its scriptures are preserved in Chinese and its general outlook is that of the Mahāyāna or 'Great Vehicle', a movement of ancient Indian Buddhist thought and practice that from about the beginning of the Christian era dubbed those who did not adopt its overall vision of Buddhism—represented today by the Theravāda—followers of the 'Lesser Vehicle' (*hīnayāna*). East Asian Buddhism is extremely diverse; it has coexisted with Confucianism, Taoism,

Shintō, and, more recently but less happily, Communism; it remains a significant religious tradition for a population of 500 million to 1,000 million.

3. The Tibetan tradition, also sometimes referred to as 'northern' Buddhism. Its scriptures are preserved in Tibetan and once more its outlook is broadly that of the Mahāyāna, but its more specific orientation is that of the 'Vehicle of the Diamond Thunderbolt' (*vajra-yāna*), also known as Tantric Buddhism. Today it is the religious tradition followed by 10 million to 20 million, principally in Tibet and Mongolia, but also in parts of Nepal and Himalayan India.

All three of these traditions look back to ancient Buddhism and the land of India, where Buddhism was born but whence it virtually disappeared over five centuries ago.

The present volume was conceived as an introduction to Buddhist thought and practice, and is intended to be accessible to the reader with no previous knowledge of Buddhism. Given its great diversity and its long history, the task of introducing Buddhism is a daunting one. As is fashionable to point out these days, 'Buddhism' is something of an intellectual abstraction: in reality there is not one Buddhism but many Buddhisms. Any writer of an introductory text to Buddhism is faced with the problem of how to do justice to the richness and diversity of Buddhism both past and present. Most of the existing introductory volumes to Buddhism offer their readers some kind of general survey of the different 'Buddhisms', and attempt to give an equal and balanced treatment of all that Buddhism has been and still is. The advantage of this approach is that, ideally if not always in practice, it avoids the pitfall of seeming to imply that one or other form of Buddhism represents a 'truer' form of Buddhism than others, or that one has somehow captured the real essence of Buddhism. Its disadvantage is that, in a volume of some 300 pages, one is in danger of saying very little about an awful lot, and of presenting the reader with what amounts to a catalogue of dates, people, places, doctrines, and practices; a reader may finish such a book, yet somehow *know* very little of Buddhism. For this reason it seems worth while trying to introduce Buddhism in a more explicitly focused way.

The approach I have adopted in the present volume, then, is to try to identify and focus on those fundamental ideas and practices that constitute something of a common heritage shared by the different traditions of Buddhism that exist in the world today. Of course, the precise nature of that common heritage is open to question. Nevertheless, the fact remains that the areas of Buddhist thought and practice outlined in the present volume —the story of the Buddha (Chapter 1), a textual and scriptural tradition (Chapter 2), the framework of the four noble truths (Chapter 3), the monastic and lay ways of life (Chapter 4), a cosmology based around karma and rebirth (Chapter 5), the teaching of no self and dependent arising (Chapter 6), a progressive path of practice leading on from good conduct and devotions through stages of meditation to a higher understanding (Chapter 7), the theoretical systems of either the Abhidharma or the Madyamaka and Yogācāra (Chapters 8 and 9), the path of the bodhisattva (Chapter 9)—are all, in one way or another, assumed by and known to all Buddhism. These are the foundations upon which Buddhism rests.

Of course, I do not mean to suggest by this that a Buddhist layman in Tokyo and a Buddhist laywoman in Bangkok, that a monk in Colombo and a nun in Lhasa, would all respond to questions on these topics precisely along the lines set out in the relevant chapters below. None the less, it is not unreasonable nor, I think, is it to commit oneself to an essentialist view of Buddhism to suggest that, whatever the nature of the Buddhist terrain, one cannot dig much below the surface without coming across some trace of the patterns of thought and practice outlined here, even if at different times and in different places the constructions built on their foundations present their own distinctive and peculiar aspects. Moreover, the fact that those patterns of thought and practice are not immediately apparent does not of itself mean that they exert no influence. That we may not always be consciously aware of particular ideas and theories, or that we may be unable to articulate them in detail, does not mean that those ideas fail to affect our view of the world. The principles of, say, Newtonian physics, Darwinian evolutionary theory, and Freudian psychology contribute to a world-view that is shared by many who have never read a word of what Newton, Darwin, or Freud wrote and would be hard pressed to explain in detail any of their ideas.

I should, however, add that I have not entirely eschewed the general-survey approach; Chapter 9, on specifically Mahāyāna ideas, and especially Chapter 10, an overview of the history of the different traditions of Buddhism in Asia, are intended to give some indication of what I have not covered and provide some form of orientation for further study.

Apart from its simply allowing a more sustained account of some significant aspects of Buddhist thought and practice, there is a further reason why I think focusing on the common heritage as indicated above is appropriate at the introductory level: it affords a perspective on the development of Buddhist thought and practice which calls into question what might be dubbed the standard 'textbook' view and is in fact more in tune with recent scholarship. This textbook view tends to see the history of Buddhism in terms of a division into two major 'sects': the Theravāda and the Mahāyāna. More specifically, according to this 'textbook' view, in origin the Mahāyāna was at once a popular religious protest against the élitist monasticism of early Buddhism and a philosophical refutation of its dead-end scholasticism; moreover, this religious protest and philosophical refutation rapidly all but marginalized earlier forms of Buddhism. The research published in the last twenty years or so has increasingly made such a view of the development of Indian Buddhist thought and practice untenable. The Mahāyāna did not originate as a clearly defined 'sect' and, far from being a popular lay movement, it seems increasingly likely that it began as a minority monastic movement and remained such for several hundred years, down to at least the fifth century CE. Moreover, what is becoming clearer is that many elements of Buddhist thought and practice that were once thought to be characteristic of the emerging Mahāyāna were simply developments within what has been called by some 'mainstream' Buddhism;[3] and while the Mahāyāna certainly criticized aspects of mainstream Buddhist thought and practice, much more was taken as said and done, and just carried over. Thus, instead of seeing Mahāyāna as simply superseding earlier forms of Buddhism in India, the approach adopted in the present volume is to try to focus on the common ground between the non-Mahāyāna and Mahāyāna in the formative phase of Indian Buddhist thought and practice, and by referring to both the Pali sources of Sri Lanka and the Sanskrit sources of northern India to present an outline of 'mainstream' Buddhist thought and practice as the foundations for developments in India and beyond. Such an approach, then, does tend to privilege what is ancient, but throughout I have attempted to give some indication of how these basic principles of Buddhist thought and practice might relate to more recent developments.

Let me add here a few words on my specific approach to my material. In describing Buddhist thought and practice, my aim has been, in the first place, simply to act as spokesman for its principles, and to try to articulate those principles as Buddhist tradition itself has understood them. In the second place, I have tried to give some indication of and pass some comment on the critical and scholarly issues that have emerged in the modern academic study of Buddhism over the last 150 years or so.

Some might question the need for yet another introductory volume on Buddhism, yet as a teacher of introductory courses on Buddhism at a university I find myself somewhat dissatisfied with the available teaching materials. Certainly there are available a number of survey-type books ranging from short and sketchy to more moderate-sized treatments. In addition there are some solid introductions to various aspects of Buddhism —the social history of Theravāda, Mahāyāna thought, Chinese Buddhism, Tibetan Buddhism—but if one looks for a volume giving a more focused account, reflecting recent scholarship, of what, for want of a better expression, one might refer to as the principles of 'mainstream' Buddhist thought and practice, there appears to be a gap. It is hoped that the present work will go some way to filling that gap.

In sum, what distinguishes the present volume is that it contains rather more sustained expositions of Buddhist cosmology, no self and dependent arising, the path of meditation, and the theoretical Abhidharma framework (which underlies all later Buddhist thought) than other introductory books. Thus there is material here which, although basic from a Buddhist point of view, is only available in specialized books and articles. I hope, then, that while the book is intended to be accessible to the novice, there may also be something here for the elders of Buddhist studies.

1

The Buddha

The Story of the Awakened One

The historical Buddha

In January 1898 an Englishman, W. C. Peppé, digging into a mound on his estate at Piprāhwā just the Indian side of the Indian–Nepalese border, unearthed a soapstone vase some six inches in height with a brief inscription around its lid. The inscription, written in the Brāhmī script and dating from about the second century BCE, was in one of the ancient Indian dialects or Prakrits collectively referred to as Middle Indo-Aryan. The precise interpretation of the inscription remains problematic, but it appears to claim that the vase is 'a receptacle of relics of the Blessed Buddha of the Śākyas'.[1] The circumstances of this find and the find itself actually reveal a considerable amount about the nature and long history of what we know today as 'Buddhism'.

Peppé was among the early excavators of ruined Buddhist *stūpas* or monumental burial mounds. Such stūpas vary considerably in size. The largest were made to enshrine the relics of the Buddha himself or of Buddhist 'saints' or *arhats* (Pali *arahat*), while smaller ones contained the remains of more ordinary men and women.[2] Today countless stūpas are to be found scattered across the Indian subcontinent (where over the past hundred years a few have been restored to something of their former glory) and also other countries where Buddhism spread. Buddhism was, then, in origin an Indian phenomenon. Beginning in the fifth century BCE, its teachings and institutions continued to flourish for some fifteen centuries on Indian soil, inspiring and moulding the intellectual, religious, and cultural life of India. During this period Buddhism spread via the old trade routes far beyond the confines of India right across Asia, from Afghanistan in the west to Japan in the east, affecting and touching the lives of millions of people. Yet by around the close of the twelfth century Buddhist institutions had all but disappeared from India proper, and it is in the countries and cultures that lie beyond India that Buddhism flourishes today. None the less all the various living traditions of Buddhism in some way look back to and revere a figure who has a certain basis in history—a figure who lived and died in northern India several centuries before the beginning of the Christian era and belonged to a people known as the Śākyas (Pali Sakya). He is Śākya-muni, 'the sage of the Śākyas', or as our inscription prefers to call him *buddho bhagavā*—'the Blessed Buddha', 'the Lord Buddha'.

So who, and indeed what, was the Lord Buddha? This is a question that might be answered in a number of different ways, a question about which both the Buddhist tradition and the historian have something to say. The nature of the Buddha is a subject that the Buddhist tradition itself has expounded on at length and to which we will return below but, in brief, the word *buddha* is not a name but a title; its meaning is 'one who has woken up'. This title is generally applied by the Buddhist tradition to a class of beings who are, from the perspective of ordinary humanity, extremely rare and quite extraordinary. In contrast to these Buddhas or 'awakened ones' the mass of humanity, along with the other creatures and beings that constitute the world, are asleep—asleep in the sense that they pass through their lives never knowing and seeing the world 'as it is' (*yathā-bhūtaṃ*). As a consequence they suffer. A buddha on the other hand awakens to the knowledge of the world as it truly is and in so doing finds release from suffering. Moreover—and this is perhaps the greatest significance of a buddha for the rest of humanity, and indeed for all the beings who make up the universe—a buddha teaches. He teaches out of sympathy and compassion for the suffering of beings, for the benefit and welfare of all beings; he teaches in order to lead others to awaken to the understanding that brings final relief from suffering. An ancient formula still used in Buddhist devotions today puts it as follows:

For the following reasons he is a Blessed One: he is an Arhat, a perfectly and completely awakened one, perfect in his understanding and conduct, happy, one who understands the world, an unsurpassed trainer of unruly men, the teacher of both gods and men, a blessed buddha.[3]

Such is a buddha in general terms, but what of the particular buddha with whom we started, whose relics appear to have been enshrined in a number of stūpas across the north of India and to whom the Buddhist tradition looks as its particular founder—the historical Buddha? Let us for the moment consider the question not so much from the perspective of the Buddhist tradition as from the perspective of the historian.

The Buddha and the Indian 'renouncer' tradition

We can know very little of the historical Buddha with any degree of certainty. Yet within the bounds of reasonable historical probability we can form quite a clear picture of the kind of person the Buddha was and the main events of his life. The oldest Buddhist sources, which provide us with a number of details concerning the person and life of the Buddha, date from the fourth or third century BCE. Unfortunately when we turn to the non-Buddhist sources of a similar date, namely the earliest texts of the Jain and brahmanical traditions, there is no explicit mention of the Buddha at all.[4] It would be a mistake to conclude, however, that non-Buddhist sources thus provide us with no corroborative evidence for the picture of the Buddha painted in early Buddhist texts. Essentially the latter present the Buddha as a *śramaṇa* (Pali *samaṇa*). This term means literally 'one who strives' and belongs to the technical vocabulary of Indian religion, referring as it does to 'one who strives' religiously or spiritually. It points towards a particular tradition that in one way or another has been of great significance in Indian religious history, be it Buddhist, Jain, or Hindu. Any quest for the historical Buddha must begin with the *śramaṇa* tradition. Collectively our sources may not allow us to write the early history of this movement but they do enable us to say a certain amount concerning its character.

The tradition is sometimes called the 'renouncer (*saṃnyāsin*) tradition'. What we are concerned with here is the phenomenon of individuals' renouncing their normal role in society as a member of an extended 'household' in order to devote themselves to some form of religious or spiritual life. The 'renouncer' abandons conventional means of livelihood, such as farming or trade, and adopts instead the religious life as a means of livelihood. That is, he becomes a religious mendicant dependent on alms. What our sources make clear is that by the fifth century BCE this phenomenon was both widespread and varied. Thus while 'renouncers' had in common the fact that they had 'gone forth from the household life into homelessness' (to use a phrase common in Buddhist sources), the kind of lifestyle they then adopted was not necessarily the same. This is suggested by some of the terms that we find in the texts: in addition to 'one who strives' and 'renouncer', we fiṇd 'wanderer' (*parivrājaka/paribbājaka*), 'one who begs his share [of alms]' (*bhikṣu/bhikkhu*), 'naked ascetic' (*acelaka*), 'matted-hair ascetic' (*jaṭila*), as well as a number of other terms.[5] Some of these wanderers and ascetics seem to have been loners, while others seem to have organized themselves into groups and lived under a teacher. Early renouncers seem to have been for the most part male, although with the growth of Buddhism and Jainism it is certainly the case that women too began to be numbered among their ranks.

Three kinds of activity seem to have preoccupied these wanderers and ascetics. First, there is the practice of austerities, such as going naked in all weathers, enduring all physical discomforts, fasting, or undertaking the vow to live like a cow or even a dog.[6] Secondly, there is the cultivation of meditative and contemplative techniques aimed at producing what might, for the lack of a suitable technical term in English, be referred to as 'altered states of consciousness'. In the technical vocabulary of Indian religious texts such states come to be termed 'meditations' (*dhyāna/jhāna*) or 'concentrations' (*samādhi*); the attainment of such states of consciousness was generally regarded as bringing the practitioner to some deeper knowledge and experience of the nature of the world. Lastly there is the development of various philosophical views providing the intellectual justification for particular practices and the theoretical expression of the 'knowledge' to which they led. While some groups and individuals seem to have combined all three activities, others favoured one at the expense of the others, and the line between the practice of austerities and the practice of meditation may not always be clear: the practice of extreme austerity will certainly alter one's state of mind.

The existence of some of these different groups of ancient Indian wanderers and ascetics with their various practices and theories finds expression in Buddhist texts in a stock description of 'six teachers of other schools', who are each represented as expounding a particular teaching and practice. Another list, with no details of the associated teachings and practices, gives ten types of renouncer. In fact two other ancient Indian traditions that were subsequently of some importance in the religious life of India (the Ājīvikas and the Jains) find a place in both these ancient Buddhist lists; the Jain tradition, of course, survives to this day.[7] But one of the most significant groups for the understanding of the religious milieu of the historical Buddha is omitted from these lists; this is the early brahmanical tradition. To explain who the brahmins (*brāhmaṇa*) were requires a brief excursus into the early evolution of Indian culture and society.

The brahmanical tradition

It is generally thought that some time after the beginning of the second millennium BCE groups of a nomadic tribal people began to move south from ancient Iran, through the passes of the Hindu Kush and down into the plains of the Indus valley. These people spoke dialects of Old Indo-Aryan, that is, of Sanskrit and they are known as the Āryas. The Āryas who moved into India were descendants of nomadic pastoralists who had occupied the grasslands of central Asia, some of whom similarly moved west into Europe.

Once in India the Āryas' cultural influence gradually spread southwards and eastwards across the plains of northern India. By the time the Buddha was born, probably early in the fifth century BCE, the Āryas had been in India perhaps a thousand years and their cultural influence extended down the Ganges valley as far as Pāṭaliputra (modern Patnā). The coming of the Āryas into India did not bring political unity to northern India, but it did bring a certain ideology that constitutes one of the principal components of Indian culture. This Aryan vision of society was principally developed and articulated by a hereditary group within Aryan society known as *brāhmaṇas* or, in the Anglo-Indian spelling, brahmins. The original literature of the brahmins is known as the *Vedas*, the oldest portions of which, found in the *Ṛg Veda*, date from about 1500 BCE. By the time of the Buddha, Vedic literature probably already comprised several different classes: the four collections (*saṃhitā*) of verses attributed to the ancient seers (*ṛsi*), the ritual manuals (also known as *brāhmaṇas*) giving instruction in the carrying out of the elaborate Vedic sacrificial ritual, and 'the forest books' (*āraṇyaka*) explaining the esoteric meaning of this sacrificial ritual. The final class of Vedic literature, the Upaniṣads, containing further esoteric explanations of the sacrificial ritual, was still in the process of formation.

Two aspects of the brahmanical vision are of particular importance, namely an understanding of society as reflecting a hierarchy of ritual 'purity', and a complex system of ritual and sacrifice. From the brahmanical perspective society comprises two groups: the Āryas and the non-Āryas. The former consists of the three hereditary classes (*varṇa*) in descending order of purity: *brāhmaṇas* (whose prerogative and duty it is to teach and maintain the Vedic tradition), *kṣatriyas* or rulers (whose prerogative and duty is to maintain order and where necessary inflict appropriate punishment), and the *vaiśyas* (whose prerogative and duty is to generate wealth through farming and trade). These three classes are termed 'twice born' (*dvija*) by virtue of the fact that traditionally male members undergo an initiation (*upanayana*) into a period of study of the Vedic tradition under the supervision of a brahmin teacher; at the end of this period of study it is their duty to maintain the household sacrificial fires and, with the help of brahmins, carry out various sacrificial rituals in accordance with the prescriptions of Vedic tradition. The non-Āryas make up the fourth class, the *śūdras* or servants, whose basic duty it is to serve the three other classes. While it is important not to confuse these four classes (*varṇa*) and the countless castes (*jāti*) of later Indian society, it is none the less the ideology of the relative ritual purity of the classes that underpins the medieval and modern Indian 'caste system'.

The brahmins' hereditary ritual status empowered them to carry out certain ritual functions that members of other classes were excluded from, but at the time of the Buddha not all brahmins were full-time 'priests'. Precisely how brahmins related to the various groups of wandering ascetics is not clear.[8] In part we can see the brahmanical vision of society and that of the wandering ascetics as opposed to each other, in part we can see the two as complementing each other. To accept the brahmanical view of the world was to accept brahmanical authority as an aspect of the eternal structure of the universe and, as such, unassailable. Yet wandering ascetics threatened brahmanical supremacy by offering rival visions of the world and society. On the other hand, within brahmanical circles we find the development of certain esoteric theories of the nature of the sacrificial ritual and philosophical views about the ultimate nature of man and his relationship to the universe at large. These theories may to some extent have drawn on ideas developing amongst the groups of wandering ascetics; at the same time they may have substantially contributed to the development of the tradition of the wanderers itself, since it is clear that brahmin circles were an important recruiting ground for the various groups of wandering ascetics. Yet it seems clear that in certain respects the Buddha's teachings were formulated as a response to certain brahmanical teachings.[9]

The Buddha and history

It is in this milieu that the historian must understand the historical Buddha as existing. And given this milieu, the bare 'facts' of the Buddha's life as presented by tradition are historically unproblematic and inconsequential.

The precise dates of the Buddha's life are uncertain. A widespread Buddhist tradition records that he was in his eightieth year when he died, and the dates for his life most widely quoted in modern published works are 566–486 BCE. These dates are arrived at by, first, following a tradition, recorded in the Pali sources of 'southern' Buddhism, that the great Mauryan king, Aśoka, was consecrated 218 years after the death of the Buddha, and, secondly, taking 268 BCE as the year of Aśoka's accession. This is done on the basis of the Aśokan rock-edict reference to rulers in the wider Hellenic world who can be dated from other ancient sources. But both the figure 218 and the accession of Aśoka in 268 BCE are problematic. In contrast to the southern 'long chronology', northern Buddhist Sanskrit sources adopt a 'short chronology', placing Aśoka's accession just 100 years after the death of the Buddha, while recent research suggests that Aśoka's accession may be plausibly placed anywhere between 280 and 267 BCE.[10] But such figures as 218 and 100 should properly be seen as ideal round numbers.[11] Moreover, as was first pointed out by Rhys Davids and more recently by Richard Gombrich, a time lapse of rather less than 218 years from the Buddha's death to Aśoka's accession is suggested by the figures associated with the lineage of teachers found in a Pali source, namely an ancient Sri Lankan chronicle, the *Dīpavaṃsa*.[12] While there is no scholarly consensus on the precise dates of the Buddha, a detailed examination of all the available data and arguments by scholars in recent years has resulted in a general tendency to bring the date of the Buddha considerably forward and place his death much nearer 400 BCE than 500 BCE.

The earliest Buddhist sources state that the future Buddha was born Siddhārtha Gautama (Pali Siddhattha Gotama), the son of a local chieftain—a *rājan*—in Kapilavastu (Pali Kapilavatthu) on what is now the Indian–Nepalese border. He was thus a member of a relatively privileged and wealthy family, and enjoyed a comfortable upbringing. While the later Buddhist tradition, in recounting the story of his youth, certainly likes to dwell on the wealth of Siddhārtha's family and the extravagance of his princely upbringing, there is something of a cultural misunderstanding involved in the notion that the Buddhist tradition presents the Buddha as born a royal prince, the son of a great king.

In representing the Buddha as a *rājan* or *kṣatriya* the tradition is effectively recording little more than that he was, in European cultural terms, a member of a locally important aristocratic family. At some point he became disillusioned with his comfortable and privileged life; he became troubled by a sense of the suffering that, in the form of sickness, old age, and death, sooner or later awaited him and everyone else. In the face of this, the pleasures he enjoyed seemed empty and of little value. So he left home and adopted the life of a wandering ascetic, a *śramaṇa*, to embark on a religious and spiritual quest. He took instruction from various teachers; he practised extreme austerities as was the custom of some ascetics. Still he was not satisfied. Finally, seated in meditation beneath an *aśvattha* tree on the banks of the Nairañjanā in what is now the north Indian state of Bihar, he had an experience which affected him profoundly, convincing him that he had come to the end of his quest. While the historian can make no judgement on the nature of this experience, the Buddhist tradition (apparently bearing witness to the Buddha's own understanding of his experience) calls it *bodhi* or 'awakening' and characterizes it as involving the deepest understanding of the nature of suffering, its cause, its cessation, and the way leading to its cessation. The Buddha devoted the rest of his life to teaching this 'way to the cessation of suffering' to groups of wanderers and ordinary householders. In the course of his wanderings across the plains that flank the banks of the Ganges he gathered a considerable following and by the time of his death at about the age of 80 he had established a well-organized mendicant community which attracted considerable support from the wider population. His followers cremated his body and divided up the relics which were enshrined in a number of stūpas which became revered shrines.

That the subsequent Buddhist tradition is founded upon and inspired by the teaching activity of a charismatic individual who lived some centuries before the beginning of the Christian era can hardly be doubted. In the words of the great Belgian scholar Étienne Lamotte, 'Buddhism cannot be explained unless we accept that it has its origin in the strong personality of its founder.'[13] Given this premiss, none of the bare details of the Buddha's life is particularly problematic for the historian—something we should bear in mind in the face of certain modern scholarly discussions of the life of the Buddha, such as André Bareau's, which, in dwelling on the absence of corroborative evidence for many of the details of the traditional life of the Buddha, introduces a note of undue scepticism with regard to the whole account.

Of course, as the Buddhist tradition tells it, the story of the life of the Buddha is not history nor meant to be. The whole story takes on a mythic and legendary character. A wealth of detail is brought in capable of being read metaphorically, allegorically, typologically, and symbolically. Much of this detail is to modern sensibilities of a decidedly 'miraculous' and 'supernatural' kind. The story of the Buddha's life becomes not an account of the particular and individual circumstances of a man who, some 2,500 years ago, left home to become a wandering ascetic, but something universal, an archetype; it is the story of all those who have become buddhas in the past and all who will become buddhas in the future, and, in a sense, of all who follow the Buddhist path. It is the story of the Buddhist path, a story that shows the way to a profound religious truth. Yet for all that, many of the details of his early life given in the oldest sources remain evocative of some memory of events from a distant time. If we persist in distinguishing and holding apart myth and history, we are in danger of missing the story's own sense of truth. Furthermore, the historian must recognize that he has virtually no strictly *historical* criteria for distinguishing between history and myth in the accounts of the life of the Buddha. And at that point he should perhaps remain silent and let the story speak for itself.[14]

The legend of the Buddha

Sources

The centrepiece of the legend of the Buddha is the story of the Buddha's life from his conception to the events of his awakening and his first teaching. This narrative must be accounted one of the great stories of the world. Part of the common heritage of Buddhism, it is known throughout Asia wherever Buddhism has taken root. The core of this story and not a few of its details are already found in the Sūtra and Vinaya collections of early Buddhist texts (see next chapter).[15] In literary works and in sculptural reliefs that date from two or three centuries later, we find these details embellished and woven together to form a more sustained narrative. The classical literary tellings of the story are found in Sanskrit texts such as the *Mahāvastu* ('Great Story', first century CE), the *Lalitavistara* ('Graceful Description', first century CE), in Aśvaghoṣa's poem the *Buddhacarita* ('Acts of the Buddha', second century CE), and in the Pali *Nidānakathā* ('Introductory Tale', second or third century CE), which forms an introduction to the commentary on the *Jātaka*, a collection of stories of the Buddha's previous births.[16] New narratives of the life of the Buddha have continued to be produced down to modern times.[17]

Tibetan tradition structures the story of the Buddha's life around twelve acts performed by all buddhas, while Theravādin sources draw up a rather longer list of thirty features that are the rule (*dhammatā*) for the lives of all buddhas.[18] The substance of these two lists is already found in the oldest tellings of the story. What follows is in effect the story of these twelve acts and (most of) the thirty features, told with a bias to how they are recounted in the early discourses of the Buddha and Pali sources, together with some comments aimed at providing a historical perspective on the development of the story.

The legend

The Buddhist and general Indian world-view is that all sentient beings are subject to rebirth: all beings are born, live, die, and are reborn again and again in a variety of different circumstances. This process knows no definite beginning and, ordinarily, no definite end. The being who becomes a buddha, like any other being, has known countless previous lives—as a human being, an animal, and a god. An old tradition tells us that the life before the one in which the state of buddhahood is reached is always spent as a 'god' (*deva*) in the heaven of the Contented (Tuṣita/ Tusita). Here the bodhisattva (Pali *bodhisatta*)—the being intent on awakening—dwells awaiting the appropriate time to take a human birth and become a buddha. Dwelling in the Tuṣita heaven is the first of the twelve acts, but how does the bodhisattva come to be dwelling here? The answer, in short, is that it is as a result of having practised 'the perfections' (*pāramitā/pāramī*) over many, many lifetimes.

Long ago, in fact incalculable numbers of aeons ago, there lived an ascetic called Sumedha (or Megha by some) who encountered a former buddha, the Buddha Dīpaṃkara. This meeting affected Sumedha in such a way that he too aspired to becoming a buddha. What impressed Sumedha was Dīpaṃkara's very presence and a sense of his infinite wisdom and compassion, such that he resolved that he would do whatever was necessary to cultivate and perfect these qualities in himself. Sumedha thus set out on the path of the cultivation of the ten 'perfections': generosity, morality, desirelessness, vigour, wisdom, patience, truthfulness, resolve, loving kindness, and equanimity. In undertaking the cultivation of these perfections Sumedha became a bodhisattva, a being intent on and destined for buddhahood, and it is the life in which he becomes the Buddha Gautama some time in the fifth century BCE that represents the fruition of that distant aspiration. Many *jātakas*—'[tales] of the [previous] births [of the Bodhisattva]'—recount how the Bodhisattva gradually developed the 'perfections'. Such stories, like the story of the Buddha's life, are deeply embedded in Buddhist culture and serve to emphasize how, for the Buddhist, the being who dwells in Tuṣita as one intent on buddhahood is a being of the profoundest spiritual qualities.

The appearance of such a being in the world may not be unique, but is nevertheless a rare and special circumstance, for a buddha only appears in the world when the teachings of a previous buddha have been lost and when beings will be receptive to his message. So it is said that surveying the world from Tuṣita the Bodhisattva saw that the time had come for him to take a human birth and at last become a buddha; he saw that the 'Middle Country' of the great continent of Jambudvīpa (India) was the place in which to take birth, for its inhabitants would be receptive to his message. The Bodhisattva was conceived on the full moon night of Āṣāḍha (July); that night his mother, Mahāmāyā, dreamt that a white elephant carrying a white lotus in its trunk came and entered her womb. The second and third acts, descent from Tuṣita and entering his mother's womb, had been accomplished.

Māyā carried the Bodhisattva in her womb for precisely ten lunar months. Then on the full moon of Vaiśākha (May), passing by the Lumbinī grove on her way to her home town, she was captivated by the beauty of the flowering *śāla* trees and stepped down from her palanquin to walk amongst the trees in the grove. As she reached for a branch of a śāla tree, which bent itself down to meet her hand, the pangs of birth came upon her. Thus, 'while other women give birth sitting or lying down', the Bodhisattva's mother was delivered of her child while standing and holding on to the branch of a śāla tree. As soon as the Bodhisattva was born he took seven steps to the north and proclaimed, 'I am chief in the world, I am best in the world, I am first in the world. This is my last birth. There will be no further rebirth.'

Such is the legend of the Bodhisattva's birth, the fourth act. By the middle of the third century BCE a site reckoned to be the place of his birth had become a centre of pilgrimage, and the great Mauryan emperor Aśoka—or, as he preferred to call himself, Piyadassi Beloved of the Gods—whose empire extended across virtually the entire Indian subcontinent, had inscribed on a pillar at Lumbinī:

> When King Piyadassi, Beloved of the Gods, had been anointed twenty years, he himself came and worshipped [here], because this is where the Buddha, sage of the Śākyas, was born.[10]

The Bodhisattva was thus born among the Śākya people into a *kṣatriya* family whose name was Gautama. Seven days after his birth his mother died and was reborn in the Tuṣita heaven. The child was named Siddhārtha—'he whose purpose is accomplished'. Despite the strange and marvellous circumstances of his birth, as he grew up the child appears to have forgotten he was the Bodhisattva: he had no memory of his dwelling in Tuṣita or any of his other previous births. However, certain predictions of his future destiny were made to his father, Śuddhodana. Soon after his birth the infant Bodhisattva was examined by brahmin specialists in 'the thirty-two marks of the great man' (*mahāpuruṣa-lakṣaṇa/mahāpurisa-lakkhaṇa*).[20] This notion may be of some antiquity in Indian tradition. These marks take the form of signs on the body that indicate that the possessor is a Great Man. Such marks may not be visible to the ordinary eye, but it is said that certain brahmins kept the knowledge that was capable of interpreting these marks. According to Buddhist tradition two destinies are open to one who possesses these marks in full: either he will become a great 'wheel-turning' (*cakravartin/cakka-vattin*) king ruling the four quarters of the earth in perfect justice, or he will become a buddha. On hearing that the brahmins had pronounced his son was one who possessed the thirty-two marks, Śuddhodana determined that his son should become a wheel-turning king. To this end he arranged matters that Siddhārtha should have no occasion to become unhappy and disillusioned with his life at home: he would be sheltered from all things unpleasant and ugly such as old age, sickness, and death; whatever he wanted to make him happy, that he should have. In this way Śuddhodana hoped that he might prevent Siddhārtha from renouncing his home-life for the life of a wandering ascetic and thus assure that he became not a buddha but a wheel-turning king. We are told that Siddhārtha married a young and beautiful wife, Yaśodharā, and had a son, Rāhula, by her.

All this relates to the fifth of the twelve acts, the Bodhisattva's enjoyment of proficiency in worldly skills and sensuality. The oldest sources say virtually nothing of the Bodhisattva's life before the time he left home. They indicate that he did indeed have a wife and son, but apart from that all we have is a stock description of a life of luxury enjoyed by the very wealthy and privileged placed into the mouth of the Buddha himself:

I was delicate, most delicate, supremely delicate. Lotus pools were made for me at my father's house solely for my use; in one blue lotuses

> flowered, in another white, and in another red. I used no sandal wood that was not from Benares. My turban, tunic, lower garments and cloak were all of Benares cloth. A white sunshade was held over me day and night so that I would not be troubled by cold or heat, dust or grit or dew . . . Yet even while I possessed such fortune and luxury, I thought, 'When an unthinking, ordinary person who is himself subject to ageing, sickness, and death, who is not beyond ageing, sickness, and death, sees another who is old, sick or dead, he is shocked, disturbed, and disgusted, forgetting his own condition. I too am subject to ageing, sickness, and death, not beyond ageing, sickness, and death, and that I should see another who is old, sick or dead and be shocked, disturbed, and disgusted —this is not fitting.' As I reflected thus, the conceit of youth, health, and life entirely left me.[21]

This brings us straight to the sixth act, disenchantment with his life of pleasure. In the developed account this experience of disenchantment with the world is related in terms of the story of the Bodhisattva's rides with his charioteer. As he leaves the confines of his luxurious apartments, he encounters for the first time in his life a decrepit old man, a severely ill man, and a corpse being carried to the funeral pyre by mourners. The experience is traumatic, and when he then sees a wandering ascetic with serene and composed features Gautama resolves that he will leave his home and take up the life of a wandering ascetic himself. The Bodhisattva's 'great going forth' (*mahāpravrajyā/mahāpabbajjā*), the seventh act, took place on the night of the Āṣāḍha full moon. Accompanied by his charioteer, Channa, he went forth on his horse, Kanthaka. According to traditional reckoning he was then 29 and this was the beginning of a six-year quest for awakening. During these six years he first spent time with and practised the systems of meditation taught by Ārāḍa Kālāma (Pali Āḷāra Kālāma) and then Udraka Rāmaputra (Pali Uddaka Rāmaputta). Although he mastered their respective systems, he felt that here he had not found any real answer to the problem of human suffering. So next, in the company of five other wandering ascetics, he turned to the practice of severe austerities. The old texts preserve a hauntingly vivid description of the results of this practice, the eighth act:

My body reached a state of extreme emaciation. Because of eating so little my limbs became like the jointed stems of creepers or bamboo; my backside became like a buffalo's hoof; my backbone, bent or straight, was like corded beads; my jutting and broken ribs were like the jutting and broken rafters of an old house; the gleam of my eyes sunk deep in their sockets was like the gleam of water seen deep down at the bottom of a deep well.[22]

But by his gruelling penance he again felt he had not found what he was searching for. Then he recalled an experience from his youth. One day seated quietly beneath the shade of a rose-apple tree his mind had settled into a state of deep calm and peace. Buddhist tradition calls this state the first 'meditation' or *dhyāna* (Pali *jhāna*). According to the later Buddhist understanding, this state is the gateway to a state of perfect mental calm and equilibrium known as the fourth *dhyāna*. As he reflected, it came to the Bodhisattva that it was by letting the mind settle in this state of peace that he might come to find what he was looking for. This required that he nourish his body and regain his strength. His five companions thought he had turned away from the quest and left him to his own devices. In the full legend this is the occasion of the young woman Sujātā's (or, according to some, Nandabalā's) offering of milk-rice to the Bodhisattva. Now nourished, he seated himself beneath an *aśvattha* or pīpal tree (*ficus religiosa*), henceforth to be known as 'the tree of awakening' or Bodhi-tree. It was once more the night of the Vaiśākha full moon and he made a final resolve: 'Let only skin, sinew and bone remain, let the flesh and blood dry in my body, but I will not give up this seat without attaining complete awakening.'[23] The gods from many different world-systems gathered around the tree sensing that something momentous was about to happen.

Again the oldest accounts describe the gaining of awakening in generally sober psychological terms, most often by reference to the successive practice of the four *dhyānas* and the gaining of three 'knowledges', culminating in the knowledge of suffering, its cause, its cessation, and the way leading to its cessation—what come to be known as 'the four noble truths'; the awakening is also described in terms of gaining insight into the causal chain of 'dependent arising'.[24] These are classic elements of Buddhist thought and we shall return to them later. Perhaps because they do not exactly make for a good story, the later legend of the Buddha recounts the awakening in terms of the story of the Bodhisattva's encounter with Māra. This is a story rather more vivid and immediately accessible than the abstract technical concepts of Buddhist meditation theory.

Māra is a being who in certain respects is like the Satan of Judaism, Islam, and Christianity. His name means 'bringer of death' and his most common epithet is 'the Bad One' (*pāpīyāṃs/ pāpimant*). Māra is not so much a personification of evil as of the terrible hold which the world—in particular the world of the senses—can have on the mind. Māra is the power of all kinds of experience to seduce and ensnare the unwary mind; seduced by Māra one remains lost in the enchantment of the world and fails to find the path that leads through to the cessation of suffering. So as the Bodhisattva sat beneath the tree firm in his resolve, Māra, mounted on his great elephant, approached. He came accompanied by his armies: desire, aversion, hunger and thirst, craving, tiredness and sleepiness, fear, and doubt. His one purpose was to break the Bodhisattva's resolve and shift him from his seat beneath the pīpal tree. The gods who had gathered around the tree in anticipation of the Bodhisattva's awakening fled at the sight of Māra's approaching armies, and the Bodhisattva was left to face Māra and his armies alone.

Some relate how at this point the beautiful daughters of Māra came before the Bodhisattva and tested his commitment to his purpose by offering themselves to him.[25] But the Bodhisattva was unmoved. Māra then sent various storms against him. When this too failed, Māra approached to claim the Bodhisattva's seat directly. He asked him by what right he sat there beneath the tree. The Bodhisattva replied that it was by right of having practised the perfections over countless aeons. Māra replied that he had done likewise and, what was more, he had witnesses to prove it: all his armies would vouch for him, but who would vouch for the Bodhisattva? The Bodhisattva then lifted his right hand and touched the ground calling on the very earth as his witness.

This is the 'earth-touching gesture' (*bhūmi-sparśa-mudrā*) depicted in so many statues of the Buddha through the ages. It signals the defeat of Māra and the Buddha's awakening. As the Buddha touched the earth Māra tumbled from his elephant and his armies fled in disarray. With the ninth and tenth acts, the defeat of Māra and the attainment of complete awakening, Siddhārtha had accomplished his goal.

The legend of the Buddha is dense and rich at this point and we must pass over many of its details. But according to tradition the Buddha spent as many as seven weeks seated beneath and in the vicinity of the Bodhi-tree enjoying the bliss of emancipation. Once a great storm arose as the Buddha was seated in meditation and a Nāga, a great serpent, came and spread its hood over the Buddha to protect him. Again this scene is often depicted, especially in images of Cambodian provenance.

The Buddha had achieved his purpose; he had come to an understanding of suffering, and had realized the cessation of suffering. In Buddhist terms, seated beneath the tree he had a direct experience of 'the unconditioned', 'the transcendent', 'the deathless', nirvāṇa (Pali *nibbāna*); he had come to know directly the deep and underlying way of things that is referred to in India as Dharma (Pali *dhamma*). It is said that at that point his mind inclined not to teach:

> This Dharma that I have found is profound, hard to see, hard to understand; it is peaceful, sublime, beyond the sphere of mere reasoning, subtle, to be experienced by the wise. But this generation takes delight in attachment, is delighted by attachment, rejoices in attachment and as such it is hard for them to see this truth, namely . . . nirvāṇa.[26]

Even the oldest tradition seems to know the story of how the great god, the Brahmā called Sahampati, or 'mighty lord', came then and stood before the Buddha and requested him to teach. The implications of this story are various. Sometimes it is suggested that it has been created as a device to show that even the gods already recognized at that time in India acknowledge the Buddha's superiority. But there are perhaps other meanings. There are reasons for thinking that the realm of Brahmā is associated with compassion in early Buddhist thought.[27] There is also a strong Buddhist tradition that the teaching should only be given to those who ask and thereby show their willingness to hear receptively. Thus even today, in certain traditions of Buddhism, when a layman makes a formal request to a Buddhist monk to teach Dharma he consciously repeats Brahmā's original request by using the very words of the ancient formula.

Then the Brahmā Sahampati, lord of the world, with joined palms requested a boon: There are beings here with but little dust in their eyes. Pray teach Dharma out of compassion for them.[28]

In a deer park outside Benares the Buddha approached the five who had been his companions when he practised austerities and gave them instruction in the path to the cessation of suffering that he had discovered. In this way he performed a buddha's eleventh act: 'setting in motion' or 'turning the wheel of Dharma' (*dharma-cakra-pravartana/dhamma-cakka-ppavattana*), and soon, we are told, there were six *arhats* in the world—six in the world who had cultivated the path to the cessation of suffering and realized the unconditioned.

For the Buddha this was the beginning of a life of teaching that lasted some forty-five years. Many stories and legends are recounted of the Buddha's teaching career. Indeed, fourteen of the thirty features given in the Pali sources as the rule for all buddhas relate to it. To a large extent these incidents are preserved by the earlier tradition in no systematic order, and it is left to later tradition to organize them into a sequential narrative.[29] Most of these legends must be passed over here but it is worth just mentioning some since they form part of the common heritage of Buddhism and are again and again alluded to by later tradition in literary texts and in paintings and stone relief. There is the story of how the Buddha gained his two greatest disciples, the monks Śāriputra and Maudgalyāyana; of how the monk Ānanda came to be his attendant; of how the Buddha performed the extraordinary 'miracle of the pairs', causing fire and water to issue from every pore of his body, and then ascended to the heaven of the 'Thirty-Three Gods' to give his profoundest teachings to his reborn mother. There is the story of the quarrelling monks at Kauśāmbī and of how the Buddha retired to the Pārileyyaka forest where he was attended by a lone elephant who had grown weary of the herd, of how a monkey came to the Buddha and offered him honey. There is the story of the dispute with his cousin Devadatta, who attempted to kill him by releasing a rogue elephant which the Buddha subdued by the strength of his 'loving kindness' (*maitrī/mettā*).

As we shall see, it is one of the great emphases of Buddhist teaching that the things of the world are impermanent and unreliable. To the extent that the Buddha is of the world then he is no exception. There is a majestic and poignant account of the Buddha's last days preserved in the ancient canon under the title of 'the great discourse of the final passing' (*Mahāparinibbāna Sutta*). According to tradition it was some time in his eighty-first year that the Buddha fell ill:

> I am now grown old, Ānanda, and full of years; my journey is done and I have reached my sum of days; I am turning eighty years of age. And just as a worn out cart is kcpt going with thc hclp of rcpairs, so it sccms is the Tathāgata's body kept going with repairs.[30]

As the Buddha lay dying between two blossoming śāla trees, it is related how the monk Ānanda, who unlike many of his other disciples had not achieved the state of arhatship or perfection, lent against a door and wept. Then the Buddha asked for him:

> Enough, Ānanda, do not sorrow, do not lament. Have I not formerly explained that it is the nature of things that we must be divided, separated, and parted from all that is beloved and dear? How could it be, Ānanda, that what has been born and come into being, that what is compounded and subject to decay, should not decay? It is not possible.[31]

The Buddha's death constituted his 'full going out' (*parinirvāṇa/ parinibbāna*), the twelfth and final act of all buddhas. Before his death the Buddha had given instructions that his remains should be treated like those of a wheel-turning monarch and enshrined in a stūpa where four roads meet. After the Buddha's body had been cremated, various messengers arrived from districts in northern India each demanding a share of his relics. The relics were thus divided into eight parts and eight different stūpas were built over them.

This is where we began this chapter. It is possible that the stūpa excavated by Peppé represents an enlargement of an older stūpa —one that the Śākyas erected over their share of the relics at Kapilavastu. The reliquary unearthed by Peppé appears to date from the second century BCE. More recent excavations at the site have unearthed further reliquaries—without any inscriptions—from deeper within the stūpa. These may date from the fourth or fifth century BCE. In that case Peppé's reliquary would seem to have been deposited when the stūpa was undergoing reconstruction some centuries after the death of the Buddha.

The nature of a buddha

The Buddha is presented to us as in certain respects simply a man: the *śramaṇa* or ascetic Gautama, the sage of the Śākya people. Yet at the same time he is presented as something much more than this: he was a *buddha*, an awakened one, the embodiment at a particular time and place of 'perfection', a Tathāgata, one who comes and goes in accordance with the profoundest way of things. At this point we need to begin to consider more fully what it is to be a buddha.

I have already referred to a generally accepted Indian view of things that sees ordinary humanity, ordinary beings, as being born, dying, and being reborn continually. This process is the round of rebirth known as *saṃsāra* or 'wandering', and it is this that constitutes the universe. Beings wander through this vast endless universe attempting to find some permanent home, a place where they can feel at ease and secure. In the realms of the gods they find great joy, and in the worlds of hell great suffering, but their sojurn in these places is always temporary. Nowhere in this universe is permanently secure; sooner or later, whatever the realm of rebirth, a being will die to be reborn somewhere else. So the search for happiness and security within the round of rebirth never ends. And yet, according to the teaching of the Buddha, this does not mean that the search for happiness and security is futile and without end, for a buddha is precisely one who finds and follows the path to the end of suffering.

Now the question of what happens to a buddha when he dies takes us to the heart of Buddhist philosophical thinking. Here Buddhist thought suggests that we must be very careful indeed about what we say, about how we use language, lest we become fooled. The Buddha cannot be reborn in some new form of existence, for to exist is, by definition, to exist at some particular time and in some particular place and so be part of the unstable, shifting world of conditions. If we say that the Buddha exists, then the round of rebirth continues for the Buddha and the quest for an end to suffering has not been completed. On the other hand, to say that the Buddha simply does not exist is to suggest that the Buddhist quest for happiness amounts to nothing but the destruction of the individual being—something which is specifically denied in the texts.[32] Hence the strict doctrinal formulation of Buddhist texts is this: one cannot say that the Buddha exists after death, one cannot say that he does not exist, one cannot say that he both exists and does not exist, and one cannot say that he neither exists nor does not exist.[33] One cannot say more here without beginning to explore certain other aspects of Buddhist metaphysics and ontology, and this I shall leave for later chapters. The important point is that a Buddha is understood as a being who has in some way transcended and gone beyond the round of rebirth. He is a Tathāgata, one who, in accordance with the profoundest way of things, has come 'thus' (*tathā*) and gone 'thus'.[34]

So what does this transcendence imply about the final nature of a buddha? If one is thinking in categories dictated and shaped by the theologies of Judaism, Christianity, and Islam, and also modern Western thought, there is often a strong inclination to suppose that such a question should be answered in terms of the categories of human and divine: *either* the Buddha was basically a man *or* he was some kind of god, perhaps even God.[35] But something of an imaginative leap is required here, for these are not the categories of Indian or Buddhist thought. In the first place, according to the Buddhist view of things, the nature of beings is not eternally or absolutely fixed. Beings that were once humans or animals may be reborn as gods; beings that were once gods may be reborn as animals or in hellish realms. Certainly, for the Buddhist tradition, the being who became *buddha* or awakened had been born a man, but equally that being is regarded as having spent many previous lives as a god. Yet in becoming a buddha he goes beyond such categories of being as human and divine.

A story is told of how once a brahmin saw on the Buddha's footprints one of the thirty-two marks, wheels complete with a thousand spokes, with rims and hubs.[36] He thought that such footprints could hardly be those of a human being and followed them. On catching up with the Buddha, he asked him whether he was a god or some kind of angel or demon. The Buddha replied that he was none of these. The brahmin then asked if he was a human being. The Buddha replied that he was not. The brahmin was puzzled. So what was the Buddha?

> Just as a blue, red, or white lotus, born in water and grown up in water, having risen above the water stands unstained by water, even so do I, born in the world and grown up in the world, having overcome the world, dwell unstained by the world. Understand that I am a buddha.

A buddha is thus a being *sui generis*: a buddha is just a buddha.[37] But, in principle, according to Buddhist thought, *any* being can follow the path of developing the perfections over countless lives, and eventually become a buddha. That is, all beings have the potential to become buddhas.

Thus something has happened to Gautama the man that means that the categories that normally apply to beings no longer properly apply. Ordinarily a human being's behaviour will sometimes be motivated by greed, hatred, and delusion and sometimes by such things as selflessness, friendliness, compassion, and wisdom. The different deeds, words, and thoughts of a being are an expression of these conflicting emotions and psychological forces. But for a buddha all this has changed. He has rooted out any sense of pride, attachment, or hostility. The thoughts, words, and deeds of a buddha are motivated only by generosity, loving kindness, and wisdom. A buddha can think, say, and do nothing that is not based on these. This is the effect or 'fruit' of what happened as he sat in meditation beneath the tree of awakening.

The bodies of the Buddha

One early Buddhist text puts it that the Buddha is 'one whose body is Dharma, whose body is Brahma; who has become Dharma, who has become Brahma'.[38] Now *dharma* and *brahma* are two technical terms pregnant with emotional and religious meaning. Among other things Dharma is 'the right way to behave', 'the perfect way to act'; hence it is also the teaching of the Buddha since by following the teaching of the Buddha one follows the path that ends in Dharma or perfect action. We have already come across the term Brahmā denoting a divine being (p. 24), but in Buddhist texts *brahma* is also used to denote or describe the qualities of such divine beings; thus *brahma* conveys something of the sense of the English 'divine', something of the sense of 'holy' and something of the sense of 'perfection'. Like the English word 'body' the Sanskrit/Pali word *kāya* means both a physical body and figuratively a collection or aggregate of something—as in 'a body of opinion'. To say that the Buddha is *dharma-kāya* means that he is at once the embodiment of Dharma and the collection or sum of all those qualities—non-attachment, loving kindness, wisdom, etc.—that constitute Dharma. Thus the nature of a buddha does not inhere primarily in his visible human body—it is not that which makes him a buddha—but in his perfected spiritual qualities.

Another passage of the ancient texts relates how the monk Vakkali was lying seriously ill on his sick-bed; when the Buddha arrives Vakkali explains to him that, although he has no sense of failure in his conduct, he is troubled by the fact that because of his illness he has not been able to come and visit the Buddha. The Buddha responds: 'Enough, Vakkali. What point is there in your seeing this decaying body? He who sees Dharma sees me; he who sees me sees Dharma.'[39]

This kind of thinking gives rise in developed Buddhist thought to various theories of 'the bodies of the Buddha'. Such theories are often presented as a distinguishing feature of later Mahāyāna Buddhism. This is misleading. Certainly, there is a rather sophisticated understanding of 'the three bodies' (*trikāya*) of the Buddha worked out and expounded in the writings of the fourth-century CE Indian Mahāyānist thinker Asaṅga (see Chapter 9). But this theory stands at the end of a process of development, and some conception of the bodies of the Buddha is common to all Buddhist thought. What is common is the distinguishing between the 'physical body' (*rūpa-kāya*) and the 'dharma-body'.

The physical body is the body that one would see if one happened to meet the Buddha. Most people, most of the time, it seems, would see a man who looked and dressed much like any other Buddhist monk. However, recalling the stories of the brahmins who examined the Buddha's body after his birth and the brahmin who followed his footprints, some people some of the time see—or perhaps, more precisely, experience—a body that is eighteen cubits in height and endowed with the thirty-two marks of the great man as described in the *Lakkhaṇa Sutta*, 'the discourse on the marks of the great man'.[40] This apparently extraordinary body appears in part to be connected with theories of the 'subtle body' developed in meditation. All this then is the physical body—the body as it appears to the senses. The Dharma-body, as we have seen already, is the collection of perfect qualities that, as it were, constitute the 'personality' or psychological make-up of the Buddha.

A Buddha's physical body and Dharma-body in a sense parallel and in a sense contrast with the physical and psychological make-up of other more ordinary beings. According to a classic Buddhist analysis that we shall have occasion to consider more fully below, any individual being's physical and psychological make-up comprises five groups of conditions and functions: a physical body normally endowed with five senses; feelings that are pleasant, unpleasant, or neutral; ideas and concepts; various desires and volitions; and self-consciousness. Any being might be considered as consisting in the accumulation of just these five 'heaps' or 'aggregates' (*skandha/khandha*) of physical and psychological conditions. And in this respect a buddha is no different. Yet a buddha has transformed these five into an expression and embodiment of Dharma. Thus rather than, or as well as, consisting in the accumulation of these five aggregates, the psychological make-up of the Buddha might be considered as consisting in the accumulation of another set of five 'aggregates', namely, the various qualities of perfect conduct (*śīla/sīla*), meditation (*samādhi*), wisdom (*prajñā/paññā*), freedom (*vimukti/vimutti*), and knowledge and understanding (*vimukti-jñāna-darśana/vimutti-ñāṇa-dassana*).[41]

Śrāvaka-buddhas, pratyeka-buddhas, and samyak-sambuddhas

In this chapter we have seen how the Buddhist tradition regards a particular historical individual—Siddhārtha Gautama—as an instance of a certain kind of rare and extraordinary being—a buddha. Such a being having resolved to become a buddha by making a vow in the presence of some previous buddha of a far distant age, practises the perfections for countless lives and finally, born as a man, attains buddhahood by finding 'the path to the cessation of suffering'; he then goes on to teach this path to the cessation of suffering to others so that they may reach the same realization as he has done, so that they too may become 'awakened' or *buddha*. Both Gautama and those who come to realization by following his teachings—the arhats—may be referred to as 'buddhas' since both, by the rooting out of greed, hatred, and delusion, have come to understand suffering and the path to its cessation. And yet, as the tradition acknowledges, some difference between Gautama and the arhats must remain. Gautama, *the* Buddha, has found the path by his individual striving without the immediate help of an already awakened being and then gone on to show others the way.[42] His followers on the other hand may have come to precisely the same understanding and realization as Gautama but they have done so with the assistance of his unequalled abilities as teacher.

We have then here two kinds of buddha: 'the perfectly, fully awakened one' (*samyak-/sammā-sambuddha*) like Gautama, and the arhat or 'one who has awakened as a disciple' (*śrāvaka-/sāvaka-buddha*). Thus while on the one hand wishing to stress that the 'awakening' of Gautama and his 'awakened' disciples is the same, the Buddhist tradition has also been unable to resist the tendency to dwell on the superiority of Gautama's achievement. Apart from becoming 'awakened' as a samyaksam-buddha or arhat, Buddhist texts also envisage a third possibility: that one might become awakened by one's unaided effort without hearing the teaching of a buddha and yet fail to teach others the way to awakening. Such a one is known as a 'solitary buddha' (*pratyeka-/pacceka-buddha*).

The sense that the achievements of these three kinds of 'buddha' are at once the same but different—the Buddha's achievement being somehow superior—is a tension that lies at the heart of Buddhist thought and, as we shall see, explains in part certain later developments of Buddhist thought known as the Mahāyāna. How does the Buddha's superiority to arhats and pratyekabuddhas manifest itself? In order to answer this question it is useful to return to a question raised earlier concerning the Buddha's nature as man or god. In the context especially of early Buddhism and Buddhism as practised today in Sri Lanka and South-East Asia, once it has been established that theoretically the Buddha is neither a god nor a 'Saviour', there has been a tendency amongst observers to conclude that the Buddha ought then to be seen by Buddhists as simply a man—as if this was the only alternative. A further conclusion is then drawn that, since Buddhism teaches that there is no 'saviour', the only way to 'salvation' must be through one's own unaided effort.

True, the Buddha did not create the world and he cannot simply 'save' us—and the Buddhist would say that it is not so much that the Buddha lacks the power as that the world is just not like that: no being could do such a thing. Yet although no saviour, the Buddha is still 'the teacher of gods and men, the unsurpassed trainer of unruly men'; in the Pali commentaries of fifth-century Sri Lanka he is often referred to as simply *the* Teacher (*satthar*). That is, we have here to do with a question of alternative religious imagery and metaphor: not the 'Father' or 'Saviour' of Judaism or Christianity, but the Teacher. If one is not familiar with the Indian cultural context it is easy to underestimate the potency of the image here. For a Buddhist no being can match the Buddha's abilities to teach and instruct in order to push beings gently towards the final truth of things. A buddha may not be able to save us—that is, he cannot simply turn us into awakened beings—yet, if awakening is what we are intent on, the presence of a buddha is still our best hope. Indeed some contemporary Buddhists would suggest that it is no longer possible to reach awakening since conditions are now unpropitious; rather it is better to aspire to be reborn at the time of the next buddha or in a world where a buddha is now teaching so that one can hear the teachings directly from a buddha. For the Buddhist tradition, then, the Buddha is above all the great Teacher; it is his rediscovery of the path to the cessation of suffering and his teaching of that path that offers beings the possibility of following that path themselves.

As Teacher, then, the Buddha set in motion the wheel of Dharma. As a result of setting in motion the wheel of Dharma he established a community of accomplished disciples, the Saṅgha. In the Buddha, Dharma, and Saṅgha the Buddhist thus has 'three jewels' (*tri-ratna/ti-ratana*) to which to go for refuge. Going to the three jewels for refuge is realized by the formal recitation of a threefold formula: 'To the Buddha I go for refuge; to the Dharma I go for refuge; to the Saṅgha I go for refuge.' Going to these three jewels for refuge is essentially what defines an individual as a Buddhist. Having considered the Buddha, let us now turn to consider his teaching and how that teaching is put into practice by those who take refuge in the three jewels.

2

The Word of the Buddha

Buddhist Scriptures and Schools

Dharma: texts, practice, and realization

The Buddha is author of no books or treatises. Moreover it is extremely unlikely that any of his immediate disciples wrote anything of his teachings down. And yet we are told that the Buddha devoted some forty-five years of his life entirely to teaching and that by the end of his life he was quite satisfied that he had succeeded in passing on his teachings carefully and exactly, such that they would long be of benefit and help to the world.[1] This state of affairs is worth reflecting on, for it reveals something of the nature of Buddhism.

Buddhism cannot be reduced to a collection of theoretical writings nor a philosophical system of thought—although both these form an important part of its tradition. What lies at the heart of Buddhism, according to its own understanding of the matter, is *dharma*. Dharma is not an exclusively Buddhist concept, but one which is common to Indian philosophical, religious, social, and political thought in its entirety. According to Indian thought Dharma is that which is the basis of things, the underlying nature of things, the way things are; in short, it is the truth about things, the truth about the world. More than this, Dharma is the way we should act, for if we are to avoid bringing harm to both ourselves and others we should strive to act in a way that is true to the way things are, that accords with the underlying truth of things. Ultimately the only true way to act is in conformity with Dharma.

The notion of Dharma in Indian thought thus has both a descriptive and a prescriptive aspect: it is the way things are and the way to act. The various schools of Indian religious and philosophical thought and practice all offer slightly different visions (*darśana*) of Dharma—different visions of the way things are and the way to act. Of course, when we examine the teachings of the various schools, we find that there is often substantial common ground and much borrowing from each other. Yet the Buddha's vision and understanding of Dharma must be reckoned to have had a profound influence on Indian culture and, to an extent unparalleled by other visions of Dharma, on cultures beyond India.

The Buddha regarded the Dharma he had found as 'profound, hard to see, hard to understand, peaceful, sublime, beyond the sphere of mere reasoning, subtle, to be experienced by the wise'. Thus knowledge of Dharma is not something that is acquired simply by being told the necessary information or by reading the appropriate texts. Knowledge of Dharma is not a matter of scholarly and intellectual study. This does mean that such study may not have a part to play, yet it can never be the whole story. In fact according to an ancient and authoritative view of the matter knowledge of Dharma comes about as a result of the interplay between three kinds of understanding (*prajñā/paññā*): that which arises from listening (*śruta/suta*), that which arises from reflection (*cintā*), and that which arises from spiritual practice (*bhāvanā*).[2] The aim of Buddhism is to put into practice a particular way of living the 'holy life' or 'spiritual life' (*brahma-cariya*) that involves training in ethical conduct (*śīla/sīla*) and meditative and contemplative techniques (*samādhi*) and which culminates in the direct realization of the very knowledge (*prajñā/paññā*) the Buddha himself reached under the tree of awakening. Therefore what the Buddha taught is often referred to in the early texts as a system of 'training' (*śikṣā/sikkhā*), and his disciples may be referred to as being 'in training' (*śaikṣa/sekha*) or 'not in need of further training' (*aśaikṣa/asekha*). Thus in certain important respects the nature of the knowledge that the Buddha was trying to convey to his pupils is more akin to a skill, like knowing how to play a musical instrument, than a piece of information, such as what time the Manchester train leaves tomorrow.

That knowledge of Dharma was conceived of in this way explains in part why the written word was not originally the medium for its communication. Practical training is difficult to impart and acquire simply on the basis of theoretical manuals; one needs a teacher who can demonstrate the training and also comment on and encourage one in one's own attempts to put the instructions into practice.[3] In fact a sense that knowledge is not properly communicated by the written word colours the traditional Indian attitude to learning in general: knowledge must be passed from teacher to pupil directly. This does not mean that at the time of the Buddha India had no literature. On the contrary, in the form of the *Ṛg Veda* India has a literature that predates the Buddha by perhaps as much as a thousand years. But this literature is 'oral'. It was composed orally, memorized, and then passed from teacher to pupil directly by a process of oral recitation for centuries, without ever being committed to writing. India's is, of course, not the only culture to have an ancient oral literature; the *Iliad* and the *Odyssey*, for example, grew out of a tradition of oral composition, yet the oral origins of traditional Indian learning continued to inform its structure long after texts had begun to be committed to writing.[4]

In presenting its teachings to the world, the Buddhist tradition would thus point towards an unbroken lineage or succession of teachers and pupils: just as the Buddha took care to instruct his pupils, so they in turn took care to instruct theirs. The visible and concrete manifestation of this succession is in the first place the Saṅgha, the community of ordained monks (*bhikkhu*) and nuns (*bhikkhunī*). Becoming a Buddhist monk or nun requires a particular ceremony that is legitimate only if properly carried out according to prescribed rules, which apparently go right back to the time of the Buddha himself. In particular the prescriptions for the ceremony require the presence of a minimum of five fully ordained *bhikkhus* of at least ten years' standing. Thus when someone ordains as a Buddhist monk there is in effect a direct link back to the presence of the Buddha himself. Of course, the principle of the passing of the teachings directly from person to person may also operate outside the Saṅgha, for members of the Saṅgha do not only teach other members of the Saṅgha, they teach lay people as well. Yet the Saṅgha remains the tangible thread of the tradition.

So the Buddha's Dharma is mediated to us via the Saṅgha—a community that ideally does not merely hand down some vague recollection of what the Buddha taught but actually lives the teaching. In the Pali commentaries written down in Sri Lanka in the fifth century CE a distinction was made between two kinds of monastic duty: that of books and that of practice (see below, pp. 104–5).[5] The former is concerned with the study of the theory as preserved in Buddhist writings. The latter is the straightforward attempt to put the Buddha's system of training into practice, to live the spiritual life as prescribed by the Buddha and his followers. Although this formal distinction is found in the writings of a particular Buddhist school, the point being highlighted holds good for Buddhism as a whole. Throughout the history of Buddhism there has existed a certain tension between the monk who is a great scholar and theoretician and the monk who is a realized practitioner. Something of the same tension is indicated in the sixth and seventh centuries in China with the arising of the Ch'an (Japanese Zen) school of Buddhism, whose well-known suspicion of theoretical formulations of the teaching is summed up by the traditional stanza:

> A special tradition outside the scriptures;
> Not founded on words and letters;
> Pointing directly to the heart of man;
> Seeing into one's own nature and attaining Buddhahood.[6]

The same kind of tension is in part reflected in a threefold characterization of Dharma itself as textual tradition (*pariyatti*), practice (*paṭipatti*), and realization (*paṭivedha*) once again found in the Pali commentaries.[7] The first refers to the sum of Buddhist theory as contained in Buddhist scriptures, the second to the putting into practice of those teachings, while the third to the direct understanding acquired consequent upon the practice. The rest of this chapter will primarily be concerned with Dharma as textual tradition.

Dharma as textual tradition goes back to the teachings heard directly from the Buddha. These teachings were, it seems, memorized by the immediate followers of the Buddha. For several generations perhaps, the teachings of the Buddha were preserved and handed down directly from master to pupil orally without ever being committed to writing. It is tempting for us in the modern world to be sceptical about the reliability of this method of transmission, but it was the norm in ancient India; the use of mnemonic techniques such as the numbered list and frequent repetition of certain portions of the material within a given text aided reliable transmission.[8] Indeed the evidence of the transmission of the Vedic texts, for example, is that oral transmission can be more reliable than a tradition of written texts involving the copying of manuscripts.[9]

In the early phase of their transmission then the only access to Buddhist 'texts' was by hearing them directly from someone who had heard and learnt them from someone else, this oral transmission of the texts being an activity that went on primarily within the community of monks. Even after these texts began to be committed to writing their study was primarily a monastic concern. Thus the ordinary lay Buddhist's access to Buddhist teachings was always through the Saṅgha: he or she learnt the Dharma by sitting in the presence of a monk or nun and listening to their exposition of the teachings. Thus, in so far as a monk or nun necessarily follows a way of life defined by the prescriptions and rules of Buddhist monasticism, the study of Buddhist theory always took place in a context of practice. It is only in the twentieth century—with the arrival of the modern printed book in traditional Buddhist societies, and the demand in the West for books and information on Buddhism—that this state of affairs has begun to change. That is, for over two millennia it was only by some form of contact with the living tradition of practice that there could be any knowledge of Buddhism.

The first recitation of scriptures: the four Nikāyas/Āgamas and the Vinaya

According to a generally accepted ancient tradition, the first attempt to agree the form of the Buddhist textual tradition, what was remembered as the authoritative 'word of the Buddha', took place some three months after the Buddha's death at the town of Rājagṛha (Pali Rājagaha) in northern India when 500 arhats took part in a 'communal recitation' (*saṃgīti*). This event is commonly referred to in modern writings as 'the first Buddhist council'. Significantly the earliest Buddhist tradition attempts to resolve any tension between theory and practice by insisting that the first communal recitation of scriptures was carried out by 500 individuals who had each realized direct and perfect knowledge of Dharma. According to the accounts of this communal recitation, what was remembered of the Buddha's teachings fell into two classes: the general discourses of the Buddha, the *sūtras* (Pali *sutta*), and his prescriptions for the lifestyle of the Buddhist monk, the 'discipline' or *vinaya*. Some accounts suggest there was a third category, *mātṛkās* (Pali *mātikā*) or summary mnemonic lists of significant points of the teaching. At any rate, later canonical collections of Buddhist writings were subsequently often referred to as 'the three baskets' (*tri-piṭaka/ti-piṭaka*): the basket of discipline, the basket of discourses, and the basket of 'further dharma' (*abhidharma/abhidhamma*), whose development is in part related to the use of the summary mnemonic lists or *mātṛkās*.

Three principal 'canons' of Buddhist scriptures survive today corresponding to the three main traditions of living Buddhism: the Pali or Theravāda canon of the southern tradition of Sri Lanka and South-East Asia, the Chinese Tripiṭaka of the eastern tradition of China, Korea, and Japan, and the Tibetan Kanjur (*bKa' 'gyur*) and Tenjur (*bsTan 'gyur*) of the northern tradition of Tibet and Mongolia. All three of these collections are extensive. Modern printed editions of the Pali canon run to some fifty moderately sized volumes; the Taishō edition of the Chinese Tripiṭaka comprises fifty-five volumes, each containing some 1,000 pages of Chinese characters; together the Tibetan Kanjur and Tenjur comprise 300 traditional *poti* volumes. When the contents of the three canons are compared it is apparent that, while significant portions of the Pali canon are paralleled in the Chinese collection, and there is considerable overlap between the Chinese Tripiṭaka and the Kanjur and Tenjur, Buddhism as a whole does not possess a 'canon' of scriptures in the manner of the Hebrew Bible of Judaism, the Old and New Testaments of Christianity, or the Qu'ran of Islam. It is also apparent that the Chinese and Tibetan canons do not represent *en bloc* translations of ancient Indian canonical collections of Buddhist texts, but rather libraries of translations of individual Indian works made over the centuries (see Chapter 10). In the case of the Chinese canon this process of translating Indian texts began in the second century CE and continued for over 800 years; the process of arranging and cataloguing these texts continues down to the present century. In the case of Tibetan Kanjur and Tenjur the translation process was carried out between the seventh and thirteenth centuries, while the precise contents and arrangement of these two collections has never been fixed.

What of the Pali canon? The use of the term 'Pali' as the name of the language of the Theravāda canon of Buddhist scriptures derives from the expression *pāli-bhāsā*, 'the language of the [Buddhist] texts'. This language is an ancient Indian language closely related to Sanskrit, the language of classical Indian culture *par excellence*. At the time of the Buddha, Sanskrit appears to have been very much the language of brahmanical learning and religious ritual. The Buddha therefore seems to have deliberately and consciously eschewed Sanskrit, preferring to teach in the ordinary vernacular—the various Middle Indo-Aryan dialects, known as Prakrit, which were spoken across the north of India in the fifth century BCE.[10] In the first century or so after the death of the Buddha, as Buddhism began gradually to spread across the Indian subcontinent, different groups of monks and the evolving schools of Buddhism appear to have preserved their own versions of the Buddha's teaching orally in their local dialect. However, as time passed there was a tendency for the language of 'the scriptures' to become frozen and increasingly removed from any actually spoken dialect. At the same time Sanskrit was becoming less an exclusively brahmanical language and more the accepted language of Indian culture—the language in which to communicate learning and literature right across India. Thus Buddhist scriptures were subject to varying degrees of 'sanskritization' ('translation' is too strong here since the order of difference between Middle Indian and Sanskrit is similar to that between modern English and Chaucer's or Mallory's English). Although basically Middle Indo-Aryan, the language of the Pali canon is thus something of a hybrid, preserving linguistic features of several dialects and showing some evidence of sanskritization.

Theravāda Buddhist tradition traces the Pali canon back to a recension of Buddhist scriptures brought from northern India to Sri Lanka in the third century BCE by Mahinda, a Buddhist monk who was the son of the emperor Aśoka. Mahinda and his company brought no books, the texts being in their heads, but the tradition is that the Pali texts were subsequently written down for the first time in the first century BCE. The historical value of this tradition is uncertain. Most scholars would be sceptical of the suggestion that the Pali canon existed exactly as we have it today already in the middle of third century BCE. We know, however, that what the commentators had before them in the fifth century CE in Sri Lanka corresponded fairly exactly to what we have now, and the original north Indian provenance and relative antiquity of much of the Pali canon seems to be guaranteed on linguistic grounds.[11] Significant portions of the material it contains must go back to the third century BCE.

How many other versions or recensions of the canon of Buddhist scriptures existed in partially or more fully sanskritized Middle Indian dialects is unclear. The Pali canon is the only one to survive apparently complete in an Indian language. Of the other ancient Indian versions of the canon, we have only isolated fragments and portions in the original Indian languages. More substantial portions are, however, preserved in translation especially in the Chinese Tripiṭaka. This, along with what Buddhist literature as a whole reveals about its own history, allows us to know something of the content of these other ancient Indian canons and also to identify the generally more archaic material—material that must be relatively close in time to the ancient Rājagṛha recitation. This material takes the form of the four primary Nikāyas or 'collections' of the Buddha's discourses

—also known as the four Āgamas or books of textual 'tradition' —along with the Vinaya or Buddhist monastic rule. These texts constitute the essential common heritage of Buddhist thought, and from this perspective the subsequent history of Buddhism is a working out of their implications. This is not to imply that Buddhism can somehow be reduced to what is contained in these texts; one must understand that this 'working out' in practice constitutes much of what Buddhism has actually been and, today, is. Nevertheless, in the quest for an understanding of Buddhist thought these texts represent the most convenient starting point.

Today we have two full versions of this Nikāya/Āgama material: a version in Pali forming part of the Pali canon and a version in Chinese translation contained in the Chinese Tripiṭaka. It is usual scholarly practice to refer to the Pali version by the term 'Nikāya' and the Chinese by the term 'Āgama'. Like the Pali canon as a whole, it is impossible to date the Pali Nikāyas in their present form with any precision. The Chinese Āgamas were translated into Chinese from Sanskrit or Middle Indo-Aryan dialects around the end of the fourth century CE, but the texts upon which they rest must like the Nikāyas date from the centuries before the beginning of the Christian era. Portions of further versions of this material also come down to us in Tibetan translation in the Tibetan Kanjur.

The four Nikāyas/Āgamas arrange the Buddha's discourses in the first place according to length. The collection of long discourses (*dīrghāgama/dīgha-nikāya*) comprises some thirty sūtras arranged in three volumes; the collection of middle-length discourses (*madhyamāgama/majjhima-nikāya*) comprises some 150 sūtras in the Pali version and 200 in the Chinese. Finally there are two collections of shorter sūtras. The first of these is 'the grouped collection' (*saṃyuktāgama/saṃyutta nikāya*) which consists of short sūtras grouped principally according to subject matter and dominated by the subjects of dependent arising, the aggregates, the sense-spheres, and the path. The oral nature of early Buddhist literature resulted in the proliferation of numbered lists, in part as mnemonic devices, and the 'numbered collection' (*ekottarikāgama/aṅguttara-nikāya*) consists of short sūtras built around such a numbered list and grouped according to number rather than topic.

In this book I generally quote from and refer to the Pali recension of these texts. Using the Pali recension is in part a matter of convenience and not a question of thereby suggesting that the traditions it preserves are always the oldest and most authentic available to us, even if it is likely that this is generally the case. The Pali versions of these texts have been translated into English in their entirety (unlike the Chinese and Tibetan versions) and are readily available. That these texts have become widely known over the past century through their Pali form has sometimes led to an attitude which sees them as presenting the peculiar perspective of Theravāda Buddhism. But, as Étienne Lamotte pointed out forty years ago, the doctrinal basis common to the Chinese Āgamas and Pali Nikāyas is remarkably uniform; such variations as exist affect only the mode of expression or the arrangement of topics.[12] Far from representing sectarian Buddhism, these texts above all constitute the common ancient heritage of Buddhism.

The failure to appreciate this results in a distorted view of ancient Buddhism, and its subsequent development and history both within and outside India. From their frequent references to and quotations from the Nikāyas/Āgamas, it is apparent that all subsequent Indian Buddhist thinkers and writers of whatever school or persuasion, including the Mahāyāna—and most certainly those thinkers such as Nāgārjuna, Asaṅga, and Vasubandhu, who became the great Indian fathers of east Asian and Tibetan Buddhism—were completely familiar with this material and treated it as the authoritative word of the Buddha. When disagreements arose among Buddhists they did not concern the authority of the Nikāya/Āgama material, but certain points of its interpretation and the authority of other quite different material, namely the Mahāyāna sūtras, which we shall return to presently.

Alongside the four primary Nikāya/Āgama collections of sūtras the ancient Indian canons like the Pali canon preserved a 'minor' (*kṣudraka/khuddaka*) collection of miscellaneous texts that were also recognized as having the authority of the Buddha's word. This fifth collection included such works as the *Dharmapada* ('sayings on Dharma') and the *Jātaka* or stories concerning the previous lives of the Buddha. The four Nikāyas together with a greater or lesser number of miscellaneous minor texts constituted 'the basket of discourses' (*Sūtra/Sutta Piṭaka*) for the earliest Buddhist schools.[13]

The Pali canon, Chinese Tripiṭaka, and Tibetan Kanjur all preserve versions of the ancient 'basket of monastic discipline' (*Vinaya Piṭaka*): the Pali canon and Kanjur one each, the Chinese Tripiṭaka four, plus an incomplete fifth. All six extant versions of the Vinaya fall into two basic parts. The first is a detailed analysis of the rules which constitute the *prātimokṣa* (Pali *pāṭimokkha*) and which govern the life of the individual monk or nun. The second comprises twenty 'sections' (*skandhaka/khandhaka*) which set out the proper procedures for conducting the various communal acts of the Saṅgha, such as ordination (see Chapter 4).[14]

Sutra and Abhidharma: the problem of textual authenticity

The Nikāyas/Āgamas are collections of sūtras or 'discourses' regarded as delivered by the Buddha. The older term for a discourse of the Buddha preserved in Pali is *sutta*. It is not clear what this term originally meant. When Buddhists started sanskritizing their texts they chose the word *sūtra*. This is a term which literally means 'thread' (compare English 'suture') but in a literary context refers especially to authoritative brahmanical texts consisting of a string of terse, aphoristic verses which a pupil might memorize and a teacher might take as the basis for exposition. Buddhist sūtras, however, are not in this form. As Richard Gombrich has pointed out, it is perhaps more likely that Middle Indo-Aryan *sutta* corresponds to Sanskrit *sūkta*, which means 'something that is well said' and was early in the history of Indian literature used to refer to the inspired hymns of the Vedic seers that make up the collection of the Ṛg Veda. Early

Buddhists can therefore be seen as claiming a status on a par with the Vedas for the utterances of the Buddha.[15]

Be that as it may, a Buddhist sūtra always begins with the words: 'Thus have I heard. At one time the Lord was staying at . . .'[16] The later tradition understands these as the words of Ānanda, the Buddha's attendant, introducing each discourse of the Buddha at the first communal recitation. The inclusion of this particular formula at the beginning of a Buddhist text indicates that the text claims the status of 'the word of the Buddha' (*buddha-vacana*). It is clear that from a very early date there is a tacit understanding that to claim this status for a text is not exactly to claim that it represents only what has actually been uttered by the Buddha in person. Even in the Nikāya/Āgama collections accepted as 'the word of the Buddha' by all ancient schools, there are sūtras presented as delivered not by the Buddha but by monks and nuns who were his chief pupils—some of them after his death.

As indicated above, the notion of a fixed canon of Buddhist scriptures is somewhat problematic. And we must be careful not to impose inappropriate notions of 'canon' and authenticity—derived, say, from Christianity—on the Buddhist tradition. Even in the accounts of the first Buddhist council we are told of a monk who, on hearing of the recitation of the Buddha's teaching by the 500 arhats, declared that he preferred to remember the teaching as he himself had heard it directly from the Buddha.[17] For several centuries as Buddhism spread across the Indian subcontinent it is clear that, while the Buddhist community accepted and preserved a common core of textual material, this material constituted a 'canon' in only a rather loose and informal sense; that each and every collection of textual material should correspond exactly was not regarded by the early community as the critical issue.

This state of affairs is reflected in the discussion of 'the four great authorities' (*mahāpadesa*) to which a monk might appeal for accepting a particular teaching as authentic Dharma: that he has heard it from the Buddha himself, from a community of elder monks, from a group of learned monks, or from one learned monk. In each case the Buddha is recorded as having instructed monks to examine and consider the teaching in order to see if it conforms to what they already know the teaching to be.[18] This is not quite as subjective as it sounds. The discourses of the Buddha as preserved in the Nikāyas do not of themselves constitute a systematic exposition of Buddhist thought with a beginning, middle, and end. Each discourse is rather presented as a more or less self-contained piece on a particular theme. And yet, the discourses as a whole do contain quite explicit indications of how these various themes relate to each other and fit together to form an overall structure and pattern.[19] The final criterion for judging a teaching lies in an appreciation and understanding of this overall structure and pattern of the teaching. Thus at times the question of who originally spoke the words appears irrelevant to the tradition: 'Whatever monk, nun, male or female layfollower, god or . . . Brahmā might teach and proclaim Dharma, it is all considered as taught and proclaimed by the Teacher [i.e. the Buddha].'[20] Nevertheless the principle that certain texts represent the primary 'word of the Buddha', while others are the secondary work of commentators and scholars, remains significant to the Buddhist tradition. And the question of just which texts are to be counted as the word of the Buddha has, at particular points in the history of Buddhism, been a critical one.

The term *abhidharma* (Pali *abhidhamma*) means approximately 'higher' or 'further' Dharma. In many ways the extant works of 'the basket of Abhidharma', the third part of the ancient canon of Buddhist scriptures, can be seen as continuing the process of systematization already evident in the Nikāyas. That some form of commentary and interpretation formed part of Buddhism almost from its inception is indicated by certain of the sūtras in the Nikāyas. The *Mahāvedalla Sutta*, for example, recounts how a nun is approached and asked to comment on certain technical terms of the Buddha's teaching;[21] in the Vinaya each rule of the monastic discipline is followed by 'a word analysis' which defines key terms of the rulings; and one of the later books of the Pali canon must be the *Niddesa* ('Exposition'), which takes the form of a commentary on a section of another work of the canon, the *Suttanipāta* ('Group of Discourses'). But it is the Abhidharma *par excellence* that represents the earliest attempt to give a full and systematic statement of the Buddha's teaching on the basis of what is contained in his discourses. The traditional understanding is thus that while the sūtras represent the Buddha's teaching applied in particular circumstances at a particular time and place, the Abhidharma is the Buddha's teaching stated in bare and general terms without reference to any particular circumstances.

Something of the Abhidharma method must go back to the lifetime of the Buddha himself. Certainly much of its outlook and many of its principles must be regarded as still forming part of the common heritage of Buddhism, alongside the Nikāya/Āgama sūtra collections and the monastic rule of the Vinaya. Yet in addition to what is common, we begin to find in the Abhidharma literature interpretations and understandings of the Sūtra material that are specific to particular schools of Buddhism. We must be careful, however, to understand this situation in the light of our knowledge of just what constituted a Buddhist 'school' in ancient India, and avoid the trap of thinking that Buddhist 'schools' evolved and defined themselves in the same way as, say, Christian 'sects' or 'denominations'.

We have substantial knowledge of the Abhidharma literature and systems of only two ancient Buddhist schools: the Sarvāstivādins and the Theravādins. The only obvious similarity between their respective Abhidharma Piṭaka collections, however, is that they both contain just seven works (see Chapter 7). Despite the great status and authority attributed to the Abhidharma and the claim that it is 'the word of the Buddha', both these schools explicitly acknowledge the work of the Buddha's chief disciples in arranging and transmitting the Abhidharma. From this point of view, the Abhidharma has for the tradition the status of a sūtra or set of headings expanded by one of the Buddha's disciples and then subsequently endorsed by the Buddha.[22] Even so, some ancient Buddhists, such as the Sautrāntikas or 'those who follow the Sūtra', came to resist the notion that the Abhidharma had the full status of 'the word of the Buddha'. Yet while such a group may have wished to deny the Abhidharma the status of the Buddha's word, it is clear that they did not seek to question the method and principles of Abhidharma in their entirety; what they were concerned to question were particular interpretations and understandings current amongst certain exponents of Abhidharma.

To sum up, a typical ancient Indian 'canon' of Buddhist texts consisted of 'three baskets' (*tripiṭaka*): the Sūtra Piṭaka or 'basket of discourses' (comprising four main collections of the discourses of the Buddha, often with a supplementary collection of miscellaneous texts), the Vinaya Piṭaka or 'basket of monastic discipline', and the Abhidharma Piṭaka or 'basket of further Dharma'. Only one such ancient Tripiṭaka survives complete in an ancient Indian language, the Pali canon of the Theravādin tradition of Sri Lanka and South-East Asia. How many other recensions of this ancient Tripiṭaka existed is unclear, but the contents and arrangement of others may be partially reconstructed on the basis of the surviving fragments in Indian languages and Chinese and Tibetan translations; in this respect we have the fullest knowledge of the canon of the Sarvāstivādins.

The origin of the ancient Buddhist schools and their exegetical literatures

In turning to the complex problem of the origin of the ancient Indian Buddhist schools, we must at the outset register that we are speaking primarily of divisions and groupings within the community of monks and nuns or Saṅgha. In most cases the basis of such divisions would have been of little or no concern to the ordinary lay Buddhist in ancient India. In other words, we are not dealing with great schisms of the kind associated with the Reformation in the history of Christianity, or with one Buddhist group accusing another of 'heresy'. In order to understand the processes at work here it is necessary first to consider the notion of formal division in the Saṅgha (*saṅgha-bheda*) from the legal perspective of the Buddhist monastic code encapsulated in the Vinaya.[23]

Two communal ceremonies are fundamental to the constitution of the Saṅgha; the first is the ordination ceremony itself, the second is the fortnightly rehearsal of the rule (*prātimokṣa/pāṭimokkha*). As I have already mentioned, for an ordination to be legitimate the participation of at least five monks of ten years' standing is required. The *prātimokṣa* ceremony involves the gathering together of the members of the Saṅgha in a given locality in order to recite the rule and confess any breaches; a valid ceremony requires a quorum of at least four monks. Since both valid ordination and *prātimokṣa* ceremonies are thus essential for any group of monks' claim to be monks, it follows that, even in the short term, only a schismatic group that includes at least four monks in its party is viable; for a schismatic group to be viable in the long term it must include five senior monks in its party. Clearly in the first century or so after the Buddha's death, as the numbers in the Saṅgha increased and it expanded across first northern India and then the whole subcontinent, the establishment of groups of monks around particular teachers, perhaps associated with particular views on certain issues of Abhidharma, was both natural and inevitable. But as long as such groups followed essentially the same Vinaya and recognized the validity of each other's ordination lineage, movement between the groups would present no problem: monks from one group could legitimately attend and participate in the ceremonies of another group; there was no question of formal division in the Saṅgha.

One should note here that holding a particular opinion or view on *any* matter—let alone on a moot point of Abhidharma philosophy—cannot be grounds for expulsion from the Saṅgha. The grounds for expulsion from the Saṅgha are sexual intercourse, taking what is not given, intentionally killing a human being, and falsely claiming spiritual attainments. The only opinion or view that is even to be censured according to the Vinaya is the view that sexual intercourse is not an 'obstacle'.[24] It is easy to see the practical reason why: it threatens the very basis of a celibate community. Since the Vinaya left monks and nuns largely free to develop the Buddha's teaching doctrinally as they saw fit, there would be little incentive to provoke a schism on purely doctrinal grounds. What was of public concern was living by the monastic rules, not doctrinal conformity. We are dealing here with orthopraxy, not orthodoxy. The implications of this state of affairs were not fully realized in the earlier scholarly studies of the formation of the Buddhist schools, such as André Bareau's important work, *Les Sectes bouddhiques du petit véhicule*.

It is not surprising to find then that the earliest indication in Buddhist writings of schismatic tendencies in the Saṅgha concerns interpretation of the Vinaya and not questions of Buddhist doctrine. As with the first 'communal recitation', the ancient sources that have come down to us via various schools are in broad agreement that one hundred years—the figure is likely to be approximate—after the death of the Buddha a dispute arose concerning ten points of Vinaya. A group of senior monks convened at Vaiśālī (Pali Vesālī), decided against the ten points, and initiated a second communal recitation of the scriptures.

The traditions preserved in the ancient sources concerning the Buddhist councils and the division of the Saṅgha into its various schools are complex and inconsistent. Despite the scholarly discussion that has been devoted to them, a satisfactory interpretation of these sources explaining the contradictions and presenting a coherent and consistent history of Buddhism in the centuries after the death of the Buddha has yet to be worked out. It seems clear that, at some point after the Vaiśālī meeting, the primitive Saṅgha formally divided into two parties each of which thenceforth had its own ordination traditions. The ancient accounts are inconsistent as to what provoked the split. Some suggest that it was the result of a dispute over five points, later associated with a monk named Mahādeva, concerning the nature of the arhat. That this was indeed the cause of the division was accepted by Bareau. Other ancient sources attribute the division to a disagreement over questions of Vinaya, and the more recent scholarship suggests that this is the explanation to be preferred. According to this view a reformist group in the Saṅgha proposed tightening discipline on certain matters of Vinaya, while the majority were happy to leave things as they stood. Since the two parties failed to come to an agreement, the Saṅgha divided into two: the reformist *sthaviras* (Pali *thera*) or 'elders' and the majority *mahāsāṃghikas* or 'those of the great community'.[25] The dating of this important event in the history of Buddhism is also extremely problematic since it hinges on the vexed question of the date of the death of the Buddha himself. With the growing scholarly consensus that dates the Buddha's death at the end of the fifth century BCE or even the beginning of the fourth, it seems that we must place the event of the first division of the Saṅgha some time around the beginning of the third century BCE before the accession of the emperor Aśoka (*c.*268 BCE); although it is not impossible that we should follow certain of our sources which suggest that the division occurred actually during the reign of Aśoka.

In the century or so following this fundamental division of the Saṅgha into the Sthaviras and Mahāsāṃghikas it is clear that further schools emerged. Yet the processes by which these schools came into being is not so clear; whether they occurred as the result of formal disagreements over some Vinaya issue that resulted in deadlock and was thus the occasion for formal division of the Saṅgha (i.e. *saṅgha-bheda*), or whether they merely represent *de facto* divisions of the Saṅgha that evolved haphazardly as the Saṅgha spread and grew, is not certain. The names of the schools variously suggest characteristic teachings, geographical location, or the followings of particular teachers. At least some of the schools mentioned by later Buddhist tradition are likely to have been informal schools of thought in the manner of 'Cartesians', 'British Empiricists', or 'Kantians' for the history of modern philosophy.[26]

The primary sub-schools of the Sthaviras focus on certain technical points of Abhidharma. The Vātsīputrīyas ('followers of Vātsīputra') and their sub-schools adopted a particular position on thc ontological status of 'the person' (*pudgala/puggala*) and were thus referred to as 'advocates of the doctrine [of the existence] of the person' (*pudgala-vādin*).

Another group developed a particular understanding of the way things exist in past, present, and future time; they were known as 'advocates of the doctrine that all things [past, present, and future] exist' (*sarvāsti-vādin*). Yet another group were known as 'advocates of the doctrine of analysis' (*vibhajyavādin*). In some contexts this last group is represented as analysing existence as either in the past, present, or future, in opposition to the Sarvāstivādins; elsewhere the exact significance of the appellation is not made clear. The Sri Lankan Theravāda or 'advocates of the doctrine of the elders' in fact traces its lineage through the Vibhajjavādins (Sanskrit *vibhajyavādin*). According to their traditions the Vibhajjavādins were the favoured party in a dispute that took place at Pāṭaliputra during the reign of the emperor Aśoka. Bareau therefore concluded that this dispute concerned the split between the Sarvāstivādins and Vibhajjavādins on the matter of the abstruse Abhidharma question of existence in the three times. The ancient accounts of this dispute are, however, confused and inconsistent.[27] Its basis, in so far as it is stated in the sources, seems to have been not so much the finer points of Abhidharma philosophy as a Vinaya matter: the fact that non-Buddhists were masquerading as Buddhist monks without being properly ordained or keeping to the rules of the Vinaya. The outcome is stated as the expulsion of the false monks from the Saṅgha and a third communal recitation (after those of Rājagṛha and Vaiśālī) of the canon of Buddhist scriptures. The latter turned on—rather incongruously given the stated nature of the dispute—the exposition by Moggaliputtatissa of the *Kathāvatthu* ('Discussion Points'), a manual of moot Abhidharma points, which was thereafter counted as one of the canonical works of the Pali Abhidhamma Piṭaka. As K. R. Norman suggests, it would appear that two different events have been conflated.

The relevance of such abstruse matters as existence in the three times of present, past, and future to the theory and practice of Buddhism may not be immediately clear to the reader, and is something I shall return to in Chapter 8. But the very technical nature of these matters makes it, I think, extremely unlikely that they were ever the real impetus behind formal division in the Saṅgha. It is inconceivable that a Buddhist monk who did or did not adopt the position of, say, *sarvāstivāda* should ever be charged with a Buddhist equivalent of 'heresy' and that this should become an issue in determining whether he could participate in the formal ceremonies of the Saṅgha. The failure to realize this is something of a shortcoming in Bareau's pioneering and scholarly study of the Buddhist councils.

Certain non-Theravādin sources are also suggestive of a dispute at Pāṭaliputra during the reign of Aśoka, but they link the dispute to the second communal recitation or, as we have seen, the question of Mahādeva's five points; only one of these sources —a relatively late one—mentions a third communal recitation in this connection.[28] Yet that some kind of dispute did occur at Pāṭaliputra during the reign of Aśoka receives some corroboration in the form of his so-called schism edict.

Ancient Buddhist sources preserve various lists of schools which invariably state the total number to be eighteen while in fact listing rather more; the number eighteen seems to be ideal and symbolic.[29] A rough assessment of the evidence in the light of the witness of inscriptional evidence, extant Vinayas, and the Chinese pilgrims, suggests that we should rather think in terms of four major groupings—the Mahāsāṃghikas, the Sthaviras, the Vātsīputrīya-Saṃmatīyas, and the Sarvāstivādins—with the Mahīśāsakas, Dharmaguptakas, and Kāśyapīyas also representing significant sub-schools of the Sthaviras.

It is legitimate, I think, to see the exposition of the basic principles and method of Abhidharma as the product of the first generation of the Buddha's disciples. As such it obviously carried great weight and authority, and for much of the tradition was indeed 'the word of the Buddha'. And yet, even while granting it the status of the Buddha's word, in acknowledging the contribution of the early disciples in its transmission, the tradition itself retains a sense that the Abhidharma is one step removed from the Teacher himself. It is in this respect that I suggest that the early Abhidharma can be seen as the original 'commentary' upon the Buddha's teaching. But as Buddhism spread across the Indian subcontinent, subsequent generations of the Buddha's disciples further refined the Abhidharma systems of thought and contributed to the gradual evolution of the different schools. Increasingly in this context the Buddhist tradition as a whole began to acknowledge freely that its new literary productions did not have the status of 'the word of the Buddha' (that is, Sūtra or Āgama), but were rather commentaries (*aṭṭhakathā*, *bhāṣya*, *vibhāṣā*) on or textbooks (*śāstra*) of the teaching of the Buddha. In all this there is no convenient point after which we can say we are dealing exclusively with self-conscious commentary. Most of the commentaries and manuals come down to us in a form that post-dates the beginning of the Christian era, yet they refer to and record the views of 'the ancient teachers', and we can be certain that some of their traditions are considerably older, although it may not always be easy to determine precisely which.

The exegetical literature of most of the ancient schools is lost. We only have significant knowledge of two traditions: the Sarvāstivādins and the Thervādins, the Sri Lankan representatives of the Sthaviras. I would like to single out two manuals that I shall be continually referring to throughout this book as providing convenient and at the same time authoritative summaries of Buddhist theory and practice. Both these manuals were produced in the fifth century CE but their authority has continued to be recognized down to the present day.

The first is the *Visuddhimagga* or 'Path of Purification', a summary statement of Theravāda teaching, whose text in English translation runs to over 800 pages.[30] It is the work of Buddhaghosa, a monk who, so the story goes, travelled from north India to Anurādhapura, the ancient capital of Sri Lanka and an important centre of Buddhist learning, where he took up residence in the Mahāvihāra (the Great Monastery). With access to earlier commentaries preserved in the Mahāvihāra, he produced, as well as the *Visuddhimagga*, definitive commentaries to the principal works of the Pali canon. The *Visuddhimagga* is one of the classic texts of the Theravāda or 'southern' tradition of Buddhism.

The second manual is the *Abhidharmakośa* or 'Treasury of Abhidharma', which takes the form of a summary statement of the teachings and traditions of the Sarvāstvādins in just less than 600 verses. Its author, Vasubandhu, a monk who lived in north India, furnished these verses with his own commentary (*bhāṣya*) which, in addition to expanding on the verses, provides a critique of the Sarvāstivāda from the perspective of the Sautrāntika school. In English translation the verses along with their commentary fill more than 1,300 pages.[31] The *Abhidharmakośa* was translated into Chinese in the sixth century and again in the seventh; later it was also translated into Tibetan. It thereby came and continues to be one of the great theoretical texts of both east Asian Buddhism and northern Buddhism.

The Mahāyāna sūtras

In this manner, in the centuries following the Buddha's death, the various ancient schools of Indian Buddhism began to evolve, preserving their distinctive recensions of the Sūtra and Vinaya Piṭakas, and developing their characteristic understandings of Abhidharma. Against this background we find, beginning around the beginning of the Christian era, a rather different kind of Buddhist literature emerging. Hitherto unknown texts that begin with the words 'thus I have heard'—the traditional opening of the discourses of the Buddha—begin to appear. In other words, these new texts present themselves not as the commentary or understanding of a particular school of Buddhism, but as actual sūtras. They thus claim the status of 'the word of the Buddha'.

The texts in question are the early sūtras of 'the Great Vehicle' (*mahāyāna*). The origins of the Mahāyāna are complex (see Chapter 9), but this was not a sectarian literature disseminated by one of the existing schools nor did it lead to the development of a formal division of the Saṅgha (*saṃgha-bheda*), with an associated Mahāyāna recension of the Vinaya. Indeed, the very idea of an exclusively Mahāyāna Vinaya seems only to have emerged in eighth/ninth-century Japan with the Tendai monk Saichō. At the time of the emergence of Mahāyāna literature in ancient India, members of the Saṅgha who were sympathetic to it followed their interest while remaining within the already existing schools and ordination lineages of the Saṅgha, almost invariably continuing to live alongside monks and nuns who did not necessarily share their interest. The question of the status and authority of the new literature was thus initially not decided along sectarian lines; monks from various of the existing schools would have been more or less favourably inclined towards the new sūtras. In time, certain schools more formally and explicitly refused to acknowledge the authority of the Mahāyāna sūtras, but such uncompromising attitudes were perhaps not relevant until as late as the fifth century CE. The reason for this was that for the most part the new sūtras represented something of a minority and esoteric interest, rather than a mass popular movement; and this appears to have remained so for at least several centuries.[32] According to the figures reported by the Chinese monk Hsüantsang, by the seventh century monks following the Mahāyāna constituted about half of the Indian Saṅgha.[33] But it is likely that this is an inflated figure.

The production of Mahāyāna sūtras spans a period of some six or seven centuries. Just as the earlier sūtras of the Nikāyas/Āgamas had already given rise to the Abhidharma and the distinctive interpretations of a number of schools, so the Mahāyāna sūtras are also associated with the production of treatises and commentaries associated with the emergence of new philosophical schools of Buddhism. Three writers should be singled out in this connection since I will be referring to them from time to time. The first is Nāgārjuna, a monk probably from the south of India who lived in the second century CE and was the author of the *Madhyamaka-kārikā* ('Verses on the Middle') as well as a number of other works. He is revered by the Buddhists of China and Tibet as the founding father of one of the principal 'Śāstra' systems of Mahāyāna philosophy, namely the Madhyamaka or Śūnyavāda. The other two authors can be taken together. Indeed, tradition has it that they were brothers. They are Asaṅga and Vasubandhu, who lived in north India at the end of the fourth or beginning of the fifth century CE. According to tradition, questioned by modern scholarship (see Chapter 7), this Vasubandhu is one and the same Vasubandhu whom I mentioned above as author of the *Abhidharmakośa*. Together these two are regarded as the founding fathers of the other great 'Śāstra' school of the Mahāyāna, namely the Yogācāra or Vijñānavāda, which expounded the theory that apart from consciousness or mind (*citta*, *vijñāna*) and the ideas and information (*vijñapti*) it processes, there is nothing.

Mahāyāna Buddhism as a more or less separate tradition of Buddhism, with its clearly defined subdivisions and philosophical schools, is to some extent the outcome of the history of Chinese and Tibetan Buddhism. As it evolved in China and Tibet, Buddhism came to adopt an exclusively Mahāyānist outlook in a way that it never did in India. As Buddhism began to fade from the Indian scene in the eleventh and twelfth centuries, the Buddhists of China, Japan, and Korea to the east, and Tibet and Mongolia to the north, were left as heirs to the Indian Mahāyānist vision. To the south the Buddhists of Sri Lanka and South-East Asia became the only surviving representatives of the perspective of the non-Mahāyāna. Yet we must remember that much of what modern Buddhists in Sri Lanka, China, or Tibet have inherited from the past was held in common by both the Mahāyāna and non-Mahāyāna tradition. And it is with this common heritage that I am mostly concerned in this book. At the same time we should not forget that the Buddhists of Sri Lanka, Burma, Thailand, Cambodia, Laos, Vietnam, China, Korea, Japan, Tibet, and Mongolia have all produced their own distinctive literatures, and continued to do so right up to the present day.

Having briefly reviewed the development of the Buddha's teaching in the form of literary texts, I wish to turn in the next chapter to the actual content of that teaching. In the first place we shall focus on those basic principles which are presented in the four Nikāya/Āgama collections of the Buddha's discourses and have been assumed and taken for granted by the subsequent Buddhist tradition.

3

Four Truths

The Disease, the Cause, the Cure, the Medicine

The orientation of the Buddha's teaching

What did the Buddha teach? The early sūtras present the Buddha's teaching as the solution to a problem. This problem is the fundamental problem of life. In Sanskrit and Pali the problem is termed *duḥkha/dukkha*, which can be approximately translated as 'suffering'. In a Nikāya passage the Buddha thus states that he has always made known just two things, namely suffering and the cessation of suffering.[1] This statement can be regarded as expressing the basic orientation of Buddhism for all times and all places. Its classic formulation is by way of 'four noble truths': the truth of the nature of suffering, the truth of the nature of its cause, the truth of the nature of its cessation, and the truth of the nature of the path leading to its cessation. One of the earliest summary statements of the truths is as follows:

> This is the noble truth of suffering: birth is suffering, ageing is suffering, sickness is suffering, dying is suffering, sorrow, grief, pain, unhappiness, and unease are suffering; being united with what is not liked is suffering, separation from what is liked is suffering; not to get what one wants is suffering; in short, the five aggregates of grasping are suffering.
>
> This is the noble truth of the origin of suffering: the thirst for repeated existence which, associated with delight and greed, delights in this and that, namely the thirst for the objects of sense desire, the thirst for existence, and the thirst for non-existence.
>
> This is the noble truth of the cessation of suffering: the complete fading away and cessation of this very thirst—its abandoning, relinquishing, releasing, letting go.
>
> This is the noble truth of the way leading to the cessation of suffering: the noble eightfold path, namely right view, right intention, right

speech, right action, right livelihood, right effort, right mindfulness, right concentration.[2]

The temptation to understand these four 'truths' as functioning as a kind of Buddhist creed should be resisted; they do not represent 'truth claims' that one must intellectually assent to on becoming a Buddhist. Part of the problem here is the word 'truth'. The word *satya* (Pali *sacca*) can certainly mean truth, but it might equally be rendered as 'real' or 'actual thing'. That is, we are not dealing here with propositional truths with which we must either agree or disagree, but with four 'true things' or 'realities' whose nature, we are told, the Buddha finally understood on the night of his awakening. The teachings of the Buddha thus state that suffering, its cause, its cessation, and the path to its cessation are realities which we fail to see as they are, and this is as true for the 'Buddhist' as the 'non-Buddhist'. The 'Buddhist' is simply one committed to trying to follow the Buddha's prescriptions for coming to see these realities as they are. This is not to say that the Buddha's discourses do not contain theoretical statements of the nature of suffering, its cause, its cessation, and the path to its cessation, but these descriptions function not so much as dogmas of the Buddhist faith as a convenient conceptual framework for making sense of Buddhist thought.[3] Thus from one point of view any piece of Buddhist theory can be considered as to do with the analysis of one or other of the four truths.

The disease of suffering

The starting point of the Buddha's teachings is, then, the reality of suffering. Yet the summary statement of the first truth quoted above should not be seen as seeking to persuade a world of otherwise perfectly contented beings that life is in fact unpleasant. Rather it addresses a basic fact of existence: sooner or later, in some form or another, no matter what they do, beings are confronted by and have to deal with *duḥkha*. This is, of course, precisely the moral of the tale of the Buddha's early life in Kapilavastu: even with everything one could possibly wish for, he had not found true happiness as long as he and those dearest to him were prey to disease, old age, and death. This is the actuality of *duḥkha*.

Rich in meaning and nuance, the word *duḥkha* is one of the basic terms of Buddhist and other Indian religious discourse. Literally 'pain' or 'anguish', in its religious and philosophical contexts *duḥkha* is, however, suggestive of an underlying sense of 'unsatisfactoriness' or 'unease' that must ultimately mar even our experience of happiness. Since any pleasant experience, whatever its basis, is ultimately unreliable and subject to loss, if we rest our hopes of final happiness in it we are bound to be disappointed. Thus *duḥkha* can be analysed in Buddhist thought by way of three kinds: suffering as pain, as change, and as conditions.[4]

The first is self-evident suffering: when we are in mental or physical pain there is no question that there is *duḥkha*. Yet when we are enjoying something, or even when there is nothing that is causing us particular unhappiness, things are always liable to change: what we were enjoying may be removed from us or something unpleasant may manifest itself—this is *duḥkha* as change. In fact everything in the world, everything we experience, is changing moment by moment. Some things may change very rapidly, some things extremely slowly, but still everything changes, everything is impermanent (*anitya/anicca*). When we begin to be affected by the reality of this state of affairs we may find the things that previously gave us great pleasure are tainted and no longer please us in the way they once did. The world becomes a place of uncertainty in which we can never be sure what is going to happen next, a place of shifting and unstable conditions whose very nature is such that we can never feel entirely at ease in it. Here we are confronted with *duḥkha* in a form that seems to be inherent in the nature of our existence itself—*duḥkha* as conditions. To put it another way, I may be relaxing in a comfortable armchair after a long, tiring day, but part of the reason I am enjoying it so much is precisely because I had such a long, tiring day. How long will it be before I am longing to get up and do something again—half an hour, an hour, two hours? Or again, I may feel myself perfectly happy and content; the suffering I hear about is a long way away, in another town, in another country, on another continent. But how close does it have to come before it in some sense impinges on my own sense of well-being—the next street, the house next door, the next room? That is, we are part of a world compounded of unstable and unreliable conditions, a world in which pain and pleasure, happiness and suffering are in all sorts of ways bound up together. It is the reality of this state of affairs that the teachings of the Buddha suggest we each must understand if we are ever to be free of suffering.

On the basis of its analysis of the problem of suffering, some have concluded that Buddhism must be judged a bleak, pessimistic and world-denying philosophy. From a Buddhist perspective, such a judgement may reflect a deep-seated refusal to accept the reality of *duḥkha* itself, and it certainly reflects a particular misunderstanding of the Buddha's teaching. The Buddha taught *four* truths and, by his own standards, the cessation of suffering and the path leading to its cessation are as much true realities as suffering and its cause.

The growth of early Buddhism must be understood in the context of the existence of a number of different 'renouncer' groups who shared the view that 'suffering' in some sense characterizes human experience, and that the quest for happiness is thus only to be fulfilled by fleeing the world. Some historians have felt that the emergence of such a view and its general acceptance in eastern India of the fourth and third centuries BCE requires a particular kind of explanation. In short, there must have been a lot of suffering about. Various suggestions have been made, from psychological unease caused by urbanization to the spread of disease.[5] Whether or not such factors played a role, I am unconvinced that as historians we are driven to seek such explanations, for this is to conclude that the *decisive* historical determinants in this case are the physical and mental well-being of society at large, rather than individual personalities. An individual's sense of suffering need not be related to the amount of suffering in society as a whole, nor even to the amount of suffering he or she has personally undergone. Nor am I convinced that the idea that suffering in some sense characterizes human experience is so extraordinary and culturally specific that it requires particular explanation; the ancient Indian sage might protest with some justification:

> Thou seest we are not all alone unhappy:
> This wide and universal theatre
> Presents more woeful pageants than the scene
> Wherein we play in.[6]

Historians seem prepared to accept that the Buddha was a charismatic personality and something of a genius. That such an individual might well have had a certain success in convincing others of the soundness of his understanding of the nature of the world, and that they in turn might have had considerable influence on the overall cultural outlook does not seem to me historically implausible.

It is worth noting, however, that the Buddhist tradition itself makes certain observations concerning the circumstances in which beings will be receptive to the teaching of *duḥkha*. According to the understanding of traditional Buddhist cosmology the universe comprises many different types of beings. Some of these beings' lives are so pleasurable that, although it is not impossible for them to appreciate that their happiness is not final or absolute, it is certainly difficult. On the other hand, other beings are preoccupied with lives of such misery that coming to understand the subtlety of the Buddha's teaching is extremely difficult. According to the ancient commentary to the *Jātaka*, it was the consideration of the circumstances in which beings would be receptive to his teachings that the Bodhisattva took into account when he was reflecting in the Tuṣita heaven on when and where to be reborn for the last time and become a buddha and teach Dharma.[7]

The Buddhist tradition has sometimes compared the Buddha to a physician and the four truths to a medical diagnosis: the truth of *duḥkha* is like a disease, the truth of the origin of *duḥkha* is like its cause, the truth of the cessation of *duḥkha* is like the disease's being cured, and the truth of the path leading to the cessation of *duḥkha* is like the medicine that brings about the disease's cure.[8] It is the wish to relieve the suffering of the disease and eradicate its cause that is the starting point of Buddhist practice. All this suggests something else that is fundamental to the orientation of Buddhist thought and practice: the wish to relieve suffering can in the end only be rooted in a feeling of sympathy (*anukampā*) or compassion for the suffering of both oneself and of others. This feeling of sympathy for the suffering of beings is what motivates not only the Buddha to teach but ultimately everyone who tries to put his teaching into practice.[9]

The Buddha's teaching thus represents the medicine for the disease of suffering. Or, according to the metaphor of the fourth truth, it is the 'path' (*mārga/magga*) or 'way' (*pratipad/paṭipadā*) that one follows in order to reach the destination that is the cessation of suffering. Or, as we saw in the previous chapter, it is a system of training in conduct, meditation, and wisdom. If one were to define Buddhism in keeping with this understanding, it would have to be as a practical method for dealing with the reality of suffering. Yet it is usual to classify Buddhism as 'a religion'. Asked to define the meaning of the word *religion*, English speakers would probably not immediately suggest 'a practical way of dealing with the reality of suffering'. Certainly this is not the kind of definition we find in contemporary dictionaries. Yet in the Indian cultural context this is essentially how many of the traditions which we today generally class as 'religious' conceive of themselves. One of the ancient and recurring images of Indian religious discourse is of 'crossing the ocean of existence', that is, crossing over from the near shore, which is fraught with dangers, to the further shore, which is safe and free from danger. This is equivalent to escaping or transcending the endless round of rebirth that is *saṃsāra* and the condition of *duḥkha*.

One contemporary dictionary definition of religion is as follows: 'belief in, worship of or obedience to a supernatural power or powers considered to be divine or to have control over human destiny'.[10] This is illustrative of a modern tendency to understand religion as principally a kind of belief system—usually revolving around a God who is both creator and saviour—that an individual takes on board and which then provides him or her with a way of looking at the world. Probably the reduction of religion to this kind of belief system should be seen as a relatively recent phenomenon—the legacy of the Reformation and the Enlightenment. Protestant theology tended to emphasize the primacy of 'faith' over 'works'; by seeming to expose the irrationality of the theoretical beliefs regarded as the underpinnings of this Christian faith, the post-Enlightenment traditions of philosophy and science appeared about to cause the collapse of religion. All this amounts to a modern preoccupation with particular beliefs as the essence of religion. Arguably the very nature of Christianity makes it predisposed to understanding itself as a particular set of beliefs; nevertheless historically Christianity has clearly been much more than its creeds—as much a question of adopting certain practices as of adopting beliefs. Theoretically the modern academic study of religion should have made us all aware of the multi-dimensional nature of religion, but cultural biases are not so easily corrected in practice.[11] Thus the tendency to understand religion as primarily involving the adoption of particular kinds of belief still informs what we expect 'religions' to be; this hinders our understanding of Christianity, let alone of Judaism, Islam, Hinduism, and Buddhism.

I am not concerned here to pronounce on a question that is sometimes asked of Buddhism: is it a religion? Obviously it depends on how one defines 'a religion'. What is certain, however, is that Buddhism does not involve belief in a creator God who has control over human destiny, nor does it seek to define itself by reference to a creed; as Edward Conze has pointed out, it took over 2,000 years and a couple of Western converts to Buddhism to provide it with a creed.[12] On the other hand, Buddhism views activities that would be generally understood as religious—such as devotional practices and rituals—as a legitimate, useful, and even essential part of the practice and training that leads to the cessation of suffering.

Buddhism regards itself as presenting a system of training in conduct, meditation, and understanding that constitutes a path leading to the cessation of suffering. Everything is to be subordinated to this goal. And in this connection the Buddha's teachings suggest that preoccupation with certain beliefs and ideas about the ultimate nature of the world and our destiny in fact hinders our progress along the path rather than helping it. If we insist on working out exactly what to believe about the world and human destiny before beginning to follow the path of practice we will never even set out.

An important incident is related in the *Cūḷa-Māluṅkya Sutta* ('short discourse to Māluṅkya') and concerns ten matters that are 'unexplained' or 'undetermined' (*avyākṛta/avyākata*) by the Buddha.[13] These ten undetermined questions are as follows: (1) is the world eternal or (2) is it not eternal? (3) is the world finite or (4) is it infinite? (5) are the soul and the body one and the same thing or (6) is the soul one thing and the body another? (7) after death, does the Tathāgata (i.e. a buddha or arhat) exist or (8) does he not exist or (9) does he both exist and not exist or (10) does he neither exist nor not exist? One evening, it seems, the monk Māluṅkyāputta felt that he had been patient with the Buddha long enough. Māluṅkyāputta went to the Buddha and declared that unless he answered these questions or straightforwardly stated that the reason he did not answer them was because he did not know the answers, he would abandon his training under the Buddha. The Buddha responded by asking Māluṅkyāputta a question: had he ever said to Māluṅkyāputta that he should come and practise the spiritual life with him and he would explain to him whether or not the world was eternal? Māluṅkyāputta confessed that he had not. The Buddha then suggested that whoever declared that he would not practise the spiritual life with the Buddha until he had explained these questions would certainly die without the Buddha having explained them; he then related a story of a man struck by an arrow.

It is as if there were a man struck by an arrow that was smeared thickly with poison; his friends and companions, his family and relatives would summon a doctor to see to the arrow. And the man might say, 'I will not draw out this arrow as long as I do not know whether the man by whom I was struck was a brahmin, a kṣatriya, a vaiśya, or a śūdra . . . as long as I do not know his name and his family . . . whether he was tall, short or of medium height . . .' That man would not discover these things, but that man would die.[14]

Why did the Buddha refuse to give categorical answers to these questions? It has been claimed by some modern scholars that the Buddha was simply not interested in metaphysical questions and that he wished to leave these matters open.[15] Such an interpretation seems to miss the point. The Buddha's refusal to answer has a philosophically more sophisticated and subtle basis. It is stated in the *Cūḷa-Māluṅkya Sutta* that one of the reasons why he did not explain these matters was because they were not connected with the goal and purpose of the path, namely the cessation of suffering; what the Buddha explained was just suffering, its cause, its cessation, and the way leading to its cessation. This leaves no doubt as to the practical intent of the Buddha's teaching, but what precisely is being said about these questions when it is declared that their explanation does not conduce to the cessation of suffering?

The Buddha might be suggesting that he neither knew the answers to these questions nor was he interested in pursuing the questions because he considered them irrelevant. Yet this is quite definitely not the understanding of the later Buddhist tradition, which tended to regard the Buddha as knowing everything; and the Buddha of the earlier texts certainly never straightforwardly admits to not knowing the answers to these questions. Thus if we take this line we are driven to the conclusion that either the Buddha himself or the authors of the early texts were embarrassed about his ignorance of these matters and sought to cover it up. Alternatively the Buddha might have had answers to these questions which he simply refused to divulge on the stated grounds that it would not help his followers in their progress in the training. Such a possibility might seem to be confirmed by another tradition that reports the Buddha as once saying that there were indeed many things which he knew and understood but did not communicate on the grounds that they did not conduce to the cessation of suffering.[16] But the passage in question gives no explicit indication that these ten questions are included in this category of things the Buddha understands but does not communicate. The third possibility would seem to be that these questions are somehow by their very nature unanswerable. It is fairly clear that this is indeed how the early texts and the subsequent Buddhist tradition understand the matter.[17] The reason why these questions are unanswerable concerns matters that lie at the heart of Buddhist thought. In simple terms the questions are unanswerable because they assume, as absolute, categories and concepts—the world, the soul, the self, the Tathāgata—that the Buddha and the Buddhist tradition does not accept or at least criticizes or understands in particular ways. That is, from the Buddhist perspective these questions are ill-formed and misconceived. To answer 'yes' or 'no' to any one of them is to be drawn into accepting the validity of the question and the terms in which it is couched—rather like answering 'yes' or 'no' to a question such as, 'Are Martians green?' One's answer may be construed in ways one had not intended. Thus the Buddha tells the insistent Māluṅkyāputta that whichever one of these views he might embrace, the real work remains:

> It is not the case that one would live the spiritual life by virtue of holding the view that the world is eternal. Nor is it the case that one would live the spiritual life by virtue of holding the view that the world is not eternal. Whether one holds the view that the world is eternal, or whether one holds the view that the world is not eternal, there is still birth, ageing, death, grief, despair, pain, and unhappiness—whose destruction here and now I declare.[18]

In fact, such views (*dṛṣṭi/diṭṭhi*) about the ultimate nature of the world are, from the Buddhist perspective, the expression of a mental grasping which is but one manifestation of that insatiable 'thirst' or 'craving' which Buddhist thought regards as the condition for the arising of suffering, and to which we will now turn.

The origin of suffering: attachment, aversion, and delusion

Why do beings suffer? What is the truth or reality of the origin of suffering? At the outset it is worth drawing attention to a point of contrast with the approach to suffering found in certain traditional Jewish, Christian, and Islamic theologies. As we have already seen, and shall see more clearly in Chapter 5, the Buddhist understanding of the world is not based upon the concept of a creator God—omnipotent or otherwise. Thus there is no need in Buddhist thought to explain the existence of suffering in the face of God's omnipotence and boundless love. The existence of suffering in the world is not to be related in some way to God's purpose in creating the world and, in particular, mankind as in the traditional Christian theodicies of Augustine and Ireneus. For Buddhist thought suffering is simply a fact of existence, and in its general approach to the problem, Buddhist thought suggests that it is beings themselves who must take ultimate responsibility for their suffering. This may come as rather depressing news, but on the other hand, to anticipate our discussion of the third and fourth truths, precisely because our suffering is something that we must each bear a certain responsibility for, it is also something that we can do something about.

This way of looking at things has sometimes been perceived by people brought up in an intellectual and cultural tradition in part moulded by Christian thought as a rather bleak view of affairs, contrasting with the message of the saving Christ proclaimed by Christianity. Yet it is important to appreciate that in its own cultural context this is most definitely presented and perceived as a message of hope. Furthermore this outlook of individual responsibility does not entail that individuals are, as it were, forever and absolutely 'on their own'. On the contrary, the message is precisely that help is at hand in the form of the Buddha's teachings and of those who have followed and are following the path. Moreover, from a Buddhist perspective, the sense that one is forever and absolutely on one's own must rest in part on a self-delusion from which one can be eventually released by the Buddha's teachings (see Chapter 6). With the Buddha's awakening 'the doors to the deathless' are once more open for those who have the faith to set out on the path.[19] As John Ross Carter has put it, there is no need of a saviour not because suffering humanity is its own saviour, but because of the efficacy of Dharma when made the integral basis of one's life.[20]

So suffering is created by beings, but how? The summary definition of the second truth states the condition for the arising of suffering as 'the thirst for repeated existence which, associated with delight and greed, delights in this and that'; this is then specified as 'the thirst for the objects of sense desire, the thirst for existence and the thirst for non-existence'. I have translated the word *tṛṣṇā* (Pali: *taṇhā*) as 'thirst'. This is its literal meaning, but in the present context it is a figurative word for strong desire or craving. In fact *tṛṣṇā* or 'thirst' belongs to the corpus of Buddhist technical vocabulary and has very specific meanings and connotations. Thus 'craving', while certainly conveying a good deal of the sense of *tṛṣṇā* in Buddhist discourse, requires a certain amount of commentary and explication.

The suggestion is that deep in the minds of beings there is a greed or desire that manifests as an unquenchable thirst which is the principal condition for the arising of suffering. As the summary quotation points out, this thirst or craving takes different forms: craving for the objects of the senses, for existence and non-existence. It is the cause of suffering because it can never be finally satisfied. This is clear with the objects of the senses: pleasure based on these is always liable to be taken from us because of their unstable and unreliable nature; on another level desire for the objects of the senses has always the tendency to increase; never content with what it has, it is always looking for new objects to satisfy itself. But craving for the objects of the senses is just a particular manifestation of craving. I may crave to be some particular kind of person, or I may crave fame and even immortality. On the other hand, I may bitterly and resentfully turn my back on ambition, craving to be a nobody; I may become depressed and long not to exist, wishing that I had never been born; in this state I may even take my own life. I may passionately believe that I possess an immortal soul and that I will exist after death; or I may be absolutely certain in my conviction that death will be the final end, and that I shall die and there will be no more of me. From the perspective of Buddhist thought all these feelings, desires, and beliefs are the products of the workings of *tṛṣṇā*, the workings of craving for existence and non-existence. Yet in a world where everything is always changing, in a world of shifting and unstable conditions, craving of whatever kind will never be able to hold on to the things it craves. This is the origin of suffering.

At first desires may be like the trickle of a stream, but they grow into a river of craving which carries us away like the current of a swiftly flowing river.[21] Craving is understood to crystallize as 'grasping' or 'attachment' (*upādāna*): the various things we like evoke desires in us; these turn to cravings; as a result of our craving we grasp at things and try to take possession of them; in short, we try to call them our own. Buddhist texts provide a stock list of four kinds of attachment: attachment to the objects of sense desire, attachment to views, attachment to precepts and vows, attachment to the doctrine of the self.[22] These suggest the complex and subtle network and web of attachment that Buddhist thought sees as enmeshing beings.

The ultimately significant thing in all this is craving and attachment rather than whatever is the object of that attachment and craving. Thus it is not the objects of sense desire that cause us suffering, but our attachment to those; it is not views, precepts and vows, and the doctrine of self that in themselves cause suffering but our attachment. This is not to say that all views, precepts and vows, and doctrines about the self are regarded as equal in Buddhist thought. Certain attachments are most definitely considered more harmful and more productive of suffering than others. Thus an attachment to the first of the five Buddhist precepts, the precept of not harming living creatures, is not to be considered as of the same order as an attachment to the habit of killing creatures. Indeed, deliberately killing living creatures is regarded as a particularly unwholesome act, and to the extent that attachment to the precept of not harming living creatures prevents us from killing, it is a positive good; nevertheless, as long as it remains an attachment—an abstract principle we tenaciously cling to—it too must remain a contributory cause of *duhkha*. The problem is that we can become attached to even useful and helpful things, even to the practice of the Buddha's teaching:

'It is as if there were a man who had set out on a long journey. He might see a great river in flood, the near shore fearful and dangerous, the far shore safe and free of danger, but there might be no ferry or bridge for crossing from one side to the other. And this man might think, "This is a great river in flood. The near shore is fearful and dangerous, the far shore safe and free of danger, but there is no ferry or bridge to cross from one side to the other. What if I were to gather together grass, sticks, branches and foliage and bind together a raft, and then using that raft, striving with my hands and feet, safely cross over to the further shore?" Thereupon that man might gather together grass, sticks, branches and foliage and bind together a raft, and then using that raft, striving with his hands and feet he might safely cross over to the further shore. Once he had crossed over it might occur to him, "This raft is very useful to me. Using this raft, striving with my hands and feet I have safely crossed over to the further shore. What if I were to now lift it on to my head or raise it on my back and set off as I pleased?" What do you think of this, monks? If the man did this with the raft would he be doing what is appropriate?'

'Not at all, lord.'

'So what might this man do with the raft in order to do what is appropriate? In this case once he had crossed over it might occur to him, "This raft is very useful to me. Using this raft, striving with my hands and feet, I have safely crossed over to the further shore. What if I were now to beach this raft on the shore or sink it in the water and go on my way as I pleased?" The man who did this with the raft would be doing what is appropriate. Even so, monks, as being like a raft, I have taught you how Dharma is for the purpose of crossing over and not for the purpose of holding on to. Those who understand the similarity to a raft will let go even of the teachings and practices (*dhammā*), let alone what are not the teachings and practices (*adhammā*)'.[23]

This does not mean that in relinquishing his or her attachment to the precept of not harming living creatures the Buddhist saint suddenly starts harming living creatures. Rather the Buddhist saint does no harm to living creatures not out of attachment to some precept or ethical principle he or she has undertaken to live by, but because of rooting out any motivation that might move him or her to want to harm living creatures. Thus as well as indicating the, as it were, horizontal range of craving and attachment, Buddhist thought draws up a vertical hierarchy of attachment which the Buddhist practitioner progressively relinquishes as he or she follows the path.

Something of this hierarchy of attachments is indicated by the ancient list of the ten 'fetters' or 'bonds' (*saṃyojana*) that bind beings to suffering and the round of rebirth: the view of individuality, doubt, clinging to precepts and vows, sensual desire, aversion, desire for form, desire for the formless, pride, agitation, and ignorance. As we shall presently see, the practice of the Buddhist path begins with the taking of ethical precepts aimed at restraining particularly damaging kinds of behaviour; these provide the basis for the cultivation of meditation practices that bring the practitioner to direct experience of the subtle worlds of 'form' and 'the formless'. Nevertheless, as the list of the ten fetters makes clear, attachment to both precepts and to the worlds of form and the formless experienced in meditation must be relinquished for the end of the path to be fully realized.

The list of ten fetters includes four items that are not prima-facie aspects of craving or attachment: doubt, aversion, agitation, and ignorance. The psychological relationship of aversion to craving is not hard to see. Unfulfilled craving and frustrated attachment become the conditions for aversion, anger, depression, hatred, and cruelty and violence which are in themselves quite manifestly unpleasant (*duḥkha* as pain) and in turn bring further suffering. But what about doubt, agitation, and ignorance? Developed Buddhist thought understands these states as having an important psychological relationship. Even in the absence of craving and aversion, we view the world through a mind that is often fundamentally unclear, unsettled, and confused. Not surprisingly we fail to see things as they truly are. At this point it begins to become quite apparent just how and why craving leads to suffering. There is a discrepancy between our craving and the world we live in, between our expectations and the way things are. We want the world to be other than it is. Our craving is based on a fundamental misjudgement of the situation; a judgement that assumes that when our craving gets what it wants we will be happy, that when our craving possesses the objects of its desire we will be satisfied. But such a judgement in turn assumes a world in which things are permanent, unchanging, stable, and reliable. But the world is simply not like that. In short, in craving we fail to see how things truly are, and in failing to see how things truly are we crave. In other words craving goes hand in hand with a fundamental ignorance and misapprehension of the nature of the world.

Thus we can state the three fundamental defilements of the mind according to Buddhist thought: greed (*rāga, lobha*), aversion (*dveṣa/dosa*), and delusion (*moha, avidyā/avijjā*). It is these that combine and interact, that manifest in different ways and result in *duḥkha*. In this way the great focus of Buddhist thought is the workings of the mind. The processes by which the mind responds to its various stimuli to bring about either the arising of *duḥkha* or the path that leads towards the cessation of *duḥkha* is considered in Buddhist thought by way of a particularly important and significant teaching that I referred to in passing in recounting the story of the Buddha's awakening. This teaching is known as 'dependent arising' or 'dependent origination' (*pratītya-samutpāda/paṭicca-samuppāda*). Dependent arising is to be understood as in certain respects an elaboration of the truth of the origin of suffering, but this difficult teaching is intertwined with other important themes of Buddhist thought and I shall postpone its full explanation until Chapter 6.

The cessation of suffering: nirvāṇa

In the normal course of events our quest for happiness leads us to attempt to satisfy our desires—whatever they be. But in so doing we become attached to things that are unreliable, unstable, changing, and impermanent. As long as there is attachment to things that are unstable, unreliable, changing, and impermanent there will be suffering—when they change, when they cease to be what we want them to be. Try as we might to find something in the world that is permanent and stable, which we can hold on to and thereby find lasting happiness, we must always fail. The Buddhist solution is as radical as it is simple: let go, let go of everything. If craving is the cause of suffering, then the cessation of suffering will surely follow from 'the complete fading away and ceasing of that very craving': its abandoning, relinquishing, releasing, letting go. The cessation of craving is, then, the goal of the Buddhist path, and equivalent to the cessation of suffering, the highest happiness, nirvāṇa (Pali *nibbāna*).

Nirvāṇa is a difficult concept, but certain things about the traditional Buddhist understanding of nirvāṇa are quite clear. Some of the confusion surrounding the concept arises, I think, from a failure to distinguish different dimensions of the use of the term *nirvāṇa* in Buddhist literature. I want here to discuss nirvāṇa in terms of three things: (1) nirvāṇa as, in some sense, a particular event (what happens at the moment of awakening), (2) nirvāṇa as, in some sense, the content of an experience (what the mind knows at the moment of awakening), and (3) nirvāṇa as, in some sense, the state or condition enjoyed by buddhas and arhats after death. Let us examine this more closely.

Literally *nirvāṇa* means 'blowing out' or 'extinguishing', although Buddhist commentarial writings, by a play on words, like to explain it as 'the absence of craving'. But where English translations of Buddhist texts have 'he attains nirvāṇa/parinirvāṇa', the more characteristic Pali or Sanskrit idiom is a simple verb: 'he or she nirvāṇa-s' or more often 'he or she parinirvāṇa-s' (*parinibbāyati*). What the Pali and Sanskrit expression primarily indicates is the event or process of the extinction of the 'fires' of greed, aversion, and delusion. At the moment the Buddha understood suffering, its arising, its cessation, and the path leading to its cessation, these fires were extinguished. This process is the same for all who reach awakening, and the early texts term it either nirvāṇa or parinirvāṇa, the complete 'blowing out' or 'extinguishing' of the 'fires' of greed, aversion, and delusion. This is not a 'thing' but an event or experience.

After a being has, as it were, 'nirvāṇa-ed', the defilements of greed, hatred, and delusion no longer arise in his or her mind, since they have been thoroughly rooted out (to switch to another metaphor also current in the tradition). Yet like the Buddha, any person who attains nirvāṇa does not remain there after forever absorbed in some transcendental state of mind. On the contrary he or she continues to live in the world; he or she continues to think, speak, and act as other people do—with the difference that all his or her thoughts, words, and deeds are completely free of the motivations of greed, aversion, and delusion, and motivated instead entirely by generosity, friendliness, and wisdom. This condition of having extinguished the defilements can be termed 'nirvāṇa with the remainder [of life]' (*sopadhiśeṣa-nirvāṇa/sa-upādisesa-nibbāna*): the nirvāṇa that comes from ending the occurrence of the defilements (*kleśa/kilesa*) of the mind; what the Pali commentaries call for short *kilesa-parinibbāna*.[24] And this is what the Buddha achieved on the night of his awakening.

Eventually 'the remainder of life' will be exhausted and, like all beings, such a person must die. But unlike other beings, who have not experienced 'nirvāṇa', he or she will not be reborn into some new life, the physical and mental constituents of being will not come together in some new existence, there will be no new being or person. Instead of being reborn, the person 'parinirvāṇa-s', meaning in this context that the five aggregates of physical and mental phenomena that constitute a being cease to occur. This is the condition of 'nirvāṇa without remainder [of life]' (*nir-upadhiśeṣa-nirvāṇa/an-upādisesa-nibbāna*): nirvāṇa that comes from ending the occurrence of the aggregates (*skandha/khandha*) of physical and mental phenomena that constitute a being; or, for short, *khandha-parinibbāna*.[25] Modern Buddhist usage tends to restrict 'nirvāṇa' to the awakening experience and reserve 'parinirvāṇa' for the death experience.[26]

So far we have considered nirvāṇa from the perspective of a particular experience which has far-reaching and quite specific effects. This is the more straightforward aspect of the Buddhist tradition's understanding of nirvāṇa. There is, however, a further dimension to the tradition's treatment and understanding of nirvāṇa. What precisely does the mind experience at the moment when the fires of greed, hatred and delusion are finally extinguished? At the close of one of the works of the Pali canon entitled *Udāna* there are recorded several often quoted 'inspired utterances' (*udāna*) said to have been made by the Buddha concerning nirvāṇa. Here is the first:

> There is, monks, a domain where there is no earth, no water, no fire, no wind, no sphere of infinite space, no sphere of nothingness, no sphere of infinite consciousness, no sphere of neither awareness nor non-awareness; there is not this world, there is not another world, there is no sun or moon. I do not call this coming or going, nor standing,

nor dying, nor being reborn; it is without support, without occurrence, without object. Just this is the end of suffering.[27]

This passage refers to the four elements that constitute the physical world and also what the Buddhist tradition sees as the most subtle forms of consciousness possible, and suggests that there is a 'domain' or 'sphere' (*āyatana*) of experience of which these form no part. This 'domain' or 'sphere' of experience is nirvāṇa. It may also be referred to as the 'unconditioned' (*asaṃskṛta/asaṃkhata*) or 'unconditioned realm' (*asaṃskṛta-/asaṃkhata-dhātu*) in contrast to the shifting, unstable, conditioned realms of the round of rebirth. For certain Abhidharma traditions, at the moment of awakening, at the moment of the extinguishing of the fires of greed, hatred, and delusion, the mind knows this unconditioned realm directly. In the technical terminology of the Abhidharma, nirvāṇa can be said to be the object of consciousness at the moment of awakening when it sees the four truths.[28] Thus in the moment of awakening when all craving and attachments are relinquished, one experiences the profoundest and ultimate truth about the world, and that experience is not of 'a nothing'—the mere absence of greed, hatred, and delusion—but of what can be termed the 'unconditioned'.

We can, then, understand nirvāṇa from three points of view: (1) it is the extinguishing of the defilements of greed, hatred, and delusion; (2) it is the final condition of the Buddha and arhats after death consequent upon the extinction of the defilements; (3) it is the unconditioned realm known at the moment of awakening. The critical question becomes the exact definition of the ontological status of (2) and (3). The earlier tradition tends to shy away from such definition, although, as we have seen, it is insistent on one point: one cannot say that the arhat after death exists, does not exist, both exists and does not exist, neither exists nor does not exist. The ontological status of nirvāṇa thus defies neat categorization and is 'undetermined' (*avyākṛta/avyākata*). None the less the followers of Sarvāstivāda Abhidharma argue that nirvāṇa should be regarded as 'real' (*dravya*), while followers of the Theravāda state that it should not be said to be 'non-existence' (*abhāva*). But for the Sautrāntikas, even this is to say too much: one should not say more than that nirvāṇa is the absence of the defilements.[29] With the development of the Mahāyāna philosophical schools of Madhyamaka and Yogācāra we find attempts to articulate the ontology of nirvāṇa in different terms—the logic of 'emptiness' (*śūnyatā*) and non-duality (*advaya*).

In the face of this some early Western scholarship concluded that there was no consensus in Buddhist thought on the nature of nirvāṇa, or persisted in arguing either that nirvāṇa was mere annihilation or that it was some form of eternal bliss.[30] If one examines Buddhist writings one will find material that can be interpreted in isolation to support the view that nirvāṇa amounts to annihilation (the five aggregates of physical and mental phenomena that constitute a being are gone and the arhat is no longer reborn), and material to support the view that it is an eternal reality. But this is not the point; the Buddhist tradition knows this. The reason why both kinds of material are there is not because the Buddhist tradition could not make up its mind. For, as we have seen, the tradition is clear on one point: nirvāṇa, as the post-mortem condition of the Buddha and arhats, cannot be characterized as non-existence, but nor can it be characterized as existence. In fact to characterize it in either of these ways is to fall foul of one of the two basic wrong views (*dṛṣṭi/diṭṭhi*) between which Buddhist thought tries to steer a middle course: the annihilationist view (*uccheda-vāda*) and the eternalist view (*śāśvata-/sassata-vāda*). Thus although the schools of Buddhist thought may articulate the ontology of nirvāṇa in different terms, one thing is clear, and that is that they are always attempting to articulate the middle way between existence and non-existence, between annihilationism and eternalism. And it is in so far as any formulation of nirvāṇa's ontolgy is judged to have failed to maintain the delicate balance necessary to walk the middle path that it is criticized. Of course, whether any of Buddhist thought's attempts at articulating the ontology of the middle way will be judged philosophically successful is another question. And again the tradition seems on occasion to acknowledge even this. Although some of the things one might say about nirvāṇa will certainly be more misleading than others, ultimately whatever one says will be misleading; the last resort must be the 'silence of the Āryas', the silence of the ones who have directly known the ultimate truth, for ultimately 'in such matters syllables, words and concepts are of no use'.[31]

What remains after all is said—and not said—is the reality of nirvāṇa as the goal of the Buddhist path conveyed not so much by the attempt to articulate it philosophically but by metaphor. Thus although strictly nirvāṇa is no place, no abode where beings can be said to exist, the metaphor of nirvāṇa as the destination at the end of the road remains vivid: 'the country of No-Birth—the city of Nibbāna, the place of the highest happiness, peaceful, lovely, happy, without suffering, without fear, without sickness, free from old age and death'.[32]

> As if, monks, a person wandering in the forest, in the jungle, were to see an ancient path, an ancient road along which men of old had gone. And he would follow it, and as he followed it he would see an ancient city, an ancient seat of kings which men of old had inhabited, possessing parks, gardens, lotus ponds, with high walls—a delightful place . . . Just so, monks, I saw an ancient path, the ancient road along which the fully awakened ones of old had gone . . . I followed it and following it I knew directly old-age and death, the arising of old-age and death, the ceasing of old-age and death and the path leading to the ceasing of old age and death.[33]

So let us now turn to the path that leads to the city of nirvāṇa.

The way leading to the cessation of suffering

So far in this chapter we have seen that Buddhist thought starts from the premiss that life presents us with the problem of suffering. The schema of the four truths analyses the nature of the problem, its cause, its solution and the way to effect that solution. The first three truths primarily concern matters of Buddhist theory; with the fourth truth we come to Buddhist practice proper. That is, the first three truths provide a framework for the application of the Buddhist solution to the problem of suffering.

The second truth suggests that we must recognize that the mind has deep-rooted tendencies to crave the particular experiences it likes, and that this craving is related to a fundamental misapprehension of 'the way things are': the idea that lasting happiness is related to our ability to *have*, to possess and take hold of, these experiences we like. In a world where everything is constantly changing beyond our control, such an outlook brings us not the happiness we seek, but discontent. Thus the third truth suggests that lasting happiness lies in the stopping of craving and grasping, in the rooting-out of greed, aversion, and delusion. Of course, these latter mental forces are varied and psychologically subtle; we can get caught in the trap of craving not to crave—of desiring what is, in a sense, desireless, namely nirvāṇa. Yet as long as we *crave* nirvāṇa or the cessation of suffering, then by definition the object of our craving is not nirvāṇa, not the 'reality' of the cessation of suffering, but a mere idea of what we imagine nirvāṇa, the cessation of suffering, to be like. Nirvāṇa is precisely the ceasing of all craving, so even the craving for nirvāṇa must be rooted out and eventually abandoned. The fourth truth is concerned with the practical means for bringing this about. But, as I have already suggested, from the perspective of the path certain cravings are less harmful than others and, to an extent, even necessary to progress along the path. Ultimately, however, as the simile of the raft indicates, attachment to even the teachings and practices of Buddhism must be relinquished.

According to Buddhist thought, just as there are various defilements of the mind—principally greed, hatred, and delusion—so there are various wholesome (*kuśala/kusala*) qualities of the mind. As well as greed, hatred, and delusion there are then their opposites, namely non-attachment (*alobha*), loving kindness (*adveṣa/adosa, maitrī/mettā*), and wisdom (*prajñā/paññā*). Were it not for these there would be no way of breaking out of the cycle of greed, hatred, and delusion, and thus no path leading to the cessation of *duḥkha*. The principal, if not only, aim of the Buddhist path is to develop and cultivate (*bhāvayati/bhāveti*) these and related wholesome qualities.

TABLE 1. *The noble eightfold path*

right view	seeing the four truths	wisdom (*prajñā*)
right intention	desirelessness friendliness compassion	wisdom (*prajñā*)
right speech	refraining from false speech refraining from divisive speech refraining from hurtful speech refraining from idle chatter	conduct (*śīla*)
right action	refraining from harming living beings refraining from taking what is not given refraining from sexual misconduct	conduct (*śīla*)
right livelihood	not based on wrong speech and action	conduct (*śīla*)
right effort	to prevent unarisen unwholesome states to abandon arisen unwholesome states to arouse unarisen wholesome states to develop arisen wholesome states	meditation (*samādhi*)
right mindfulness	contemplation of body contemplation of feeling contemplation of mind contemplation of dharma	meditation (*samādhi*)
right concentration	practice of the four *dhyānas*	meditation (*samādhi*)

In the earliest Buddhist texts the noble truth of the path to the cessation of suffering is most frequently summed up as the 'noble eightfold path': 'perfect', 'right', or 'appropriate' (*samyak/sammā*) view, intention, speech, conduct, livelihood, effort, mindfulness, and concentration. The basic meaning of these eight items is clearly explained in a number of places in the early Buddhist texts (see Table 1), but the interpretation of the overall structure of the eightfold path is perhaps not so straightforward.[34] We all have certain views, ideas, beliefs, and opinions about ourselves, others, and the world (1); depending on these we turn towards the world with various intentions and aspirations (2); depending on these we speak (3), act (4), and generally make our way in the world (5). So far so good, but the meaning of the last three items of the eightfold path is not so transparent. Effort (6), mindfulness (7), and concentration (8) are in effect technical terms of Buddhist meditation practice whose expression in everyday language is less obvious. In practice they relate to one's underlying state of mind or, perhaps better, emotional state. In other words, the list of eight items suggests that there is a basic relationship between one's understanding, one's actions, and one's underlying emotional state.

The eight items of the path are not, however, to be understood simply as stages, each one being completed before moving on to the next. In fact, when we look at the extensive treatment of the eightfold path in Buddhist literature, it becomes apparent that view, intention, speech, conduct, livelihood, effort, mindfulness, and concentration are presented here as eight significant dimensions of one's behaviour—mental, spoken, and bodily—that are regarded as operating in dependence on one another and as defining a complete way (*mārga/magga*) of living.[35] The eight items are significant in that they focus on the manner in which what one thinks, says, does, and feels can effect—and affect—the unfolding of the path to the cessation of suffering. Ordinarily these eight aspects of one's way of life may, at different times, be either 'right' and 'appropriate' (*samyak/sammā*) or 'wrong' and 'inappropriate' (*mithyā/micchā*); that is, they may either be out of keeping with the nature of things, leading one further away from the cessation of suffering, or they may be in keeping with the nature of things, bringing one closer to the cessation of suffering. By means of Buddhist practice the eight dimensions are gradually and collectively transformed and developed, until they are established as 'right', such that they constitute the 'noble' (*ārya/ariya*) eightfold path. Strictly, then, the *noble* eightfold path represents the end of Buddhist practice; it is the way of living achieved by Buddhist saints—the stream-attainers, once-returners, non-returners, arhats, and bodhisattvas who have worked on and gradually perfected view, intention, speech, conduct, livelihood, effort, mindfulness, and concentration. For such as these, having perfect view, intention, speech, action, livelihood, endeavour, mindfulness, and concentration is not a matter of trying to make their behaviour conform to the prescriptions of the path, but simply of how they are in all they think, say, and do. We are talking of an inner transformation at the deepest levels of one's being.

Alongside the eightfold path, Buddhist texts present the path that ends in the cessation of suffering as a gradual and cumulative process involving a hierarchical progression of practice, beginning with generosity (*dāna*), moving on to good conduct (*sīla/śīla*), and ending in meditation (*bhāvanā*); alternatively we find the sequence: good conduct (*śīla/sīla*), meditative concentration (*samādhi*), and wisdom (*prajñā/paññā*). According to this kind of scheme, the early stages of the practice of the path are more concerned with establishing good conduct on the basis of the ethical precepts; these provide the firm foundation for the development of concentration, which in turn prepares for the perfection of understanding and wisdom. This outlook is the basis of the important notion of 'the gradual path' which finds its earliest and most succinct expression as 'the step by step discourse' (*anupūrvikā kathā/anupubbi-kathā*) of the Nikāyas/Āgamas:

> Then the Blessed One gave instruction step by step . . . namely talk on giving, talk on good conduct, and talk on heaven; he proclaimed the danger, elimination and impurity of sense desires, and the benefit of desirelessness. When the Blessed One knew that the mind [of his listener] was ready, open, without hindrances, inspired, and confident, then he gave the instruction in Dharma that is special to buddhas: suffering, its origin, its cessation, the path.[36]

The psychological understanding that underlies this is not hard to see. In order to see the four truths, the mind must be clear and still; in order to be still, the mind must be content; in order to be content, the mind must be free from remorse and guilt; in order to be free from guilt, one needs a clear conscience; the bases of a clear conscience are generosity and good conduct.

The eight items of the eightfold path can also be analysed in terms of the three categories of good conduct, concentration, and wisdom: the first two items of the path (view and intention) are encompassed by the third category, wisdom; the next three (speech, action, and livelihood) by the first category, good conduct; and the final three (effort, mindfulness, and concentration) by the second category, meditative concentration.[37] That the sequence of the items of the path does not conform to the order of these three categories of practice highlights an understanding of the spiritual life that sees all three aspects of practice as, although progressive, none the less interdependent and relevant to each and every stage of Buddhist practice. The practice of the path is not simply linear; in one's progress along the path it is not that one first exclusively practises good conduct and then, when one has perfected that, moves on to meditative concentration and finally wisdom. Rather the three aspects of the practice of the path exist, operate, and are developed in a mutually dependent and reciprocal relationship. In other words, without some nascent sense of suffering and what conduces to its cessation one would not and could not even begin the practice of the path. This is not necessarily a conscious understanding capable of being articulated in terms of Buddhist doctrine, but is perhaps just a sense of generosity and good conduct as in some way constituting 'good' or wholesome (*kuśala/kusala*) behaviour—behaviour that is in accordance with Dharma and conduces to the cessation of suffering for both oneself and others. The details of the cultivation of the path to the cessation of suffering form the subject matter of Chapter 7, but let us now turn to consider Buddhist practice more generally: the way of life of Buddhist monks, nuns, and lay followers.

4

The Buddhist Community

Monks, Nuns, and Lay Followers

The Buddha's followers and the origin of the Buddhist order

As we saw in Chapter 1, Buddhism grew out of the ancient Indian 'renouncer' tradition; the Buddha's own teachers were such renouncers, as were those to whom he first addressed his teachings. Thus in presenting a system of training and practice geared to the eradication of greed, aversion, and delusion as the root causes of suffering, the Buddha's teaching suggests that the ideal basis for this training is the way of life followed by the Buddha himself, the life of a homeless, mendicant wanderer—in short, the life of a Buddhist monk (*bhikṣu/bhikkhu*) or nun (*bhikṣuṇī/bhikkhunī*). Indeed, while the earliest texts allow that one may achieve full awakening and arhatship without first formally becoming a monk, an old tradition argues that in such a case one inevitably either joins the Buddhist order or dies the same day.[1]

The basis of the renouncer's lifestyle lies in two things: (1) renunciation of the household life for the sake of the religious life, and (2) dependence upon the generosity of the population at large for the provision of material needs—food, clothing, and dwellings. The success of early Buddhism thus assumes both a desire on the part of certain members of the population to give up 'normal society' or 'the household life', and sufficient good will on the part of those remaining in normal society to allow them to do so. The followers of a teacher such as the Buddha thus fell into two socially distinct categories: homeless wanderers and lay supporters. Buddhist texts talk of the four 'assemblies' (*pariṣat/parisā*): of monks, nuns, male lay followers, female lay followers.

Buddhists have, then, always understood the Buddha's message not only as an invitation to give up the household life and join the Buddha's group of monks, but also as an invitation to the wider community to support the religious life. The Buddhist understanding of the nature of the lifestyle of 'one gone forth' sees the Buddhist monastic community as a significant part of society as a whole. Thus when the Buddha is reported, shortly after his awakening, as instructing his growing group of newly 'awakened' monastic followers to set off, never two by the same way, to teach Dharma that is 'lovely in the beginning, lovely in the middle, and lovely in the end', 'for the benefit and happiness of the many, out of sympathy for the world, for the good, benefit, and happiness of gods and men', this represents more than simply a recruitment drive for the Saṅgha or Order of monks and nuns.[2] The presence of Buddhist monks and nuns within a society has been seen as in itself a positive good and of benefit for all. Let us turn now to consider the members of the assemblies of the monks and nuns.

The procedures governing ordination, along with the rule governing life as a Buddhist monk or nun, are set out in the Vinaya, the division of Buddhist scriptures devoted to monastic 'discipline'. As we saw in Chapter 2, a number of different versions of this survive from ancient times. Only three are in actual use today. In Sri Lanka and South-East Asia monks in principle follow the rule of the Pali Theravādin Vinaya; in East Asia (China, Korea, and Japan) monks follow the rule of the ancient Dharmaguptaka Vinaya, translated into Chinese from an Indian original in the fifth century; in Tibet and Mongolia monks follow the rule of the Mūlasarvāstivāda, a branch of the Sarvāstivāda school, translated into Tibetan in the ninth century.[3] The Vinayas fall into two basic parts: (1) a set of rules governing the life of the individual monk or nun known as the *prātimokṣa* (Pali *pāṭimokkha*); and (2) regulations concerning the communal ceremonies and corporate 'acts' of the Saṅgha (i.e. an 'act' that is confirmed after having been formally proposed before a chapter of the Saṅgha either just once or three times, depending on the type of proposal), beginning with admission to the order.[4]

While there is considerable variation in the details of the surviving Vinayas, there is a fundamental agreement in structure and core content.

Ordination and the Buddhist monastic ideal

According to tradition, becoming a Buddhist monk could initially be accomplished without much ceremony; 'going forth' (*pravrajyā/pabbajjā*)—from the household life into homelessness—and 'ordination' (*upasampadā*) involved only a request to the Buddha and its acceptance by him with the words, 'Come, monk. Well taught is the Dharma. Live the spiritual life for the complete ending of suffering.'[5] Subsequently 'going forth' and ordination proper were distinguished as two distinct ceremonies; by undergoing the former ceremony of *pravrajyā* one becomes a 'novice' (*śrāmaṇera/sāmaṇera*), while the latter ceremony of *upasampadā* renders one a *bhikṣu* proper.[6] The ordination and discipline of the Buddhist nun (*bhikṣuṇī/bhikkhunī*) follows essentially the same pattern.

The Theravādin Vinaya specifies that the candidate for *pravrajyā* must be old enough to scare crows away, usually taken as meaning 7 or 8.[7] Going forth involves formally requesting that a monk of at least ten years' standing becomes one's preceptor (*upadhyāya/upajjhāya*) and teacher (*ācārya/ācariya*). The novice's head is shaved, and he puts on ochre robes. He then recites the formula of going for refuge to the Buddha, Dharma, and Saṅgha, and takes the ten precepts or 'rules of training' (*śikṣā-/sikkhā-pada*): (1) to refrain from harming living creatures, (2) to refrain from taking what is not given, (3) to refrain from all sexual activity, (4) to refrain from false speech, (5) to refrain from intoxicants that cause heedlessness, (6) to refrain from eating after midday, (7) to refrain from attending entertainments, (8) to refrain from wearing jewellery or using perfumes, (9) to refrain from sleeping on luxurious beds, (10) to refrain from handling gold and silver.[8]

One becomes a candidate for full ordination at the age of 20.[9] The *upasampadā* ceremony requires the participation of at least five properly ordained *bhikṣus* of at least ten years' standing. For someone over the age of 20 the *pravrajyā* and the *upasampadā* may be performed together at one occasion.

At the end of his ordination ceremony a Buddhist monk is informed that the four basic 'resources' (*niśraya/nissaya*) that he can count on for the four 'requisites' (*pariṣkāra/parikkhāra*) of food, clothing, lodging, and medicine are food offered to him as alms, robes made of discarded rags, the foot of a tree, and fermented urine respectively. Another list of requisites allows the monk eight items as his personal possessions: three robes, an alms-bowl, a razor, a needle, a belt, and a water-strainer.

The ideal of the Buddhist monk then is of one who steps out from ordinary society: his appearance is different (his head is shaved and he wears monastic robes); he renounces the ordinary household life of wife, children, and family and takes a vow of complete sexual abstinence; in adopting the way of life of the monk he abandons any profession or means of livelihood; his personal possessions are minimal and for the little he can expect in the way of creature comforts he is dependent on the generosity of others.

While in the course of the Saṅgha's long history in India and beyond there has been some adaptation and local variations have developed, the basic pattern of ordination set out in the Vinaya remains relevant to the monastic traditions of Theravāda Buddhism, East Asian Buddhism, and Tibetan Buddhism.[10] The most visible variation is that Theravādin monks wear orange or brown robes, while the monks of East Asia wear grey or black robes, and the monks of Tibet wear maroon robes. In Tibet (and sometimes in China) there has been a tendency for a considerable proportion of the Saṅgha to remain as *śrāmaṇeras* and never take full ordination.[11] In China *pravrajyā* ordination has been extended by separating initial tonsure, sometimes by many years, from formal taking of the ten precepts, while higher ordination has usually involved, in addition to the rules of the *prātimokṣa*, taking the fifty-eight 'bodhisattva vows' set out in the Chinese 'Brahma's Net' sūtra (*Fan-Wang-Ching*).[12] In South-East Asia temporary ordination as a monk for a year or even just a few months has become widespread.

After *upasampadā* one becomes a *bhikṣu*—a Buddhist monk proper—and as such one's life is governed by the complete set of rules which constitute the *prātimokṣa*. The precise number of rules that make up the monk's *prātimokṣa* varies; for the Theravāda there are 227 rules, for the Mūlasarvāstivāda (followed by the Tibetans) there are 258, for the Dharmaguptakas (followed in East Asia) there are 250, but the basic structure of the rules and the individual rules involving serious offences are held in common. In principle the rules simply elaborate a way of life based on keeping the ten precepts of the novice, distinguishing between serious and less serious breaches of these precepts. In this way the rules fall into eight categories. Four offences involve 'defeat' (*pārājika*), i.e. expulsion from the saṅgha: sexual intercourse, taking what is not given, killing another human being, and falsely laying claim to spiritual attainments of any sort.[13] These four *pārājika* offences map out the theoretical basis of the monastic way of life: celibacy and reliance on the generosity of lay support. The failure to keep his vow of celibacy undermines one of the defining characteristics of the Buddhist monk: he has renounced the ordinary 'household' life of wife, children, and family; furthermore sexual abstinence is associated with channelling one's energies towards spiritual attainments. To seek to solve the problem of suffering by killing other human beings is the grossest manifestation of greed, hatred, and delusion. To take from society what is not freely given betrays the fundamental relationship of trust between the monk, who undertakes to live the life of the ascetic wanderer, and those who in good faith offer their material support. Since any monk thought to be spiritually accomplished is likely to become the object of lay admiration and even devotion, to lie about spiritual attainments equally betrays the trust of lay supporters.

The second category of rules comprises thirteen *saṃghāvaśeṣa* (Pali *saṃghādisesa*) offences which are punishable by a period of probation involving loss of full status as a member of the Saṅgha; these involve sexual impropriety of various sorts, as well as the building of certain types of dwelling, making false accusations, promoting schism in the Saṅgha, refusing to accept the admonishments of the Saṅgha, and corrupting families. The thirteen *saṃghāvaśeṣas* are followed by two further rules concerning charges of possible sexual impropriety whose penalty is not fixed but must be determined by the Saṅgha according to circumstances. Next come thirty *niḥsargika* (Pali *nissaggiya*) rules which mostly concern inappropriate use of robes, rugs, money, bowls, and medicines; the offence should be confessed and the item given up. A further ninety or ninety-two minor *pāyantika* (Pali *pācittiya*) rules prohibit various kinds of lying, physical violence, and abusive speech, as well as further regulating the use of the monk's requisites, and his conduct in a monastery or in the presence of women; breach of these rules only requires confession. A further four miscellaneous offences merely require confession (*prātideśanīya/pāṭidesaniya*). The category of minor rules of training (*śaikṣa/sekhiya*) varies from 66 to 113, depending on the recension of the Vinaya, and covers the general decorum and manners of a monk as he eats, walks, dresses, and so forth. The *bhikṣu's prātimokṣa* concludes with seven rules concerned with the settling of disputes. Traditionally all members of the Saṅgha in a given locality gather on the fortnightly *poṣadha* (Pali *uposatha*) days—the days of the new and full moon—to recite the rules that make up the *prātimokṣa* and to confess any breaches.

A note on Buddhist nuns

Tradition relates how the nuns' or *bhikṣuṇīs*' order was founded after a request to the Buddha from Ānanda on behalf of women wanting to take up the spiritual life.[14] On that occasion the Buddha explained his reluctance to ordain women not because he regarded them as incapable of attaining arhatship, but because their ordination would hasten the decline of the Dharma. This attitude has often been interpreted as betraying a negative view of women, although in part it might be read simply as reflecting a realistic view of what happens when men and women who have undertaken the celibate life live in close proximity. None the less, the Buddha is represented as laying down eight special rules (*garudhamma*) subordinating the nuns' order to that of the monks.

However, it has been argued on the grounds of inconsistencies in the nuns' Vinaya that these eight rules represent a later interpolation.[15] Otherwise the *prātimokṣa* of Buddhist nuns is similar in broad outline to that of the monks, although in all recensions it comprises rather more rules.

The Buddhist canon contains a whole collection of verses, the *Therīgāthā*, attributed to female arhats as well as numerous examples of accomplished female religious teachers. At the same time, while allowing that women may become arhats, a canonical tradition represents the Buddha as denying that it was possible that a woman could be a buddha; the same passage also denies the possibility of a woman's being Māra.[16] Of course, such an understanding assumes also the reality of rebirth; the status of Māra or Buddha is thus not denied finally to any being since a being born as a woman—or a Brahmā (who is strictly without sex)—in one life may be born as a man in another. Inscriptional evidence from the early centuries CE points to the active role of both Buddhist nuns and lay women.[17]

At some point the Theravāda order of nuns died out, perhaps as early as the eleventh century in Sri Lanka, while the full nun's ordination lineage may never even have been established in Tibet. This means that fully ordained Buddhist nuns are only found today within East Asian Buddhism. Nevertheless, in the Theravāda and Tibetan traditions a significant number of women still effectively live as nuns by permanently keeping the ten precepts of the novice nun or the eight precepts of the committed female lay disciple; some continue to be regarded as respected teachers of meditation.[18] There is a movement to re-establish the *bhikkhunī* ordination lineage in Theravāda Buddhism, although the attitude of some 'nuns' towards this is ambivalent, since full ordination as a *bhikkhuṇī* brings with it the eight special rules mentioned above.

The underlying concerns of the Vinaya

It is possible, I think, to identify four particular concerns in the Buddhist monastic rule as set out in Vinaya: (1) the unity and cohesion of the Saṅgha, (2) the spiritual life, (3) the dependence of the Saṅgha upon the wider community, and (4) the appearance of the Saṅgha in the eyes of that community. These require some elaboration.

The Buddhist monastic community is the prerequisite for the existence of Buddhism in a given society. As we saw in Chapter 2, in a traditional Buddhist society it is only through contact with the monastic community that laity can have any knowledge of the Buddha's teachings. The Saṅgha lives the teaching, preserves the teaching as scriptures, and teaches the wider community. Without the Saṅgha there is no Buddhism. The Vinaya thus attempts to provide a framework which renders the Saṅgha a stable and viable institution, showing considerable concern for unity and the settling of disputes. The Saṅgha's constitution as set out in the Vinaya provides for no formal head or leader; authority rests in the agreement and consensus of bodies of senior monks. The formal hierarchy of the Saṅgha is based on seniority calculated from the time and date of one's ordination. The existence and survival of the Saṅgha for well over two millennia in diverse cultures is a measure of the Vinaya's success in establishing a structure that is tight enough to prevent disintegration of the community, but flexible enough to allow for adaptation to particular circumstances.

If the life as a monk is fundamental to the Buddhist vision of the spiritual life, then it follows that one of the Vinaya's prime concerns must be to regulate a way of life that conduces to the realization of the Buddhist path. The Vinaya's success in this respect is perhaps harder to gauge; there are, alas, no statistics for the number of realized 'saints'—bodhisattvas, stream-attainers, once-returners, never-returners, and arhats—it has fostered. Yet the widespread view that, for example, the Thai monk Acharn Mun who died in 1949 was an arhat indicates that 'enlightenment' is still regarded by some as a realistic aspiration for the Buddhist monk, even if the prevalent attitude in some circles is that arhatship is no longer possible.[19] The sanctity, or otherwise, of past and present members of the Saṅgha is hardly a matter to be determined by academic enquiry; nevertheless the

Vinaya's concern with the minutiae of a monk's handling of the requisites exhibits an awareness of human foibles as well as of the mind's ingenuity and even deviousness in the face of rules and regulations designed to curb greed, aversion, and delusion. Anyone genuinely attempting to put this way of life into practice is very soon likely to be made aware of the multifarious ways in which his or her greed, aversion, and delusion work. Furthermore the number of minor rules concerning more general behaviour seem intended to make for a certain alertness or mindfulness, one of the mental qualities to be cultivated in meditation.

The final two concerns of the Vinaya—the dependence of the Saṅgha upon the wider community, and the appearance of the Saṅgha in the eyes of that community—are interlinked. The Buddhist monk may be one who renounces society, but the genius of the Vinaya is that having invited the monk to give up society it then requires him to live in dependence upon it, thereby forcing him back into a relationship with it. It has sometimes been suggested that the Buddha originally intended to institute only a movement of committed ascetics removed from society; these are the true and original Buddhists. From this perspective the involvement of lay followers represents something of an afterthought on the part of the Buddha. If the basic conception of the Vinaya is attributable to the Buddha himself, then such an interpretation is hardly sustainable, for the interaction of the monastic and lay communities is integral to the way of life set out by the Vinaya.

Many of the rules of the Vinaya concerned with food, for example, are clearly designed to force members of the Saṅgha to be dependent on lay support. That is, if the Vinaya was intended to regulate the life of a self-sufficient community of ascetics who had no contact with society at large, it could have been structured differently. Instead it specifies that a monk should not handle money;[20] he should not eat food that he has not received from someone else;[21] he should not dig the ground or have it dug, and so is effectively prohibited from farming;[22] strictly he should not store food unless sick, and then only for seven days;[23] finally he is discouraged from cooking.[24] If called on to preach or attend to a lay supporter in various ways, then the community of monks should provide someone.[25] All these rules have the effect of drawing the Buddhist monk into a relationship with society, and balancing any tendency towards becoming a movement of eremitic ascetics.

The lifestyle of the Buddhist monk is thus founded on a relationship of trust between himself and his supporters. In accepting lay support in the form of robes, food, and lodgings, the monk enters into a kind of social contract; it becomes his responsibility to live in a certain way, namely to live the holy or spiritual life (*brahmacarya*) to the best of his ability. If Buddhism is unthinkable without the Saṅgha, then it is also true that the Saṅgha is unthinkable without lay support. The texts are thus at pains to point out that certain kinds of behaviour become inappropriate in the light of this contract; to spend one's time playing games or at entertainments; to spend one's time practising astrology and various kinds of divining. The concern here seems not so much to condemn these practices as such but merely to reinforce the principle that as a Buddhist monk one accepts lay support in order to practise the spiritual life. As a Buddhist monk one is deserving of lay support to the extent one attempts to put into practice the teachings of the Buddha, and *not* because of one's skills as an astrologer or doctor. Thus to lie about one's spiritual attainments is, as we have seen, undermining of this relationship of trust. Yet if the responsibility resting on the shoulders of the Buddhist monk should appear too heavy, the Buddha is recorded as reassuring them that if one dwells for even a finger-snap absorbed in meditation on loving kindness, then one has not eaten the country's alms food in vain.[26]

Other Vinaya rules are concerned to make sure that a monk avoids behaviour that might be misconstrued by the laity; his conduct should be in all respects beyond reproach. Thus talking in private with a woman or spending the night in the same house as a woman are prohibited.[27] The monk should also avoid behaviour that might be considered bad manners or give offence in some other way.

From wandering to settled life: forest dwellers and town dwellers

The ideal that the lifestyle of the Buddhist monk is founded upon is that of the homeless wanderer who, having renounced all possessions and gone forth from the household life, dresses in robes made from discarded rags, begs for his food, and takes as his dwelling the forest, a mountain cave, or the foot of a tree. Perhaps one of the most uncompromising descriptions of the renouncer's lifestyle is that found in a poem near the beginning of the *Suttanipāta*. Here the renouncer is advised to wander alone, free from any ties of family and friendship, 'like the [single] horn of the Indian rhinoceros'.[28] Although Buddhist tradition has not seen this account as a general prescription for Buddhist monastic life, there has been a tendency for modern scholarship to take the kind of picture it presents at face value. The history of the Saṅgha in ancient India can then be read as a series of compromises that amount to a gradual corruption of the ancient ideal. On this view, the monks at first wandered completely homeless in their single-minded intent on the goal of nirvāṇa. Increasing numbers of spiritually inexperienced and immature monks made it necessary for the Buddha to lay down more rules and regulations. Step by step this led to the institutionalization of the Saṅgha. Particularly significant in this process was a rule which is said to have been laid down in response to complaints that Buddhist monks wandering about during the monsoon rainy season were causing damage to plants and small creatures; this rule therefore requires monks to take up residence in one place for the three months of the rains. The consequence of this was the establishment of residential monasteries and the gradual evolution of a more settled way of life.[29]

But there are problems with such a model of the evolution of the Saṅgha. To begin with, as the more recent work of Mohan Wijayaratna and Gregory Schopen has shown, the Vinaya texts as we have them certainly already assume the development of a settled way of life and the picture of the typical monk's way of life reflected in them is not exactly that of the homeless wanderer. Schopen takes this as reason to conclude that the Vinaya texts as we have them reflect a state of affairs long after the death of the Buddha and in their present form must belong to a rather later period than is usually assumed—the early centuries of the Christian era. And yet, as Steven Collins has pointed out in his introduction, Wijayaratna's study of the early Pali sources brings out the extent to which they contain a coherent, developed, and well-integrated conception of monastic life, and this suggests that we must redraw our picture of the Buddhist monk as exclusively a homeless forest dweller even in the lifetime of the Buddha. Schopen might respond that in pushing the existence of a settled monastic way of life too far back in time, we assume too much development in too short a period of time and deny the Saṅgha any history.[30] But the fact remains that we are still unclear of the extent to which the Saṅgha can be regarded as having a 'pre-Buddhist' history. That is, a comparison with Jain monastic organization indicates that certain rules and principles, including the institution of a residential rains, are held in common. This suggests that either Buddhism and Jainism have borrowed from each other or that both have drawn on a common heritage. It may well be the case that the varied 'renouncer' tradition from which both Jainism and Buddhism emerge had already developed certain institutional patterns by the time of the Buddha, and that these have been drawn upon and adapted to suit the characteristically Buddhist vision of a mendicant order.

Again as Gregory Schopen has made clear, if we want to form some idea of the reality of ancient Buddhism, in addition to the evidence of ancient texts, we must take into account the archaeological evidence of ancient inscriptions and other artefacts. Dating from the third or second centuries BCE, these reflect the reality of how Buddhism was actually practised less problematically than the ideals of the texts. Once again the picture that can be drawn on the basis of these makes it clear that the homeless mendicant wanderer, meditating in the forest, intent on nirvaṇa, was neither the only, nor probably the numerically dominant, actuality.

For a general picture of Buddhist monastic life in ancient India and Sri Lanka through the centuries of the first millennium

CE, the most generally useful textual sources, apart from the various Vinayas, are the Pali commentaries and the records of three Chinese Buddhist pilgrims: Fa-hsien, who spent some fifteen years travelling in northern India and Sri Lanka at the beginning of the fifth century (399–414), Hsüan-tsang, who travelled throughout India, in the first half of the seventh century (630–643), and I-tsing, who visited India and the Malay archipelago towards the end of the seventh century (671–695).[31] Archaeological and inscriptional evidence comes from a great variety of monastic sites across India and from Sri Lanka.

These sources suggest that monks lived as more or less permanent residents in monasteries (*vihāra*, *ārāma*) that usually consisted of a number of buildings: residential quarters, a teaching hall, and a *poṣadha* hall (for the fortnightly recitation of the monastic rule). The religious heart of a monastery was threefold: a stūpa (containing relics, ideally of the Buddha or of some acknowledged 'saint'), a Bodhi-tree (an *aśvattha* or *ficus religiosa*—the type of tree the Buddha gained awakening under—often growing on a platform), and finally a shrine hall or image house.[32] All three would have been the object of considerable devotional practice by monks and laity alike. Monasteries varied enormously in size. Fa-hsien records that the Abhayagiri Vihāra at Anurādhapura, the ancient capital of Sri Lanka, housed 5,000 monks, while I-tsing states that at the famous monastic university of Nālandā in eastern India there were some 3,000 residents.[33] Such monastic establishments included kitchens, refectories, latrines, bathing facilities, and libraries. Whether or not the figures of the Chinese pilgrims are exaggerated, the remains of these ancient monastic complexes are impressive in themselves and bear witness to their grand past. Patronized by royalty and the wealthy, many monasteries had considerable endowments in the form of property, lands, and other material goods. Thus in both India and Sri Lanka we find the development of a system (already adumbrated in the Vinaya itself) whereby monasteries' requirements for food were provided by the produce of land farmed on behalf of the monastery by laity who received a share in return.[34] Large monasteries also employed considerable numbers of lay servants of various sorts in order to handle donations of money and goods and oversee their running. The canonical Vinaya sources refer to the office of *kappiya-kāraka* (Sanskrit *kalpi-kāra*), a layman who makes 'allowable' (*kappiya*) gifts that would otherwise, according to the strictures of the Vinaya, not be permissible. This is relevant especially to donations of land and money, which individual monks and nuns are strictly forbidden from accepting or handling, but which the *kappiya-kāraka* could receive and administer on their behalf.[35] The Saṅgha could thus become the effective owner of considerable property, wealth, and resources, while individual monks also came to exercise rights over property which in certain circumstances extended to being able to leave it to their monastic pupils.[36]

A situation where a monk lives in a wealthy monastery effectively enjoying personal rights of ownership over a share of that monastery's wealth is somewhat removed from the ideal of the homeless mendicant, wandering from village to village with alms-bowl and dressed in rag robes retrieved from a dust heap, intent on his spiritual quest. But we must remember that there were also monks, perhaps the majority, who lived in more modest small village monasteries. There were also those, no doubt a small minority, who continued to be inspired by the ascetic ideal, setting off for the forest, living in caves, or donning robes made from rags discarded on rubbish heaps.

In the context of developed Buddhist monasticism, dwelling in the forest or wearing robes made of rags from a dust heap became two of a set of twelve or thirteen specialized ascetic practices (*dhuta-guṇa/dhutaṅga*) that an individual monk might undertake for a shorter or longer period.[37] These forest-dwelling (*āraṇyaka/āraññika*) or rag robe-wearing (*pāṃsu-/paṃsu-kūlikā*) monks are contrasted with the town-dwelling (*gāma-vāsin*) monks. Although the numbers of forest monks may have been relatively small, their strict practice meant that they attracted the support of the laity and that they enjoyed considerable prestige and influence.[38] Ironically this meant that they did not always succeed in maintaining their ascetic practice and that in ancient Sri Lanka, for example, monks belonging to nominally Āraññika or Paṃsukūlika groups did not necessarily dwell in the forest or wear rag robes. The tendency of the laity to direct their special gifts and particular devotions towards monks whose lifestyle approximates most closely to the traditional ascetic ideal at once invests them with power and threatens to undermine the basis of that power. Their monastic establishments become the most prosperous and, as a consequence, their ascetic tradition was most in danger of being compromised.[39] Yet the ideal of the wanderer intent on the Buddhist monk's traditional spiritual quest continued to be seen as embodied in the forest-dwelling or rag robe-wearing monk, and the periodic attempt to re-establish the ancient ascetic ideal is one of the defining features of the history of Buddhist monasticism. But, as the following story illustrates, it is the spirit of that ancient ideal that inspires the tradition, not the letter.

Two friends, it seems, were ordained as monks at Thūpārāma (one of the monasteries belonging to the Mahāvihāra) in Anurādhapura, the ancient capital of Sri Lanka.[40] One went off to Pācīnakhaṇḍarāji, a forest monastery in the east; the other remained at Thūpārāma. Ten years passed by. One day it occurred to the monk at Pācīnakhaṇḍarāji that he should invite his old friend to come and practise at this secluded forest monastery. He set off for Anurādhapura. There he was welcomed by his former companion. Over the course of the day the visiting monk was continually waiting for choice foods and other comforts to be provided by servants, attendants, and lay supporters. But none was forthcoming. Instead they wandered through Anurādhapura and got only a ladleful of gruel. As the two wandered through the town, the visiting monk enquired whether his friend always lived in such a frugal manner. When he was told that he did, the visitor reminded him that Pācīnakhaṇḍarāji was comfortable and suggested that they go there. As they passed the gate of the city the other elder took the road to Pācīnakhaṇḍarāji.

'Why do you take this road?' asked the visitor.

'Didn't you just recommend Pācīnakhaṇḍarāji?'

'But don't you have some extra possessions in this place where you have lived so long?'

'Yes, I have the bed and chair belonging to the Saṅgha, which have been put away. There is nothing else.'

'But I have left my staff, my oil tube, and my sandal bag.'

'Have you collected so much living here for one day?'

Humbled, the visitor declared, 'For those such as you everywhere is a forest dwelling.'

A note on the Saṅgha and the state

Strictly speaking the Saṅgha is an autonomous organization and no provision is made within the Vinaya for formal links with the state or government. But this does not mean that in practice close links and associations between the Saṅgha and the state have not developed. The history of Buddhism in all the regions of the world where it has taken root, from ancient times down to the present day, affords numberous examples of such links and associations.

For much of its history the Saṅgha has existed in countries ruled by a king or emperor. A king may become a patron of the Saṅgha granting it his support. Theoretically he may do this as an individual lay follower (*upāsaka*), and his individual support should be possible to distinguish from official state support. In practice this distinction becomes hard to maintain. For Buddhist tradition it is the figure of the Indian emperor Aśoka who has become the archetype of a Buddhist king. Aśoka reigned *c.*268–231 BCE and extended the Mauryan empire across nearly the entire Indian subcontinent. Aśoka's rock and pillar edicts, which have been found in various locations throughout India, indicate that after a particularly bloody military campaign in Kaliṅga (eastern India) he turned to Buddhist teachings and came to regard himself as a committed lay supporter (*upāsaka*) of the Saṅgha. His edicts subsequently go on to self-consciously promote Dharma throughout his empire and beyond, commending in particular the non-injury of living creatures, the provision of medical care for the sick, and tolerance among all religious groups, while at the same time highlighting his own efforts in these directions. Although he seems personally to have favoured Buddhism, he continued to support other religious groups. His edicts are not so much a bid to convert his subjects to Buddhism as an attempt to put into practice some of its principles in his role as emperor. Thus while his vision of Dhamma is not couched in narrow and exclusively Buddhist terms it does appear to owe much to his personal understanding of Buddhist teaching. Buddhist tradition claims Aśoka as its own and many legends about his life are recounted in the *Aśokāvadāna* and the Sinhalese chronicles (*Dīpavaṃsa* and *Mahāvaṃsa*).[41]

Once a king has become involved in supporting the Saṅgha, then the avenues are open not only for state interference in and control of the affairs of the Saṅgha, but also for the Saṅgha to become involved in the affairs of the state and political intrigue. The state may seek to justify its actions—including war—in the name of support for the Buddha, Dharma, and Saṅgha; it may seek to support the sections of the Saṅgha that it judges as representing the true Dharma; the Saṅgha may connive in this, with different factions appealing for state support. Thus an ancient Sri Lankan chronicle, the *Mahāvaṃsa*, seeks to justify Duṭṭhagāminī's war against the Tamil king, Eḷāra, as a victory for Dharma; in medieval Japan rival gangs of Tendai 'monks' (some armed) clashed in the struggle for political influence; in Tibet Sa-skya Paṇḍita's meeting with the Mongol Khan in 1249 paved the way for a 'patron–priest' relationship (*yon mchod*) with political overtones; in modern times Buddhism has been closely linked to the legitimation of power in Sri Lanka and South-East Asia.[42]

The spiritual life: the practice of 'meritorious action'

The heart of Buddhist spiritual life, whether lay or monastic, is *puṇya* (Pali *puñña*). This term is usually translated as 'merit' and refers to certain significant kinds of action that are regarded as auspicious and potent deeds. Essentially, merit is good 'karma' (*karman*/*kamma*): wholesome (*kuśala*/*kusala*) deeds which plant seeds that bear fortunate and pleasant fruits, whether in this life or lives to come, and thereby create conditions for further meritorious action in the future.[43] These are the kinds of action that conduce to the development of the qualities of the eightfold path. Moreover it is making merit that binds the lay and monastic communities together. The traditional 'bases of merit' are generosity (*dāna*), ethical conduct (*śīla/sīla*), and meditation (*bhāvanā*).

In its widest sense 'generosity' is understood as embracing all acts performed with a generous and giving spirit, but it also has a more specific application: it refers especially to the generosity of the laity in supporting the Saṅgha materially. This first basis of merit is thus regarded as of particular concern to the laity. Yet as the recipients of the laity's material gifts, members of the Saṅgha have a special responsibility, namely to act as the 'field of merit' (*puṇya-kṣetra/puñña-kkhetta*) for the gifts of the laity. A monk is only a fertile and productive field of merit as long as he lives according to the Vinaya, behaving as a monk should. One of the principles of Buddhist ethics is that the unwholesome or wholesome quality of one's acts is also affected by their object: to kill a human is a weightier unwholesome act than killing a dog; a gift to a spiritually accomplished monk is a more powerful wholesome act than a casual gift to one's neighbour. Of course, preoccupation with a recipient's worthiness to receive gifts on the part of the donor is liable to be bound up more with the motivations of greed and delusion than with generosity and wisdom, and should thus be avoided as undermining the very act of giving. The principle is more important for the one who receives a gift than the donor. Thus the onus is on a monk to make himself a suitable recipient of the laity's gifts. So long as a monk lives in accordance with the basic precepts of the Vinaya, he fulfils his obligation to society and renders himself a field of merit for the laity. The more fully a monk lives out the spiritual life, the more fruitful a field of merit he becomes for the laity's gifts; thus the Saṅgha consisting of the different kinds of 'noble persons' (*ārya-pudgala/ariya-puggala*) of stream-attainers, once returners, never-returners, and arhats—the Buddhist saints—becomes the 'unsurpassable field of merit'.

The practice of generosity is, however, also relevant to the Saṅgha. As I suggested above, in becoming a monk one enters into a contract with society: in return for material support one undertakes to live the spiritual life and to give in return the gift of Dharma.[44] As a medieval Sinhalese work advises monks:

'Householders continually provide you with gifts of material goods, and in return you must provide them with the gift of Dharma.'[45] To an extent just living the life of a monk is a teaching in itself, a gift of Dharma to society. But the Saṅgha's gift of Dharma is conceived in broader terms.

As a 'field of merit' the Saṅgha is under some obligation simply to make itself available to the laity. One of the principal ways in which the Vinaya brings this about is by requiring monks to receive food from the laity every day. Moreover, the Vinaya stipulates that the Saṅgha is normally bound to accept the laity's invitations, especially when a building or land is being offered to the Saṅgha, or when a lay follower has built a new house, gets married, or dies. In such circumstances the Saṅgha should send some representative. A monk's presence on such occasions has the effect of rendering them auspicious; they become opportunities for acts of merit. In the first place a monk can be offered food and simply act as a field of merit, but they became, and in the countries of Theravāda Buddhism continue to be, primary occasions for members of the Saṅgha to offer the gift of Dharma to the laity by preaching the Dharma directly to them and chanting 'blessings of protection' (*rakṣā/paritta*) to ward off the dangers of accident and disease (see pp. 168–9). It should be noted in this context, however, that the Buddhist monk does not traditionally act as a 'priest' on these occasions: marriages and funerals do not involve rituals or 'sacraments' that require the participation of an ordained member of the Saṅgha to consecrate them.[46] Again blessings chanted by the laity are still effective, although, in line with the kind of thinking outlined above, those chanted by a group of spiritually accomplished monks are likely to be considered more auspicious and potent.

For a member of the Saṅgha, the basis of merit that consists in ethical conduct centres on his following the prescriptions of the Vinaya, and this I have already discussed. What of the Saṅgha's practice of 'meditation'? In the ancient period it is tempting to associate serious devotion to the practice of meditation with the forest-dwelling tradition, but not all 'forest-dwellers' lived in the remote jungle, and (as our story illustrated) it is not necessarily the case that the life of monks in the larger well-endowed city monasteries was lax or especially comfortable; some of these monasteries kept up a strict regime of spiritual practice.[47] Moreover all monks would have participated alongside the laity in the various devotional practices which are associated with the 'recollections' (*anusmṛti/anussati*) (see p. 179) and which are intended to arouse and cultivate religious emotions that are an aspect of 'calm' (*śamatha*) meditation. Essentially such devotional practices take the form of worship (*pūjā*) by means of prostrations, circumambulation, and making offerings of flowers, incense, and lamps to 'relics' (*dhātu*) of the Buddha. These may be of three kinds: actual physical remains of the body of the Buddha (or some other Buddhist saint); articles 'used' by the Buddha, such as his bowl or the Bodhi-tree; and 'reminders', such as images of the Buddha.[48] Worship of the first two types of relic centred principally around the veneration of the stūpas enshrining such relics—though images too might enshrine relics—and of the Bodhi-trees normally found in each monastery.

In addition to this kind of worship, monks also seem to have participated in other activities along with the laity, commissioning and even sometimes making images of the Buddha, and other Buddhist monuments. The making of works of art was an act of merit, and the ancient inscriptions record that often the merit from such acts was dedicated or 'transferred' to parents or even to the benefit of all sentient beings.[49]

In Chapter 2 I drew attention to a distinction made in later Pali sources between two main duties: the 'task of spiritual insight' (*vipassanā-dhura*) and the scholarly 'task of books' (*gantha-dhura*).[50] This distinction indicates that as well as having the responsibility of putting the teaching into practice by keeping the Vinaya and cultivating meditation, the Saṅgha has also traditionally been responsible for the preservation and study of the scriptures. Some Buddhist monasteries have thus also been great centres of learning and scholarship, which has taken in not only the study of Buddhist and other systems of philosophical and religious thought, but also the study of such disciplines as medicine, grammar, literature, astronomy, and astrology.[51] This distinction between the vocations of practice and scholarship corresponds in part with that between forest-dwelling and town-dwelling. But these two vocations should not be seen as mutually exclusive in that an individual monk might in the course of his monastic career at one time spend a period meditating in the forest and at another devote himself to scholarship in a large monastery.

While the very success of the Saṅgha may have in certain respects compromised the original ascetic ideal of the Buddhist monk, it would be a mistake to conclude that it extinguished it. The ascetic ideal remained alive and not only continued to inspire the life of the Saṅgha, but continued to be realized. Of course the grand monasteries of the 'city-dwelling' (*grāma-vāsin*) monks patronised by royalty and the wealthy will inevitably leave more substantial remains than the abodes of 'forest-dwelling' (*āraṇya-vāsin*) monks; the literary activities of scholar (*gantha-dhura*) monks leave material evidence in the form of manuals and treatises; monks who commission statues or stūpas and dedicate the merit to their deceased parents leave behind inscriptions. But the signs left by anonymous monks following the path of meditation (*vipassanā-dhura*) in the forest are harder to trace and follow. This makes problematic Schopen's assertion that the literary and archaeological evidence forces us to the conclusion that the ascetic ideal of the forest monk became early in the history of Buddhist monasticism merely 'a dead letter'.[52] The history of Buddhist monasticism can be seen in the light of a continued interplay, and sometimes tension, between the town-dwelling monks and the forest monks, between the scholar monks and the practitioners. Although the former may have been numerically more significant, the ideal of the forest saint has continued to exercise a considerable power over the imaginations of both the Saṅgha and the laity down to the present day, with the consequence that there have always been significant attempts to put that ideal into practice.[53]

I have been talking in broad terms and of the past. What of the present actuality? The various studies that have been made of Theravāda Buddhist practice in Sri Lanka and the countries of South-East Asia suggest that the general pattern of monastic practice and its organization are not entirely dissimilar from the historical pattern. Indeed, one of the significant conclusions of Richard Gombrich's important study of traditional Buddhism in the rural highlands of Sri Lanka in the 1960s was that things appeared to have changed rather little over the previous fifteen hundred years (although the significance of modernist tendencies among the urban middle classes of Colombo and Bangkok should not be underestimated).[54] It is dangerous to generalize about the reality of Buddhist monasticism in such diverse settings as Sri Lanka, Cambodia, China, Japan, and Tibet. There are, nevertheless, features of the practice of Buddhist monasticism in these different settings that amount to a certain continuity of tradition, and suggest that the picture that can be drawn on the basis of the ancient sources is not merely of archaeological and antiquarian interest. Moreover, the basic pattern is similar. What we tend to find throughout Buddhist history and throughout the Buddhist world are a number of grand, important and wealthy monasteries (especially in capital cities and large urban centres), many more smaller local village monasteries, together with a small but always significant group of monks following a more secluded way of life in the forest, in caves, or in more isolated monasteries. Individual monks may gravitate towards one kind of lifestyle or another, but the tendency to view Buddhist monastic practice in terms of a stark polarization between the meditating forest monk and the town-dwelling scholar monk should be tempered with the reminder that these are ideal abstractions. In the course of a monastic career in all Buddhist traditions monks are likely to move between monasteries and ways of life.[55]

While this pattern remains generally relevant one should bear in mind that Buddhist monastic practice has developed characteristic features in various places at various times. Strict adherence to the letter of the Vinaya have been affected both by individual temperaments and local circumstances. For example, everywhere today there is certain laxity with regard to the rule prohibiting the handling of money, although some Theravādin forest monks will strictly adhere to it; the practice of not eating solid food after midday is more strictly followed in Theravāda monasticism than in East Asian and Tibetan;[56] among the Ch'an monks of China it became the norm for monks to farm and grow their own food in accordance with the additional code of Pai-chang and Ta-chih Huai-hai (720–814), laying down that monks should perform some productive labour every day;[57] the alms round, which remains common in South-East Asia but rarer in Sri Lanka, became very rare in China where, however, begging for money has been more common;[58] Chinese monasticism involves a more definite tradition of physical austerities (such as the burning of incense cones on one's head at ordination); in the context of Japanese Pure Land tradition we find the transformation of the monastic Saṅgha into what is effectively a married priesthood, while following the Meiji Restoration of 1868 the Japanese government decreed that monks should marry;[59] in certain schools of Tibetan Buddhism a tradition of lay teachers and practitioners has become more developed and formalized.

So while it is possible to read the history of the Buddhist Saṅgha as the process of the gradual compromising of its ascetic ideal, it is also possible that we should see the compromise as inherent in the characteristically Buddhist vision of the life of the homeless wanderer. That is, the tendency to leave society is deliberately balanced in the Vinaya by rules which force the monk back into a relationship with society. The dynamic of the Buddhist monastic way of life is then to be seen as rooted in the interaction between a more settled monastic lifestyle and the ideal of the forest-dwelling wanderer.

The lay community

As I have already indicated, the support of a lay community is essential to the existence of the Buddhist Saṅgha and thus to Buddhism. The Buddhist lay community is traditionally said to comprise the two 'assemblies' of male (*upāsaka*) and female lay disciples (*upāsikā*). An *upāsaka/upāsikā* is one who formally declares that he or she goes to the Buddha, the Dharma, and

Saṅgha as refuge, and we can see this act as loosely defining an individual as a 'Buddhist'. In ancient India the Buddhist Saṅgha probably received considerable support from 'householders' who would not have regarded themselves as formally Buddhist *upāsakas* or *upāsikās*; moreover becoming even an *upāsaka* or *upāsikā* did not necessarily involve an exclusive commitment to the Buddhist Saṅgha.[60] Some householders seem to have supported wanderers of various groups—Jains, Ājīvikas, Buddhists—rather indiscriminately, with little awareness of their different teachings, seeing them all as 'holy men' and as such deserving of some support. Other householders and their families clearly developed a sense of loyalty and commitment to one particular group or teacher, seeking out their company and requesting them to teach. But even this need not have involved exclusive allegiance. Thus we are told that when a supporter of the Jain order took refuge in the Buddha, Dharma, and Saṅgha, the Buddha suggested that he should honour the traditions of his family and not withdraw all support from the Jains.[61] Historically the degree of commitment and support offered to the Saṅgha, the degree of interest taken in Buddhist teachings and practice by lay supporters must have varied a great deal. Much the same state of affairs prevails in Buddhist cultures today. Thus in Theravāda practice today the term *upāsaka* or *upāsikā* implies a commitment to and involvement with Buddhist practice beyond what is implied by the routine taking of the refuges; in East Asian and Tibetan Buddhism formally 'going for refuge' often becomes an expression of a particular commitment to Buddhist practice.

As we saw at the close of Chapter 3, the Buddhist path can be summed up in terms of the progressive development of generosity (*dāna*), good conduct (*sīla/śīla*), and meditation (*bhāvanā*). The very act of giving is seen in general as loosening attachment, turning the mind away from selfish concerns. From the point of view of Buddhist psychological theory, generosity is an expression of two of the wholesome 'roots' or fundamental motivating forces of the mind: non-attachment and friendliness. Many of the stories of the Buddha's previous lives (*jātaka*) tell of the Bodhisattva's heroic acts of generosity. One of the most famous relates how he offered his flesh to a hungry tigress in order that she might have the strength to succour her young.[62] Another well-known tale tells of Prince Vessantara, who gave away even that which is most precious: his children and family.[63] Such heroic acts of generosity are expressions of a bodhisattva's practice of 'the perfection of generosity', inspiring faith rather than providing examples of behaviour to be emulated. In everyday practice, generosity is developed by the laity especially by acts of generosity directed towards the Buddhist religion itself. This takes the form of supporting Dharma by donating money, time, and effort for the building of monasteries and temples, and for the general support of the Buddhist monastic community, for the copying or publication of Buddhist writings. In the countries of Theravāda Buddhism the term *dāna* refers in particular to the act of giving alms directly to Buddhist monks either by offering food at a monastery or by placing it directly into the bowls of monks who still undertake a traditional alms round.

Relevant to the cultivation of generosity are two practices which are not, however, exclusively lay: the transference of merit and the rejoicing in the merit of others. The practice of the transference of merit—the giving of one's merit—is an ancient and extremely widespread and common Buddhist practice. What it indicates is that spiritual practice is to be entered into in a generous spirit, not for the sake of acquiring merit exclusively for oneself but for the benefit of others too. Indeed, only acts undertaken in this spirit are truly meritorious in the first place. The rejoicing in the merit of others also indicates that, in undertaking meritorious acts, it is one's state of mind that is crucial: thus if one gives grudgingly, with an ungenerous heart, the auspiciousness of one's acts is compromised; on the other hand, if one gives nothing at all but is deeply moved by another's act of generosity, then that in itself is an auspicious occasion, an act of merit. Thus for many Buddhists it is customary at the end of Buddhist devotions and rituals to offer the merit generated during the ceremony for the benefit of other beings—either specific beings such as dead relatives, or all sentient beings—and in so doing to invite all present (whether they have directly participated in the ceremony or not, whether they have physical presence or are unseen ghosts or gods) also to rejoice in the merit of the ceremony.

The practice of good conduct takes the form of commitment to the five precepts usually recited in conjunction with the three refuges: (1) to refrain from harming living creatures, (2) to refrain from taking what is not given, (3) to refrain from sexual misconduct, (4) to refrain from false speech, (5) to refrain from intoxicants that cause heedlessness (see pp. 170–2). In addition the lay disciple may on special occasions (traditionally the full moon 'observance' days) or for longer periods take the eight precepts, replacing the third precept (refraining from sexual misconduct) with complete sexual abstinence and adding (6) refraining from eating after midday, (7) refraining from attending entertainments and using perfumes, etc., and (8) refraining from using luxurious beds. In taking the eight precepts the lay follower takes on a discipline that approximates to the ten precepts of novice members of the Saṅgha.

As far as the lay cultivation of meditation is concerned, practice can be seen as centring around the various kinds of offerings (*pūjā*) which arouse the religious emotion of faith (*śraddhā/saddhā*) and conduce to the development of the initial stages of calm meditation (see p. 179). Pilgrimages to the sites associated with the events of the Buddha's life and also to local holy places and shrines are another significant feature of lay Buddhist practice, as too are festivals of various sorts. These again fit into the general pattern of arousing religious emotion. The fact that Buddhist devotions centred on stūpas, Bodhi-trees and images of the Buddha, the finest and most sacred of which were generally to be found in the grounds of monasteries, meant that monasteries were also centres of lay religious activity.

Spiro's schema: apotropaic, kammatic, and nibbānic Buddhism

In an important anthropological study of post-war Burmese Buddhist practice, Melford Spiro proposed a distinction between three forms of Buddhism: 'apotropaic', 'kammatic', and 'nibbānic'.[64] By the first he meant Buddhist activity that is concerned with day-to-day 'protection' of a community and individual and improving conditions in the here and now. By the second he meant Buddhist practice that is concerned with acquiring 'merit' and producing a better rebirth. By the third he meant Buddhist practice that aims directly at the attainment of nirvāṇa (Pali *nibbāna*) and release from the cycle of birth, death, and rebirth that is saṃsāra. The first Spiro regards as basically using 'magical' means such as chants, amulets, and so forth; the second involves the traditional practice of generosity and ethical conduct; the third the practice of meditation. While based on his observation of Burmese Buddhism, such a schema can, with certain qualifications, be seen as more generally relevant. As a number of writers have pointed out, Spiro, although recognizing that these three complexes are not entirely distinct, nevertheless has a tendency to present them as such. Moreover, he also tends to see their goals as incompatible and even contradictory; only the goal of nirvāṇa represents a truly Buddhist goal, while apotropaic and kammatic Buddhist practice represent a corruption and compromise respectively of the true and original ideal of Buddhism. Yet, as we shall see, the use of protective chants is certainly ancient (see p. 168) and the appeal to powerful beings for short-term help and protection is not necessarily in conflict with the principles of Buddhism; what is, is the notion that an all-powerful being might bring one ultimate salvation. Equally the association of the practice of meditation with certain extraordinary 'magical' powers is normative in the ancient texts (pp. 185–6); their practice is not generally condemned, only their display by monks for money or to win converts. Moreover, the practice of at least some of what Spiro identifies as 'apotropaic' Buddhism can be seen as part of creating an environment of protection conducive to the practice of calm meditation. Again, as we shall see (p. 179), there is no sharp divide between certain merit making activities of *pūjā* and certain of the traditional subjects of calm meditation. Finally one should avoid the conclusion that what Spiro calls apotropaic and kammatic Buddhism are the strict preserve of the layman and nibbānic Buddhism the preserve of the monk. In practice many, perhaps most, monks are equally concerned with apotropaic and kammatic Buddhism and a few lay followers with nibbānic.

5

The Buddhist Cosmos

The Thrice-Thousandfold World

Of space and time: world-systems

In Chapter 3 we saw how the Buddha's teaching seeks to address the problem of *duḥkha* or 'suffering'. For Buddhist thought, whatever the circumstances and conditions of existence—good or bad—they are always ultimately changeable and unreliable, and hence *duḥkha*. Complete understanding of the first noble truth is said to consist in the complete knowledge of the nature of *duḥkha*. One of the preoccupations of Buddhist theory, then, is the exhaustive analysis of all possible conditions and circumstances of existence. Buddhist thought approaches the analysis of *duḥkha* from two different angles, one cosmological and the other psychological. That is, it asks two different but, in the Buddhist view of things, fundamentally related questions. First, what are the possible circumstances a being can be born, exist, and die in? And second, what are the possible states of mind a being might experience? The complete Buddhist answer to these questions is classically expressed in the Abhidharma systems. In this chapter I want to look primarily at the first question, though, as I have just suggested, this cannot be entirely separated from the second. To begin with, however, I shall return to certain of those questions raised by the monk Mālunkyāputta.

As we have seen, among the questions he demanded that the Buddha answer were whether or not the universe was eternal, and whether or not it was finite. The Buddha refused to give categorical answers, but that does not mean that he had nothing to say on the subjects raised by these questions. I have already introduced the bare concept of saṃsāra or the round of rebirth. But when did it all begin? How long, according to Buddhist thinking on the matter, have you and I together with other beings been wandering from birth to death through saṃsāra?

In response to just this question the Buddha is said to have declared that saṃsāra's beginning was inconceivable and that its starting point could not be indicated; he went on to ask the group of monks he was addressing which they thought was greater, the mother's milk they had drunk in the course of their long journey through saṃsāra or the water in the four great oceans. 'Certainly the mother's milk drunk by you is greater,' they were told.[1] We have, it seems, been wandering in saṃsāra for aeons. But how long is an aeon? When asked this question, the Buddha refused to answer in terms of numbers of years, or hundreds or even thousands of years; instead he gave a simile:

> Suppose there was a great mountain of rock, seven miles across and seven miles high, a solid mass without any cracks. At the end of every hundred years a man might brush it just once with a fine Benares cloth. That great mountain of rock would decay and come to an end sooner than ever the aeon. So long is an aeon. And of aeons of this length not just one has passed, not just a hundred, not just a thousand, not just a hundred thousand.[2]

If this is how the age of the universe is to be conceived, what of its spatial extent? On another occasion the Buddha told a householder, Kevaddha, of a monk who wished to discover just where the four elements of earth, water, fire, and wind ceased completely.[3] We can understand this as wishing to discover the limits of the physical universe. The monk was a master of meditation (*samādhi*) and so was able to attain a state of concentration in which he was able to visit the realms of various *devas* or 'gods' and put his question to them. First he approached the gods of the Four Kings; they were unable to answer his question but directed him to yet higher gods who in turn passed him on to still higher gods: the gods of the Thirty-Three, the Yama gods, the Contented gods, the gods who Delight in Creation, the Masters of the Creations of Others, the gods of Brahmā. None could answer his question. Finally he approached Great Brahmā himself, who repeatedly answered only that he was Great Brahmā, 'mighty, unconquerable, all-seeing, master, lord, maker, creator, overseer, controller, father of all who are and will be'. In the face of the monk's persistence, Great Brahmā eventually took him aside and confessed that he too did not know where the elements cease and suggested that the monk return to the Buddha and put the question to him. The Buddha's answer, we are told, was that where the four elements cease completely is in the consciousness that knows nirvāṇa.[4]

This story from the *Kevaddha Sutta* ('Discourse to Kevaddha') indicates how in the traditional Buddhist view of things the universe is not to be thought of as just inhabited by the beings that make up the human and animal world but also by various classes of *deva* or 'god' that form a hierarchy of increasing subtlety and refinement. Thus the world comprises 'its gods, its Māra and Brahmā, this generation with its ascetics and brahmins, with its princes and peoples'.[5] Moreover, elsewhere, the earliest texts inform us that there is not just one such world with its gods, its Māra and Brahmā; in fact the universe as a whole comprises vast numbers of 'world-spheres' or 'world-systems' (*cakra-vāḍa/ cakka-vāḷa*) each with its gods, its Māra and Brahmā. Clusters of a thousand 'world-spheres' may be ruled over by yet higher gods, called Great Brahmās, but it would be wrong to conclude that there is any one or final overarching Great Brahmā—God the Creator. It may be that beings come to take a particular Great Brahmā as creator of the world, and a Great Brahmā may himself even form the idea that he is creator, but this is just the result of delusion on the part of both parties. In fact the universe recedes ever upwards with one class of Great Brahmā being surpassed by a further, higher class of Great Brahmā.[6]

So how many world-systems are there in all? The early Nikāya/ Āgama texts sometimes talk in terms of 'the thousandfold world-system', 'the twice-thousandfold world-system', and 'the thrice-thousandfold world-system'. According to Vasubandhu, the last of these embraces a total of 1,000,000,000 world-systems, according to Buddhaghosa, 1,000,000,000,000.[7] But even such a vast number cannot define the full extent of the universe; it is merely the highest explicit number of world-systems reported in the tradition. There is no spatial limit to the extent of world-systems:

Buddhaghosa tells us in the *Atthasālinī* ('Providing the Meaning') that if four Great Brahmās from the realm of the Supreme Gods were to set off in the four directions at a speed which allowed them to traverse a hundred thousand world-systems in the time it takes a swift arrow to pass over the shadow of a palm tree, they would reach nirvāṇa without ever finding the limit of world-systems.[8] Great Brahmās of the realm of the Supreme Gods are beings in their last existence who are certain of reaching final nirvāṇa at the end of their lives, which last 16,000 aeons. Bearing in mind the simile for the length of an aeon, I leave it to the reader to ponder how many hundreds of thousands of world-systems these Great Brahmās might traverse in 16,000 aeons.

The earliest strata of Buddhist writings, the Nikāyas/Āgamas, do not provide a systematic account of the Buddhist understanding of the nature of the cosmos, but they do contain many details and principles that are systematized into a coherent whole by the Abhidharma traditions of Buddhist thought. Two great Abhidharma traditions have come down to us, that of the Theravādins, which has shaped the outlook of Buddhism in Sri Lanka and South-East Asia, and that of the Sarvāstivādins, whose perspective on many points has passed into Chinese and Tibetan Buddhism. The elaborate cosmological systems detailed in these two Abhidharmas are, however, substantially the same, differing only occasionally on minor points of detail. This elaborate and detailed cosmology is thus to be regarded as forming an important and significant part of the common Buddhist heritage. Moreover, it is not to be regarded as only of quaint and historical interest; the world-view contained in this traditional cosmology still exerts considerable influence over the outlook of ordinary Buddhists in traditional Buddhist societies. In the one or two instances in what follows where the Sarvāstivādin and Theravādin traditions differ, I have, as a matter of convenience, presented what is handed down in the Theravādin texts.

According to the developed cosmology of the Abhidharma, saṃsāra embraces thirty-one levels or realms of existence—that is, there are thirty-one basic classes of beings comprising the round of rebirth, and any being may be born at any one of these levels (see Table 2). Indeed, one should rather say that every being has

TABLE 2. *The thirty-one realms of existence according to the Pali sources*

WORLD (*dhātu*)		COSMOLOGY			PSYCHOLOGY		
		REALM (*bhūmi*)		LIFE SPAN	KARMA (leading to rebirth in corresponding realm)		
FORMLESS WORLD (*arūpa-dhātu*)		Neither Consciousness nor Unconsciousness (*nevasaññānâsaññâyatana*)		84,000 aeons	Formless attainments (*arūpa-samāpatti*)		FORMLESS-SPHERE MIND (*arūpāvacara*)
		Nothingness (*akiñcaññâyatana*)		60,000 aeons			
		Infinite Consciousness (*viññāṇañcâyatana*)		40,000 aeons			
		Infinite Space (*ākāsânañcâyatana*)		20,000 aeons			
		The Supreme (*akaniṭṭha*)	PURE ABODES (*suddhâvāsa*)	16,000 aeons	Path of non-return (*anāgāmi-magga*) or transcendent 4th *jhāna*	Fourth *jhāna*	
		The Clear-sighted (*sudassin*)		8,000 aeons			
		The Lovely (*sudassa*)		4,000 aeons			
		The Serene (*atappa*)		2,000 aeons			
		The Durable (*aviha*)		1,000 aeons			
		Unconscious Beings (*asañña-satta*)		500 aeons	*asañña-samāpatti*		
		Great Reward (*vehapphala*)		500 aeons	Ordinary 4th *jhāna*		
WORLD OF PURE FORM (*rūpa-dhātu*)	⇑ destruction by wind	Complete Beauty (*subha-kiṇha*)		64 aeons	Third *jhāna*		FORM-SPHERE MIND (rūpāvacara)
		Boundless Beauty (*appamāṇa-subha*)		32 aeons			
		Limited Beauty (*paritta-subha*)		16 aeons			

	⇑	Streaming Radiance (*ābhassara*)		8 aeons	Second *jhāna*	
	destruction by water	Boundless Radiance (*appamāṇābha*)		4 aeons		
		Limited Radiance (*parittābha*)		2 aeons		
	⇑	Great Brahmā (*mahābrahmā*)		1 aeon	First *jhāna*	
	destruction by fire	Brahmā's Ministers (*brahma-purohita*)		1/2 aeon		
		Brahmā's Retinue (*brahma-pārisajja*)		1/3 aeon		
WORLD OF THE FIVE SENSES (*kāma-dhātu*)		The Masters of the Creations of Others (*paranimmita-vasavattin*)	HAPPY DESTINIES (*sugati*)	128,000 divine years	10 courses of wholesome karma motivated by non-attachment, friendliness and wisdom	SENSE-SPHERE MIND (*kāmāvacara*)
		Those who Delight in Creation (*nimmāṇa-ratin*)		64,000 divine years		
		The Contented (*tusita*)		16,000 divine years		
		The Yama Gods (*yāma*)		8,000 divine years		
		The Thirty-Three Gods (*tāvatiṃsa*)		2,000 divine years		
		The Gods of the Four Kings (*cātummahārājika*)		500 divine years		
		Human Beings (*manussa*)		variable		
		Jealous Gods (*asura*)	DESCENTS (*apāya*)	unspecified	10 courses of unwholesome karma motivated by attachment, aversion and delusion	
		Hungry Ghosts (*petti-visaya*)		unspecified		
		Animals (*tiracchānayoni*)		unspecified		
		Hell Beings (*niraya*)		unspecified		

Note: Table 2 is based on Vibhaṅga 422–6, Visuddhimagga vii. 40–4, xiii. 29–65; Abhidhammattha-saṅgaha 22–4.

during the course of his or her wandering through saṃsāra at some time or another been born in every one of these conditions apart, that is, from five realms known as 'the Pure Abodes'; beings born in these realms, such as the Great Brahmās of the realm of the Supreme Gods just mentioned, have reached a condition in which they inevitably attain nirvāṇa and so escape the round of rebirth. The most basic division of the thirty-one realms is threefold. First there is the world of the five senses (*kāma-dhātu, -loka*), which comprises eleven realms ranging from the realms of hell and 'the hungry ghosts', through the realms of animals, jealous gods, and human beings, to the six realms of the lower gods; the common characteristic of beings in all these realms is that they are all endowed with consciousness and five physical senses. Above this there is 'the world of pure form' (*rūpa-dhātu, -loka*) which consists of sixteen realms (the highest of which are the Pure Abodes just mentioned) occupied by various higher gods collectively known as Brahmās; these refined beings have consciousness but only two senses—sight and hearing. Finally there are the four realms of 'the formless world' (*arūpa-dhātu, -loka*) occupied by a further class of Brahmās who have only consciousness. These thirty-one realms, from bottom to top, thus reflect a basic movement from gross to subtle.

It is the lower levels of the universe, that is the world of the five senses, that arrange themselves into the various distinct 'world-spheres' or *cakra-vāḍas*. At the centre of a *cakra-vāḍa* is the great world mountain, Meru or Sineru. This is surrounded by seven concentric rings of mountains and seas. Beyond these mountains, in the four cardinal directions, are four continents. The southern continent, Jambudvīpa or 'the continent of the rose-apple tree', is the continent inhabited by ordinary human beings; the southern part, below the towering abode of snows (*himālaya*) is effectively India, the land where buddhas arise. In the spaces between world-spheres and below are various hells, while in the shadow of the slopes of Mount Meru dwell the jealous gods called Asuras, expelled from the heaven of the Thirty-Three by its king Śakra (Pali Sakka). On the slopes of Mount Meru itself and rising above its peak are the six realms inhabited by the gods of the sense-sphere. A Great Brahmā of the lower realms of pure form may rule over a thousand such world-spheres, while Brahmās of the higher realms of the form-sphere are said to rule over a hundred thousand.

What determines in which realm a being is born? The short answer is *karma* (Pali *kamma*): a being's intentional 'actions' of body, speech, and mind—whatever is done, said, or even just thought with definite intention or volition. In general, though with some qualification, rebirth in the lower realms is considered to be the result of relatively unwholesome (*akuśala/akusala*), or bad (*pāpa*) karma, while rebirth in the higher realms the result of relatively wholesome (*kuśala/kusala*), or good (*puṇya/puñña*) karma. Correspondingly, the lower the realm, the more unpleasant and unhappy one's condition; the higher the realm the more pleasant, happy, and refined one's condition. One should note, however, that this hierarchy does not constitute a simple ladder which one, as it were, climbs, passing out at the top into nirvāṇa. In fact, nirvāṇa may be obtained from any of the realms from the human to the highest of the Pure Abodes and the four formless realms, but not from the four lowest realms. Yet, rather than attaining nirvāṇa, beings generally rise and fall, and fall and rise through the various realms, now experiencing unhappiness, now experiencing happiness. This precisely is the nature of saṃsāra: wandering from life to life with no particular direction or purpose.

Cosmology and psychology: macrocosm and microcosm

It is easy to conclude that the detailed enumeration of realms is the result of an overactive scholastic imagination and is thus of no practical interest, but to begin to understand the system we must turn to the subtle and exact psychological insights of the Abhidharma understanding of consciousness and the processes governing its occurrence.

The key to understanding the Buddhist cosmological scheme lies in the principle of *the equivalence of cosmology and psychology*. I mean by this that in the traditional understanding the various realms of existence relate rather closely to certain commonly (and not so commonly) experienced states of mind. In fact Buddhist cosmology is at once a map of different realms of existence and a description of all possible experiences. This can be appreciated by considering more fully the Buddhist understanding of the nature of karma. At root karma or 'action' is considered a mental act or intention; it is an aspect of our mental life: 'It is "intention" that I call *karma*; having formed the intention, one performs acts (*karma*) by body, speech and mind.'[9] Thus acts of body and speech are driven by an underlying intention or will (*cetanā*) and they are unwholesome or wholesome because they are motivated by unwholesome or wholesome intentions. Acts of body and speech are, then, the end products of particular kinds of mentality. At the same time karma can exist as a simple 'act of will', a forceful mental intention or volition that does not lead to an act of body or speech.

The nature of bad action is usually illustrated by reference to a list of the ten courses of unwholesome action (*karma/kamma-patha*) which consist of three bodily courses of action (taking life, taking what is not given, sexual misconduct), four vocal courses of action (lying, divisive speech, hurtful speech, frivolous speech), and three mental courses of action (covetousness, ill-will, wrong view).[10]

In the commentarial literature the notion of a course of action is explained with reference to an action's being performed with full intention and full awareness of what one is doing. Thus in order for the unwholesome course of action of killing to have occurred, five conditions must have been fulfilled: there must be a living creature, one must know the creature is living, one must intend to kill the creature, one must perform the necessary action, and finally the creature must actually die.[11] The nature of good action is similarly summed up in terms of the ten courses of wholesome action which consist in rcfraining from the seven courses of unwholesome bodily and vocal action and, for the mental courses of action, desirelessness, kindness, and right view.

Essentially the psychological states that motivate the ten unwholesome courses of action—strong greed, hatred, and delusion—lead to rebirth in the unhappy destinies or 'descents': in a hell realm, as a hungry ghost, an animal, or a jealous god. In fact rather a precise correlation exists here: dominated by greed one becomes a hungry ghost, a class of beings ever discontent and anguished because of being unable to satisfy their greed; dominated by hatred one enters one of the hell realms where one suffers terrible pain; dominated by ignorance one becomes an animal ruled by the instincts of food and reproduction.[12] On the other hand the psychological states that give rise to the ten wholesome courses of action—desirelessness, friendliness, and wisdom—lead to rebirth in the happy realms: as a human being or in one of the six realms of the gods immediately above the human realm where beings enjoy increasingly happy and carefree lives. Wholesome action can also be characterized by way of the triad of terms that are often used to sum up the practice of the Buddhist path: generosity (*dāna*), ethical conduct (*śīla/sīla*), and meditation (*bhāvanā*). The first two essentially embrace conduct already covered by the ten wholesome courses of action; the third term takes us into rather different territory and refers to the cultivation of various spiritual exercises of contemplation and meditation in order to develop states of deep peace and concentration (*śamatha/samatha, samādhi, dhyāna/jhāna*) and insight and wisdom (*vipaśyanā/vipassanā*, *prajñā/paññā*). As result of attaining these states to different degrees one is reborn as a Brahmā in one of the realms of pure form; essentially such beings are thus conceived of as existing absorbed in states of meditation.[13]

In their analysis of consciousness into a hierarchy of various classes the Abhidharma systematizations further bring out the way in which cosmology is essentially a reflection of psychology and vice versa. The basic structure of this hierarchy of consciousness parallels quite explicitly the basic structure of the cosmos. Irrespective of which cosmological realm a being inhabits, its state of mind might, at different times, be classified as belonging either to the sense-sphere (*kāmāvacara*), the form-sphere (*rūpāvacara*), or the formless-sphere (*arūpāvacara*), corresponding to the way in which beings exist either in the sense-world (*kāma-loka*), the form world (*rūpa-loka*), or formless world (*arūpa-loka*). Moreover, in detailing the types of consciousness or states of mind that beings reborn in the various realms are able to experience (or have access to), the Abhidharma provides a further indication of the parallelism between the psychological order and the cosmological order.[14] Beings in the lowest realms (hell, animal, hungry ghosts, Asuras) can only experience sense-sphere consciousness; beings in the human realm and the heavens of the sense-sphere characteristically experience sense-sphere consciousness but can in special circumstances (i.e. when attaining *dhyāna*) experience form and formless-sphere consciousness; the basis of existence in the form and formless worlds is form and formless-sphere consciousness respectively, but the beings born there also experience certain forms of both wholesome and unwholesome sense-sphere consciousness, but not those associated with hatred and unpleasant feeling. The logic governing this arrangement is as follows. A being in one of the lower realms must experience at least a modicum of wholesome consciousness, for otherwise he or she would be stuck there forever, never able to generate the wholesome karma necessary to bring about rebirth in a higher realm. Similarly beings in the Brahma worlds must experience some unwholesome consciousness, otherwise they would be for ever reborn in these blissful realms where no unpleasant bodily or mental feeling ever occurs, escaping *duḥkha* permanently rather than only temporarily (albeit for an aeon or two). Finally, beings such as humans who are in the middle are evenly poised; they may experience the most unwholesome kinds of consciousness or they may experience the most wholesome—they may go right to the bottom or right to the top.

Thus in sum one can say that Buddhist cosmology takes the form of a hierarchy of certain realms of existence related to certain kinds of mentality. The dynamics of the system viewed from the perspective of the human realm might be stated along the following lines. When a human being experiences unpleasant mental states, such as aversion, hatred, or depression, then there is a sense in which that being can be said to be experiencing something of what it is like to exist in a hell realm—in other words, he makes a brief visit to the hell realms; when those unpleasant states pass (as they inevitably will), the being will return to the mental state natural to human beings—a mental state which is understood to be essentially wholesome and pleasant. But if those states of aversion, hatred, and depression become the habitual states of mind for that being, the danger is that he will end up visiting the hell realms for rather longer than he might have envisaged—in other words, when the wholesome conditions that placed him in the human realm are exhausted and he dies, he might find himself not just visiting hell but being reborn there. Similarly, if a human being should have a somewhat intense experience of such happy states of mind as friendliness and generosity, then that is to experience briefly how it feels to be a *deva* in one of the various heaven realms immediately above the human realm; once more, if those states of mind become habitual and second nature to that being, he is likely to be reborn among those *devas*. If a being experiences the even more subtle and refined states of mind associated with the various levels of meditation—the so called *dhyānas*—he temporarily visits the Brahma worlds; if he becomes a master of *dhyāna*, he can be reborn as a Brahmā.

Such is a world-system, but world-systems are not static; they themselves go through vast cycles of expansion and contraction across the vast aeons of time. According to the Abhidharma and commentarial traditions of both the Theravādins and Sarvāstivādins, world-systems contract in great clusters (Buddhaghosa in his *Visuddhimagga* speaks of a billion world-systems contracting at a time); and when they contract, they contract from the bottom upwards, the lower realms of world-systems disappearing first.[15] An ancient passage introduces this process of expansion and contraction as follows:

> Now there comes a time when after a long period of time this world contracts. When the world contracts beings are for the most part born in the realm of Radiance. There they exist made of mind, feeding on joy, self-luminous, moving through the air, constantly beautiful; thus they remain for a long, long time.[16]

According to both traditions the passage quoted, referring as it does to the rebirth of beings in the realm of Radiance (a realm corresponding in the psychological hierarchy to the level of the second *dhyāna*) at the time of world-contraction, describes this contraction as the result of destruction by fire. This fire starts in the lower realms of the sense-sphere and, having burnt up these, it invades the form realms; but, having burnt up the realms corresponding to the first *dhyāna*, it stops. The realms corresponding to the second, third, and fourth *dhyānas* and the four formless realms are thus spared the destruction. But destruction by fire is not the only kind of destruction, merely the most frequent—water and wind also wreak their havoc. When the destruction is by water, the three realms corresponding to the second *dhyāna* are included in the general destruction. The destruction by wind invades and destroys even the realms corresponding to the third *dhyāna*. Only the seven realms corresponding to the fourth *dhyāna* and the four formless realms are never subject to this universal destruction.

What becomes of the beings that occupy the lower realms when fire, water, and wind wreak their destruction? They cannot just disappear from the round of rebirth, for the only way to achieve that is to gain awakening as buddhas and arhats do. So these beings must go somewhere. Opinions differ as to what precisely happens to them. Some say that all the beings occupying the lower realms should be understood as being reborn in those higher Brahma worlds that escape the destruction—this is true even of the beings in the lowest hell realms. But rebirth in the Brahma worlds can only be gained as the result of the appropriate karma, namely the achievement of *dhyāna*. Such states of peace and calm are impossible in the lower realms, but Buddhaghosa explains that there is no being in saṃsāra that has not at some time or other performed the karma necessary for rebirth in the happy realms of the sense-sphere. Thus even beings born in hell realms as the result of the severest unwholesome karma will always have a latent good karma that can come to fruition at the time of the pending contraction of the world-system. Once reborn in a sense-sphere heaven, they subsequently cultivate the *dhyāna* leading to rebirth in the Brahma-worlds. On this view all beings must at some time have dwelt in the Brahma-realms corresponding to the second, third, and fourth *dhyānas*, and periodically—though the periods may be of inconceivable duration—all beings return to these realms. But according to others, such as Vasubandhu and Dhammapāla, at the time of destruction hell beings whose unwholesome karma is not exhausted are reborn in a world-system not in the process of contraction.

Such mythic accounts may seem fantastic, yet embedded within them are important points of Buddhist thinking, such as, for example, the suggestion that all beings have the latent potential to attain—and indeed have some distant knowledge and experience of—the condition of the fourth *dhyāna*. The condition of the mind in the fourth *dhyāna* is, according to the classical theory of the stages of the Buddhist path, pivotal to the attainment of the awakening knowledge itself. The fourth *dhyāna* represents a particular clear and open state of mind in which the awakening knowledge can arise. The suggestion that every being in saṃsāra in some sense already knows such a state introduces a theme that becomes particularly significant in certain strands of Indian Mahāyāna Buddhist thought, and which is especially emphasized in Japanese Zen. I am referring to the notion of *tathāgata-garbha* or the inherent 'Buddha-nature' of all beings, about which I shall say more in Chapter 9.

In a certain sense the elaborate and fantastic traditional cosmology of Buddhism is nothing more than a full account of all possible experience: this is the world, the universe in its entirety. It may not be circumscribed spatially and temporally but there is no possible manner of being or conceivable experience that is not included here. Wherever one goes, whatever one experiences, it is encompassed by this map of saṃsāra. For Buddhist theory the cosmological scheme defines the round of rebirth—the uncertain, unstable, changing conditioned world of time and space—in its entirety. Thus just as in day-to-day experience one fails to find any physical or mental condition that is not changeable, that can give permanent satisfaction and happiness, so, even if one is reborn in the condition of a Brahmā living 84,000 aeons, the calm and peaceful condition of one's existence is not ultimately lasting or secure. Just as our ordinary happinesses are in this sense *duḥkha*, so too are the lives of the Brahmās even though they experience no physical or mental pain.

It is a curious fact of the developed cosmological scheme that it comprises just thirty-one realms. There is some reason for thinking that the number thirty-two connotes completion and fulfilment in Buddhist thought: the body is described as consisting of thirty-two parts; the Great Man has a body with thirty-two marks. Yet saṃsāra has only thirty-one realms. What is missing is nirvāṇa. But then nirvāṇa is precisely not a state or condition that can be defined spatially or temporally; one cannot be reborn in nirvāṇa, nor can one come to nirvāṇa however far or long one journeys:

> That the end of the world where one is not born, does not age, does not die, does not pass away, does not reappear is to be known, seen or reached by travelling—that I do not say . . . And yet I do not say that one makes an end of suffering without reaching the end of the world. Rather in this fathom-long body, with its perceptions and mind, I declare the world, the arising of the world, the ceasing of the world, and the way leading to the ceasing of the world.[17]

The Buddhist cosmological account represents the complete description of the conditioned world—the whirling circle (*vaṭṭa*) of saṃsāra. This is *duḥkha* on the macrocosmic scale. One's personal day-to-day experiences, on the other hand, are *duḥkha* on the microcosmic scale. In short, what we experience from day to day is a microcosm of the cosmos at large. As we shall see in Chapter 6, for Buddhist thought the law that governs the workings of both the microcosm of individual experience from moment to moment and also the birth and death of beings across vast aeons is one and the same: 'dependent arising' (*pratītya samutpāda/ paṭicca-samuppāda*).

Cosmology, folk religion, and modern science

I have suggested that the elaborate Buddhist cosmological schema that we have been considering is in part to be understood by reference to Buddhist psychology. The equivalence between psychology and cosmology is old and to be regarded as intrinsic to the system and not a stratagem employed by Buddhist modernist apologetics in order to render a primitive, pre-modern understanding of the world palatable to contemporary tastes. Yet this should not be taken as meaning that Buddhist cosmological descriptions were traditionally read simply as accounts of mental states in symbolic and imaginative language. Quite clearly they were not, nor are they so read in traditional Buddhist cultures today. For many Buddhists, in the present as in the past, the beings and realms described in the cosmology are as 'real' as the Queen of England and Buckingham Palace. Yet equally clearly there can be intellectually more naïve and more sophisticated ways of understanding the Buddhist cosmological world-view. But again we should avoid coming to the conclusion that somehow the psychological interpretation represents the 'real' Buddhist understanding, whereas a literal understanding feeds the popular imagination and, as such, must be suffered by sophisticated intellectuals. What we have to do with here is a question of a different conception of the nature of 'reality': a conception that allows what we would call a psychological and symbolic interpretation to coexist with a literal interpretation. Whatever ultimate interpretation one puts on traditional Buddhist cosmology, it remains a flexible framework within which to make sense of a rich spectrum of experience.

Nevertheless at another practical level this cosmological framework has allowed Buddhism to accommodate and take under its wing certain aspects of what might be called, for want of a better term, 'folk religion'. This process of accommodation is as old as Buddhism itself—perhaps older. Many of the gods and different kinds of being found in the ancient cosmology have been absorbed into the Buddhist scheme of things from pre-existing folk and religious traditions. In precisely the same way they have been absorbed and adapted by Jain and Brahmanical tradition. Thus figures such as Brahmā and Śakra or Indra, such classes of being as Asuras, Gandharvas (celestial musicians), Yakṣas and Yakṣinīs, Rākṣasas (types of demon and nymph), Nāgas (mythical serpents), Garuḍas (mythical birds), and other classes of minor deities dwelling in forests, groves, and trees—all these form part of a vast Indian mythical and folk-religious heritage that the various Indian traditions draw upon.

Each tradition preserves slightly different accounts of these beings; in each tradition they are adapted and reinterpreted, taking on slightly different characters and acquiring particular associations, while still retaining certain common features. In the fully developed Buddhist cosmology, these sorts of beings are generally associated with the gods of the lower sense-sphere heavens. But their presence in the Buddhist scheme of things in part reflects a simple fact of the cultural milieu in which Buddhism grew. We are concerned here with something which is in principle as relevant to Indian religion today as it was 2,000 years ago. Then as now most people lived in a world alive with fairies, demons, goblins, ghosts, nymphs, dragons, angels, as well as various gods. Such beings are as real to people's experience as any human being. For the most part in the context of the practice of contemporary Hinduism, the interaction and dealings with such beings concerns matters of day-to-day living rather than questions of the ultimate cessation of suffering. Thus such beings are seen as causing various kinds of disease by 'possessing' one; or they may be able to grant fulfilment of certain aspirations, help with a harvest or passing an exam; the acknowledgement of these beings assists the smooth running of day-to-day matters and grants a measure of protection against calamity.[18]

The various cultures beyond India where Buddhism has established itself over the last 2,500 years have been very similar to India herself in this respect. The existence of various kinds of beings has been taken for granted, as has the fact that they may be able to assist in limited ways with everyday human affairs. In this manner Buddhism has been able to accommodate and coexist with a considerable range of local and indigenous religious practice wherever it has established itself. Thus the Buddhists of Sri Lanka visit the shrines of various local and Hindu gods, the Buddhists of Burma have various rites associated with a class of being known as *nats*, while the Thais seek the assistance of the *phiis*; Japanese Buddhists worship at the Shintō shrines of the *kami*; Tibetan Buddhists acknowledge the existence of various kinds of spirit and god, invoking the presence of some as 'protectors of Dharma' (*chos skyong*).[19] Such behaviour troubled some early Western observers of the practice of Buddhism in its traditional cultures and led them to conclude that the people who participated in these practices were not 'true' Buddhists. This conclusion was based in part on a failure to appreciate the nature of the relationship between this kind of practice and the cultivation of the Buddhist path; in part on an image of Buddhism artificially constructed from a selective reading of early Buddhist texts; and in part on an exclusivist conception of the nature of 'a religion'—one is either a Hindu or a Buddhist, one cannot be both—which is inappropriate to the Asian context.

It has sometimes been claimed that the belief that such beings can answer one's pleas for assistance flies in the face of the Buddhist theory of karma: expecting a god to provide the cure for an illness must be inconsistent with the belief that falling ill is the inevitable result of one's own previous unwholesome actions.[20] But this is to misunderstand the Buddhist theory of action and result, which is not a species of determinism. From the Buddhist perspective certain experiences in life are indeed the results of previous actions; but our responses to those experiences, whether wished for or unwished for, are not predetermined but represent new actions which in time bear their own fruit in the future. The Buddhist understanding of individual responsibility does not mean that we should never seek or expect another's assistance in order to better cope with the troubles of life. The belief that one's broken leg is at one level to be explained as the result of unwholesome actions performed in a previous life does not mean that one should not go to a doctor to have the broken leg set. There was and is no need in Buddhist theory to deny the existence of 'divine' beings or to repudiate the Buddhist villager's efforts to get their help. The only comment that Buddhist theory has to make in this context is that divine beings—like doctors—won't be able to get to the root of the problem: they may help one get what one wants in the short term, but they are unable to bring about the final cessation of suffering.

The world of the earliest Buddhist texts is a world, like the contemporary Indian villager's, alive with various kinds of being. The Buddha and his followers are represented as being visited by these various beings, as having discussions with them, as teaching them, as being questioned by them, and as being honoured by them. Yet in their reading of the texts many nineteenth- and early twentieth-century scholars felt inclined to treat such accounts of 'supernatural' beings as later mythical additions to an earlier more sober and purely philosophical stratum of Buddhist literature that was originally uncluttered by such material. Indeed this outlook continues to influence the approach of some scholars. Yet the fact remains that these so-called mythical elements are so embedded in, so entangled with the conceptual, ethical, and philosophical dimensions of early Buddhist literature that the task of extricating them is extremely problematic. The arguments for excising the mythic material often become circular: we know that the mythic passages are later because early Buddhist teaching was a purely ethical and philosophical system uninterested in myth, and we know that early Buddhist teaching was devoid of myth because the mythic passages are later.

What can be said with certainty is that we have no evidence, either in the ancient texts or in the different contemporary traditions, for a 'pure' Buddhism that does not recognize, accommodate, and interact with various classes of 'supernatural' being. Such a pure Buddhism is something of a theoretical and scholarly abstraction. This point needs particular stress in relation to Theravāda Buddhism since the notion that the Theravāda tradition represents—or *ought* to represent—a pure, unadulterated tradition of precisely this kind is widespread and yet is a largely theoretically constructed model of what Theravāda Buddhism is.

I suggested above that a Buddhist's dealings with and interaction with ghosts, demons, and spirits is for the most part tangential to his or her practice of the Buddhist path. This is certainly so, and yet the separateness of these two dimensions of a Buddhist's life can be over-emphasized. In the earliest texts the world of the Yakṣas, Nāgas, Gandharvas, and so on merges with the world of the sense-sphere *devas*. Such beings precisely acquire ethical and spiritual associations in the theory and practice of ancient Buddhism, and such associations are not irrelevant to our appreciation of the role of the gods in the practice of contemporary Buddhism. A traditional Buddhist contemplative meditation exercise involves the recollection of the qualities of the gods (*devatānussati*) as beings who have arrived at a fortunate and happy condition as a result of their good karma;

> There are the gods of the Four Kings, the gods of the Thirty-Three, the Yāma gods, the Contented gods, the gods who Delight in Creation, the Masters of the Creations of Others, the gods of Brahmā, and yet higher gods. Endowed with faith those gods passed away from the human realm and were reborn in that condition; such faith is present in me too. Endowed with virtue, learning, generosity, and wisdom those gods passed away from the human realm and were reborn in that condition; such virtue, learning, generosity, and wisdom are present in me too.[21]

The kind of thinking indicated by this passage suggests how the world of ghosts, demons, spirits, and gods merges and blends with the world of Buddhist practice. But perhaps the most graphic illustration of this comes from Buddhist art. Early stone reliefs depicting the Buddha's enlightenment show the gods of various kinds gathering around the tree of awakening. The Great Stūpa at Sāñcī (second century BCE), a representation of the cosmos itself, is encircled by a walkway entered by four gateways; here the decoration depicts animals, Yakṣas and Yakṣinīs, Nāgas and Gandharvas, and the gods; at the centre is the great dome of the stūpa enshrining sacred relics. The interior of Buddhist shrine rooms through the ages has similarly often been decorated with murals depicting the various realms and beings of the cosmos.

In conclusion it is worth considering briefly Buddhist and Indian cosmology in relation to the cosmology of the West. Clearly the Buddhist conception of the spatial and temporal extent of the universe contrasts markedly with the traditional Judaeo-Christian conception of a single world beginning with its creation at a particular point—a point that has on occasion been defined very precisely: Archbishop Ussher (1581–1656) calculated it as 4004 BCE. Whereas from the Buddhist perspective there are countless world-systems passing through vast cycles of expansion and contraction, in the Judaeo-Christian perspective there is one world whose 'history' begins at one point and moves towards one final doomsday, and is to be read, moreover, as the working out of God's purpose. There is a point of real contrast here that is not of purely theoretical interest; these two traditional cosmologies give rise to quite different cultural perspectives on matters of social and political progress. This is a complex subject, and I merely draw the reader's attention to it.

A number of writers over the last twenty years have suggested that there is a certain affinity between aspects of traditional Indian cosmology and the findings of modern astronomy and physics.[22] Some caution is needed here. Quite clearly the conception of the *cakra-vāḍa* taken as a literal description of the geography of the world (which it clearly was and is by many) is as inaccurate from a scientific perspective as anything found in the biblical Judaeo-Christian cosmologies. Curiously though, the traditional conception of the *cakra-vāḍa* persisted in Indian thought even after the realization, early in the Christian era, that the world was in reality a globe.[23] The fact that these two quite different conceptions of the world continued to live side by side suggests that in part their functions are somewhat different. Nevertheless, the notion of Mount Meru can fare no better in the eyes of modern science than that of the Garden of Eden. Yet Buddhist cosmology's understanding of the age and size of the universe, its countless world-systems, the absence of a creator God, do perhaps sit more comfortably with certain of the notions of modern astronomy and physics than a Judaeo-Christian biblical cosmology. Yet it would be naïve to suggest that they somehow anticipate such modern scientific theories. The language of Buddhist cosmology is not the language of modern physics. If we wish to understand it, the Buddhist tradition itself suggests that we should look no further than our own minds, for in many respects the workings of the vast cosmos are nothing other than the workings of our minds writ large.

6

No Self

Personal Continuity and Dependent Arising

The Buddhist critique of self as unchanging

The story of the journeying monk in the *Kevaddha Sutta* (see above, pp. 113–14) is in fact a very precise parable of Buddhist thought. To understand the nature of *duḥkha* is precisely to reach the limits of the world. Ultimately the monk in the story is directed to the nature of the mind itself, for it is here that the secret of the arising of the world, the ceasing of the world, and the way leading to the ceasing of the world is to be found. Thus, although from a particular perspective the elaborate cosmology outlined in the previous chapter does indeed represent the complete Buddhist description of *duḥkha*, nevertheless it is in the analysis of individual experience of the world—this fathom-long body with its perceptions and mind—that *duḥkha's* ultimate nature is to be penetrated. In this chapter I wish to turn to the basic principles of that Buddhist understanding of our individual experience of the world, and of consciousness and its workings.

The Buddhist critique of the notion of 'self' or *ātman* is rooted in a specific historical context and initially directed towards particular understandings of the notion of self. The evidence of brahmanical, Jain, and Buddhist sources points towards the existence in north India of the fifth century BCE of a considerable variety of views and theories concerning the ultimate nature of the individual and his destiny.

Among the questions the early brahmanical texts known as the Upaniṣads seek to explore are: to whom or what the various experiences and parts of a being belong; who or what controls them; what is the ultimate nature of a being's self. The standard term that the Upaniṣads use for the 'self' in its ultimate nature is *ātman*, which, although also employed as the ordinary word for 'self' in Sanskrit, may etymologically be derived from a word originally meaning 'breath'. For the early Upaniṣads such as the Bṛhadāraṇyaka and Chāndogya (sixth century BCE), the self in its ultimate nature is a mysterious, ungraspable entity; it is the unseen seer, the unheard hearer, the unthought thinker, the unknown knower; it is the inner controller; it is what is immortal in us.[1] Although it is much easier to say what it is not than to specify it concretely, certain quite definite things can be said of it. This ultimate metaphysical self is the unchanging constant underlying all our various and unstable experiences. As such it is indestructible and ultimately unaffected by any specific experience and quite beyond suffering:

> The self is not this and not that. Ungraspable it is certainly not grasped; indestructible it is certainly not destroyed, without clinging it is certainly not clung to; unbound it comes to no harm, it does not suffer.[2]

Furthermore the immortal indestructible *ātman* that is the ultimate self is, according to the early Upaniṣads, to be identified with the underlying ground of all reality known as *brahman*. In the final analysis I am not something different from the underlying ground of the universe itself. This is the famous Upaniṣadic equation of *ātman* and *brahman*.[3]

This does not appear to be the only notion of the *ātman* known to Buddhist texts. In later Indian thought we find the concept of a plurality of eternal unchanging 'selves', each corresponding in some way to individual beings in the world. Such a teaching is characteristic of the Indian schools of philosophy known as Sāṃkhya and Yoga and seems to be adumbrated in the Upaniṣad of Śvetāśvatara.[4] What we have, then, in the notions of both the universal and individual *ātman* is an assumption of an unchanging and constant self that somehow underlies and is the basis for the variety of changing experiences; moreover this unchanging self is to be identified as what we ultimately are and as beyond suffering. It is this general understanding of the self that early Buddhist thought seeks to examine and question.

While this specific historical context dictates the terms of reference, it is none the less the case that the issues raised by the Buddhist critique of self touch on universal problems of personal identity. Our everyday linguistic usage of terms such as 'I' amounts in practice to an understanding of self as precisely an unchanging constant behind experiences. Thus when someone declares, 'I was feeling sad, but now I am feeling happy,' he or she implies by the term 'I' that there is a constant, unchanging thing that underlies and links the quite different experiences of happiness and sadness. Linguistic usage and no doubt certain emotional and psychological circumstances predispose us to an understanding of personal identity and selfhood in terms of an 'I' that exists as an autonomous individual and who has various experiences. In this way I assume—perhaps unconsciously—that although *my* experiences may vary there is something—*me*—that remains constant. In other words, it only makes sense to talk in terms of my having experiences if there is a constant 'I' that can somehow be considered apart from and separately from those experiences.[5] It is in this conceptual framework that Buddhist thought begins to ask various questions about the nature of the 'I', the constant unchanging self underlying experience.

One task that Buddhist thought attempts is a descriptive analysis of the nature of experience, or, to put it simply, of just what it is that seems to be going on all the time. This exercise is in fact one of the preoccupations of Buddhist thought and it offers a number of ways of analysing the nature of experience which are integrated in the complex Abhidharma systems of the developed schools of Buddhist thought. Perhaps the most important analysis of individual experience found in the early texts and carried over into the Abhidharma is an account in terms of the five 'aggregates' or 'groups' (*skandha/khandha*) of physical and mental events.

The list and description of the five *skandhas* represent a response to such questions as: what is a being? what is going on? what is there? In the first place I can say that I seem to have a body with five senses of sight, hearing, smell, taste, and touch. There is then the physical world, what the Buddhist texts call 'form' (*rūpa*). In the second place there is variety of mental activity going on, much of it in direct response to the various physical stimuli. Thus my experiences continuously produce in me pleasant, unpleasant, or indifferent feelings (*vedanā*). I am also continuously classifying and sorting my experiences such that, confronted by various sense stimuli, there can be recognition (*saṃjñā/saññā*) of something as an 'apple' or a 'cup of tea'.[6] Furthermore, my experiences seem to provoke various desires, wishes, and tendencies—volitional 'forces' or 'formations' (*saṃskāra/saṃkhāra*); thus, if I perceive an apple when I am hungry, quite strong desires may arise which may lead to my being unable to resist reaching out and taking it; in fact, given a variety of circumstances, the emotions produced in response to my experiences may lead to all sorts of actions from self-sacrifice to vicious murder. Finally we can say that there is a basic self-consciousness (*vijñāna/viññāṇa*)—an awareness of ourselves as thinking subjects having a series of perceptions and thoughts. In this way my individual experience can be analysed as consisting of various phenomena that can be conveniently classified as forming five collections or aggregates: bodily phenomena, feelings, labelling or recognizing, volitional activities, and conscious awareness.

Buddhist thought presents these five aggregates as an exhaustive analysis of the individual. They are the world for any given being—there is nothing else besides. The question now arises whether any given instance of these five groups of phenomena can qualify as a 'self'—an unchanging, constant underlying experience. Steven Collins effectively identifies three arguments for the denial of the self in early Buddhist texts.[7]

One of the Upaniṣadic characterizations of the self was as the 'inner controller', and the first argument employed is that in fact we have no ultimate control over any of the five aggregates:

> Body is not a self. If body were a self then it might be that it would not lead to sickness; then it might be possible to say, 'Let my body be like this, let my body not be like this.' But since body is not a self, so it leads to sickness, and it is not possible to say, 'Let my body be like this, let my body not be like this.'[8]

The same can be said of feeling, recognition, volitions, and conscious awareness. It is simply ridiculous to take things that are bound up with change and sickness, and over which we have no ultimate control as self.

A second argument against the self is to be found in the following exchange between the Buddha and his monks, which occurs frequently in the earliest Buddhist texts, sometimes buttressing the argument from lack of control. The Buddha asks:

> 'What do you think, monks? Are body . . . feeling . . . recognition . . . volitions . . . conscious awareness permanent or impermanent?'
>
> 'Impermanent, lord.'
>
> 'But is something that is impermanent painful or unpainful?'
>
> 'Painful, lord.'
>
> 'But is it fitting to regard something that is painful, whose nature it is to change as "this is mine, I am this, this is my self"?'
>
> 'Certainly not, lord.'
>
> 'Therefore, monks, all body . . . feeling . . . recognition . . . volitions . . . conscious awareness whatsoever, whether past, present or future, whether gross or subtle, inferior or refined, far or near, should be seen by means of clear understanding as it really is, as "this is not mine, I am not this, this is not my self".'[9]

That something which is impermanent must be regarded as 'painful' (*duḥkha*) follows, of course, from principles we have already found expressed in the second of the four noble truths: if we become attached and try to hold on to things that will inevitably change and disappear, then we are bound to suffer. This argument also seems to be aimed directly at the early Upaniṣadic notion of the self as an unchanging, eternal absolute that is free from all suffering; in the phrase 'this is not mine, I am not this, this is not my self' there appears to be a deliberate echo and rebuttal of the Chāndogya Upaniṣad's 'this is the self, this is what you are'.[10]

A third argument centres on the meaninglessness of the term 'self' apart from particular experiences.[11] There are three possibilities: one must regard the self as the same as experience, or one must regard the self as something apart from experience, or one must regard the self as having the attribute of experience.

But none of these ways of viewing the self is coherent. The first method, in failing to distinguish the self from changing experiences, ends up with a self that continuously changes as our experiences change; but a self, by definition, is something that does not change as experiences change, it is the unchanging thing behind those experiences. The second method makes no sense either since (in a kind of inversion of the Cartesian 'I think therefore I am'), apart from experiences, how can one possibly think of oneself as existing? So we are left with the third possibility, namely a self that is something different from experience, yet not without experience; a self that experiences or has the attribute of experience. Such a self must still in some sense be distinguishable from experiences, yet there is no basis upon which to make such a distinction, since it remains the case that apart from particular experiences it is not possible to think of oneself as existing.

The gist of the Buddhist critique of the notion of 'self' is then this. It cannot be denied that there is a complex of experience going on; this can be conveniently analysed by way of the five aggregates. But where precisely in all this is the constant, unchanging self which is having all these experiences? What we find when we introspect, the Buddha suggests, is always some particular sense datum, some particular feeling, some particular idea, some particular wish or desire, some consciousness of something particular. And all these are constantly changing from one moment to the next; none of them remains for more than a mere moment. Thus, apart from some particular experience, I never actually directly come across or experience the 'I' that is having experiences. It is something entirely elusive. This looks suspicious. How can I know it is there? For it is impossible to conceive of consciousness apart from all these particular changing details, and if we abstract all the particular details of consciousness we are not left with a constant, individual 'self' but a blank, a nothing.

The early Upaniṣads themselves acknowledged that the self was something of a mysterious, ungraspable entity, but—and here Buddhist thought lays down its challenge—perhaps its nature is actually so mysterious and ungraspable that it does not make any coherent sense at all. Thus Buddhist thought suggests that as an individual I am a complex flow of physical and mental phenomena, but peel away these phenomena and look behind them and one just does not find a constant self that one can call one's own. My sense of self is both logically and emotionally just a label that I impose on these physical and mental phenomena in consequence of their connectedness. In other words, the idea of self as a constant unchanging thing behind the variety of experience is just a product of linguistic usage and the particular way in which certain physical and mental phenomena are experienced as connected.

An ancient Buddhist text, the *Milindapañha* ('Milinda's Questions') records the meeting of a Buddhist monk and the local Bactrian Greek king, Milinda or Menander. The monk introduces himself as Nāgasena, but then adds that this is just a convenient label, for in reality no 'person' can be found. The king is puzzled and accuses the monk of talking nonsense. Nāgasena then asks how the king came to this hermitage, and the king replies that he came in a chariot. 'But what is a chariot?', asks Nāgasena. Is it the pole? Is it the axle? Is it the wheels, or the framework, or the yoke, or the reins? King Milinda is forced to admit that it is none of these. Nevertheless, he persists, it is not meaningless to talk of a 'chariot', for the term is used as a convenient label in dependence upon pole, axle, wheels, framework, yoke, reins, etc. Just so, responds Nāgasena, it is not meaningless to talk of 'Nāgasena', for terms such as 'Nāgasena' or 'being' are used as convenient labels when all the relevant constituents—the five aggregates—are present, yet there is no such independent thing as 'Nāgasena' or 'a being'.[12]

Language and the fact that experiences are somehow connected fools us into thinking that there is an 'I' apart from and behind changing experiences—apart from the fact of experiences being connected. In reality, as we shall presently see, for Buddhist thought there is only their 'connectedness'—nothing besides that. The fact that experiences are causally connected is not to be explained by reference to an unchanging self that underlies experience, but by examining the nature of causality.

The problem of personal continuity: self as 'causal connectedness'

We have seen how Buddhist thought criticizes the concept of an unchanging self as incoherent; however, both ancient and modern critics have argued that to do away with the self in the manner of Buddhist thought in fact creates insurmountable philosophical and moral problems. How can the experienced facts of personal continuity—after all it is I who remember getting up this morning and going to the shops, not you—be accounted for? Again, central to the Buddhist world-view is the notion of rebirth, but surely for this to be meaningful some part of a person must remain constant and be reborn, which is precisely what the teaching of no self seems to deny. Furthermore, if there is no self, is not the whole foundation of morality undermined? If I am not the same person as the one who robbed the bank yesterday, how can I be held responsible? In fact does not the teaching of no self render life meaningless and is it not tantamount to a doctrine of nihilism? For its part, Buddhist thought claims that it has adequate answers to these questions and has always categorically denied the charge that it is a species of nihilism.[13] The answers to these questions are all in one way or another to be referred to the particular Buddhist understanding of the way in which things are causally connected.

We have seen how Buddhist thought breaks down an individual into five classes of physical and mental events known as *skandhas* or 'aggregates'. But the list of five aggregates represents only one of various possible ways of analysing the constituents of a being. An alternative analysis sees the individual as comprising twelve 'spheres' (*āyatana*): the six senses (five physical senses and mind) and the six classes of object of those senses; a variation of this talks of eighteen 'elements' (*dhātu*): six senses, six classes of sense object, and six classes of consciousness.[14] For Buddhist thought the physical and mental events that comprise a being and his or her experiences can be analysed, grouped, and viewed from a number of different perspectives. But whatever the perspective, the concern is to show that physical and mental events occur in various relationships to each other. As such, physical and mental events or phenomena are termed *dharmas* (Pali *dhamma*). This is a term whose full discussion must be reserved for Chapter 7, but it can be defined in the present context as an ultimate 'event' or 'reality' that, in combination with other ultimate events or realities, constitutes the basis of reality as a whole. The occurrence of physical and mental events is not just arbitrary or random; on the contrary there is a deep and real relationship of causal connectedness between events or phenomena. And it is the concern with the nature of this causal connectedness that lies at the heart of Buddhist philosophy and which is seen as validating all Buddhist practice.

A story has it that the wanderer Śāriputra's introduction to the teaching of the Buddha was in the form of a summary verse recited to him by the monk Aśvajit:

> Of those dharmas which arise from a cause, the Tathāgata has stated the cause, and also the cessation; such is the teaching of the Great Ascetic.

Hearing this verse, Śāriputra immediately gained a profound insight into the Dharma, although he was not to become an awakened arhat for another fortnight.[15] The verse thus encapsulates the Buddha's teaching and as such states the secret of the cessation of suffering—if we could but understand it. Later Buddhist tradition regarded this verse as possessing an almost magical potency, and in ancient times, throughout the Buddhist world, it was inscribed on bricks, metal plates, and images to make a protective amulet that might be worn or enshrined in stūpas.[16] Another succinct formula states the principle of causality (*idaṃ-pratyayatā*) as 'this existing, that exists; this arising, that arises; this not existing, that does not exist; this ceasing, that ceases'.[17] But the most important statement of the Buddhist understanding of how causality operates is in terms of the twelve links (*nidāna*) of the chain of 'dependent arising' (*pratītya-samutpāda/paṭicca-samuppāda*):

> Conditioned by (1) ignorance are (2) formations, conditioned by formations is (3) consciousness, conditioned by consciousness is (4) mind-and-body, conditioned by mind-and-body are (5) the six senses,

conditioned by the six senses is (6) sense-contact, conditioned by sense-contact is (7) feeling, conditioned by feeling is (8) craving, conditioned by craving is (9) grasping, conditioned by grasping is (10) becoming, conditioned by becoming is (11) birth, conditioned by birth is (12) old-age and death—grief, lamentation, pain, sorrow, and despair come into being. Thus is the arising of this whole mass of suffering.[18]

The verse and the succinct formula state baldly that the secret of the universe lies in the nature of causality—the way one thing leads to another. The chain of twelve links goes rather further; it attempts to reveal the actual pattern and structure of causal conditioning. And we are told in the ancient texts that he who sees dependent arising—this pattern of conditioning—sees Dharma itself.[19]

According to Buddhist analysis a person should be seen as five classes of physical and mental events that arise dependently at any given moment in time and also over a period of time. What this means then is that the causal connectedness of events is such that events occur in certain quite specific clusters and patterns. From this perspective a 'person' is a series of clusters of events (physical and mental) occurring in a 'human' pattern, as opposed to, say, the canine pattern of a 'dog'. Furthermore, causal connectedness is such that the patterns in which events occur tend to reproduce themselves and so are relatively stable over a period of time. Thus it does not happen that a man is a man one moment and a dog the next, rather over a period of time a baby becomes a child, and a child an adult. So although I am not now the same person as I was when I was 3 years old in that there is no single part of me that is the same as it was, there is nevertheless a continuous causal connectedness between the clusters and pattern of physical and mental events that occurred thirty-five years ago, and those occurring now. The 'person' that is me thus subsists not in some entity remaining constant for thirty-five years but merely in the fact that certain clusters of physical and mental events are linked causally.

In other words, Buddhist thought understands change not in terms of a primary substantial essence remaining constant while its secondary qualities change, but solely in terms of the causal connectedness of different qualities. There is no primary substance to remain constant:

There is neither identity nor difference in a sequence of continuity. For if there were complete identity in a sequence of continuity there would be no curds produced from the milk; if there were complete difference the owner of the milk would not own the curds. This is the case with all conditioned things.[20]

What is more, this causal connectedness of events does not suddenly cease at the death of a 'person'. In fact death from the perspective of the Buddhist understanding of the causal connectedness of events is simply the breaking up of a particular configuration of those events. As I have said, the stability of particular configurations of events is only relative; eventually it must break down. But the nature of the causal connectedness of physical and mental events is such that as soon as one particular configuration breaks down events begin to build themselves into a new one. This then is 'rebirth'. The new pattern of events, although certainly connected with the old, may be of a different kind. A man may be reborn as an animal; a god may be reborn as a man.

Although I have been talking in terms of physical and mental events, one should note that in the breaking down of a particular configuration of events that is death, it is the mental events that are crucially determinative of the nature of the new pattern of events, for as we saw in the previous chapter, the workings of karma, of action and result, are essentially a matter of intention. We have now returned from the microcosm of a person consisting of patterns of events arising and ceasing to the macrocosm of the universe of beings passing through cycles of birth, death, and rebirth.

Let me sum up the Buddhist response to the questions I posed at the beginning of this section. The basic experienced facts of personal continuity are to be explained not with reference to an enduring substantial self, but with reference to the particular way in which the phenomena that make up a being are causally connected. And just as this causal connectedness is the basis of continuity within a particular life, so it is the basis of continuity between lives. Just as no substantial self endures during a lifetime, so no substantial self endures from death to rebirth. None the less there is a causal connection between the phenomena that constitute a being at the time of death and the phenomena that constitute a being at the start of a new life. This linking (*pratisandhi/paṭisandhi*) of different lives into a causal series, such that we can speak of someone being reborn as someone else, is understood as a particular function of mental phenomena (rather than physical phenomena); death is then not an interruption in the causal flow of phenomena, it is simply the reconfiguring of events into a new pattern in dependence upon the old. Thus, when asked whether the one who is reborn is the same or different from the one who died, the Buddhist tradition replies that strictly he (or she) is neither the same nor different.[21]

The way in which phenomena are causally connected is also seen as sufficient to account for moral responsibility. The monk Nāgasena put it as follows to King Milinda. Suppose that someone should steal some mangoes from another man's trees; if he were to claim in his defence that the mangoes he stole were not the mangoes the other man planted, we would point out that the mangoes he stole nevertheless arose in dependence upon the mangoes that were previously planted. Similarly I cannot, by appeal to the teaching of no self, claim that it was not I who robbed the bank yesterday but some other person who no longer exists, since the teaching of no self states quite categorically that the 'I' who exists today only exists by virtue of its dependence upon the 'I' that existed yesterday; there is a definite causal connection.

Properly understood the principle of the causal connectedness of phenomena is sufficient, claims Buddhist thought, to answer critics of the teaching of no self and redeem Buddhism from the charge of nihilism. Of course, philosophers, ancient and modern, Indian and Western, need not necessarily accept that this is the end of the matter and that Buddhist thought has dealt with the problems of the theory of no self once and for all. Throughout its history Buddhist philosophy has continued to try to refine both its treatment of these problems as well as its own critique of the notion of enduring substances, but this is as far as we need pursue the matter at present. I shall, however, mention two further dimensions to the teaching of no self here. The first concerns the notion of 'the middle way' and the second the notion of two kinds of truth.

The understanding that sees a 'person' as subsisting in the causal connectedness of dependent arising is often presented in Buddhist thought as 'the middle' (*madhyama/majjhima*) between the views of 'eternalism' (*śaśvata-/sassata-vāda*) and 'annihilationism' (*uccheda-vāda*).[22] If we understand a 'person' as subsisting in an unchanging, constant self that underlies different experiences, then, since we have postulated something that endures without change, we have fallen prey to the view of 'eternalism'; if on the other hand we understand that there is no real connection between the person at one point in time and another point in time, then we have fallen prey to the view of 'annihilationism'. In other words, if we deny that there is a real connectedness between events this is annihilationism, but if we understand that connectedness in terms of an unchanging self this is eternalism; the middle way is that there is only the connectedness, there is only dependent arising.

Part of the Buddhist critique of the concept of self involves the claim that language predisposes us towards and indeed confuses us into thinking that an enduring self does in fact exist. Sentences such as 'I am going to London tomorrow' suggest that there is something constant to which the term 'I' refers, namely, my 'self'; yet in reality, claims Buddhist thought, such a self is not to be found. However, this does not mean that the terms 'self', 'I', and so forth are to be systematically removed from all truly Buddhist discourse. Indeed, such terms are perfectly normal in Buddhist discourse. Developed Buddhist thought articulates what is involved here in terms of a distinction between conventional (*saṃvṛti/sammuti*) and ultimate (*paramārtha/paramattha*) truth. From this perspective the Buddhist denial of self is not an absolute denial of self as such, but a quite specific denial of self as an enduring substance. As we have seen, for Buddhist thought terms like 'self', 'being' and 'person' are conventional labels for what in reality is a mass of constantly changing, causally connected physical and mental phenomena. The problem is not with the words in themselves but with what we understand by the words: we are misled by their conventional usage into thinking that selves, beings and persons have an ultimate existence in their own right. The Buddha, on the other hand, makes use of such words without holding on to them and being led astray.[23] Thus when a Buddha, or any other awakened being, says 'I', he or she merely uses the term as a matter of convenience, rather than saying 'this particular group of five aggregates'—just as a nuclear physicist will refer to a 'table' rather than 'a mass of subatomic particles'. So it is not that it is not *true* to say that I exist, but that it is only conventionally true; from the ultimate point of view there are only five aggregates of physical and mental phenomena.

Ignorance, attachment, and views of the self

The Buddhist critique of the notion of a self rests on the claim that we never in fact experience an unchanging self, and that there is therefore no reason to posit an unchanging self underlying experience. In other words, the idea that one exists as a permanent, unchanging self is born of faulty reasoning based on the failure to perceive the world as it actually is. This notion of self is born of delusion (*moha*) or ignorance (*avidyā/avijjā*). But there is another strand to the Buddhist critique of the notion of self which sees it as intimately bound up with craving (*tṛṣṇā/taṇhā*) and attachment (*upādāna*).

A passage from the early Buddhist scriptures that I referred to earlier concludes by stating that someone who succeeds in neither regarding the self as the same as experience, nor as something that is apart from experience, nor as something which has the attribute of experience is thereby one who 'does not grasp at anything in the world, and through not grasping he craves no longer, and through not craving he effects complete nirvāṇa'.[24] Thus for Buddhist thought, to understand the world in terms of self is not only to see it wrongly but to be led by greed, desire, and attachment. One's sense of 'self' springs not only from delusion, but from the desire to identify and claim some part or parts of the universe as one's own, as one's possession, and say of them 'this is mine, I am this, this is my self'. To identify with the five aggregates, either collectively or individually, is a kind of conceit—the conceit 'I am' (*asmi-māna*).

As a function of both ignorance and greed, the belief in self is something that we construct, not only at a conscious and intellectual level, but also at a deep psychological and emotional level. We continually crave to be particular kinds of person. In so far as they are entangled with craving, the notions of self and of personal identity can, from the Buddhist point of view, only lead to suffering—for both ourselves and others. The appropriating of some part or parts of the universe as mine, as opposed to yours, the desire to construct my 'self' or personal identity, must lead inevitably to self-*ish* concerns. It drives me to accumulate 'possessions'—both physical and psychological—that define and reinforce my sense of my own selfhood as student, teacher, banker, lawyer, politician, craftsmen, Buddhist monk—as some kind of person as opposed to some other kind of person. And when I feel that what I regard as my self, that what I regard as by rights mine, is in danger of being taken from me, I become angry, frustrated, fearful; I may even be driven to violence and kill. And yet disease, old age and death for sure will take from me all that I have regarded as mine—body, feelings, ideas, volitions, mind. Indeed an ancient image compares our identifying ourselves with any of the five aggregates to trying to grasp at various kinds of grass, reeds, and rushes as we are being swept along in a river's fierce current: they all slip from our grasp or break away from the bank.[25] My continued grasping at self in the face of this fact sets my self over and against others' selves. We all become rivals in the fruitless struggle of trying to find something in the universe which we can grasp and call 'mine'. Selves thus cause problems for all concerned, and the aim of Buddhism is therefore to realize selflessness, both metaphysically and ethically; or, to borrow the title of Steven Collins's comprehensive study of the teaching of no self, the goal of the Buddhist path is to become a truly 'self-*less* person'.

The idea of belief in self as something conditioned by greed is stated as the fourth of the four kinds of grasping mentioned in the previous chapter: grasping at the doctrine of self. There are then these two complementary aspects to the Buddhist critique of self: the claim that the notion is based on a faulty understanding of the world; and the claim that it is a function of deep-seated greed and attachment. Conditioned by these two things the notion of self brings only suffering into the world.

The Buddhist critique of self is directed at all theories or views of the self that imply some sort of unchanging self whether that self is conceived of as eternal, immortal, or merely subsisting unchanged for the duration of a particular lifetime, or any period of time. As Professor Norman has shown, the refutation of the Upaniṣadic identification of the *ātman* with the world is the primary focus of the critique of self contained in the *Alagaddūpama Sutta* ('discourse on the simile of the water-snake').[26] Elsewhere Buddhist texts attack a whole range of views concerning the self. We saw above (pp. 137–8) how three specific ways of regarding the self are dismissed. In another extremely important and famous text, the *Brahmajāla Sutta* ('discourse on the supreme net'), the Buddha gives an account of sixty-two different views, fifty-four of which concern ways of perceiving the self.[27] Many of these views involve the misinterpretation of meditation experience: someone experiences some subtle and sublime level of consciousness in meditation and takes this as the unchanging self underlying other experiences. Another often repeated passage gives four different ways of constructing a view of self based on each of the five aggregates, making twenty varieties of the view that the individual exists (*satkāya-dṛṣṭi/sakkāya-diṭṭhi*): one regards the body as the self, or the self as possessing body, or body as in the self, or the self as in body, and so forth.[28] Yet another passage describes how someone, tortuously preoccupied with understanding the nature of self, falls prey to one of six views about the self:

Thus someone reflects inappropriately, 'Did I exist in the past? Did I not exist in the past? What was I in the past? How was I in the past?

> ... Will I exist in the future? Will I not exist in the future? What will I be in the future? How will I be in the future?' Or he is uncertain about himself in the present, 'Do I exist? Do I not exist? What am I? How am I? From where has this being come, and where will it go?' To one reflecting inappropriately in this way one of six views occurs. The definite and firm view arises, 'I have a self' or, 'I do not have a self' or, 'By the self I perceive what is self' or, 'By the self I perceive what is not self' or, 'By what is not self I perceive what is not self' or, 'That which is my self here, which speaks, feels, and which experiences at different times the results of good and bad deeds, will become permanent, constant, eternal, not subject to change.' This is called being lost to views, the grip of views, the jungle of views, the turmoil of views, the commotion of views, the bond of views. Bound by the bond of views the ignorant ordinary man is not freed from birth, old age and death, from distress, grief and suffering.[29]

In this way Buddhist thought sees us as being seduced by greed and ignorance into constructing all manner of views, opinions, and beliefs about our selves. Sometimes the view is founded on elaborate but, from the Buddhist perspective, faulty reasoning; for some it is everyday experiences that mislead them into believing in a self, for others it is the more subtle experiences of meditation that mislead.

The elaboration of the teaching of dependent arising

I introduced above the notion of dependent arising and the formula of twelve links that most commonly describes it. In the earliest Buddhist texts there are a number of variations on this list, some omitting links, some changing the order. This has led some modern textual scholars to speculate as to the possible stages in the evolution of the formula. These problems need not concern us here. Whatever its history, it is clear that the twelvefold formula became standard early in the development of Buddhist thought. But curiously, apart from stating the formula and using it in a variety of contexts, the earliest texts give very little explanation of how the formula is to be understood. For that we must turn to the later manuals of the fifth century CE such as Buddhaghosa's *Visuddhimagga* and Vasubandhu's *Abhidharmakośa*.[30]

Both Vasubandhu and Buddhaghosa present as standard a way of taking the twelvefold formula as relating to three different lives of a being (cf. Table 3). In our previous life we have performed various actions, we have been prey to the various volitions, impulses, and activities of the mind, both meritorious and unmeritorious, wholesome and unwholesome, and these are collectively summed up in the formula as (2) 'formations' (*saṃskāra/saṃkhāra*); although some of our actions have been wholesome, we never entirely succeed in freeing ourselves from a fundamentally distorted and partial seeing of the way things are; like a blind man we stumble from the right road to the wrong road without really understanding what we are doing;[31] thus (1) 'ignorance' (*avidyā/avijjā*), as a positive misconception and not the mere absence of knowledge,[32] forms the background to all our past actions, and so the formula begins, 'conditioned by ignorance are formations'. In the present we are heirs to these past deeds. In the process of rebirth at the moment of conception in our mother's womb we come into existence with (3) a mind or consciousness (*vijñāna/viññāṇa*) that is directly conditioned by these past deeds; in turn this consciousness gives rise to (4) our basic mental and physical make-up (*nāma-rūpa*) which in turn conditions the physical and mental capacities with which we turn to the world, (5) our five physical senses, and the mind (*āyatana*). Vasubandhu's *Abhidharmakośa* relates these last two links to the gradual development of the foetus in the womb. From the moment of birth by way of these six senses (6) various sensations (*sparśa/phassa*) and experiences come to us leading to (7) pleasant, unpleasant, and neutral feelings (*vedanā*); Vasubandhu relates this link to the stage in its development when a child learns to distinguish clearly those things which will bring pleasure and those that will bring pain. This world of feelings, some of which we like, some of which we dislike, some of which we are indifferent towards, gives rise to (8) craving (*tṛṣṇā/taṇhā*) for more of the pleasant feelings and fewer of the painful feelings. For Vasubandhu this link is particularly associated with the awakening of sexual passion at puberty. In response to our craving we determine on and (9) cling to (*upādāna*) various courses of action as the means to bring about the particular pleasant experiences we repeatedly crave;[33] and so we carry out these particular courses of action; as we repeatedly carry them out they (10) become our particular ways of being (*bhava*). And so a future (11) birth (*jāti*) conditioned by these very courses of action must occur, and whatever is born will once more (12) age and eventually die (*jarā-maraṇa*). So the process goes on without any known beginning or end.

Buddhaghosa gives us the following vivid image of dependent arising. A blind man (ignorance) stumbles (formations) and falls (consciousness); as a result of the fall a swelling develops (mind and body) and on that swelling there forms an abscess which weeps (six senses); this abscess gets continually knocked and bruised (contact) causing terrible pain (feeling) which the man longs to remove (craving); in consequence he seizes on (grasping) and applies (becoming) to the swelling various remedies that he thinks will relieve the pain; but instead of relieving the pain their effect is simply to change the condition of the swelling for the worse (birth) and finally the whole swelling bursts (old age and death).[34]

Theravāda commentaries preserve some further points of analysis of the formula that can be best set out in the form of a table (see Table 3). In the first place there are three main transition points (column 2) that divide the twelve links of the formula into four sections (column 3). Thus our previous ignorance and formations represent the 'past cause' of the 'present fruit' which consists of the consciousness, mind and body, six senses, sense-contact, and feeling which we presently experience; the way we react to this fruit in the present, by way of craving, grasping and becoming, constitutes the 'present cause' that will bear fruit in the form of the conditions of our future birth, ageing, and death. Viewing the formula in this way also reveals a certain symmetry: if links 1 and 2 (ignorance and formations) were active in the past, then inevitably links 8, 9, and 10 (craving, grasping, and becoming) were also active in the past; similarly if links 8, 9, and 10 are active in the present, so must links 1 and 2 (ignorance and formations); and the future existence of links 11 and 12

TABLE 3. *Dependent arising*

12 LINKS	3 TRANSITIONS	4 SECTIONS	20 FACTORS		3 TIMES
1. ignorance 2. formations	first transition	PAST CAUSE	1. ignorance 2. formations	8. craving 9. grasping 10. becoming	PAST LIFE
3. consciousness 4. mind and body 5. six senses 6. sense-contact 7. feeling	second transition	PRESENT FRUIT	3. consciousness 4. mind and body 5. six senses 6. sense-contact 7. feeling		PRESENT LIFE
8. craving 9. grasping 10. becoming	third transition	PRESENT CAUSE	8. craving 9. grasping 10. becoming	1. ignorance 2. formations	
11. birth 12. old age & death		FUTURE FRUIT	3. consciousness 4. mind and body 5. six senses 6. sense-contact 7. feeling		FUTURE LIFE

(birth, old age, and death) is a shorthand way of referring to the coming into being and subsequent decay of links 3, 4, 5, 6, and 7 (consciousness, mind and body, six senses, sense-contact, and feeling) in a future life. In this way, each of the four sections of column 3 can be seen as comprising five factors, making a total of twenty, instead of twelve, links.

The formula of dependent arising states that 'conditioned by' a certain phenomenon a certain other phenomenon comes into being. The Theravādin tradition analyses in some detail the ways in which a phenomenon can be a condition for another phenomenon by applying a scheme of twenty-four possible types of condition to each of the twelve links and detailing which are relevant in each case.[35] Another important point made in the exegetical literature is that, although the formula states just one condition for each subsequent link, this should not be taken as suggesting that a single cause is a sufficient condition for the arising of each further link. Each condition is stated as a representative and significant cause; the Theravāda tradition records here as a fundamental axiom the principle that a single cause does not give rise to either a single result or several results; nor do several causes give rise to just one result; but rather several causes give rise to several results.[36]

The details of all this need not concern us here, and if it sounds complicated, it is and deliberately so. Yet what is conveyed is how we as individual beings—our lives and experience—consist of a complex web of conditions built around the interaction of passive fruits and active causes. I said above that the formula of dependent arising is intended to reveal the actual pattern and structure of causality. Buddhist thought does not understand causality in terms similar to, say, Newtonian mechanics, where billiard balls rebound off each other in an entirely predictable manner once the relevant information is gathered. First, the Buddhist attempt to understand the ways of causal conditioning is concerned primarily with the workings of the mind: the way in which things we think, say, and do have an effect on both our selves and others. Second, Buddhist thought sees causal conditioning as involving the interaction of certain fixed or determined effects and certain free or unpredictable causes. If, presented with a situation, I deliberately kill another human being, this action must lead to some unpleasant result in the future; it may also make it easier for me to kill in the future, eventually establishing something of a habit; and this may lead me into circumstances—life as a bandit, say, or rebirth as a tiger—where the only way to live is by killing; and yet in some measure the freedom not to kill, not to act in accordance with established habits, remains.

On the one hand, we are born with a certain mental and physical make-up, and are presented with various experiences over which we have no control; on the other hand, we continually choose certain courses of action in response to what is given us. We like or do not like our experiences, ourselves, and our bodies, and we decide to act in certain ways in order to try to change our lives. But from the Buddhist perspective, because of the fundamental condition of ignorance, we fail to act effectively and lose our way in the labyrinth of conditions that constitutes our being. That dependent arising is indeed presented by the Buddhist tradition as something profound and, in a sense, difficult and complicated is aptly summed by a saying attributed to the Buddha himself:

> Profound is this dependent arising and profound too is its appearance. It is through not knowing its nature, not penetrating its nature that beings become like a tangled skein, like a knotted ball of thread, like a weave of grass and rushes and fail to pass beyond saṃsāra with its descents, unhappy destinies, and perdition.[37]

While the method of taking the twelvefold formula as describing a process over three lives is common to the ancient schools, it is also clear that it should be taken on a number of different scales—as describing, for example, the process whereby in response to some circumstance we determine upon and carry out one particular course of action.[38] The Abhidharma tradition of both the Theravādins and Sarvāstivādins points out that the formula should also be applied to each moment of consciousness—that is, every thought that occurs arises in accordance with this twelvefold formula. Dependent arising describes the structure of reality however, wherever, and whenever we dissect it. The application of the formula to a thought moment has some interesting implications. The formula describes a process, and we usually conceive of processes as by definition taking place over a period of time, and yet for the Abhidharma such a process occurs quite literally in one moment: the twelve links arise simultaneously. This is something that touches upon complex tensions and issues in the history of Buddhist thought. The point that is being made is that reality is at heart something dynamic, something fluid; however one looks at it, reality is a process; analyse reality down to its smallest possible components or constituents, and what one finds are, not static building blocks, but dynamic processes. This is vividly summed up in the notion of 'death' as something we live through in each moment:

> From the standpoint of ultimate truth the moment of a being's life is extremely short—just the occurrence of a single thought. Indeed just as the rolling wheel of a cart rolls on just one point of its rim, and resting rests on just one point, exactly so the life of a being lasts but the moment of one thought, and as soon as that thought has ceased the being has ceased . . . Life, personality, pleasure and pain all come together in a single thought—the moment passes swiftly; the aggregates of one who dies or of one who remains are all alike—gone never to be met with again. Without the occurrence of thought the world is not born, with its arising it lives, with its passing it dies. This is understanding in the ultimate sense.[39]

Yet again we move from the macrocosm of beings dying and being reborn to the microcosm of our changing thoughts. But the fact that reality is at heart a process relates also once more to the notion of the middle way. True process, true change cannot be explained either in terms of eternalism (a thing exists unchanging) or annihilationism (a thing exists for a time and then ceases to exist). The process of change as described by dependent arising is thus a middle between these two extremes, encapsulating the paradox of identity and difference involved in the very notion of change.

Buddhaghosa thus records that the teaching of dependent arising makes four points.[40] (1) It shows that there is continuity and identity in the process of change and thereby denies the view of annihilationism; if we misunderstand the nature of this identity, however, we fall into the trap of eternalism. (2) By indicating how various different phenomena condition each other, dependent arising also shows that there is difference and diversity involved in the process of something changing, and thereby denies the view of eternalism; but when this aspect of dependent arising is not correctly grasped, we are drawn to the view of annihilationism. (3) By indicating that actions are to be understood not as the work of an autonomous self but rather as the outcome of the complex interaction of diverse impersonal conditions, the view of selfhood is denied; but an incorrect grasp of this aspect of the teaching can lead to the view that actions are not real and have no moral consequences. (4) Finally, by indicating that appropriate consequences follow from specific causes, both the view that actions are not real and the view that causality is not real are abandoned; but wrongly grasped this aspect of dependent arising can lead both to the view of determinism and the view that causality is not real. In all this, then, views that see the world as random chaos, or as mechanically determined, or see individuals as having absolute free will or as having no choice whatsoever and simply being prey to random conditions or fixed destiny, are understood as cut through by the middle way of dependent arising.

All this may sound very conceptual, abstract, and philosophical but it is related rather precisely to the Buddhist understanding of spiritual practice. For there is one more aspect of the teaching of dependent arising that I have so far left unmentioned. The twelvefold formula I quoted above is in accordance with the arising of suffering, but when the formula is quoted in Buddhist texts it is nearly always quoted with a second version in the order of the ceasing of suffering:

> With the utter fading away and ceasing of ignorance is the ceasing of formations, with the ceasing of formations is the ceasing of consciousness, with the ceasing of consciousness is the ceasing of mind-and-body, with the ceasing of mind-and-body is the ceasing of the six senses, with

the ceasing of the six senses is the ceasing of sense-contact, with the ceasing of sense-contact is the ceasing of feeling, with the ceasing of feeling is the ceasing of craving, with the ceasing of craving is the ceasing of grasping, with the ceasing of grasping is the ceasing of becoming, with the ceasing of becoming is the ceasing of birth, with the ceasing of birth is the ceasing of old age and death—grief, lamentation, pain, sorrow and despair cease. Thus is the ceasing of this entire mass of suffering.

Thus not only does dependent arising hold the key to the way in which beings become enmeshed in suffering, it also points to the way in which they can free themselves from suffering. Precisely because all things occur in accordance with the law of dependent arising, small changes in the nature of the conditions that constitute the process can produce different effects. And because the mind contains the seeds of wholesome action—namely non-attachment, friendliness, and wisdom—as well as of unwholesome action, the root causes of suffering—namely ignorance and craving—can be gradually undermined and eradicated. It is because selfhood or personal continuity resides in the causal conditioning that is circumscribed by dependent arising that we can change, that we can bring about the cessation of suffering. Indeed, if I were an unchanging 'self', what would be the point of trying to change myself? The spiritual life would be meaningless. The work of Buddhist practice then is quite simply to cultivate those conditions that set in motion and bring about the process of the ceasing of ignorance leading to the ceasing of suffering. A significant ancient variation on the formula of dependent arising, having detailed the standard sequence of conditions leading to the arising of this whole mass of suffering, thus goes on to state that:

Conditioned by (1) suffering, there is (2) faith, conditioned by faith, there is (3) gladness, conditioned by gladness, there is (4) joy, conditioned by joy, there is (5) tranquillity, conditioned by tranquillity, there is (6) happiness, conditioned by happiness, there is (7) concentration, conditioned by concentration, there is (8) knowledge and vision of what truly is, conditioned by knowledge and vision of what truly is, there is (9) disenchantment, conditioned by disenchantment, there is (10) dispassion, conditioned by dispassion, there is (11) freedom, conditioned by freedom, there is (12) knowledge that the defilements are destroyed.[41]

FIGURE 1. *The Tibetan 'Wheel of Existence'*

This version of the formula introduces some of the technical terminology of Buddhist meditation which will be discussed in the next chapter. But what we must understand here is that Buddhist thought envisages that there are essentially two currents of the mind, one leading towards the arising of suffering, and one leading towards its cessation; both function according to the process of dependent arising, since this describes the way things are, whether or not there is any buddha or Buddhist teaching in the world to draw it to our attention. The law of dependent arising is the way things are, it is Dharma—even when there is no buddha in the world to point this out.[42]

The chain of dependent arising is sometimes referred to in Buddhist texts as 'the wheel of becoming' (*bhava-cakra/-cakka*). There is an old tradition of representing this graphically. Indeed, instructions for this are included in the Mūlasarvāstivādin Vinaya, although nowadays the tradition is continued only in Tibetan Buddhism (see Figure 1).[43] The wheel itself is shown clutched in the hands and jaws of Yama, the god of death. The outer circle shows the twelve links: a blind man (ignorance), a potter fashioning a pot (formations), a monkey picking a fruit (consciousness), a boat on a journey (mind and body), a house with six windows (the six sense-spheres), a couple embracing (sense contact), a man struck in the eye by an arrow (feeling), a man drinking (thirst), a man taking hold of a fruit (grasping), a pregnant woman (becoming), a woman in labour (birth), a man carrying a corpse to a charnel ground (old age and death). The next circle in shows six basic realms of rebirth: at the top, the heavenly realms of the gods, moving clockwise, the jealous gods, animals, hells, hungry ghosts, and humans. Moving inwards again we see beings rising (on the left) and falling (on the right). At the hub, driving the whole process, are a cock (greed), a snake (hatred) and a pig (ignorance).[44]

Did the Buddha deny the existence of the self?

I have been discussing just what is involved in the Buddhist denial of the self, and some of the possible philosophical difficulties that arise from conceiving of persons in terms of sequences of causally connected physical and mental events rather than enduring substances. As I have indicated, the philosophical and conceptual elaboration of the teaching of no self in conjunction with that of dependent arising is one of the hallmarks of Buddhist thought. But the view that the teaching of no self annihilates the individual and with it the basis of morality has been a feature of the work of a number of nineteenth- and twentieth-century scholars of Buddhism. Some of these accept the conclusion that the teaching of the Buddha is thus irredeemably nihilistic. Others have argued that the Buddhist elaboration of the teaching of no self is the work of later scholastics who have misunderstood what the Buddha actually taught.[45] Such scholars generally proceed by pointing to the fact that in the earliest texts the Buddha certainly uses the term 'self' and at the same time fails to deny categorically the existence of the self. Much in the manner of certain Upaniṣadic teachers, the Buddha is merely represented as stating what is not the self. Thus, it is claimed, when the aggregates are said not to be self, only the things that constitute our ordinary experience are denied as self; the door is left open for a metaphysical, absolute self that underlies or is beyond those experiences —the mysterious, ungraspable *ātman* of the Upaniṣads. The argument here is that, as a pragmatic teacher, either the Buddha was an agnostic as far as a metaphysical self was concerned, or he did indeed accept its existence but wished to avoid becoming involved in unnecessary speculations concerning its ultimate nature.

The point that the Buddha uses the term 'self' in the earliest texts has in effect already been dealt with above since it is to be referred to the distinction between conventional and ultimate truth. Moreover, it should be noted in this connection that the word *ātman* is used in Sanskrit as an ordinary reflexive pronoun: thus if one wants to say, 'he threw himself into the river' in Sanskrit, one says that he threw his *ātman* into the river without any suggestion that it is his eternal and immortal soul that has been thrown into the river.

The point that the Buddha fails to deny the self, but only states what it is not, is more interesting. In one particular passage of the Nikāyas we are told how the Buddha was once asked by the wanderer Vacchagotta whether the self existed.[46] The Buddha remained silent. Vacchagotta asked whether the self did not then exist. The Buddha once again remained silent. The Buddha then explained to the curious Ānanda that if he had answered that the self exists it would have been to side with those ascetics and brahmins who hold the doctrine of 'eternalism'; moreover it would not have been in accordance with his understanding that all phenomena (*dharma*) are not self. On the other hand if he had answered that the self does not exist it would have been to side with those ascetics and brahmins who hold the doctrine of 'annihilationism'; moreover it would have thrown poor Vacchagotta into even more confusion, as he would have concluded that formerly he had a self but now he did not.

Essentially this refusal to answer Vacchagotta categorically must be seen in the same light as the refusal to give unequivocal answers to the ten undetermined questions; that is, the terms in which the question is couched are not accepted. Furthermore, we should note that, while the Buddha may refuse to give a categorical answer when asked whether or not the self exists, he is nevertheless recorded as stating that all those ascetics and brahmins who contemplate the self in various ways in fact contemplate the five aggregates or one of them, and on the basis of this come to the conclusion, 'I exist'.[47] This makes it clear, I think, that to talk of a self that exists apart from the five aggregates is meaningless for the Buddha. Thus the Buddha's silence here is not about leaving the door open for some mysterious, ungraspable absolute self. The Buddha's suggestion to Ānanda that if he had told Vacchagotta that the self does not exist he would have become even more confused is revealing.

What is at issue here is not so much the question of the existence or non-existence of the self, but that in seeking to answer the question of its existence the ordinary unawakened mind that is not free from grasping inevitably gets entangled in views and theories about the self. As we have seen, the awakened mind, on the other hand, breaks free from all views about the self. Part of the problem here stems from a failure on the part of some modern scholars to appreciate the relationship between the intellectual (cognitive) and emotional (affective) dimensions of the teaching of no self. From the Buddhist perspective, the mind needs to give up all attachment to any view about the self. That is, to think 'I do not exist' reveals no less preoccupation and entanglement with the notion of my self and its existence than to think 'I exist'. Buddhist thought is thus concerned with both our conscious intellectual theories about our 'selves' and also the way in which our minds and emotions cling to the idea of our individual existence at a subconscious level. This is well illustrated by the story of the monk Khemaka who informs a group of monks that, although he does not view any one of the aggregates as the self, yet the idea of his own existence in the subtle form of the 'the conceit "I am"' clings to the aggregates as a faint smell of dirt might still cling to washed clothes.[48]

7

The Buddhist Path

The Way of Calm and Insight

Introductory remarks

The previous two chapters have focused on the Buddhist understanding of the nature of the world and of the individual; we have seen how Buddhist thought sees the world of our experience as constructed in dependence upon a variety of conditions, the most crucial of which are greed, hatred, and delusion. The discussion of cosmology, the self, and dependent arising in effect represents an elaboration of the first and second of the four noble truths, namely suffering and its arising. This discussion has at times touched on quite technical areas of Buddhist intellectual theory. We come now to the fourth truth, the path leading to the cessation of suffering, the practice of Buddhism. In this connection also, Buddhist tradition provides us with rather elaborate theoretical accounts, this time focusing on the stages of the path. There is sometimes the idea in the West that Buddhism is an overly philosophical and intellectual religion, but we should be careful not to mistake Buddhism's intellectual theories for Buddhism itself—just as we should not confuse learning to swim with gaining an understanding of the theory of buoyancy and propulsion, or being able to play a musical instrument with an exact theoretical knowledge of where one has to put one's fingers on a fretboard or keyboard to produce a certain melody. Such theoretical knowledge may be useful in the process of learning, but the experience of practice is never quite what one's understanding of theory leads one to expect.

Buddhist theory is, then, the soil in which understanding may grow.[1] It should, moreover, be considered as intended more for the benefit of monks or committed lay followers, who already have some basis in ordinary, everyday Buddhist practice, than for the beginner. The vast majority of Buddhists today, as in the past, do not concern themselves with intellectual theory but with basic Buddhist practice. There are, furthermore, traditions in Buddhism that are somewhat critical of theory, suggesting that too much at the wrong time may clutter our minds and actually get in the way of the practice that can eradicate attachment and bring true wisdom. With this in mind let us turn to the theoretical account of the path that leads to the cessation of suffering.

As we saw in Chapter 3 (pp. 81–2), in the earliest Buddhist texts the noble truth of the path to the cessation of suffering is most frequently summed up as the noble eightfold path: right view, right intention, right speech, right action, right livelihood, right effort, right mindfulness, and right concentration. But rather than presenting it as equivalent to Buddhist practice in general, Buddhist writings usually understand the noble eightfold path in a more restricted sense, implied by the epithet 'noble' (*ārya/ariya*). The term indicates that one who has established these eight qualities has in fact found the way to the cessation of suffering—like one finding a path in the jungle leading to a beautiful city. But the 'ordinary man' (*pṛthagjana/puthujjana*) who is plagued by greed, hatred, and delusion cannot simply call into being the right view of such 'noble ones' (*ārya/ariya*) who have found the path. He cannot, as it were, simply open the door and set out on the noble eightfold path, first he must negotiate the jungle of his views, behaviour, and emotions in order to find the eight qualities. Much of the Buddhist path is thus concerned not so much with *walking* the noble eightfold path as with *finding* the noble eightfold path. The Buddhist practitioner thus sets out on the ordinary path of Buddhist practice in order gradually to transform view, intention, speech, action, endeavour, mindfulness, and concentration into the eight qualities of the noble path; once on the noble path he may further develop and perfect these eight qualities and follow the path to the complete cessation of suffering.

It is the structure of the 'the step-by-step discourse' (*anupūrvikā kathā/anupubbi-kathā*), rather than the eightfold path, that informs the general accounts of the Buddhist path as a gradual progression from the fundamental practices of generosity (*dāna*) and conduct (*sīla/śīla*), to the cultivation of concentration (*samādhi*) and wisdom (*prajñā/paññā*) by means of meditative development (*bhāvanā*) (see above, pp. 83–4). The often repeated step-by-step discourse represents perhaps the most succinct statement of this gradual path in the Nikāyas/Āgamas. An equally early but fuller expression is found in the schema of 'the fruits of asceticism' (*śrāmaṇya-phala/sāmañña-phala*), an essentially stock account of the path, which is again repeated with slight variations in a number of places in the Nikāyas/Āgamas. This schema is assumed and, in one way or another, adapted by the later manuals such as the *Visuddhimagga*, the *Abhidharmakośa*, Kamalaśīla's *Bhāvanākrama* ('Stages of Meditation', eighth century) and also Chinese and later Tibetan works such as Chih-i's *Mo-ho chih-kuan* ('Great Calm and Insight') and *Hsiu-hsi chih-kuan tso-ch'an fa-yao* ('The Essentials for Sitting in Meditation and Cultivating Calm and Insight', sixth century), sGam-po-pa's *Thar-pa rin-po-che'i rgyan* ('Jewel Ornament of Liberation', twelfth century) and Tsong-kha-pa's *Lam rim chen mo* ('Great Graduated Path', fourteenth century). It is within this basic framework that I shall set out Buddhist practice. I will be referring to the details as set out by Buddhaghosa in his *Visuddhimagga* and Vasubandhu in his *Abhidharmakośa*, since both these accounts acquired a certain authority for those that followed. It must be emphasized, however, that the Buddhist meditation tradition is extremely rich, and the material I am presenting embodies a tradition of creative adaptation that continues down to the present day. Important approaches to the practice of Buddhist meditation that I am forced to pass over include Ch'an (Japanese Zen) and esoteric systems of Tibetan tantra, Chinese Chen Yen (Japanese Shingon), and the less well-known esoteric Theravāda tradition (see Chapter 10).

The role of faith

While the *noble* eightfold path may be understood as strictly relevant only to the practice of the 'noble ones', nevertheless its basic structure can still be seen as revealing something general about the nature of the spiritual path: the basic dependence of one's actions (items 3–5) upon one's beliefs and aspirations (items 1–2), and, in turn, of one's basic emotional state (items 6–8) upon one's actions. In fact here is a certain parallelism between the structure of the eightfold path and the chain of dependent arising, where ignorance conditions certain actions which in turn condition one's rebirth. The parallelism is clearer when, as often in the early texts, we find talk of wrong view, wrong intention, wrong speech, wrong action, wrong livelihood, wrong endeavour, wrong mindfulness, wrong concentration. Moreover, as the positive sequence of dependent arising begins with faith (*śraddhā/saddhā*), so the sequence of the eightfold path begins with right view (*samyag-dṛṣṭi/sammā-diṭṭhi*). Without some initial trust in the fact that there is a way out of suffering, without some seed of understanding of the nature of suffering and its cessation, we would never begin to look for the path and we would have no hope of finding it.

An ancient formula describes the beginning of the path in the following terms:

> A Tathāgata appears in the world . . . He teaches the Dharma that is beautiful in the beginning, beautiful in the middle, and beautiful in the end. A householder or a householder's son or someone born into some family hears that Dharma. And hearing the Dharma, he gains faith in the Tathāgata.[2]

Faith or confidence in the Buddha, his teaching (*dharma/dhamma*) and the community (*saṅgha*) of those who have followed and realized the teaching is the starting point of the Buddhist path that is assumed both by the earliest texts and by those brought up in traditional Buddhist cultures today. Yet those of us whose sensibilities have been moulded by more recent Western intellectual traditions are often uncomfortable in the presence of religious faith and its devotional and ritual expression. Indeed nineteenth- and early twentieth-century enthusiasts have on occasion presented Buddhism as the answer to the modern world's 'crisis of faith': a religion devoid of belief in God and the saving power of rituals, whose truths are not accepted on the authority of scripture, but verified by direct experience.

Certainly the Buddha counsels the Kālāmas not to reject or accept things because tradition, scripture, reasoning, logic, or argument tells them to do so, nor out of respect for some ascetic, but rather because of their own direct knowledge.[3] Yet a preoccupation with the *Kālāma Sutta* as a repudiation of faith betrays a misunderstanding of the very nature of faith and its devotional and ritual expression in Buddhism. As the Buddhist scholar Edward Conze has commented:

This sceptical age dwells anyway far too much on the intellectual side of faith. *Śraddhā*, the word we render as 'faith', is etymologically akin to Latin *cor*, 'the heart', and faith is much more a matter of the heart than the intellect.[4]

Conze's comment highlights a distinction that is sometimes made between faith as 'cognitive' and faith as 'affective'. Faith in its cognitive mode is a putative knowledge or awareness that amounts to belief in propositions or statements of which one does not, or cannot, have direct knowledge. Faith in its affective mode, on the other hand, is a positive emotional response to someone or something one has heard or read. The Buddhist understanding of 'faith' is almost entirely affective. In other words, Buddhist texts understand faith in the Buddha and Dharma not so much as a matter of intellectual assent to certain propositions about the world in the form of a Buddhist creed, as of a state of trust, confidence, affection, and devotion inspired by the person of the Buddha and his teachings—a confidence that there is indeed a path leading to the cessation of suffering which has been walked by the Buddha and his followers.

The traditional expression of one's faith, one's commitment to the Buddhist path, is the act of going to the three 'jewels' of the Buddha, Dharma, and Saṅgha for refuge, realized by the formal recitation of the threefold formula set out at the end of Chapter 1 (see p. 34).[5] Going for refuge implies the adopting of one of two broad approaches to Buddhist practice: the way of the lay follower (*upāsaka*) and the way of the ordained monk (*bhikṣu/bhikkhu*) or nun (*bhikṣuṇī/bhikkhunī*). In practice, the strength of commitment of both may vary, but generally, of course, the monastic way of life represents the ultimate commitment to the religious life, the ultimate expression of faith. But for lay follower and monastic alike, the three 'jewels' remain powerful objects for the ritual and devotional expression of their faith.

The precise form the earliest devotions took is unclear, but they centred around the worship of stūpas. Thus the Buddha himself is presented as recommending that faithful monks, nuns, laymen, and laywomen visit the four sites where he was born, gained awakening, first taught Dharma, and died; he adds that any one who dies with a serene heart in the course of making such a pilgrimage will gain a good rebirth.[6] Given the Indian cultural context, worship no doubt took a form not entirely dissimilar from more contemporary Buddhist practice: the making of offerings —especially of flowers, incense, and lamps—and the chanting of verses and formulas as the basis for the recollection of the qualities of the Buddha, Dharma, and Saṅgha.[7] Early Buddhist art is often described as 'aniconic' since it avoided representing the Buddha in human form, using instead various symbols (an empty seat beneath the tree of awakening or the wheel of Dharma), but from the second century CE the Buddha image increasingly became a focus for such devotions and meditations. Another ancient ritual practice important for the subsequent history of Buddhism and which seems to be witnessed already in the earliest writings is the recitation of certain sūtras as protective charms (*rakṣā/paritta*).[8] The Vinaya describes monks circumambulating a monastery and chanting to protect the Buddha when they believe his life is threatened.[9] One of the oldest such protective chants is the *Āṭānāṭiya Sutta*, a charm to protect the monk meditating in the forest from unsympathetic demons (*yakṣa/yakkha*).[10] Alongside specific charms for the protection of women in childbirth or the pacifying of dangerous snakes, for example, chanting Buddhist texts and formulas, such as the refuges and precepts, in general came to be regarded as effective in protecting one against the dangers of disease and accident. The second- or first-century BCE *Milindapañha*, while acknowledging the inability of such charms to give us absolute protection from the effects of our bad karma, nevertheless defends their efficacy in certain circumstances.[11] The different traditions of Buddhism in Sri Lanka and South-East Asia, in East Asia, and in Tibet have all developed their own distinctive forms of devotional and protective ritual, yet these derive from a common ancient ancestry.

The Buddha of the early texts may be critical, then, of certain kinds of brahmanical ritual, especially those involving the sacrifice of animals; he may also deny that faith and rituals can of themselves bring about the final cessation of suffering. But there is no real evidence in the early texts to suggest a negative attitude to faith and its ritual and devotional expression; indeed we even find the Buddha apparently approving of worship at non-Buddhist shrines.[12] Faith and the activities which express that faith are, in fact, seen as performing a spiritually crucial function: they soothe and settle the mind thereby arousing the confidence to continue the practice of the path. Moreover, the mind that is quietly confident and trustful of the power of the Buddha, Dharma, and Saṅgha is its own protection. Two ancient images for faith are worth noting. Faith is compared to a gem which, when thrown into a stream that has just been stirred up by the passing of an emperor's army, immediately causes the sand, silt, and mud to settle. Or if one were standing at the bank of a river in spate unable to judge whether it might be possible to leap over it and someone should come along and indeed jump across, then there might arise the confidence that it is indeed possible to cross the torrent. So faith has two characteristics: it causes the mind to become settled and composed and it inspires it with the confidence to leap forward.[13] In sum, devotional and ritual practice constitute a preliminary meditation practice, settling and composing the mind in preparation for the higher stages of Buddhist meditative practice.

Good conduct

I have already briefly discussed generosity and good conduct as bases of 'auspicious action' or 'merit' (*puṇya/puñña*) above (see pp. 101–2). In the present context I wish to comment further on the Buddhist understanding of 'good conduct' or 'virtue' (*śīla/sīla*). It is useful here to make a distinction between the good conduct as the refraining from various deeds that are considered unwholesome and harmful to both oneself and others, and the perfected conduct of one who is awakened, such as a buddha or arhat. The ordinary unawakened person sometimes acts in a wholesome, sometimes in an unwholesome manner. The goal of the Buddhist path is to eradicate the unwholesome motivations that cause harmful behaviour. To achieve this the mind needs to be 'trained'. Part of the training involves the undertaking of various precepts, literally principles or bases of training (*śikṣāpada/sikkhāpada*), in order to try to restrain the mind and draw it back from the grosser kinds of unwholesome behaviour. For one who is awakened such precepts are redundant, not because he or she is now permitted these kinds of behaviour, but because conduct is now perfected and the temptation or rather the motivation at the root of such kinds of behaviour has gone. That is, the ordinary unawakened person's actions are sometimes motivated by greed, aversion, and delusion and sometimes by non-attachment, friendliness, and wisdom. Since a buddha or arhat has completely eradicated the defilements and any latent tendency to attachment, aversion, or delusion, he or she acts exclusively from non-attachment, friendliness, and wisdom.

As part of the practice of the path, it is traditional for the lay follower to take on five precepts: to refrain from harming living creatures, taking what is not given, sexual misconduct, false speech, intoxicants that cause heedlessness. On occasion, for limited periods, the committed lay follower may take on eight precepts, while the monk's good conduct is founded on ten basic precepts elaborated in terms of the the 200 plus rules of the *prātimokṣa* (see Chapter 4); much of this elaboration in principle involves distinguishing between serious and less serious breaches of the ten precepts.

The five precepts are for the most part self-explanatory, although there is a certain subtlety in their definition. The first precept is usually taken as specifically referring to killing, although a wider definition is not excluded. The second refers in simple terms to stealing, although once more the wider definition begs the question of what precisely constitutes 'what is not given'. The third precept is traditionally taken as referring to sexual intercourse with partners who are prohibited—in other words, adultery; but again, the precept raises the question of what exactly constitutes sexual misconduct (and even, since a literal translation of the expression might be 'misconduct with regard to sensual desire', questions about more general sensual indulgence). The fourth precept refers specifically to lying but the question of right speech is elaborated upon in Buddhist texts (see below). The fifth precept also has wider implications. Heedlessness is interpreted by Theravādin commentators as the absence of 'mindfulness' (*smṛti/sati*), an important psychological quality. It is not the taking of alcohol or other drugs as such that is problematic, but the state of mind that it generally induces: a lack of mental clarity with an increased tendency to break the other precepts. The fifth precept also highlights once more that what we have to do with here are 'principles of training' and what is of paramount importance in the Buddhist conception of spiritual training is mental clarity: this helps to create the conditions that conduce to seeing the way things truly are. The additional precepts in the lists of eight and ten are similarly principles of training seen as helpful in the cultivation of the path, rather than prohibitions against intrinsically unwholesome ways of conduct.

The kinds of behaviour that the five precepts are intended to prevent one from committing are outlined by the list of ten courses of unwholesome action: harming living creatures, taking what is not given, sexual misconduct, false speech, divisive speech, harsh speech, frivolous speech, covetousness, anger, wrong view (see above, pp. 120–1). In these ten actions—three of body, four of speech, and three of thought—we find speech further elaborated, while the particular emphasis on actions of thought and the mind draws attention once again to the Buddhist focus on karma as essentially a matter of the mind and intention: what is important is one's state of mind, and a moment of intense anger and hatred, even if it does not lead to actual physical violence or verbal abuse, nevertheless constitutes a real 'deed' or karma.

The five precepts and the ten courses of action essentially define for us right speech and action of the eightfold path. What of 'right livelihood', the third item of the eightfold path that bears on good conduct? This is basically understood as making one's living by means that avoid activity infringing the five precepts. Such occupations as that of the soldier, butcher, or trader in alcohol are therefore called into question. Yet in approaching questions of good conduct and the precepts, Buddhist tradition has generally shown an attitude of practicality and flexibility. In order to illustrate this it is worth briefly considering the question of vegetarianism in the light of the first precept.

The ethical ideal that underlies the precepts is considered to be rather exalted, such that only someone very advanced on the path (a stream-attainer, or even a buddha or arhat) could really live up to it. Indeed, good conduct is ultimately understood in Buddhist thought not in terms of adherence to external rules, but as the expression of the perfected motivations of non-attachment, friendliness, and wisdom. Thus the arhat is described as simply being incapable of intentionally acting in a manner that is not in accordance with the precepts and ten courses of wholesome action.[14] In other words, ordinary beings cannot hope to keep the precepts perfectly; rather they abide by the precepts as rules of training in order to curb the grosser forms of bad conduct. At a deeper level there is also perhaps a sense in which no one, not even a buddha, can hope to live in the world and cause absolutely no harm to any living being. That is, it is almost impossible to isolate and disassociate oneself absolutely from activities that indirectly cause harm to living creatures. That this is so is an aspect of the deepest level of the first noble truth: the world, saṃsāra, is by its very nature an imperfect place, a place where suffering is always lurking in one form or another. The question of acting ethically then becomes one of where to draw the line.

In respect of harming living creatures Buddhist thought has generally and in the first place drawn the line at direct and intentional killing. Of course, this does not mean that harm that falls short of killing is ethical, or that by only giving the order to kill one is free of blame. Yet there is no direct prescription against the eating of meat in the earliest Buddhist texts. Buddhist monks and nuns, who are dependent on what is offered to them, are encouraged not to be too fussy and are permitted to accept meat provided it has not been specifically slaughtered to feed them (though certain kinds of flesh such as that of humans, snakes, and horses are never allowable).[15] On the other hand there is also an ancient and widespread Buddhist attitude that regards vegetarianism as the appropriate response to the first precept. Although many Buddhists in traditional Buddhist cultures are not strict vegetarians, eating no meat is respected as furthering the aspiration to live without harming living creatures that underlies the first precept. The Mahāyāna *Laṅkāvatāra Sūtra* explicitly argues at length against meat-eating, and its outlook has been influential especially in East Asian Buddhism, where vegetarianism has often been the norm for members of the Buddhist monastic community and committed lay followers.[16]

But there is also in the Buddhist attitude to good conduct the suggestion that adherence to 'moral' principles for their own sake may be an expression of rigid views and attachment—'clinging to precepts and vows' (*śīla-vrata-parāmarśa/sīla-bbata-parāmāsa*) —rather than of true compassion. Ultimately Buddhism teaches that the nature of good conduct is subtle and complex—so complex that it precisely cannot be solved by reference to precepts and rules of conduct. It can only be solved by following a path of training that ends in rooting out greed, aversion, and delusion. Ethical precepts are a necessary part of the training that constitutes that path, but attachment to those precepts, like all attachments, must itself be given up.

As with faith, the practice of good conduct is once more orientated towards meditation practice. An important aspect of meditation practice is the stilling and calming of the mind. Apart from the harm they cause to others, and the unpleasant results they will bring upon us through the operation of the law of karma and the process of rebirth, the ten courses of unwholesome action are also seen as damaging to one's own sense of well-being, resulting in feelings of guilt and remorse. At a subtler level they are seen as intrinsically disturbing. Keeping the precepts, on the other hand, frees the mind from guilt and also has a strong protective quality, warding off danger. Thus it is said that the one who abides by the precepts 'experiences a blameless happiness within'.[17] In fact, as expressions of deep faith and trust in the Buddha's teaching, Buddhist devotional and ritual acts (going for refuge, taking the precepts, chanting sūtras, etc.) are generally seen as having a protective quality, keeping the mind free of fear and warding off danger.[18] We have here an understanding that verges on the magical.

The practice of calm meditation

Basic principles of Buddhist meditation

We come now to the subject of meditation and its role in the Buddhist spiritual path. Curiously it is difficult to find a precise equivalent of the term 'meditation' in Buddhist technical terminology. The two principal candidates are *bhāvanā* and *yoga*. The first of these is the older, specifically Buddhist term and means literally 'bringing into being'; it refers to mental or spiritual exercises aimed at developing and cultivating wholesome mental states that conduce to the realization of the Buddhist path. Such exercises may centre on sitting quietly in a cross-legged posture, but should not be reduced to that. The second term means approximately 'effort' or 'work' and relatively early in the history of Indian religion came to refer to specifically spiritual work and techniques. In this sense the term is one of very varied application, there being many different approaches to yoga within Indian tradition from those such as *haṭha-yoga* which focus on the practice of different bodily postures (*āsana*) to those such as Buddhist yoga which focus on contemplative techniques while sitting in some form of the cross-legged posture.

Buddhist tradition comes to consider meditation by way of two different but complementary aspects, namely calm (*śamatha/samatha*) and insight (*vipaśyanā/vipassanā*), which are geared to the cultivation of deep states of concentration (*samādhi*) and wisdom (*prajñā/paññā*) respectively. Some modern scholars have seen these two kinds of meditation as reflecting tensions and even disagreements within the earliest Buddhist tradition concerning the nature of the Buddhist path. I shall return to this matter presently. But, whatever their early history and origins, it is clear that in developed Buddhist theory the two aspects of meditation, calm and insight, are seen as together forming the basis for the realization of the Buddhist goal: when calm and insight meditation are brought together (*yuga-naddha*), the unconditioned may be experienced.

According to a cardinal principle of Buddhist psychology our minds are fundamentally clear and pure; they have become stained by the operation of adventitious defilements (*kleśa/kilesa*).

> Radiant is the mind, monks, but sometimes it is defiled by defilements that come from without. The ordinary man without understanding does not know it as it truly is.[19]

The goal of Buddhist practice is to bring to an end the operation of these defilements. The basic method is to restore to the mind something of its fundamental state of clarity and stillness. This clarity of mind provides the opportunity for seeing into the operation of the defilements and the mind's true nature, for seeing things as they really are, for fully awakening. The way of returning the mind to its state of clarity is by the use of the techniques of calm meditation, which can temporarily suppress or block the immediate defilements that disturb the mind; the way of seeing clearly into the nature of the mind is by the methods of insight meditation, which, in association with calm, can finally eradicate those defilements.

The way of Buddhist meditation is, then, to look deep into ourselves to see the very nature of our minds. The principal immediate mental defilements that constitute the obstacles to the path are known as the five 'hindrances' (*nīvaraṇa*): sensual desire, ill-will, tiredness and sleepiness, excitement and depression, and doubt. An ancient simile compares the mind that is continually prey to the five hindrances to a bowl of water disturbed or contaminated in five ways: mixed with red dye, steaming hot, full of moss and leaves, ruffled by the wind, muddied and in a dark place. If someone should look down into a bowl of water contaminated in any one of these five ways, then he would not be able to see a clear and true reflection of himself. On the other hand, if one were to look down into a bowl of water that is free of such contaminations, one would see a clear and true reflection. Likewise, the mind that is disturbed by the hindrances will never succeed in coming to know its true nature.

This then is the basic theory of Buddhist meditation stated in the terms of the oldest texts. While later schools and traditions may change and adapt the terminology used, while they may elaborate the stages and techniques in a number of different ways, while they may give distinctive technical accounts of the content of the knowledge gained in insight meditation, the basic principle for the most part holds good: one stills and clears the mind and then turns it towards investigation and insight.

Stilling the mind

The techniques of calm meditation involve counteracting the tendency of the mind to restlessly seek out new and different objects of the senses. This is accomplished by developing a basic capacity of the mind to rest undisturbed on an object of perception. This capacity, termed 'concentration' (*samādhi*), is in fact understood as a prerequisite of all thought, but in normal consciousness it functions only minimally. When this capacity is developed in meditation practice, however, it brings the mind to a condition of stillness in which it finds complete contentment with just one object of contemplation. In this condition the mind enters into quite different states of consciousness from its habitual, ordinary states. These states of consciousness may themselves be termed *samādhi*, or alternatively they are known as the *dhyānas* (Pali *jhāna*), a term which means something like 'deep thought' or 'meditation'. In Buddhist technical terms, the mind has temporarily escaped from 'the sphere of the senses' (*kāmāvacara*)—its normal preoccupation with thoughts that are in some way bound up with the objects of the five senses—to the subtle 'sphere of pure form' (*rūpāvacara*)—a refined world of pure, abstract 'forms' (*rūpa*). The experience of this refined world of pure form comprises four increasingly subtle *dhyānas* corresponding to the sixteen Brahmā realms of the Buddhist cosmos (Chapter 5).

To begin to still the mind by the practice of calm meditation one needs, then, a suitable object of contemplation. Drawing on the earlier Nikāyas/Āgamas, later manuals such as Upatissa's *Vimuttimagga* ('Path of Freedom') and Buddhaghosa's *Visuddhimagga* give standardized lists of thirty-eight and forty objects of meditation (*kammaṭṭhāna*) respectively; Vasubandhu's *Abhidharmakośa* focuses on a more limited number of meditation objects. Upatissa and Buddhaghosa initially discuss the subjects of meditation from two points of view: (1) their suitability for the practice of the preliminary or advanced stages of calm meditation, and (2) their suitability for different personality types (see Table 4).[20]

Certain objects—the six recollections (*anusmṛti/anussati*) of the Buddha, the Dharma, the Saṅgha, good conduct, generosity, and the gods, along with mindfulness of death—are suited to the preliminary practice of calm known as 'access concentration' (*upacāra-samādhi*), which is a level of concentration considered to be on the brink of full *dhyāna* or 'absorption' (*appanā*). Others —the ten 'devices' (*kasiṇa*), along with mindfulness of breathing (*ānāpāna-smṛti/-sati*)—are suitable for both the preliminary and more advanced stages. Yet others, such as the four 'formless' (*arūpa*) meditations, can only be cultivated by the advanced practitioner of calm. Certain meditation subjects are also traditionally regarded as particularly suited to different character types. Thus someone with a strong tendency towards sensual desire should balance this by cultivating the ten meditations on 'ugliness' (*aśubha/asubha*), that is, on the body in ten different degrees of putrefaction; someone with strong faith will respond to the first six recollections; while for someone with a tendency to intellectualize and get lost in speculations, mindfulness of breathing is particularly recommended as cutting off discursive thinking; someone whose temperament is irritable and who tends towards states of anger and hatred might take one of the four coloured

TABLE 4. *The forty subjects of calm meditation according to Buddhaghosa*

SUBJECT	PERSONALITY	LEVEL
10 KASINAS		
earth		
water	all personality types	
fire		
air		
blue		1st–4th *jhāna*
yellow	hate	
red		
white		
light	all personality types	
limited space		
10 UGLINESSES		
the bloated		
the livid		
the festering		
the cut-up		
the gnawed	greed	1st *jhāna*
the scattered		
the hacked and scattered		
the bleeding		
the worm-infested		
the skeleton		
repulsiveness of food	intelligent	access
determining the 4 elements		

SUBJECT	PERSONALITY	LEVEL
10 RECOLLECTIONS		
of the Buddha		
of the Dharma		
of the Saṅgha	faith	
of good conduct		access
of generosity		
of the gods		
mindfulness of death	intelligent	
mindfulness of the body	greed	1st *jhāna*
mindfulness of breathing	delusion/discursive	1st–4th *jhāna*
of peace	intelligent	access
4 IMMEASURABLES		
loving kindness		1st–3rd *jhāna*
compassion	hate	
sympathetic joy		
equanimity		4th *jhāna*
4 FORMLESS MEDITATIONS		
boundless space		
boundless consciousness		
nothingness	all personality types	4th *jhāna*
neither perception nor non-perception		

discs as a meditation subject. Upatissa and Buddhaghosa go into some detail concerning the analysis of different character types and how the way one carries out various tasks (how one eats or walks, for example) reveals the tendencies of one's personality. In this connection, they also emphasize the need for a meditation teacher—the good friend (*kalyāṇa-mitra/-mitta*)—who can suggest and teach a suitable meditation subject. The importance of the teacher is, of course, one of the great themes of Buddhist practice. The teacher of meditation stands in the place of the Buddha himself and, just as one should have faith and trust in the Buddha and his teachings, so one must have faith and trust in the meditation teacher and his instructions; without such faith it is impossible to put the teacher's instructions into practice with the necessary sense of commitment. Thus kneeling before one's teacher and paying him appropriate respect are recommended as generating faith.

It is sometimes suggested in scholarly studies that 'meditation' is traditionally the preserve of a minority and élite group of Buddhist monastics.[21] Obviously the question of which Buddhists 'meditate' depends on how one defines 'meditation'. As I suggested above, it is not entirely clear which Buddhist technical term the English word 'meditation' corresponds to. But it is clear that much of ordinary, everyday Buddhist devotional practice takes the form of some kind of recollection of the Buddha, Dharma, and Saṅgha, and also the other recollections of good conduct, generosity, and the gods.[22] For Upatissa and Buddhaghosa such recollection practice constitutes the preliminary stage of calm meditation. There is, then, a real sense in which nearly all Buddhists—lay or monastic—can be considered 'meditators'. Even if the term *bhāvanā* is taken to imply the systematic cultivation of a particular meditation subject, the line between Buddhist devotions and formal, systematic meditation is not sharp. Devotions arouse faith and compose the mind; to this extent they form a preliminary stage of calm meditation, settling the mind in a state close to *dhyāna*, technically termed 'access concentration'. To fully develop calm, however, one must cultivate a further subject of meditation.

The hindrances and the limbs of dhyāna

The basic instructions for beginning meditation are very simple. One finds a quiet place and sits down in a cross-legged position and arousing the appropriate motivation one gently places the mind's attention on whatever is the particular object of meditation. Inevitably the meditator finds that his or her mind wanders and the attention must be repeatedly brought back to the object of meditation. The reason the mind fails to become absorbed in the object of meditation is twofold. On the one hand, the mind is prey to the five hindrances already mentioned. On the other hand, it has not developed sufficient skill in bringing the object to mind or, in technical terminology, the five 'limbs' of *dhyāna* are not sufficiently strong.

In principle, something of the process of overcoming the hindrances and developing the factors of *dhyāna* can be observed whenever the mind is applied to any new task that requires a certain mental application and dexterity. Take the example of learning to play a musical instrument. In order to progress one needs to practise regularly and patiently. Almost inevitably, at times other less taxing activities seem much more attractive and pleasurable than struggling with one's practice. This is the first hindrance of desire for the objects of the senses. At times one may become frustrated, irritated, and angry, seeing faults in one's musical instrument or teacher, or using the fact the neighbours are making too much noise as a reason for not persevering with one's practice. This is the second hindrance of ill will. Or the very thought of one's practice may make one feel tired and drowsy, yet when one thinks of doing something else that the mind finds more interesting, suddenly one feels wide awake and alert. This is the third hindrance of tiredness and sleepiness. Or one may suddenly become over-excited at one's progress, or depressed at what one sees as one's lack of progress. This is the fourth hindrance of excitement and depression. Finally one may doubt the whole enterprise, asking oneself what the point is in learning to play a musical instrument anyway. Just as anyone wishing to make progress in the learning of a musical instrument must acquire some measure of control over such hindrances, so the meditator intent on developing his meditation subject must deal with these immediate defilements of the mind.

Again, at the outset of learning to play the guitar or piano, the beginner must very consciously think where to put each individual finger. At the same time one must begin to pay attention to the subtler aspects of just how one places a finger on a key or plucks a string; one must pay attention to the subtle differences this gives to the quality and length of a note. These two aspects of paying attention to an object of consciousness are referred to in Buddhist psychology as *vitarka/vitakka* and *vicāra*, which can be rendered very approximately as 'application of thought' and 'examining'; these are the first two of the five limbs of *dhyāna*. When these two aspects of thinking are developed in the context of a particular skill we are trying to learn, a certain kind of quickening occurs: suddenly the mind is enlivened by its facility in the task at hand and begins to take pleasure in it; in consequence it begins to feel more at ease and content. This is the arising of the next two limbs of *dhyāna*, joy (*prīti/pīti*) and happiness (*sukha*). And as the mind feels happy and content it becomes less distracted and more absorbed in whatever it is doing. This is the arising of the fifth limb of *dhyāna*, namely 'one-pointedness of the mind' (*cittaikagratā/cittass'ekaggatā*) which is another term for 'concentration' or 'collectedness' (*samādhi*) itself. In the case of meditation practice, the mind ceases to seek out new objects of consciousness and becomes unified, resting on one object of consciousness without any tendency to move.

The signs and the stages of joy

The overcoming of the five hindrances and the coming into balance of these five limbs of *dhyāna* is, according to the later manuals, equivalent to the mind becoming settled in 'access' concentration, a state of mind on the threshold of *dhyāna*.[23] The manuals describe the stages leading to access concentration in two different ways (see Table 5). In effect, Upatissa and Buddhaghosa give an account in terms of three successive mental images or 'signs' (*nimitta*) and five stages of joy (*pīti*), while Asaṅga

TABLE 5. *Ascending stages of calm meditation*

meditational powers/higher knowledge/insight/formless attainments			
	4th *jhāna*		
	3rd *jhāna*		
	2nd *jhāna*		
	1st *jhāna*		*dhyāna*
suffusing joy	access concentration	counterpart sign	concentrating
			unifying
transporting joy			complete calming
			calming
descending joy		acquired sign	settling
			complete stilling
momentary joy			thorough stilling
			continued stilling
slight joy		preparatory sign	stilling the mind
5 stages of joy		3 'signs'	
	Buddhaghosa's stages of calm		Asaṅga's stages of calm

and Vasubandhu, the fathers of the Yogācāra tradition of Mahāyāna thought, detail nine stages of the settling of the mind (*citta-sthiti*), although they too make reference to the mental images (*pratibimba*) seen in meditation. I will not go into the details of the latter account here, but it has come to have great authority for Tibetan manuals of meditation.[24]

The concept of the *nimitta* is most easily explained with reference to meditation on the coloured disks. To undertake this kind of meditation the meditator should first prepare a disk of the appropriate colour. He should then set it up in front of him and, sitting down, begin to try to place his attention on the disk. The 'initial' or 'preparatory sign' (*parikamma-nimitta*) is the gross physical object. After some practice, the meditator will no longer need the actual physical object to contemplate, but will be able to visualize the object in his mind directly; the object of meditation is now the 'acquired sign' (*uggaha-nimitta*). As the meditator investigates and explores the acquired sign, there eventually arises the 'counterpart sign' (*paṭibhāga-nimitta*). The arising of the counterpart sign is concurrent with the attainment of access concentration. Whereas the acquired sign is a mental visualization of the physical object exactly as it appears—an eidetic image—the counterpart sign is a purified conceptual image free of any marks or blemishes. In the case of, say, the white or red disk the mind becomes completely absorbed in the concept of 'whiteness' or 'redness'. The arising of the counterpart sign is compared to the moon coming out from behind clouds.

I have already mentioned how, as the mind becomes familiar with the object of meditation, it is enlivened and begins to feel more at ease. The stages of this process are charted rather exactly in the list of the five kinds of joy. Thus the initial stage of 'slight joy' simply raises the hairs of the body; 'momentary joy' comes like repeated flashes of lightning, while 'descending joy' is stronger and washes over the body again and again and then subsides; 'transporting joy' has the power to lift the body into the air. A Thai meditation manual written at the turn of the last century describes it as follows:

> When transporting joy arises it is very strong; it makes the whole body shake and tremble. The meditator will fall to the left or to the right, bow down, clap hands and feet, sit down, stand up, and then run around filled with strange emotions. The meditators will cry and laugh and will not be able to shut their eyes or mouths. The veins will protrude and the blood feel hot and cold. The body will feel as if it is expanding and will levitate the length of a finger span, a cubit, an arm's length.[25]

We are counselled that such phenomena are not a sign of madness. Rather they indicate the progress of one's meditation practice. Eventually, the mind settles in 'suffusing joy'; this kind of joy pervades the whole body touching every part and is likened to water flooding into a rock cave. The spiritual (*nirāmisa*) joy felt in meditation is contrasted by the tradition with carnal (*sāmisa*) joy. The point here seems not so much to suggest sexual pleasure as a mere metaphor for spiritual joy, but rather to indicate that the increasing joy experienced as the mind gradually becomes settled and calm in meditation parallels in a real sense the stages of sexual excitement and enjoyment. Indeed, it is in such terms that some contemporary Buddhist monks describe their meditation experience.[26] The kinds of joy and 'signs' are in fact indicative of the variety of visual and physical phenomena that may accompany meditation.[27] Such phenomena seem to be something of a universal in the experience and lives of contemplatives from whatever religious tradition.

With the suppression of the five hindrances and the arising of the counterpart sign, or, in Asaṅga's terms, with the attainment of the ninth stage of the settling of the mind, consciousness reaches the relative peace and quiet and clarity of 'access concentration'. This is distinguished from absorption or *dhyāna* proper by virtue of the fact that, although fully present, the five limbs of *dhyāna* are weak and unstable and liable to fail the meditator who will then fall from the state of concentration rather like a child who takes his first tentative steps and then falls in a heap. With practice the meditator achieves skill in absorption. The most ancient description of this process is as follows:

> Abandoning these five hindrances which are defilements of the mind and weaken understanding, quite secluded from the objects of sense-desire and unwholesome states, he attains the first *jhāna*, a state of joy and happiness born of seclusion and accompanied by application of thought and examining. He soaks, pervades, fills and suffuses this very body with that joy and happiness born of seclusion such that there is no part of his whole body that is not suffused by that joy and happiness born of seclusion. It is as if a skilled bath attendant or his apprentice, having sprinkled bath-powder onto a bronze tray, were to knead it together evenly with drops of water such that the ball of bath-powder is covered and filled with moisture, is suffused with moisture within and without, and yet does not drip.[28]

The stages of dhyāna

The initial attainment of meditative absorption or *dhyāna* is characterized by the presence and balancing of five mental qualities, the limbs of *dhyāna*. But this initial attainment can be further refined. The process of refinement seems once again best understood by reference to some such process as that of learning to play a musical instrument. In the initial stage of competence the mind will still have to pay attention in the way described above: it will have to think consciously what to do. However, as one's facility develops the process will become increasingly automatic and unconscious—that is, the concert pianist does not have to think consciously where to put his hands or how to place her fingers, she just does it; nevertheless he is still fully aware of what he is doing. In much the same way, it seems, the meditator becomes able to attain states of concentration by simply adverting to the object of meditation. Attaining to states of concentration in this way without 'application of thought' or 'examining' is the characteristic of the second *dhyāna*, which thus has only three remaining limbs of *dhyāna*: joy, happiness, and one-pointedness of mind. From here the state of concentration can be further refined. Joy is experienced as something that in itself can disturb the mind. With the subsiding of joy one attains the third *dhyāna*. In a similar manner the meditator eventually lets go of happiness too, and finally attains the fourth *dhyāna*, a state of purified equanimity and balance.

The fourth *dhyāna* represents something of a turning point in the theory of the Buddhist path. In attaining the fourth *dhyāna* the process of stilling and calming the mind is essentially complete. Although the theory allows for the further refining and stilling of the mind in the meditative attainments known as the four formless (*arūpa*) attainments, these are presented as essentially modifications and refinements of the fourth *dhyāna*.[29] The fourth *dhyāna* also forms the basis for the development of various meditational powers: the *ṛddhis* (Pali *iddhi*) or 'higher knowledges' (*abhijñā/abhiññā*). The meditator is able to produce 'mind-made' bodies:

> Being one he becomes many, being many he becomes one; unhindered he passes into . . . an invisible state, through house-walls, through city-walls, and through mountains, as if through space; he goes down into the earth and comes up, as if through water; he goes over firm water, as if over earth; he travels through the sky cross-legged, as if he were a bird with wings; he touches and strokes with his hand the sun and

the moon . . . he has mastery with his body as far as the world of Brahmā.

Or he has knowledge of distant sounds, knowledge of the state of others' minds, knowledge of his own and others' past lives.[30]

The place of the various meditational powers in Buddhist practice is a question of some dispute.[31] Sometimes it is suggested by scholars that these powers are regarded as entirely peripheral and even disparaged in the earliest texts. There is no real evidence for such a view. In fact, although it is quite true that both the earliest texts and the later manuals do not present the meditational powers as an essential or necessary part of Buddhist practice, they nevertheless regard them as useful complements to the meditator's practice that may facilitate his practice of the higher stages of the path. More significantly, with the attainment of the final goal of awakening, skill in the meditational powers becomes a means for teaching and helping others. We thus find stories of the Buddha and his awakened disciples using their ability in meditational powers to aid others in the practice of the path. In other contexts they are simply presented as a natural by-product or consequence of the practice of calm meditation. Stories of such meditational powers are everywhere part of the Buddhist tradition; they are told of the tantric *siddhas* of Tibet, (see Chapter 10) and of the modern saints and practitioners of South-East Asia.[32]

The brahma-vihāras

One group of ancient meditation practices that the Theravādin meditation manuals accommodate to the scheme of *dhyānas* (but which it has been suggested were originally conceived as a path to complete awakening in their own right) are the four 'immeasurables' (*apramāṇa/appamañña*) or 'divine abidings' (*brahma-vihāras*).[33] The underlying motivation for the practice of the Buddhist path is generally understood to be the benefit and welfare of both oneself and others. Thus according to Theravādin Abhidharma the wholesome mind always contains the seed of 'loving kindness' (*maitrī/mettā*). It is this seed that can be taken as a subject of meditation and developed as a 'divine abiding'. Loving kindness is understood as the wish for all beings—oneself and others—to be well and happy. It is likened to the feelings of a mother towards her child. Loving kindness is the basis of the second 'divine abiding', compassion (*karuṇā*), which is the wish for the suffering of all beings to cease, and is likened to the feelings of a mother towards her sick child. The third divine abiding is 'sympathetic joy' (*muditā*), the delight in the good fortune of others and the wish for it to continue; this is likened to the feelings of a mother at her child's successes. The final divine abiding is 'equanimity' (*upekṣā/upekkhā*), a state of calm balance with regard to the sufferings and pleasures of beings; it is likened to the attitude of a mother to a child that is busy with its own affairs, indicating that equanimity should not be misunderstood as mere indifference.[34]

The four divine abidings are described as being developed by beginning with the wish for one's own well-being and happiness; this feeling is then gradually extended—through a dwelling, a town, across a country—to other beings, until the meditator dwells pervading all directions with a mind that is imbued with loving kindness and free from enmity.[35]

The stages of insight meditation

With the essential work of calming the mind completed, with the attainment of the fourth *dhyāna*, the meditator can focus fully on the development of insight and the wisdom that understands the four truths. Insight meditation aims at understanding three aspects of the nature of things: that they are impermanent and unstable (*anitya/anicca*), that they are unsatisfactory and imperfect (*duḥkha/dukkha*), and that they are not self (*anātman/anattā*). The philosophical nuances of these three terms may be expressed differently in the theoretical writings of various Buddhist schools, but in one way or another the higher stages of the Buddhist path focus on the direct understanding and seeing of these aspects of the world.

The culmination of calm meditation is the attainment of a state of calm where the mind rests in complete ease and contentment —either access concentration or one of the four *dhyānas*; the culmination of insight meditation is likewise a state of calm and ease—one of the *dhyānas* or also (according to the Sarvāstivādins) the state of access concentration. But the difference is that in the final stage of insight meditation the mind settles not with an abstract concept as its object, but in the direct seeing of suffering, its cause, its cessation, and the path leading to its cessation. There are thus two varieties of concentration—one achieved solely as a result of calm meditation, the other achieved as a result of both calm and insight meditation. The latter may be either ordinary (*laukika/lokiya*) or transcendent (*lokottara/lokuttara*) depending on whether it involves a direct experience of nirvāṅa or not.

The point at which a meditator actively turns to the contemplation of phenomena as impermanent, suffering, and not self is not fixed either for the ancient manuals or in modern practice. The theoretical models of the paths set out in the classical manuals of Upatissa, Buddhaghosa, and Vasubandhu accommodate two basic approaches: one in which the meditator practises the *dhyānas* fully before turning to the development of insight and one in which the meditator attempts to cultivate insight with only a minimal basis of calm.

Just as the manuals provide various schemata for the stages of calm meditation, so also they provide different accounts of the stages of insight meditation. After Buddhaghosa, the Theravādin tradition works primarily with a system of seven 'purifications' (*visuddhi*) alongside a series of eight (or sometimes ten) knowledges. From the north Indian tradition, and especially the writings of Vasubandhu and Asaṅga, the Mahāyāna traditions of China and Tibet inherit a system of five paths (*mārga*) and four 'stages of penetrative insight' (*nirvedha-bhāgīya*) which comes to be set alongside a system of ten 'levels' (*bhūmi*) of the bodhisattva paths to buddhahood (see Tables 6 and 7).

The scheme of the seven purifications

In the system of seven purifications, the first two ('purification of conduct' and 'purification of consciousness') are concerned with good conduct and the practice of calm meditation in the manner just described. Together these two purifications are seen as the roots for the five purifications directly concerned with insight. The first of these is 'purification of view', also referred to as 'the analysis of formations'. At this stage the practitioner is concerned with beginning to break down his sense of a substantial self. To this end he contemplates any given experience in terms of the five aggregates, or the six senses and their respective objects. The purpose here is to impress upon the mind that, when we look at any particular experience, what we find is not a substantial person or being but just mind and body in dependence upon each other. Like two sheaves of grass propped up against each other, if we remove one the other falls. But in undertaking this practice we are warned to be careful. Some may be unresponsive to this teaching, but others may go too far and think that the task is to annihilate themselves.

Having established a sense of experience as subsisting in the interdependence of mind and body, the practitioner moves on to the fourth purification, that of 'crossing over doubt'. The practice at this stage is referred to as 'comprehension of conditions'. In the previous stage the practitioner contemplated the interdependence of mind and body in any given experience; here he broadens the meditation to take in the past, present, and future. In other words, the practice moves from the contemplation of the particular to the general, and one begins to see that what is in operation is a universal 'law'—the law of dependent arising; one begins to see that, just as mind and body are interdependent now in the present, so they have been in the past and so they must be in the future. One sees that mind and body, although existing, have not been created or brought into being out of nothing by some creator God. Thus there is no particular beginning to their existence and no end. The law of dependent arising alone is a sufficient explanation of their existence. Direct insight into this process is presented as deeply affecting the meditator. His outlook on the world is profoundly changed. His understanding of the teaching has ceased to be purely theoretical and become a matter of direct experience which cannot be denied. Thus the meditator is said to cross over doubt and thereby complete the fourth purification to become a 'lesser attainer of the stream'.

The meditator now moves on to a more committed and deeper level of insight practice in which he contemplates the world as made up of various categories and groupings of phenomena that are all alike impermanent, suffering, and not self. This results in knowledge based on 'taking dharmas in groups'; from this he passes on to 'the contemplation of rise and fall'. At this stage he begins to experience directly a world made up not, as we normally assume, of substantial beings and objects, but of patterns of events rising and falling, coming into existence, and passing out of existence. A feeling for the meditator's experience at this stage is well evoked by the images (drawn from the earlier texts) that Buddhaghosa gives in this connection: the world is no longer experienced as consisting of things that are lasting and solid but rather as something that vanishes almost as soon as it appears—like dew drops at sunrise, like a bubble on water, like a line drawn on water, like a mustard-seed placed on the point of an awl, like a flash of lightning; things in themselves lack substance and always elude one's grasp—like a mirage, a conjuring trick, a dream, the circle formed by a whirling firebrand, a fairy city, foam, or the trunk of a banana tree.[36]

This experience is profoundly peaceful and with it the mind begins to settle into a state of peace close to *jhāna*. Drawing on an earlier list, Buddhaghosa describes the mind at this time as characterized by ten qualities: illumination, knowledge, joy, tranquillity, happiness, commitment, resolve, alertness, equanimity, and, significantly, attachment. Because of the presence of the last these ten qualities are collectively referred to as 'the ten defilements of insight'. What is being said here is that the mind being so deeply affected by its experience grasps at it and takes it for the experience of awakening itself. In other words, the practitioner mistakenly concludes that he has reached the end of the path. The texts warn that the meditator may live for many years convinced that he or she has attained arhatship. Only when some experience—like the arising of strong anger or fear—dissuades him or her from this view does the meditator complete the fifth purification of 'knowing and seeing what is the path and not the path'; the meditator then passes to the sixth purification of 'knowing and seeing the way'.

So the meditator returns to the practice of the contemplation of the rise and fall of dharmas, which had been disabled by the ten defilements of insight. Now, like the lion, king of beasts, who finds delight, not when put in a golden cage, but only in the three-thousand-league expanse of the Himalayas, the meditator sees delight not in the pleasant rebirths of the sense, form, or formless realms, but only in his three contemplations of impermanence, suffering, and no self.[37] In addition to the knowledge (1) of seeing the rise and fall (of dharmas), the sixth purification is said to embrace seven other knowledges, making eight in all: the knowledge (2) of contemplating breaking up (of dharmas), (3) of the presence of danger, (4) of contemplating distress, (5) of contemplating disenchantment, (6) of the desire for release, (7) of contemplating with discernment, (8) of equanimity with regard to formations. This sequence of knowledges may be illustrated by the story of a man who set out to catch a fish:

Taking his fishing net, he sank it into the water. When he put his hand into the mouth of the net and seized hold of a snake by the neck, he thought he had caught a fish and was delighted. Thinking that he had caught a big fish, he lifted it out to take a look but when he saw the three markings and realised it was a snake he became frightened. Seeing that he was in danger, he felt distaste for what he had grasped and wished to be released. Devising a way of getting free, he unwrapped [the coils] from his arm, beginning with the tip of the tail, and then, raising his arm and swinging the snake round his head two or three times in order to weaken it, he flung it away thinking, 'Be gone damn snake!' Then without delay he climbed up the bank of the pool and stood there looking back at the way he had come thinking, 'Goodness! I have escaped from the mouth of a huge snake!'[38]

A person's initial satisfaction with his sense of his own individuality is likened to the man's initial delight at grasping a snake. A meditator's seeing the three marks of impermanence, suffering, and no self through (1) seeing the rise and fall and (2) the breaking up of phenomena is like the man's seeing the three markings on the snake. Just as the man became frightened, so the meditator (3) knows the presence of danger; just as he knew fear, so the meditator (4) contemplates his distress; just as he felt distaste for what he had grasped, so the meditator (5) contemplates disenchantment; just as he desired to be free of the snake, so too the meditator (6) desires release; and just as he devised a means of letting go, so the meditator (7) discerns all dharmas to be impermanent, suffering, and no self such that they cannot appear to him again as lasting, pleasant, beautiful, and self. So with the eighth knowledge, all formations are seen as empty (*suñña*).

The eight knowledges culminate at a point where the mind is once more settled and at peace. One should not be misled by the rather elaborate and complex descriptions that are given of what happens next. In part they seem intended to present the profound and subtle nature of an experience which happens very rapidly. With the mind having reached a point of balance, it settles in transcendent *jhāna* and in a moment it directly sees and understands suffering, its arising, its cessation, and the way leading to its cessation; it directly sees and experiences nirvāṇa. According to the Theravādin sources this understanding quite literally occurs in one moment: the conditioned world that is saṃsāra (suffering and its cause) and nirvāṇa and the transcendent path (cessation and the path leading to cessation) are finally fully known in a single flash of transcendent insight and peace. This is the culmination of previous practice and this moment is itself termed 'path' (*magga*); in this moment all the conditions that contributed to the development of the path are at once fulfilled. Frequently these conditions are listed as thirty-seven in all: four establishings of mindfulness, four right endeavours, four bases of success in concentration, five spiritual faculties, five spiritual powers, seven 'limbs' of awakening, and the eightfold path itself. The 'path' moment is understood as being immediately followed by a transcendent *jhāna* of similar qualities, this time termed 'fruit' (*phala*).

The theoretical models of the path allow a number of possibilities concerning precisely what happens when the mind settles in transcendent *dhyāna*. In the first place, the mind may

TABLE 6. *The stages of insight according to Buddhaghosa's Visuddhimagga*

PURIFICATION	KNOWLEDGE
7. by knowing and seeing	of the paths & fruits of stream attainment etc.
	of the lineage [of the Noble Ones]
	conforming [to the truth]
	8. of equanimity with regard to formations
	7. of contemplating with discernment
6. by knowing and seeing the way	6. of desire for release
	5. of contemplating disenchantment
	4. of contemplating distress
	3. of the presence of danger
	2. of contemplating breaking up
5. by knowing and seeing what is path and not path	1. of seeing the rise and fall [of dharmas]
(10 defilements of insight)	taking in groups
4. by crossing over doubt (the lesser stream-attainer)	(comprehension of conditions)
3. of view	(analysis of formations)
2. of consciousness	
1. of conduct	

settle at a level of concentration equivalent to any one of the four *dhyānas*. When the mind settles in transcendent *dhyāna*, defilements are not merely temporarily suppressed as in ordinary *dhyāna*, they are once and for all eradicated. The attainment of the transcendent path thus changes one into a different person in the most radical of senses: one ceases to be an ordinary person (*pṛthagjana/puthujjana*) and becomes one of the nobles (*ārya/ariya*), that is one of those who has directly seen the four truths.

From an early period the texts seem to have envisaged that the attaining of the transcendent path may not necessarily eradicate all defilements immediately. Basically there are four possibilities, depending on which defilements are actually eradicated. The possibilities are usually set out with reference to the list of ten bonds or fetters (*saṃyojana*) which bind one to rebirth (see above, pp. 72–3). By the abandoning of the first three fetters one becomes a 'stream-attainer' (*srotāpanna/sotāpanna*), that is, one whose final awakening is assured within a maximum of seven rebirths. By the abandoning of the first three and the permanent weakening of the next two one becomes a 'once-returner' (*sakṛdāgāmin/sakadāgāmin*), that is, one whose final awakening is assured and who will be reborn as a human being no more than once. By the complete abandoning of the five lower fetters one becomes a 'non-returner' (*anāgāmin*), that is, one who at death will not be reborn as a human being but in one of five 'Pure Abodes' (realms corresponding to the fourth *dhyāna*) where he will gain final awakening. By the complete abandoning of all ten fetters one becomes an arhat, never to be subject to rebirth again. The attainment of any of these four successive paths of stream-attainment, once-return, non-return, and arhatship constitutes the seventh purification of 'knowledge and seeing'.

What precisely governs which of these four states is attained is not clear in the earliest texts. Two basic possibilities seem to be envisaged: either (1) that, at the first arising of the transcendent path, depending on individual circumstances, one may attain any one of the four states immediately; or (2) that one must attain each state successively, either in one life or over a series of lives. The interpretation of the later tradition is also not entirely clear. Buddhaghosa seems closer to the latter understanding, although one may attain each state in such rapid succession that one in effect goes straight from being an ordinary being to being an arhat. As we shall presently see, Vasubandhu seems closer to the former.

The scheme of the five paths

The classical north Indian manuals of Vasubandhu and Asaṅga map out the path according to a system of five paths: the path of equipment (*sambhāra-mārga*), the path of application (*prayoga-mārga*), the path of seeing (*darśana-mārga*), the path of development (*bhāvanā-mārga*), and the path of completion (*niṣṭhā-mārga*) or of the adept (*aśaikṣa-mārga*).[39] The path of equipment covers the general basis of the spiritual life in the form of faith, generosity, good conduct, and the preliminary development of calm and insight. The path of application consists of the further development of calm and particularly insight. The path of seeing involves a direct seeing of the four truths in the manner of the seventh purification of Buddhaghosa's scheme. The path of development is twofold: either ordinary (*laukika*) or transcendent (*lokottara*). The ordinary path of development consists in mastery of calm, the attainment of the *dhyānas* and formless attainments. The transcendent path of development consists in the final eradication of attachment to these meditative attainments and the realms of the cosmos that correspond to them. The ordinary path of development may thus precede or succeed the paths of application and seeing: in the case of a practitioner who develops the *dhyānas* before turning to insight it precedes, and in the case of one who develops them after stream-attainment (accomplished by the path of seeing) it succeeds. The path of completion is equivalent to the final attainment of arhatship. As we shall see in Chapter 9, in the Mahāyāna this scheme of five paths becomes the basis for the ten stages of the bodhisattva path (see Table 7).

In his *Abhidharmakośa*, Vasubandhu describes the immediate preparation for the path of application in terms of the practice of calm meditation based either on meditation on the different types of 'ugliness' or on mindfulness of breathing. The practitioner develops one of these until he or she attains concentration (*samādhi*); Vasubandhu does not specify of what degree but no doubt access or *dhyāna* is intended. The meditator then turns the mind towards insight by means of the practice of the four 'establishings of mindfulness' (*smṛtyupasthāna/satipaṭṭhāna*). This is an extremely old and important set of meditations based on different contemplations: of the body, of feeling, of the mind, and fourthly of physical and mental processes (*dharma*).[10]

Essentially what is assumed by the practice of the four 'establishings of mindfulness' is that one attains a certain degree of mental clarity and calm and then turns one's attention first of all to watching various kinds of physical phenomena and activities,

TABLE 7. *The scheme of the five paths and the ten bodhisattva stages*

WHOLESOME ROOT CONNECTED WITH PENETRATIVE INSIGHT	PATH	BODHISATTVA STAGE	PERFECTION
	of the adept	Buddhahood	
	of cultivation	10. cloud of Dharma	10. knowledge
	of cultivation	9. excellent	9. strength
	of cultivation	8. unshaking	8. determination
	of cultivation	7. far-reaching	7. skill in means
	of cultivation	6. face-to-face	6. wisdom
	of cultivation	5. invincible	5. dhyāna
	of cultivation	4. resplendent	4. vigour
	of cultivation	3. radiant	3. patient acceptance
	of cultivation	2. stainless	2. good conduct
	of seeing	1. joyful	1. generosity
highest ordinary state	of application		
summit	of application		
acceptance	of application		
initial glimmering	of application		
	of equipment		

then to watching feeling as pleasant, unpleasant, or neutral, then to watching one's general mental state; and finally, at the fourth stage, to integrating the previous three stages so that finally one watches the totality of physical and mental processes. This final stage is equivalent to watching the five aggregates: the world is seen as consisting simply in the interplay of five groups of physical and mental events.

Vasubandhu presents this set of contemplations as involving a gradual movement from the gross to the subtle. His presentation corresponds closely to Buddhaghosa's presentation of the insight practice involved at the stage of the 'purification of view'. As the meditator contemplates the world of dharmas his mind eventually settles in a state of concentration which involves an initial direct seeing of the four truths. This attainment is described as the 'heat' or 'glow' (*uṣmagata*) of wisdom and it marks the first stage of the path of application. The attainment of 'the glow' is the first of four 'stages of penetrating insight' (*nirvedha-bhāgīya*); the subsequent three stages are known as summit (*mūrdhan*), acceptance (*kṣānti*), and the highest ordinary state (*laukikāgra-dharma*).

The first three of the four stages of penetrating insight are each divided into three stages of weak, medium, and strong, making ten stages of penetrative insight in all. These stages represent successive attainments of states of concentration through the practice of the fourth manifestation of mindfulness in which the meditator's direct understanding of the four truths in all their aspects is gradually deepened. The culmination of this process is a single moment of insight—the highest 'ordinary' state. This is immediately followed by a direct vision of the four truths in sixteen aspects—'the path of seeing'. In contrast to the Theravādins, the Sarvāstivādins suggest that it takes sixteen 'thought' moments to see the truths. This appears to be a theoretically constructed notion, in part connected with the idea that, since one can only know one thing at a time, one could not directly know saṃsāra and nirvāṇa (suffering and its cessation, the conditioned and the unconditioned) in a single moment of thought. Interestingly the Theravādins suggest one can. But the length of a moment of thought is understood as so short that even for the Sarvāstivādins the path of seeing is still understood as in effect instantaneous. Strictly the path of seeing endures for only fifteen moments, and is once more understood as the fulfilment of all the thirty-seven conditions contributing to awakening; the sixteenth moment is taken as belonging to the transcendent path of development and constitutes the attainment of the transcendent 'fruit'.

What happens in the attainment of the transcendent path and fruit is said to depend on one's previous practice. The meditator who has previously mastered the attainment of the *dhyānas* (by the ordinary path of development) and thereby already established a certain ability to let go of craving as far as the world of the five senses is concerned will, in the path of seeing, once and for all abandon that craving and become either a once-returner or a never-returner. The meditator who has not previously mastered the *dhyānas* eradicates by the path of seeing the grosser defilements associated with craving for the world of the five senses and thereby becomes a stream-attainer. By the successive attainment of the various *dhyānas* and abandoning of subtler and subtler kinds of attachment by means of the ordinary and transcendent paths of development, the meditator subsequently becomes a once-returner and non-returner. Finally by means of the path of 'completion' or the 'adept' and the attainment of the diamond-like concentration, he or she eradicates all defilements and becomes an arhat.

All these lists of stages can seem to the modern mind like scholastic excess. But what they seem intended to indicate is the gradual and cumulative process of the spiritual path which is kept going by the meditator's repeated and persistent practice of essentially the same exercise: contemplating the world in terms of dharmas or watching the rise and fall, the coming and going of phenomena in dependence upon each other. Gradual though the process is, it is distinguished by various landmarks which the lists of stages are intended to indicate; what is more it culminates in a more or less sudden and immediate understanding of the world which has the effect of changing one for good. Some of the ancient similes for the progress of meditation practice evoke the experience of this rather more vividly than all our lists of stages.

As a mason or a mason's apprentice, when inspecting the handle of his chisel, sees the impressions of his fingers and thumb and yet has no knowledge that so much of the handle has been worn away on that day, so much the day before, so much previously, but when the last bit has been worn away then he has knowledge—just so the monk who lives engaged in the practice of meditation has no knowledge that so much of the defilements has been worn away that day, so much the day before, so much previously, but when the last bit has been worn away then he has knowledge.[41]

The relationship of calm and insight

We have seen how developed Buddhist theory envisages two basic possibilities as far as meditation is concerned. In the first place, by the practice of calm meditation one abandons the gross for the sake of the subtle. That is, by seeing certain experiences as disturbing, the mind seeks peace in the subtler and subtler experiences of the *dhyānas*. This has the effect of weakening attachment to experiences tied up with the world of the five senses, but in subtler experiences there lurk subtler attachments which may not be recognized for what they are. So although defilements are controlled they are not rooted out. In the second place, by the practice of insight meditation one sees experiences as inherently flawed because of the characteristics of impermanence, suffering, and no self, and thus, instead of letting go of the gross merely to grasp at the subtle, one lets go of them completely. In this unqualified letting go of the conditioned one experiences the unconditioned, nirvāṇa. Yet in practice in order to see things as inherently characterized by impermanence, suffering, and no self one's mind must be clear and undisturbed; more significantly in order to relinquish the subtlest forms of attachment one must see the subtle experiences of the *dhyānas* as impermanent, suffering, and not self; and to achieve this one must generally first of all actually experience them. In this way the practice of calm and insight meditation are bound up together.

Although the theoretical position of the classical meditation manuals seems basically clear, the precise relationship of calm meditation and insight meditation is a live issue for both contemporary historical scholarship and contemporary Theravāda practice. Let me begin with the latter issue. Within contemporary Theravāda practice there is a broad movement of insight meditation that has had considerable influence in the West. The tendency of this movement is to take the view that since the *dhyānas* are only impermanent, relatively pleasant states, the meditator should not strive to attain *dhyāna* but aim at developing insight from the outset. Moreover, there is a Buddhist tradition of seeing the highest understanding of other religions as based on misinterpreted *dhyāna* experiences. From this perspective, the *dhyānas* can thus even be seen as in a sense not characteristically 'Buddhist', since they can be attained in the absence of the liberating insight which brings direct knowledge of nirvāṇa. At the academic level this kind of thinking is reflected in an authoritative modern scholarly treatment of Theravāda meditation by Winston King that presents the *dhyānas* as taken over by the Buddhist tradition from pre-existing Indian brahmanical yogic practices.[42] What Buddhism added was the practice of insight meditation.

In a controversial but at least in part convincing study, Johannes Bronkhorst has argued precisely the opposite: what is innovative and distinctive about early Buddhist meditation is the attainment of peaceful and pleasant states through the practice of the *dhyānas*.[43] There is no evidence that this kind of meditation existed in India prior to the appearance of Buddhism, and non-Buddhist Indian writings conceive of meditation or yoga not as something peaceful and pleasant, but rather as a painful austerity which burns off accumulated karma and thereby eventually removes the cause of further rebirths and thus brings liberation from saṃsāra.

Bronkhorst, like a number of scholars such as La Vallée Poussin, Frauwallner, Schmithausen, Vetter, Griffiths, and Gombrich, goes on to see certain inconsistencies in the early texts' presentation of, on the one hand, the *dhyānas* as the path of meditation leading to arhatship and, on the other hand, discriminating insight into the four truths, dependent arising and the three marks as the way to arhatship.[44] For such scholars what underlies the early texts is a certain tension between the advocates of the practice of meditation in the form of the *dhyānas* and the advocates of a more intellectual and rational approach. The later systematic accounts of the path would thus represent a compromise which tries to reconcile what were in origin quite different conceptions of the nature of the Buddhist path.

The arguments and textual analyses of these scholars are complex and often extremely philologically sophisticated and I cannot begin to review them here; a general comment will have to suffice. That some tension between rival approaches underlies the texts may be so. Yet, as Lance Cousins has indicated, from the point of view of the later manuals it is a mistake to see the tension in terms of *either* the practice of calm *or* the practice of insight: the question for them is rather how much calm and how much insight are required at the various stages of the path.[45] Even if there is an increased willingness to countenance the possibility of complete awakening without the the prior basis of the *dhyānas*, the later manuals are all agreed that the meditator needs both, and that the culmination of the path consists in a meditation attainment that consists in the coming together of calm and insight. To see a certain tension in early Buddhism between those who emphasize the importance of the *dhyānas* and those who advocate the development of insight without the prior basis of *dhyāna* is not unreasonable. Such a tension does seem to underlie the later systematic accounts and is also apparent among contemporary practitioners. We also perhaps see such a tension reflected elsewhere, in the history of Mahāyāna Buddhism: the Mādhyamika approach to 'emptiness' appears more orientated to insight in comparison to the Yogācārin focus on the stages of calm and the deep, hidden levels of the mind; similarly, in Tibetan Buddhism, the dGelugs emphasis on analytic meditation on emptiness contrasts with the rNying ma practice of *rdzogs chen* (see Chapters 9 and 10). Yet it is not necessary to see such tensions as originating in fundamentally opposed conceptions of the nature of the Buddhist path. Such a view assumes, in part at least, a rather intellectual and rational conception of the nature of insight meditation. It is also perhaps to confuse the issue with another tension in the history of the practice of Buddhist monasticism: the tension between the life of the monk as a forest-dwelling meditator and a town-dwelling scholar (see above pp. 95–100).

The systematic and theoretical accounts of the path that I have focused on in this chapter may not always represent the final word on meditation practice for practitioners today. Some schools of China and Tibet have adapted them to bring them in line with certain principles of Mahāyāna Buddhism; others such as the Ch'an and Zen schools on the surface apparently ignore such elaborate theoretical accounts. But in one way or another these systematic accounts and the ways of thinking that underlie them have influenced the forms of Buddhist meditation practice of whatever school.

8

The Abhidharma

The Higher Teaching

Stories, legends, texts, and authors

It is told by some that after the Buddha gained awakening he sat beneath the tree of awakening for seven days contemplating the Dharma which he had penetrated. Then he got up from his seat and for seven days he stood gazing with unblinking eyes at the seat thinking, 'On this seat I gained knowledge.' At that time the gods thought that perhaps the Buddha still had something to accomplish as it appeared he had not abandoned attachment to the seat of awakening. So the Buddha performed the miracle of the pairs, emitting streams of fire and water from every pore of his body. Then for seven days he walked up and down between the seat of awakening and where he had been standing. Now, twenty-one days after he had gained awakening, he sat in the House of Jewels, so called because here, over seven days, he conceived the seven books of the Abhidharma—the jewels of the Dharma. On the seventh day, when he began to contemplate the contents of the seventh book, the Great Book, his body began to emit rays of six colours: blue, yellow, red, white, maroon, clear. And as he contemplated this infinite and immeasurable Dharma, the rays emitted from his body lit up the earth, the waters, and the skies. They lit up the realms of the gods and flooded beyond throughout billions of world systems.

The Buddha did not, it seems, immediately teach the Dharma in this full form in which he had conceived it while seated in the House of Jewels. Many years later in response to a challenge from teachers of other schools the Buddha once again performed the miracle of the pairs, emitting streams of fire and water from every pore of his body. Having performed this miracle he considered what previous buddhas had done after performing this miracle. It came to his mind that they had ascended to the heaven of the Thirty-Three gods to teach the Dharma to their mothers. And so, in keeping with this tradition, the Buddha ascended to the heaven of the Thirty-Three gods and there, seated beneath the Coral Tree on the rock called Paṇḍukambala, the throne of the great god Sakka, for the three months of the rains he taught his mother and the assembled gods the seven books of the Abhidharma.

At that time the Buddha would create a mind-made Buddha to carry on teaching while he went to gather alms food in the distant land of Uttarakuru. Then he would sit down on the shores of Lake Anotatta, eat his meal, and retire to sit in meditation in a forest of sandal trees. And Sariputta, the disciple chief in wisdom, would come and the Buddha would teach him the method of Abhidharma. Sāriputta in turn taught it to five hundred of his own pupils. They say that many aeons ago in the time of the Buddha Kassapa they had been born as bats and, hanging in a cave, they had one day heard the sound of two monks reciting the Abhidharma. Of course, as bats they were unable to understand the meaning of what they heard, yet even so it seems that the very sound of the Abhidharma left an impression. So they were reborn in the world of the gods, where they remained for the vast interval of time between one Buddha and the next. Finally they were born as men and became monks and the pupils of Sāriputta, who, teaching them the seven books, made them masters of Abhidharma.[1]

The term *abhidharma* (Pali *abhidhamma*) means approximately 'higher' or 'further' Dharma. For Buddhist tradition it refers to two things: first, a set of books regarded by most ancient schools as 'the word of the Buddha' and as such forming the contents of the third basket of scriptures, the Abhidharma Piṭaka; secondly, the particular system of thought and method of exposition set out in those books and their commentaries. The above legend of the genesis of the Abhidharma is drawn from Theravādin sources, but the sentiment is indicative of a more general traditional attitude to the Abhidharma.[2] The Abhidharma is thought out and taught only by a buddha. Hearing it being recited—even without understanding it—can have a far-reaching effect. The Abhidharma catches the very essence of the Dharma, which means that its sound can operate almost as a charm or spell.

The suggestion in the legend that the form in which the Abhidharma has come down to us has been mediated through the person of Śāriputra perhaps reflects the historical reality that the canonical Abhidharma works must be regarded as somewhat later than the sūtra material of the Nikāyas/Āgamas, and in part explains why some schools of thought, such as the Sautrāntikas ('those who follow the teaching of the sūtras'), later declined to give the Abhidharma works the status of 'the word of the Buddha' (see Chapter 2). The two canonical Abhidharma collections that survive are those of the Theravādins and the Sarvāstivādins, the latter only in Chinese translation. All the books of the Theravādin Abhidharma, with the exception of the *Yamaka*, have been translated into English; the Sarvāstivādin canonical Abhidharma works remain untranslated into a modern European language.

Both these collections consist of seven books but their titles and contents vary considerably. None the less they share two tasks in common. In the first place they attempt to give a systematic and exhaustive account of the world by breaking it down into its constituent physical and mental events (*dharma/dhamma*). Secondly, they both contain works which address various points of dispute that arise out of the preceding exercise. Although the status of the Abhidharma as word of the Buddha may have been challenged, the stamp that the Abhidharma systems, methods, and debates have left on subsequent Buddhist thought is indisputable. They provide the terms of reference and determine the agenda which result in the Mahāyāna schools of Madhyamaka and Yogācāra.

Apart from the canonical Abhidharma, a great variety of Abhidharma manuals exist. These manuals aim at introducing the essentials of the complicated canonical systems. For the Theravādins, Buddhaghosa's comprehensive *Visuddhimagga* contains much of their Abhidharma system; chapters 14 to 17 form a self-contained

TABLE 8. *The Abhidharma Piṭaka*

THE ABHIDHAMMA OF THE THERAVĀDINS	THE ABHIDHARMA OF THE SARVĀSTIVĀDINS
Dhammasaṅgaṇi ('Enumeration of Dhammas')	*Jñānaprasthāna* of Kātyāyana ('The Foundation of Knowledge')
Vibhaṅga ('Analysis')	*Prakaraṇapāda* of Vasumitra ('The Treatise')
Dhātukathā ('Discourse on Elements')	*Vijñānakāya* of Devakṣema/Devaṣarman ('Compendium of Consciousness')
Puggalapaññatti ('Designation of Persons')	*Dharmaskandha* of Maudgalyāyana/Śāriputra ('Compendium of *Dharmas*')
Kathāvatthu of Moggaliputtatissa ('Points of Discussion')	*Prajñaptiśāstra* of Maudgalyāyana/Mahākātyāyana ('Manual of Concepts')
Yamaka ('Pairs')	*Dhātukāya* of Vasumitra/Pūrṇa ('Compendium of Elements')
Paṭṭhāna ('Conditions')	*Saṃgītiparyāya* of Mahākauṣṭhila/Śāriputra ('Discourse on the Collective Recitation')

section entitled 'the ground of understanding' (*paññā-bhūmi*) which is essentially an introduction to the Theravādin Abhidharma. A more direct introduction to the canonical Theravādin Abhidharma is the *Abhidhammāvatāra* ('Introduction to Abhidharma') written in the fifth century by Buddhadatta, a contemporary of Buddhaghosa. But the most commonly used introductory manual in the countries of Theravāda Buddhism today is a twelfth-century work of Anuruddha, the *Abhidhammattha-saṅgaha* ('Compendium of the Topics of Abhidharma').

In the second or third century CE, Sarvāstivādin Ābhidharmikas ('exponents of Abhidharma') in north-west India began compiling an authoritative Abhidharma commentary or *vibhāṣā*. This survives in Chinese translation in three different recensions. Of particular influence were the views of the Kāśmīra Sarvāstivādins, who are often simply referred to as the Vaibhāṣikas (exponents of the Vibhāṣā). In the early centuries of the Christian era the Sarvāstivādins also produced a number of summary Abhidharma manuals such as the **Abhidharma-hṛdaya* ('The Heart of Abhidharma') of Dharmaśrī and the **Abhidharmāmṛtarasa* ('The Taste of the Deathless') of Ghoṣaka.[3] But by far the most influential manual for later Chinese and Tibetan Buddhism is Vasubandhu's *Abhidharmakośa* ('Treasury of Abhidharma'). The influence of this work is to be explained in part by the fact that for the Chinese and Tibetans its author is none other than Vasubandhu, brother of Asaṅga and author of some of the seminal treatises of the Yogācāra, one of the principal schools of Mahāyāna Buddhist thought. This traditional view has been disputed by modern scholarship, notably by Frauwallner, who has argued that the Mahāyānist Vasubandhu, author of Yogācārin treatises, lived in the fourth century CE and must be distinguished from the Vasubandhu who is author of the *Abhidharmakośa* and lived in the early part of the fifth century. The question is unresolved.[4] Whoever he was, Vasubandhu's *Kośa* gives a masterly survey of Sarvāstivāda-Vaibhāṣika Abhidharma supplemented by his own critique of certain positions, which often betrays a Sautrāntika sympathy. Such was the authority of the *Abhidharmakośa* that Paramārtha's and Hsüan-tsang's Chinese translations (in the sixth and seventh centuries respectively) led to the formation of a significant, if relatively short-lived, school of Sino-Japanese Buddhism named, after the text, the Kośa or, in Chinese and Japanese, the Chü-shê/Kusha school. Vasubandhu's criticism of certain Vaibhāṣika positions prompted further works that attempted to address his points of criticism, such as Saṅghabhadra's **Abhidharma-samaya-pradīpika* ('Illumination of Abhidharma') and **Nyāyānusāra* ('In Accordance with Method'), and the anonymous *Abhidharma-dīpa* ('The Lamp of Abhidharma').

A number of Indian Abhidharma texts that belong neither to the Theravādin nor to the Sarvāstivādin Abhidharma also survive in Chinese translation, principally the *Śāriputrābhidharma-śāstra* ('Treatise on the Abhidharma of Śāriputra') and Harivarman's **Satya-siddhi-śāstra* ('Treatise on the Demonstration of Truth'), but in such texts we do not have a full system in the manner of the Theravādin or Sarvāstivādin Abhidharma. A third complete system of Abhidharma is, however, elaborated in certain of the works of the Mahāyāna Yogācāra tradition, principally in Asaṅga's *Abhidharma-samuccaya* ('Compendium of Abhidharma') and in Hsüan-tsang's commentary on Vasubandhu's *Triṃśikā* ('Thirty Verses'), the *Ch'eng-wei-shih lun* or *Vijñapti-mātratā-siddhi* ('Demonstration of the Theory of Mind Only'). While this Yogācārin Abhidharma owes much to the Sarvāstivādin system, it also incorporates and adapts certain aspects of other Abhidharma systems in order to present a complete Abhidharma in accordance with a Mahāyānist outlook and the view that mind (*vijñapti*) alone is ultimately 'real'.

The Abhidharma as a system of Buddhist thought

As a system of thought Abhidharma is to be contrasted with Sūtrānta (Pali *suttanta*), the system of the sūtras or discourses of the Buddha. Sūtrānta is regarded as the application of the principles of the Buddha's teaching to a particular situation: each sūtra preserved in the Nikāya/Āgama collections is a discourse delivered by the Buddha, or one of his disciples, at a particular time, in a particular place, and to a particular person or group. Sūtrānta teachings are embellished with poetic language, with similes and metaphors that inspire the listener. The Abhidharma method, in contrast, presents the Buddha's teachings without making concessions to time or place or audience, and in technical terms that are precisely defined to ensure analytical exactitude. The contrast between the methods of Sūtrānta and Abhidharma coincides in part with other distinctions sometimes made in the texts between types of teachings. Some teachings are said to be expressed in terms whose meaning must be determined (*neyārtha/neyyattha*), while others are expressed in terms whose meaning is already determined (*nītārtha/nītattha*). Some teachings are expressed in conventional terms (*saṃvṛti/sammuti*), others are expressed in ultimate terms (*paramārtha/paramattha*). The point of these distinctions is to draw attention to the fact that, as we have seen in Chapter 6, if we come across a Buddhist text that talks in terms of persons and selves, we should not immediately assume that the teaching of no self is being undermined; it is rather that that particular text is talking in conventional terms whose ultimate meaning needs drawing out. The later tradition would regard the Nikāya/Āgama collections of sūtras as in fact containing teachings of both kinds.

What is distinctive about the Abhidharma is that it is an attempt to give a comprehensive statement of the Buddha's teachings exclusively in ultimate terms. A useful analogy, I think, for the relationship between the Abhidharma and the Sūtrānta is that of the relationship between a grammar book of a language and the language as spoken and used. In the same way as a grammar book aims at giving a bare account of how a particular language works, its structure and forms of expression, based on observation of the actual use of that language, so the Abhidharma is an attempt to lay bare and describe accurately and precisely, allowing for all circumstances and eventualities, the underlying structure of the Dharma as found in the discourses of the Buddha. Indeed, the pages of certain Abhidharma texts, with their lists of terms and definitions, might be mistaken for the pages of a grammar book, and in the same way that reading a grammar book may not seem the most inspiring of pastimes, so too may the study of Abhidharma. Yet a good grammar book may impress one with its clear and intelligent account of a language; it may bring one to a better understanding of that language and equip one to recognize unexpected forms of words and modes of expression. In a similar way the sheer cleverness and intricacy of aspects of the Abhidharma is impressive in itself. Indeed, one scholar has described the seventh book of the Theravādin Abhidharma, the *Paṭṭhāna* ('Causal Relations'), as 'one of the most amazing productions of the human mind'.[5] Moreover it is the study of Abhidharma that allows the practitioner to extrapolate from the peculiarities of his own experience to the peculiarities of another's. These days the study of grammar may not be very fashionable and some may point out that grammarians and lexicographers do not always make the best poets, writers, or orators. But just as the theoretical understanding of language cannot be achieved without the study of grammar, so the theoretical understanding of Buddhism must be based in the study of some form of Abhidharma.

Abhidharma represents the theoretical counterpart to what the meditator actually experiences in meditation. It can be summed up as the attempt to give a systematic and exhaustive account of the world in terms of its constituent physical and mental events. This enterprise has two aspects: first, to categorize all possible types of event; secondly, to consider all possible ways in which those mental events can interact and so categorize the various kinds of causal relationships.

Physical and mental events are known as dharmas (Pali dhamma). The relationship between Dharma and dharmas might be stated as follows. Dharma is the way things ultimately are; it is also the Buddha's teaching since this is in accordance with the way things ultimately are. Physical and mental events are the ultimate building blocks of the way things ultimately are; thus to understand the Buddha's teaching and see Dharma is to see things in terms of dharmas.

Ultimately dharmas are all that there is. In this respect dharmas are very like atoms (when atoms were regarded as the ultimate 'bits' of matter). Thus just as a table might be analysed by a chemist as consisting of innumerable atoms, so a person is analysed by Abhidharma as consisting of innumerable dharmas. While the analogy of atoms is a useful one, we must always bear in mind that dharmas embrace both physical and mental things, not just physical ones. These mental and physical events that are dharmas fall into various classes. Again this is analogous to the way atoms are of different types: there are hydrogen atoms, oxygen atoms, lead atoms, gold atoms, and so on. In fact chemistry tells us that the physical world is constructed out of one hundred or so basic types of atom. So, just as the wood that makes up a table can be analysed into atoms of various elements, a person's mind and body can be analysed into dharmas of various classes. Again we should be careful in using this analogy. In so far as we think of atoms as bits of matter there is a tendency for the layman to conceive of them as inert enduring things, despite what modern nuclear physics tells us to the contrary. Similarly, as we saw in the context of insight meditation, dharmas are not enduring substances, they are evanescent events, here one moment and gone the next—like dewdrops at sunrise or a bubble on water, like a mirage or a conjuring trick.

Just as there is a more or less finite number of elements, so there is a more or less finite number of classes of dharmas. But we should also note that the term dharma is used both of a particular instance of a class of dharma and of the whole class. Thus according to the Sarvāstivādins the number of dharmas is seventy-five, meaning not that there are only seventy-five events in the world—given the duration of a dharma the world would be over in a very short time—but that there are only seventy-five possible types of event. The Yogācārins count some one hundred classes, while later Theravādin sources give eighty-two classes of dharma.[6] Let us take a closer look at the Theravādin analysis, the basic principles of which are shared with the other Abhidharma systems.

Eighty-one types of dharma are 'conditioned' (*saṃkhata*). That is to say, the conditioned world of saṃsāra from the lowest hell realms to the highest heavens of the Brahma world is constructed from the combination of these dharmas. The eighty-second dharma is the unconditioned (*asaṃkhata*), namely nirvāṇa. Conditioned dharmas fall into three main groups: consciousness (*citta*), associated mentality (*cetasika*), and physical phenomena (*rūpa*). The first, consciousness, constitutes a single class of dharma; the second, associated mentality, comprises fifty-two classes of dharma; the third, physical phenomena, comprises twenty-eight classes of dharma. Each of these eighty-one classes of dharma is precisely defined by, among other things, a distinctive characteristic (*lakkhaṇa*). For example, greed (*lobha*) is one particular class of dharma. The nature of greed may vary from a mild wanting as one gazes through a shop window to an unstoppable craving. Yet all dharmas that are instances of 'greed' share the distinctive characteristic of 'grasping at some object';

this is what defines them as greed as opposed to some other dharma.

In this technical sense of a dharma the characteristic of 'consciousness' is the bare sense of being aware of some object: it is the phenomenon of being conscious of something. We can never actually experience just this bare consciousness, for 'consciousness' never arises as a single isolated dharma; according to the Abhidharma, for the mind to be aware of some object it needs the help of a number of associated mental factors, some of the fifty-two dharmas of the associated mentality group. The minimum number of associated mental factors required is seven. In other words, to be conscious in fact requires the occurrence of a minimum of eight dharmas: consciousness, contact, feeling, recognition, volition, one-pointedness, life-faculty, and bringing-to-mind.

I shall pass over the precise technical definitions that the Abhidharma supplies for each of these dharmas, but the basic Abhidharma conception of how the mind functions is this: a collection of at least eight dharmas (consciousness and associated mental factors) arises for a moment and then falls away to be immediately followed by the next combination of consciousness and associated mental factors. Each combination is conscious of just one object. The arising and passing of each moment of consciousness is understood to occur extremely rapidly—so rapidly that a countless number passes even in a finger-snap. The flow of consciousness is thus analogous to the rapid sequence of the frames of a movie film; consciousness is experienced as a continuous flow, but is in fact made up of the rapidly occurring sequence of consciousness moments, each with a particular object. We may think that we are thinking of two or three things at once, but according to the Ābhidharmikas we are just very rapidly turning from one thing to another and back again. Similarly we experience each moment of consciousness as unified, yet rather like the way in which a colour photograph in a printed book is seen as an unbroken whole when it is in fact made up of countless tiny dots of just four colours, so consciousness is made up of separate dharmas. Thus, to extend the analogy, the infinite variety and richness of the mind is to be explained by the combination of just eighty-one classes of dharma. Indeed, according to an old image, the mind is far more complex, subtle, and varied than any painting.[7] Moreover the arising of dharmas is seamless and the difficulty of distinguishing different kinds of dharma in actual experience is compared to tasting the waters of the sea and knowing that certain water comes from one river and certain water from another river.[8]

The term *citta* or consciousness is used in two senses: (1) as a name for one of the eighty-one classes of dharma, namely the bare phenomenon of consciousness; (2) as a term for a given combination of consciousness and its associated mental factors. Consciousness in this second sense might be compared to a hand: the hand excluding the fingers is like the bare dharma of consciousness (the first sense), while the fingers are like the various associated mental factors; a given arising of consciousness is thus analogous to consciousness experiencing or picking up and handling a particular object by means of the associated mental factors. The flow of consciousness involves the mind picking up and putting down successive objects by means of successive sets of associated mental factors. In fact an old image from the sūtras compares the mind to a monkey swinging quickly through the trees in the forest: as soon as it lets go of one branch it grasps another.[9]

Although there is a total of fifty-two types of associated mental factor, only certain combinations of these are possible; for example it is impossible for the mental factors of greed and aversion to arise together in the same moment of consciousness for the simple reason that it is not possible to want something and not want it in the same moment—this does not, of course, mean that we cannot want something one moment and not want it the next. As I have already mentioned, for the Theravādins the simplest kind of consciousness that can occur involves seven associated mental factors. More complex consciousnesses involve up to a maximum of thirty-six types of associated mental factor. The Theravādin Abhidharma tabulates a system of eighty-nine basic classes of consciousness based on possible combinations of consciousness and associated mental factors. Normal human consciousness involves forty-five of these classes of consciousness. Of the other forty-four, eighteen concern the mind that has attained ordinary *jhāna* (either in meditation or as a result of rebirth in one of the Brahma worlds), eight concern the mind that has attained transcendent *jhāna* (at the moment of attaining one of the paths and fruits of stream-attainment, once-return, non-return or arhatship), and eighteen are restricted to the consciousness of one who is awakened.

The forty-five classes of normal consciousness fall into four broad groups: seventeen rootless (*ahetuka*), twelve unwholesome (*akusala*) consciousnesses, eight wholesome (*kusala*) classes of consciousness, and eight consciousnesses that are the karmic results (*vipāka*) of wholesome consciousness. The seventeen rootless classes of consciousness are so called because they are motivated neither by greed, aversion or delusion, nor by non-attachment, friendliness, or wisdom; they are considered to operate in a largely mechanical way in the processes of simply seeing, hearing, smelling, tasting, or touching something. Of the remaining kinds of consciousness, the unwholesome and wholesome are bound up with the way we react to what we experience through the senses, while the eight resultants principally operate as *bhavaṅga*, our basic state of mind when no active mental process is occurring (for example, in deep, dreamless sleep). Thus if we crave or cling to what we see, hear, smell, taste, or touch then we experience one of the eight types of consciousness rooted in greed; if we feel annoyed or irritated by it we experience one of the two types of consciousness rooted in aversion; if we simply feel dull or confused then we experience one of the two types of consciousness rooted in delusion. On the other hand, instead of feeling attached, irritated, or dull, we may feel generous, friendly, and awake.

One aspect of the Buddhist conception of a wholesome or 'healthy' mind is made particularly clear in the Abhidharma. That is that we should not confuse enjoyment with greed or desire. According to the Buddhist analysis feeling is of five basic types: painful physical sensation, enjoyable physical sensation, mental pleasure, mental displeasure, and neutral feeling. Painful or enjoyable sensations are neither wholesome or unwholesome, but considered to be the results of previous unwholesome or wholesome karma respectively. Mental displeasure only occurs in unwholesome consciousness rooted in aversion. In fact it is the distinctive characteristic of these types of consciousness. Thus, if there is mental displeasure, then we know that there is unwholesome consciousness. Mental pleasure and neutral feeling are more subtle. They can accompany both consciousness rooted in greed and consciousness rooted in non-attachment, friendliness, and wisdom. Accordingly mental pleasure may be a characteristic of both unwholesome and wholesome consciousness. That wholesome consciousness is, on the Buddhist view, associated with pleasant states of mind is in line with the Buddhist goal of finding a complete cessation of suffering. Thus Buddhist thought would resist any suggestion that, in teaching that the world is *dukkha* or 'suffering,' it presents a bleak and depressing outlook on the world. What Abhidharma analysis makes clear is that wholesome states of mind—those that conduce to relinquishing of attachments, those that possess the seeds of understanding and wisdom, those that resemble most closely the states of mind of one who is awakened—are precisely not unpleasant states of mind. This is not to say that one who attempts to put Buddhist teaching into practice immediately leaves behind all unpleasant and unwholesome states of mind—certainly the mind may experience much pain and suffering before it finally relinquishes its attachments. Yet it is not necessarily so.

According to another Abhidharma classification there are those whose practice is unpleasant and who take a long time to come to understanding; there are those whose practice is unpleasant but who come to understanding quickly; on the other hand there are those whose practice is pleasant who come to understanding slowly; and there are those whose practice is pleasant and who also come to understanding quickly.[10] The point I am making here by way of reference to the Abhidharma is essentially the same point as was made by Bronkhorst on the basis of historical arguments about the nature of Buddhist meditation which we met at the end of the last chapter. The Buddhist path aims at the cultivation of happy and balanced states of mind as the basis for the gaining of the understanding that liberates the mind by rooting out greed, aversion, and delusion.

The consciousness process, karma, and rebirth

For the Theravādin Abhidharma there are two basic modes of the mind: the mind that is involved in process (*vīthi-citta*) and the mind that is free of process (*vīthi-mutta*). The mind that is in process is the mind that is actively perceiving objects and reacting to those objects; the mind that is free of process is resting in the inactive mode known as *bhavaṅga*. This inactive mode characteristically occurs in deep, dreamless sleep. However, according to the theory of consciousness process, the mind momentarily returns to the inactive mode of *bhavaṅga* between each consciousness process. The mind in this inactive mode of *bhavaṅga* is compared to a spider resting in the middle of its web.[11] The web extends out in different directions and when one of the threads of the web is struck by an insect the spider in the middle stirs, and then runs out along the thread and bites into the insect to drink its juice. Similarly, when one of the senses is stimulated, the mind, like the spider, wakes up and adverts to the 'door' of the particular sense in question. Like a spider running out along the thread, the mind is then said in due order to perceive the object, receive it, investigate it, and establish its nature. Finally, again like our spider, the mind enjoys and savours the object. As I have already indicated, this whole process occurs extremely rapidly. In fact what one would ordinarily experience as the simple awareness that one is, say, looking at a beautiful lotus flower is understood to be constructed from countless sense-door consciousness processes of the type just described, as well as mind-door processes internalizing the information received through the senses.[12]

In the simple consciousness process the functions of perceiving, receiving, and investigating an object are said to be performed by classes of rootless resultant consciousness. That is to say, the nature of the sense data presented to our minds is regarded as determined by our previous actions. Whenever I see, hear, smell, taste, or touch something that is intrinsically 'desirable' (*iṭṭha*) or pleasing, I experience a result of previous wholesome consciousness; whenever I see, hear, smell, taste or touch something that is intrinsically 'undesirable' (*aniṭṭha*) or unpleasing I experience a result of previous unwholesome consciousness. The basic experiences that I have are thus the result of my previous karma and beyond my immediate control; they come to me whether I wish for them or not. But in each consciousness process the mind has a choice in how it will react to the experienced object. It is only the final stage when the mind has chosen to enjoy and savour its object in some way that actively unwholesome or wholesome consciousness plays its part and sows the seeds that will bear future results. In this way the Abhidharma in effect provides an exact small-scale analysis of the process of dependent arising.

The theory of *bhavaṅga* consciousness requires some further comment.[13] *Bhavaṅga* is the state of mind a being is born with and it is the state of mind to which a being returns in deep, dreamless sleep and in between every consciousness process. More strictly it is the state of mind that arises at the moment of conception in the womb, forming the link (*paṭisandhi*) between one life and the next. The particular characteristics of a *bhavaṅga* consciousness are unique to an individual being; a particular *bhavaṅga* thus reproduces itself and recurs throughout a being's life, defining that being as an individual. For human beings the function of *bhavaṅga* is performed by one of eight general classes of wholesome resultant consciousness. Like the consciousnesses that perceive, receive, and investigate an object, these kinds of consciousness are the results of previous karma. But unlike the former they are not rootless; rather they have the roots of non-attachment, friendliness, and sometimes also wisdom. They are therefore much richer and complex kinds of consciousness.

The basis of a rebirth as a human being is then one of these eight types of consciousness that are the result of previous wholesome karma. This wholesome karma may have been performed many lifetimes ago; more often it is wholesome karma done in the immediately previous life that is significant. What is said to be crucial in the process of rebirth is one's state of mind at the time of death. It is understood that at death significant acts performed during one's life tend to present themselves to one's mind. Certain kinds of action—for example, certain types of murder—are regarded as so 'weighty' that they cannot but come to mind at the time of death. In the absence of these what tends to come to mind are one's habitual actions or the actions that one performs close to the actual time of death. The widespread Buddhist understanding that actions performed at the time of death can be of crucial significance in determining the nature of one's rebirth relates to various customs aimed at turning the mind of a dying person to some meritorious action that he or she has performed. Thus flowers, incense, lamps, or chanting may be offered on the dying person's behalf. And because the dead person's new state may be short-lived or, in the Tibetan view, a temporary 'in-between state', relatives and friends may continue to perform actions for his or her benefit for some time after death.[14] The Tibetan belief in the *bar-do* or 'in-between state' (*antarābhava*) is inherited from the Sarvāstivādin Abhidharma and is associated with the elaborate practices of the *Bar-do Thos-grol*, the so-called Tibetan Book of the Dead. This notion of the 'in-between state' was a subject of dispute among ancient Indian schools of Buddhism; the Theravādins denied that it was coherent from an Abhidharma perspective, since an in-between existence must be another kind of existence.[15]

Essentially Abhidharma is a device for promoting mindfulness and understanding. The study of Abhidharma encourages the practitioner to pay attention to the kinds of mental states that are occurring whatever he or she is doing. It also draws the practitioner's attention to the way in which the spiritual process is understood to unfold. To this extent it can be seen as simply the elaboration of the analysis of the five aggregates and the twelvefold chain of dependent arising.

One cannot make oneself think nice things or have beautiful wholesome thoughts by simply wishing it. The mind works according to certain laws and principles that are in significant respects beyond our conscious control. That is to say, certain things happen to us because of previous actions; we react to things in certain ways because of past tendencies and patterns of thought which nurture deep-rooted habits. Thus I may decide that aggressive behaviour is unwholesome and that I will no longer indulge my temper; yet when provoked, when the conditions arise, I still find myself unable to control my temper. We react in unwholesome and unhealthy ways because greed, hatred, and delusion have not been rooted out. These tendencies lurk in our minds, and when the appropriate conditions arise they come to the fore. On the other hand there are also present in the mind the seeds of wholesome and healthy states of mind. According to the theory of the Buddhist path these must be gradually and patiently nurtured and cultivated. The process is compared to the way in which a hen cannot simply hatch her chicks by a mere wish; she must sit patiently nurturing the eggs until suddenly they finally hatch.[16]

Some Abhidharma problems

The Abhidharma analysis represents a continuation of two aspects of Buddhist theory: the breaking down of the individual into its constituent parts and the analysis of the causal relations that exist between those parts. As we saw in the account of 'no self' in Chapter 6, the first is characterized by the analysis of a being into the five *skandhas* or aggregates of physical and mental phenomena; the second by the analysis of causality in terms of the twelve links of dependent arising. The first counters the 'eternalist' tendency of beings to cling to the view that their existence is substantial and enduring; the second the 'nihilist' tendency to see the world and their own existence as chaotic and meaningless. Again, as we saw in Chapter 6, past and present critics of Buddhist theory argue that the breaking up of the individual into parts cannot account for the experienced facts of personal continuity and ends in devaluing the moral status of the individual. Buddhist thought counters that such a criticism does not take proper account of the causal continuity that exists between the parts, and that anyway it is true that we must relinquish attachment to our own individuality in order to act selflessly.

The rigorous Abhidharma analysis of the mind and body in terms of linear series of momentary dharmas arising and ceasing in every moment meant that Buddhist thought was required to give an equally rigorous intellectual account of the processes that govern psychological and bodily continuity. For example, I can remember past events, but if the dharmas that constituted those events no longer exist, what is it that I remember? More significantly, how can something that no longer exists have an effect in the present? Buddhist practice is based on the fact that actions have various kinds of results. Wholesome and unwholesome actions lead to pleasant and unpleasant results in the future—sometimes in far distant future lives. Yet how can an action performed many lifetimes ago suddenly have an effect now? Moreover, according to Buddhist thought, actions are habit-forming, creating tendencies in the mind. Yet if actions begin and cease in every moment how do these tendencies accumulate, how do we learn to do things? And how is it that an acquired skill like swimming or speaking a language can be retained when it is not used, even for many years? And crucially, where is the potentiality for anger when it is not active? Suppose that I am sitting peacefully experiencing thoughts of generosity and friendliness towards the world. At that time, according to Abhidharma, there is no occurrence of thoughts motivated by greed, aversion, or delusion, but only of thoughts motivated by non-attachment, friendliness, and wisdom; therefore my mental state should not be distinguishable from an arhat's or even a Buddha's. Yet if Māra should send his armies against me or if his daughters should appear before me, it would probably not be long before a state of fear or hatred or desire arose in me. So here is the difference: in me there is a potentiality for greed, hatred, and delusion that is not found in a Buddha or arhat. But how does the potentiality for unwholesome thought suddenly emerge from wholesome thoughts, and how do wholesome dharmas operate as a condition for unwholesome dharmas?

One of the most intellectually creative explanations of these related sets of questions is expounded by the Sarvāstivādins. Their theories are in the first place based on a radical understanding of the nature of time, the view that all three times—present, past, and future—exist (*sarvāsti-vāda*). According to this view, to say of dharmas that they are future or past is not to say that they do not exist; they exist, but they happen to exist in the past or the future, just as other dharmas happen, for a moment, to exist in the present. Time is thus conceived as a kind of dimension through which dharmas travel. Four different ways of understanding this are associated with the names of four Sarvāstivādin theorists of the early centuries CE. From the perspective of modern philosophy Buddhadeva's suggestion that a dharma can be said to be 'present', relative to simultaneous dharmas, 'past' relative to dharmas that come after and 'future' relative to dharmas that come before—like a woman who is daughter and mother—is perhaps the most philosophically subtle.[17] Nevertheless it was the view of Vasumitra that apparently carried the most authority: a dharma moving through the different times does not change in essential nature but only in position (*avasthā*), just as in decimal counting a 'one' signifies 'one', 'ten' or 'one hundred' according to position.

In connection with their understanding of the existence of dharmas in the three times, the Sarvāstivādins proposed two dharmas that governed the operation of dharmas. As an ordinary unenlightened person, when one experiences, say, desire, there is a 'possession' (*prāpti*) of present desire; but when it is past, although there may be no 'possession' of present desire, there is still a 'possession' of past desire and also one of its future results; this 'possession' of the future result will continue to reproduce itself from moment to moment until it matures into a 'possession' of a present result. For an unenlightened person there is also 'non-possession' (*aprāpti*) of certain kinds of wholesome dharmas associated with the higher stages of meditation and the Buddhist path; such 'non-possession' is not the mere absence of these wholesome dharmas but a real dharma in itself which must be destroyed, along with the 'possessions' of unwholesome dharmas, by the practice of the path. Critics of the Sarvāstivādins objected that if 'possession' is a dharma like other dharmas then it must require 'possession' in order to operate: there would have to be possession of 'possession' of 'possession' and so on, *ad infinitum*. The Sarvāstivādins responded with the notion of a 'secondary possession' (*anuprāpti*) that both possessed and was in turn possessed by the primary possession.

For certain Buddhist theorists the intellectual sophistication, not to say abstraction, of the Sarvāstivādin analyses rendered them problematic. Among the critics of the Sarvāstivāda a group styled the Sautrāntikas or 'those who follow the method of the sūtras' are especially important for the subsequent history of Buddhist thought. Although the Sautrāntikas did not accept the Abhidharma as the 'word of the Buddha', it would be wrong to think of them as rejecting the Abhidharma method in its entirety. In fact the basic Abhidharma system is largely assumed by their criticisms; it is particular doctrines characteristic of the Vaibhāṣika-Sarvāstivāda Abhidharma that they took issue with. Two theories are especially associated with their name: the theory of the radical momentariness of dharmas and the theory of seeds.

Rejecting the idea of dharmas existing in the three times of present, past, and future, Sautrāntikas criticized the Sarvāstivādin conception of the duration of a dharma in the present moment. For the Sarvāstivādins dharmas are substantial realities (*dravya*), existing in their own right, which for a moment operate in the present. From this perspective, the present moment although a very short period of time, is none the less a period of time. There is no Sarvāstivādin consensus on the length of a moment but figures given in the texts work out at between 0.13 and 13 milliseconds.[18] Yet, object the Sautrāntikas, if something endures unchanged for even a moment, then the fundamental Buddhist principle of impermanence is compromised. If things are truly impermanent, then they must be changing continuously and cannot remain static for any period of time, however short.[19] This kind of thinking led to the conception of moments as point instants of time which, just as geometric points have no extension in space, have no duration in time. It is in the light of this that we should understand the Abhidharma account of the twelve links of interdependent arising occurring in a moment: analyse reality down to the shortest conceivable moment of time and what we still find is a process rather than inert, or static bits.

Instead of the theory of 'possession' the Sautrāntikas proposed that the mechanism whereby dharmas produce effects long after they cease to exist can be understood by reference to the images of seeds and 'perfuming'.[20] When I perform an action motivated by greed, it plants a 'seed' in the series of dharmas that is my mind. Such a seed is not a thing in itself—a dharma—but merely the modification or 'perfuming' of the subsequent flow of dharmas consequent upon the action. In the course of time this modification matures and issues in a particular result, in the same way as a seed does not produce its fruit immediately, but only after the 'modifications' of the shoot, stem, leaf, and flower. The Sautrāntikas also suggested that there are two types of seed. In addition to seeds that are planted by our wholesome and unwholesome deeds, there are certain seeds that subsist in the mental continuum of beings from time immemorial; such seeds constitute an innate potentiality for wholesome behaviour that can never be destroyed. In the Sautrāntika theory of seeds we have the precursors of two extremely important concepts of later Mahāyāna Buddhist thought: the Yogācārin 'store consciousness' (*ālaya-vijñāna*) and the notion of 'the embryo of the Buddha' (*tathāgata-garbha*) or Buddha-nature, the innate capacity in all beings to gain enlightenment. The latter concept was to prove particularly influential in the development of certain tendencies of East Asian Buddhist thought.

For their part the Theravādin Ābhidharmikas seem to have referred the answer to the kinds of problem we have been considering to their understanding of the consciousness process, outlined briefly above. Between each active consciousness process the mind returns to a basic state of consciousness (*bhavaṅga*) that defines a being as an individual before emerging once more in response to some physical or mental stimulus. Thus instead of referring the continuity of character traits and habitual tendencies to a continuously present (but still always changing) underlying state of mind, which the Sautrāntikas and later the Yogācārins tended to do, the Theravādins refer it to a continually intervening state of mind.[21]

As a footnote to this discussion of Abhidharma problems, I should mention the theory of one more Buddhist school, the Pudgalavādins or 'those who affirm the existence of the person'. Their ideas seem to have been formed in the context of early Abhidharma discussions of the undetermined questions, karma and rebirth, the unconditioned, and the nature of consciousness.[22] To some extent the 'person' of the Pudgalavādins might be seen as performing an analogous function to 'possession', seeds, or *bhavaṅga*. While other schools accused them of having smuggled in an *ātman* or 'self', they vigorously denied that their person was a 'self': it cannot be said to be the same or different from the five aggregates; it is not susceptible to annihilation nor is it eternal; in fact it is strictly ineffable (*avaktavya*). The writings of the Pudgalavādins themselves hardly survive and our knowledge of their ideas is largely based on the refutations of other schools.[23] Although the affirmation of the person can hardly be regarded as characteristic of mainstream Buddhist thought, it is associated particularly with the Vinaya lineage named after the monk Vātsīputra, the Vātsīputrīya-Sammatīyas. According to the Chinese pilgrim Hsüan-tsang who visited India in the seventh century, around a quarter of the monks in India belonged to this school. Of course, that a monk had been ordained into a particular ordination lineage need not have meant that he automatically subscribed to the doctrinal positions associated with that ordination lineage. Not all monks ordained as Sammatīyas need have been *pudgalavadins*, just as not all Sarvāstivādin monks need necessarily have been *sarvāstivādins*. This last point is aptly illustrated by the fact that the contemporary Tibetan monks are ordained in the tradition of the Mūlasarvāstivādins (a sub-school of the ancient Sarvāstivāda), yet none would subscribe to the view that dharmas exist in the three times.

9

The Mahāyāna

The Great Vehicle

The beginnings of the Mahāyāna

The production of Buddhist sūtras or texts claiming to be 'the word of the Buddha' is something that continued for many centuries after the death of the Buddha. Although different schools of Buddhism gradually developed a sense of defined collections of scriptures having the authority of the word of the Buddha, the notion of a fixed canon seems to have remained somewhat loose. As the history of Theravāda Buddhism in Sri Lanka and South-East Asia illustrates, even where there exists a defined canon it is quite possible for 'non-canonical' sūtras to continue to circulate and be used.[1] But around the beginning of the Christian era there began to emerge scriptures that challenged certain established Buddhist teachings and ways of understanding, and which advocated what is represented as a superior path of practice leading to a superior understanding.

The defining idea of the vision of Buddhist teaching presented in these sūtras is one that I outlined at the end of Chapter 1: the superiority of Gautama's awakening to that of his disciples. Gautama's awakening is characterized by the perfect development of *all* spiritual qualities, and as such it exceeds the accomplishment of his disciples. The path followed by Gautama is thus the *mahā-yāna*—the 'great vehicle'—or the vehicle of the Bodhisattva (*bodhisattva-yāna*) ending in the perfect awakening of the fully awakened *samyak-sambuddha* as opposed to 'the inferior vehicle' (*hīna-yāna*), the vehicle of the disciple (*śrāvaka-yāna*), ending in arhatship.

The dating of the earliest Mahāyāna sūtras, like that of all ancient Indian texts, is extremely problematic. The earliest firm date we have for their existence is the late second century CE when a number of Mahāyāna sūtras were translated into Chinese by Lokakṣema. Many Mahāyāna sūtras as we have them show evidence of a particular kind of literary history: an older core text is expanded and elaborated; thus the sūtras translated by Lokakṣema originated possibly a century or so earlier in India. Most scholars push the date of the earliest Mahāyāna sūtras back into the first century BCE, but the production and elaboration of Mahāyāna sūtras certainly continued for a number of centuries. For their part, however, the Mahāyāna sūtras present themselves as teachings which, having been originally delivered by the Buddha himself, were not taught until the time was ripe.

Modern scholars have sometimes sought to connect their production with particular areas of India (either the south or the north-west), but the evidence is problematic and inconclusive. Following the lead of certain later Mahāyāna writers themselves, some modern scholars have also sometimes traced the origins of the sūtras to a particular school of the ancient Saṅgha, namely the Mahāsāṃghikas; but more recent scholarship tends to stress the fact that Mahāyāna was not in origin a sectarian movement. Rather than causing a schism within the Saṅgha, Mahāyāna teachings were esoteric teachings of interest to small groups of monks from various of the ancient schools (see above pp. 56–8). Again, while earlier scholarship has tended to represent Mahāyāna as a movement inspired by popular lay religiosity and stūpa worship, more recent scholarship has suggested that we might see the origins of the Mahāyāna in the activity of forest-dwelling ascetic monks attempting to return to the ideals of original Buddhism.[2] Other writers have also connected the rise of the Mahāyāna with a growing cult of the book.[3]

The most important Mahayana sutras can be conveniently grouped according to the characteristic ideas they expound:

- Sūtras setting out the stages of the bodhisattva path: the *Bodhisattva-piṭaka*, the *Daśabhūmika Sūtra*.
- The 'perfection of wisdom' (*prajñā-pāramitā*) sūtras. These are among the earliest Mahāyāna sūtras, and of these the

earliest is probably the *Aṣṭasāhasrikā* or 'Perfection of Wisdom in 8,000 Lines'. The characteristic teaching is the 'emptiness' of dharmas.

- The 'ideas only' (*vijñapti-mātra*) sūtras. These sūtras introduce the idealist doctrine that the 'mind', 'ideas' or 'information' (*vijñapti*) alone is real. The most important early sūtra is the *Saṃdhinirmocana Sūtra* but its teachings along with associated theories are found developed in the next group of sūtras.
- The 'embryo of the Tathāgata' (*tathāgatagarbha*) sūtras: the *Tathāgatagarbha Sūtra, Mahāparinirvāṇa Sūtra, Laṅkāvatāra Sūtra, Śrīmālādevī-siṃhanāda Sūtra.*
- Two sūtras of particular importance in East Asian Buddhism are the *Saddharmapuṇḍarīka Sūtra* ('Discourse of the Lotus of the True Dharma', commonly referred to simply as the 'Lotus Sūtra'), which expounds the notion of the 'one vehicle' (see p. 228), and the (*Buddha-*) *Avataṃsaka Sūtra* (incorporating the *Gaṇḍavyūha* and *Daśabhūmika Sūtras*), which develops the notion of the 'interpenetration of all phenomena' (see pp. 264–5).
- The 'pure land' sūtras: the smaller and larger *Sukhāvatī-vyūha Sūtras*, the *Amitāyur-dhyāna Sūtra*. These sūtras describe the 'pure land' of the Buddha of Boundless Light and become the basis for the Pure Land school of East Asian Buddhism.
- Meditation sūtras: *Pratyutpanna-buddha-sammukhāvasthita-samādhi Sūtra, Samādhi-rāja Sūtra, Śūraṅgama-samādhi Sūtra.* These sūtras describe particular meditation practices.

Such a list indicates only in outline the nature and scope of a few of the most important Mahāyāna sūtras. Let us now turn to the summary exposition of the ideas articulated in these sūtras and the related expository manuals or *śāstras*.

The vehicle of the bodhisattva

That all Buddhism has a bodhisattva path follows from the fact that all Buddhism knows the story of the ascetic variously named as Megha (in the *Mahāvastu*) or Sumedha (in Pali sources) and his meeting with a previous buddha, Dīpaṃkara. Megha could have chosen to become a disciple of Dīpaṃkara and followed the path to awakening, and thus become an arhat in that very life. If he had done so that would have been the end of the matter: there would have been no Gautama Buddha, only the arhat Megha. But he did not follow the path to immediate arhatship; instead he chose to practise the perfections (*pāramitā/pāramī*) and so eventually—many, many lifetimes, many, many aeons later—he became the *samyaksam-buddha*, Gautama. The reason for Megha's decision is that he was inspired by the compassionate ideal of the bodhisattva path: having become awakened himself, he would lead others to awakening.[4] The traditional notion of the arhat is that he becomes awakened and then effectively disappears from saṃsāra; the bodhisattva, on the other hand, spends many aeons in saṃsāra perfecting spiritual qualities, and, in the process, working for the benefit of sentient beings; eventually he becomes a fully awakened buddha, but only when the teaching of the previous buddha has disappeared from the world. In choosing the path of the bodhisattva, Megha thus forgoes his own immediate release from suffering, as an arhat, in order to become a buddha and teach the path to the cessation of suffering to other beings.

This basic distinction between the career of the disciple and the career of the bodhisattva is thus presupposed by all Buddhist thought. But the earlier tradition tends to emphasize that as far as the fundamental liberating knowledge of the four noble truths is concerned the Buddha and his disciples are equal. But a gap between the Buddha and arhat none the less exists. We can trace in Buddhist literature generally an increasing tendency to exalt the figure of the Buddha and to dwell on the description of his incomparable virtues and superhuman powers; lists such as the ten powers of the Tathāgata and the eighteen special qualities of a Buddha are common to all Buddhist schools. But with a text such as the *Lokānuvartanā Sūtra* ('discourse on conforming to the world') the Buddha is seen less and less as a historical personality and more and more as a transcendent being who merely appears to conform to the conventions of worldly existence.[5] And the more this happens, the greater the opportunity for the suggestion that the attainments of his arhat disciples fall somewhat short of the complete awakening of the Buddha. What is characteristic of the Mahāyāna vision of Buddhism is the view that the attainment of the disciple falls so far short of full Buddhahood that it cannot be considered as a worthy spiritual goal; contrary to the traditional formula which states the arhat 'has done what has to be done', he or she in fact has further work to do. Thus for the earlier tradition, as for the Theravāda today, the normal route to awakening was considered the path of arhatship, and the heroic path of the bodhisattva an option for the few.[6] The parting of the two ways of the bodhisattva and *śrāvaka* is illustrated by the traditional story of Megha. For the Mahāyāna, however, the path to arhatship appears tainted with a residual selfishness since it lacks the motivation of the great compassion (*mahākaruṇā*) of the bodhisattva, and ultimately the only legitimate way of Buddhist practice is the bodhisattva path.

The traditions of Indian Buddhism that resisted the Mahāyāna vision continued to think in terms of three approaches to what was essentially one and the same final release from suffering, nirvāṇa: the path of the *śrāvaka* or 'disciple' leading to arhatship, the path of the *pratyeka-buddha* and the path of the bodhisattva leading to the attainment of the *samyak-sambuddha* (see above, pp. 32–4). The Mahāyāna sūtras express two basic attitudes to this.[7] The first is that the path of the disciple and the path of the *pratyeka-buddha* do lead to a kind of awakening, a release from suffering, nirvāṇa, and as such are real goals. These goals are, however, inferior and should be renounced for the superior attainment of buddhahood. The second attitude, classically articulated by the Lotus Sūtra, sees the goal of the disciple and the *pratyeka-buddha* as not true goals at all.[8] The fact that the Buddha taught them is an example of his 'skill in means' (*upāya-kauśalya*) as a teacher.[9] These goals are thus merely clever devices (*upāya*) employed by the Buddha in order to get beings to at least begin the practice of the path; eventually their practice must lead on to the one and only vehicle (*eka-yāna*) that is the *mahāyāna*, the vehicle ending in perfect buddhahood.

From this perspective the difference between *hınayana* and *mahāyāna* is effectively the difference between progressive stages of the same path. This kind of understanding is expressed in the classic Tibetan presentations of 'the gradual path' (*lam rim*) to awakening.[10] Thus even 'Mahāyānists' (people who accept the Mahāyāna vision) do not necessarily begin their spiritual practice with the motivation of the bodhisattva simply established in their hearts; they must first undertake various practices in order to arouse and cultivate this motivation in the form of 'the mind of awakening' (*bodhi-citta*): spiritual practice begins by letting go of the delights of this world, by arousing a sense of the pain and suffering of saṃsāra and desiring release; it is only then that the motivation of the bodhisattva becomes crucial.[11] That is to say, at the beginning of the path we are almost inevitably primarily motivated by the wish to rid ourselves of our own individual suffering; it is only as we progress along the path that we come to understand that, in fact, suffering is above all something that beings share in common; with the dawning of this realization we are moved by compassion and the desire to help others; our motivation for following the path shifts and we enter the Mahāyāna proper. The bodhisattva thus at once turns away from saṃsāra as a place of suffering and at the same time turns back towards it out of compassion for the suffering of the world:

> And he who hopes for the welfare of the world thinks to himself: Let me undertake religious practice, that I may bring welfare and happiness to all beings. And he sees the aggregates (*skandha*) as like a magic show, but he does not wish to disown the aggregates; he sees the senses (*dhātu*) as like a poisonous serpent, but he does not wish to disown the senses; he sees sensory awareness (*ayatana*) as like an empty village, but he does not wish to disown sensory awareness.[12]

The Mahāyāna texts may emphasize that the motivation of the bodhisattva is quite different from that of the *śrāvaka* or disciple, but in *practice* the two paths are not so different: one develops essentially the same spiritual qualities, but to the perfect degree of a buddha. The bodhisattva's practice, like the *śrāvaka's*, consists of the development of good conduct, concentration, and wisdom: he stills the mind by means of calm meditation and then turns the mind to insight. A new scheme of ten stages or levels (*bhūmi*) of the bodhisattva path, as set out in such texts as the *Daśabhūmika* ('On the Ten Levels'), is superimposed on the older map of five paths (see Table 7 above), giving a scheme of thirteen spiritual stages. As I have just indicated, the bodhisattva path is seen as beginning with a series of meditations aimed at arousing the 'awakening mind' (*bodhi-citta*). What is meant here is the arousing and establishing in one's heart of a genuine desire to become a buddha, and this is brought about by an awareness of the sufferings of beings. As a result one is truly affected by their anguish and deeply moved by compassion. The arousing and establishing of *bodhi-citta* correspond to the paths of equipment and application, and arc thus spiritual attainments of some depth. With the 'path of seeing'—the point, on the path of the *śrāvaka*, at which one became a stream-attainer—one has reached the first of the ten levels of the bodhisattva path and begun the development of the six perfections (*pāramitā*): generosity (*dāna*), good conduct (*śīla*), patient acceptance (*kṣānti*), vigour (*vīrya*), meditation (*dhyāna*), wisdom (*prajñā*). This standard list of six perfections is correlated with the first six levels; an additional four perfections of skill in means (*upāya-kauśalya*), determination (*praṇidhāna*), strength (*bala*), and knowledge (*jñāna*), are then related to the final four levels. The practice of all ten perfections constitutes 'the path of development' ending in the tenth level, the 'Cloud of Dharma', and the attainment of buddhahood; beyond is the path of 'one in need of no further training', a buddha.[13]

Thus whereas from the non-Mahāyāna perspective the path of seeing is the point at which the meditator sees the four truths directly and attains 'the stream' that ends in arhatship, from the perspective of the Mahāyāna path this path of insight is the point of establishing oneself on the first of ten levels that culminate in full buddhahood.

Reaching the first level corresponds to stream-attainment; at the sixth level the bodhisattva has reached the stage when he could attain the nirvāṇa of arhatship, but the journey to full buddhahood is not yet complete and he must pass on to the seventh level.

The bodhisattva of these higher *bhūmis* is a quite extraordinary being who works ceaselessly for the benefit of all beings. Born as god in the realms of the devas or of Brahmā, he in fact already has many of the powers and qualities of a buddha.[14] Indeed according to some sources the bodhisattva already manifests created bodies which perform all the twelve acts of a Buddha (see Chapter 1) at the tenth stage:

At will he displays the array of the realms of all the Buddhas at the end of a single hair; at will he displays untold arrays of the realms of the Buddhas of all kinds; at will in the twinkling of an eye he creates as many individuals as there are particles in untold world-systems . . . In the arising of a thought he embraces the ten directions; in a moment of thought he controls the manifestation of innumerable processes of complete awakening and final nirvāṇa . . . In his own body he controls countless manifestations of the qualities of the Buddha fields of innumerable Blessed Buddhas.[15]

If this is what tenth-stage bodhisattvas do, then what do buddhas do? The short answer is much, much more of the same—such that one cannot properly begin to conceive of what buddhas truly do. Nevertheless it appears that we are to understand that at some point in the process—the repeated process of manifesting the acts of buddhas and carrying out their work—these tenth-stage bodhisattvas do actually become buddhas. But for the Mahāyāna buddhahood this final attainment occurs in the Akaniṣṭha (Pali Akaniṭṭha) realm, the highest of 'the Pure Abodes' (see above p. 118).

Transcendent buddhas

In the earlier tradition the Tathāgata, or 'the one who has gone thus', teaches the Dharma and at death attains parinirvāṇa or 'final nirvāṇa'. Although after death he strictly cannot be said to exist, not exist, both exist and not exist, or neither exist nor not exist, effectively he disappears from saṃsāra never to be seen again. The Buddha of the Mahāyāna, however, continues to be present and in some way active. Strictly, for all Buddhism, we cannot speak of a buddha as 'existing' in any ordinary sense, since to exist in an ordinary sense means to be born as an individual being in a particular realm; Buddhas have precisely transcended the round of rebirth, so cannot be said to exist at a particular time and place as 'individuals'. For the Mahāyāna becoming a Buddha generally involves attaining what is characterized as the 'unestablished' or 'non-abiding' (*apratiṣṭhita*) nirvāṇa: on the one hand the knowledge of a buddha that sees emptiness, is not 'established' in saṃsāra (by seizing on birth as an individual being, for example), on the other hand the great compassion of a buddha prevents the complete turning away from saṃsāra. So ultimately he abides neither in saṃsāra nor in nirvāṇa.[16] Thus, while it may appear that a buddha takes birth as an individual being like the rest of us, in truth he does not. What we ordinarily see here on earth, as it were, is merely a body created by the Buddha, a *nirmāṇa-kāya*. Where is the Buddha really?

In the process of following the path the bodhisattva gradually develops the ability to magically transform himself and the world around him for the benefit of beings. The Indian yogic and meditation theory generally recognizes the development of various powers (see pp. 185–6), but in the context of the development of the bodhisattva path the ability is perfected and becomes of a different order. In a sutta in the Pali canon the Buddha is described as having a body endowed with thirty-two marks. But these marks are obviously not marks of the Buddha's ordinary body that we normally see. They are the marks of a body gradually developed over many aeons by the practice of perfections. Again, various kinds of 'subtle bodies' are universal to Indian meditation theory. For the yogin his other body (even if more subtle), developed and experienced in the stages of meditation, comes to be more real than his ordinary physical body. So there is a sense in which the yogin gradually becomes this other body. For the bodhisattva the end point of this development is the 'enjoyment body' (*sambhoga-kāya*) of a buddha teaching the Dharma in a 'buddha-field' (*buddha-kṣetra*). This enjoyment body is closer to what a buddha really is and may, indeed, be seen by some; for the rest of us, we must be content with the grosser manifestations of the Buddha's bodies of magical creation (*nirmāṇa-kāya*). Yet the enjoyment body is, again hardly what the Buddha ultimately is. What a buddha is in 'himself' is the *dharma-kāya*. This expression originally seems to have meant that a buddha is ultimately the sum (*kāya*) of perfected good qualities (dharma) that constitute a Buddha. But the expression comes to be interpreted, at any rate in the Yogācāra tradition, as referring to the ultimate truth of the way things are: the eternal, unchanging truth perceived by a buddha, 'thusness' (*tathatā*).[17] Buddhas in the world, *nirmāṇa-kāyas*, come and go, live and die, as Gautama did in the fifth century BCE; cosmic buddhas, *sambhoga-kāyas*, spend countless aeons teaching in their pure lands and manifesting *nirmāṇa-kāyas*; strictly *dharma-kāyas* do not do anything at all.

For the earlier non-Mahāyāna tradition there can only be one buddha at any given time and we must wait until his teaching has disappeared for the next to arise. Previous buddhas, although recognized and the object of devotions and rituals, are, like the Buddha Gautama, doctrinally at least beings of the past rather than the present.[18] Maitreya (Pali Metteyya), universally acknowledged as the bodhisattva who will become the next buddha, must already be far advanced along the path, but his time is yet to come. For the Mahāyāna all this changes; the notion of the *sambhoga-kāya* is developed and exploited, emphasizing that there must, in the infinite universe, be buddhas now teaching in their pure lands and buddha-fields.[19] These buddhas—the 'unshakeable' Akṣobhya, the 'medicine' Buddha Bhaiṣajya Guru, the boundless radiance of Amitābha—and their lovely pure lands are accessible to us, through either meditation or rebirth. Moreover the Mahāyāna conception allows that numerous advanced bodhisattvas are now working for the benefit of beings—not only Maitreya, but also Avalokiteśvara, the lord who looks down with compassion, the charming Mañjuśrī, bodhisattva of wisdom, and the 'saviouress' Tārā.[20] Indeed, according to the Lotus Sūtra, Gautama, Śākyamuni Buddha, is still around.

The development of the worship of various buddhas and bodhisattvas is a feature of Mahāyāna Buddhist practice, and it continues especially in East Asian Pure Land Buddhism and in Tibetan Buddhism. Yet this development can be seen as a continuation of the practice of the recollection and visualization of the Buddha and his qualities (*buddhānusmṛti/buddhānussati*), and the contrast with contemporary Theravādin attitudes can be overstated. While the Theravādin doctrinal position on the ontological status of the Buddha and arhats of the past (which, we should remember, includes the stricture that we should not say that they do not exist) remains, in practice the power of the Buddha Gautama is thought of as somehow persisting until the final disappearance of all his relics, which, it is thought, in the last days of the Dharma will spontaneously come together at the site of the Buddha's awakening and vanish (the tradition of *dhātu-parinibbāna*).[21] The devotional cult of arhats is ancient, and the presence of the arhats is invoked in South-East Asia, and one whom many regarded as a twentieth-century arhat, Ajahn Mun, is described as meeting and conversing with the arhats of the past.[22]

Emptiness (*śūnyatā*) and the 'perfection of wisdom' (*prajñāpāramitā*)

Mahāyāna sūtras see the motivation underlying the arhat's attainment as lacking the great compassion (*mahā-karuṇā*) of a buddha; of equal concern to the sūtras is perfect wisdom. Together, wisdom and compassion become the two great themes of Mahāyāna thought.

The 'Perfection of Wisdom' (*prajñāpāramitā*) literature evolved over many centuries and comprises a variety of texts, including some of the oldest Mahāyāna sūtra material. Edward Conze, a pioneer of the scholarly study of this literature, considered the oldest and most basic text to be the *Aṣṭasāhasrikā-Prajñāpāramitā* ('Perfection of Wisdom in 8,000 Lines'), which he dates from the first century BCE. Subsequent centuries saw the production of vast expanded versions, such as those of 100,000 lines, 25,000 lines, and 18,000 lines, as well as shorter versions, such as the *Vajracchedikā* and *Hṛdaya* (the 'Diamond' and 'Heart' Sūtras), although it now appears that the last, a text only a few lines in length, was originally composed in Chinese and only subsequently rendered into Sanskrit.[23]

In the century or so prior to the appearance of the Perfection of Wisdom literature, Buddhism had, in the form of Abhidharma, begun to evolve increasingly detailed and sophisticated theoretical accounts of the nature of reality and of the stages of the path to awakening. Central to the Abhidharma is the distinction between the conventional truth (that persons and selves exist) and the ultimate truth (that persons and selves are ultimately simply aggregates of evanescent dharmas—physical and mental events). The main teaching of the Perfection of Wisdom is that, from the perspective of perfect wisdom, even this account of the way things are is *ultimately* arbitrary.

Since we fail to see things as they really are—impermanent, suffering, and not self—we grasp at them as if they were permanent, as if they could bring us lasting happiness, as if we could possess them as our very own. Thus the cultivation of calm and insight involves breaking up the seemingly substantial and enduring appearance of things. Things—our very own selves, our own minds—are actually nothing but insubstantial, evanescent dharmas (see above, p. 190). Abhidharma theory and the associated meditations thus provide a way of getting behind appearances to a world that is quite different from the one ordinarily experienced—a way of easing the mind from the ways and patterns of thought it habitually uses to understand the world. So far so good, but the currents of craving run deep, and the habitual ways and patterns of thought are subtle and devious. Our minds have a predilection to the formulation of views (*dṛṣṭi/diṭṭhi*), to conceptual proliferation (*prapañca/papañca*), and to the manufacture of conceptual constructs (*vikalpa*); it is these which we tend to confuse with the way things are and to which we become attached. In other words, we are always in danger of mistaking our own views and opinions for a true understanding of the way things are. This danger—and this is the really significant point—may apply to views and opinions based on the theoretical teachings of Buddhism (the Abhidharma and the account of the stages of the path) no less than to views and opinions derived from other theoretical systems. Perfect wisdom, however, is what sees through the process of the mind's conceptual construction and is not tainted by attachment to any view or opinion. In particular, it is not attached to the views and conceptual constructs of Buddhist theory: unwholesome and wholesome qualities, the levels of meditation or *dhyāna*, the stages of insight, the attainment of the Buddhist path, nirvāṇa itself, the general theory of dharmas. From the perspective of perfect wisdom all these are seen for what they ultimately are: empty (*śūnya/suñña*). That is, the conceptual constructs of Buddhist theory are *ultimately* no less artificial and arbitrary entities than the conceptual constructs of the ordinary unawakened mind which sees really existing persons and selves. The mind can grasp at the theory of dharmas and turn it into another conceptual strait-jacket. Thus the Large Sūtra can state that:

> there is no ignorance and no cessation of ignorance . . . no suffering and no knowledge of suffering, no cause and no abandoning of the cause, no cessation and no realization of cessation, and no path and no development of the path . . . It is in this sense, Śāriputra, that a bodhisattva, a great being who practises perfect wisdom, is called one devoted [to perfect wisdom].[24]

The teaching of emptiness should not be read, as it sometimes appears to be, as an attempt to subvert the Abhidharma theory of dharmas as a whole. After all it applies to the constructs of all Buddhist theory, including the Mahāyāna and, crucially, itself: there are no bodhisattvas and no stages of the bodhisattva path. Two points are of importance here. First, we are concerned here with the *perfection* of wisdom, how the world is seen by the awakened mind. Secondly the perfection of wisdom texts present what they have to say about wisdom not as an innovation but as a restatement of the original teaching of the Buddha.

The wisdom or understanding of ordinary beings becomes tainted by attachment to views and conceptual construction; this attachment manifests as a certain rigidity and inflexibility of mind; the perfect wisdom of a buddha is free of all attachment and clinging. In carving up reality into dharmas in the manner of the Abhidharma, we are essentially constructing a theoretical 'model' or map of the way things are. Like any model or map, it may be useful and indeed help us to understand the way things are. In a provisional or conventional way, it may actually correspond to the way things are. Some maps and models will reflect the way things are better than others, but they nevertheless remain models and maps. As such, none should be mistaken for the way things are. Thus for the Perfection of Wisdom, just as persons and beings are ultimately elusive entities, so too are all dharmas. In fact the idea that *anything* exists of and in itself is a simply a trick that our minds and language play on us.

The great theme of the Perfection of Wisdom thus becomes 'emptiness' (*śūnyatā/suññatā*)—the emptiness of all things that we might be tempted to think truly and ultimately exist of and in themselves. To see any dharma as existing in itself is to grasp at it, to try to hold on to it, but dharmas are like dreams, magical illusions, echoes, reflected images, mirages, space; like the moon reflected in water, a fairy castle, a shadow, or a magical creation; like the stars, dewdrops, a bubble, a flash of lightning, or a cloud —they are there, but they are not there, and if we reach out for them, we find nothing to hold on to.[25] Some of these similes and images are older than the Perfection of Wisdom, and in referring and adding to them the literature is not so much suggesting that the theory of dharmas is wrong as that it must be understood correctly.[26]

The term 'emptiness' is not new to the Perfection of Wisdom literature; it is already employed, albeit somewhat loosely and only occasionally, in the Nikāyas/Āgamas and the canonical Abhidharma texts to characterize the experiences of meditation, and the five aggregates and dharmas.[27] But the emphasis on perfect wisdom as that which understands emptiness becomes the hallmark of the Perfection of Wisdom literature and its philosophical explication by Nāgārjuna.

Nāgārjuna and the 'middle' (Madhyamaka) school

Nāgārjuna, who probably lived in the second century CE, is the father of the Madhyamaka or 'middle' school of Buddhist philosophy. The Madhyamaka was to become one of the two great philosophical traditions of the Mahāyāna, but lest there be confusion let me remind the reader that a philosophical school of thought is quite a distinct matter from a division and grouping of the monastic Saṅgha (*nikāya*); in India the Madhyamaka was not and never becomes a school in the sense of the Mahāsāṃghika, Theravāda, Sarvāstivāda, or Sammatīya. In fact, as a Buddhist monk, Nāgārjuna was presumably ordained into one of these four main ordination lineages, though which is not known, and remained in that tradition for the rest of his monastic life. The Madhyamaka was a philosophical outlook that, like the Mahāyāna in general, would have crossed the boundaries of the various ordination lineages of the Saṅgha.

This philosophical school is named after Nāgārjuna's principal work, *Mūla-Madhyamaka-Kārikā* or 'Root Verses on the Middle', and refers to the way in which Nāgārjuna presents 'emptiness' as equivalent to that fundamental teaching of the Buddha, 'dependent arising', and, as such, as articulating the 'middle' between the extremes of eternalism and annihilationism. If something arises in dependence upon some other thing, as a dharma is supposed to, then how, Nāgārjuna asks, can it be defined in the manner that certain Abhidharma theorists want, as that which exists of and in itself, as that which possesses its own existence (*svabhāva/sabhāva*)? For if something is sufficient to explain its own existence, then it must exist as itself for ever and ever, and could never be affected by anything else, since as soon as it was affected it would cease to be itself. And if things cannot truly change, then the whole of Buddhism is undermined, for Buddhism claims that suffering arises because of causes and conditions and that by gradually eliminating unwholesome conditions and cultivating wholesome conditions we can change from being unawakened to being awakened. Thus the one who claims that dharmas ultimately exist in themselves must either fall into the trap of eternalism by denying the possibility of real change, or, if he nevertheless insists that change is possible, fall into the trap of annihilationism since, in changing, what existed has gone out of existence. Therefore, concludes Nāgārjuna, the teaching of the Buddha is that everything is empty of its own inherent existence.

But Nāgārjuna was quick to point out that we should not conclude that emptiness itself is equivalent to the view that nothing exists; in fact those who see in emptiness some kind of annihilationism have a faulty view of emptiness, and 'when it is wrongly seen, emptiness destroys the dull-witted, like a snake that is wrongly grasped or a magical spell that is wrongly cast'.[28] It is not that nothing exists, but that nothing exists as an individual essence possessed of its own inherent existence. In particular, to see 'emptiness' as undermining the teaching of the Buddha is to fail to take proper account of the basic Abhidharma distinction between conventional truth and ultimate truth. The point is that, for Nāgārjuna, the Abhidharma account of the world in terms of dharmas cannot be the ultimate description of the way things are; rather it still falls within the compass of conventional truth. The ultimate truth about the way things are is emptiness, but conventional truth is still *truth*, not conventional falsehood, and without it the Buddha's teaching is hopeless:

> The buddhas' teaching of Dharma depends equally on two truths: ordinary conventional truth and truth from the point of view of the ultimate; those who do not perceive the difference between these two truths do not perceive the deep 'reality' (*tattva*) in the teaching of the buddhas. Without resorting to ordinary conventions, what is ultimate cannot be taught; without recourse to what is ultimate, nirvāṇa is not attained.[29]

But nirvāṇa is not some 'Absolute Reality' existing beyond the phenomenal conditioned world, behind the veil of conventional truth, for again this would commit us to eternalism. Emptiness is the ultimate truth of reality and of nirvāṇa—it too is empty of its own existence, it is not an existent. It follows that nirvāṇa cannot be understood as some *thing*, some existent, which is other than the conditioned round of existence, saṃsara:

> There is nothing that distinguishes saṃsāra from nirvāṇa; there is nothing that distinguishes nirvāṇa from saṃsāra; and the furthest limit of nirvāṇa is also the furthest limit of saṃsāra; not even the subtlest difference between the two is found.[30]

In emptiness, then, Nāgārjuna attempts to articulate very precisely what he sees as the Buddha's teaching of dependent arising and the middle between annihilationism and eternalism: emptiness is not a 'nothing', it is not nihilism, but equally it is not a 'something', it is not some absolute reality; it is the absolute truth about the way things are but it is not *the* Absolute. For to think of emptiness in terms of either an Absolute or a Nothingness is precisely to turn emptiness into a view of either eternalism or of annihilationism. But in fact the Buddha taught Dharma for the abandoning of all views and emptiness is precisely the letting go of all views, while those for whom emptiness is a view are 'incurable'.[31]

Tibetan tradition has identified two basic schools of thought in the history of Madhyamaka in India after Nāgārjuna. The first is the *prāsaṅgika* or method 'of consequences', exemplified by Buddhapālita (sixth century) and Candrakīrti. This involves drawing out the undesirable and contradictory consequences that follow from attempting to take up a philosophical position on some issue. The classic form of this method amounts to a kind of *reductio ad absurdum* of four possibilities (*catuṣ-koṭi*), that something is the case, is not the case, both is and is not the case, neither is nor is not the case. All four are shown to be untenable, and 'emptiness' follows directly from this. Thus, for example, chapter 12 of Nāgārjuna's *Mūla-Madhyamaka-Kārikā* tries to demonstrate the incoherence of maintaining that suffering is produced by oneself, that it is produced by another, that it is produced by both oneself and another, that it is produced by neither. The method is thus primarily negative, there being no attempt to adduce independent (*svātantrika*) positive arguments aimed at establishing the philosophical 'position' of emptiness. This alternative *svātantrika* method is associated with the name of Bhāvaviveka (sixth century).

The term 'view' (*dṛṣṭi/diṭṭhi*) becomes crucial for the Perfection of Wisdom and Nāgārjuna. The Nikāyas and Āgamas distinguished between 'wrong' view (e.g. that our actions have no results, that the self exists) and 'right' views (e.g. that actions do have results and that all things are not self) and recommend the latter. At the same time these early Buddhist texts stress that the arhat transcends and is free of all views and opinions. What the Perfection of Wisdom and Nāgārjuna are concerned to articulate is that there is a level at which views in general—even 'right' ones—should be seen as a form of mental rigidity, a form of opinionatedness: that is, we become attached to our right understanding. Thus the awakened mind is free of all views—even right views; it simply sees that dharmas are empty, it simply sees the way things are; the unawakened mind grasps at or fixes upon particular conceptual understandings or verbal expressions. This does not mean that 'right' views are somehow wrong, only that theoretical understanding should not be confused with real seeing. Right views and opinions are ultimately merely devices to bring about perfect understanding itself; the theory is for the sake of understanding. That is, a buddha cannot strictly be said to hold the view, opinion, or belief that all dharmas are empty; strictly speaking he does not hold any views or opinions, he simply sees the way things are. That is, the mind that sees emptiness (as opposed to the mind that merely has a theoretical grasp) is free of any tendency to impose some sort of conceptual construct on the way things are. On the other hand, although we may be convinced by Nāgārjuna's argument and form the view that it is certainly true that all things are empty of inherent existence, nothing actually changes for us and our minds continue to grasp at objects of experience, whether physical or emotional, as if they were so many possessions to have or to reject.

Like the Prajñāpāramitā in general, Nāgārjuna's analysis has often been presented in modern scholarly discussions as subverting the whole Abhidharma enterprise. This is to simplify Nāgārjuna to the point of distortion. Nāgārjuna's discussion is couched in Abhidharma technical terminology and assumes a thorough understanding of Abhidharma principles of analysis. Nāgārjuna is not attempting to show that Abhidharma is somehow wrong, just as he is not attempting to show that the four noble truths, or any of the other categories of Buddhist teaching, are wrong. Rather Nāgārjuna is concerned with a particular Abhidharma issue, namely the ontology of a 'dharma': how is one to define what a 'dharma' is? What he wants to point out, by appeal to fundamental principles that all Buddhist thought takes for granted, is that a 'dharma' certainly cannot be defined as that which possesses its own inherent existence (as opposed to the conventional existence of the 'self', for example). An account of reality in terms of ultimately real, self-existent dharmas cannot have the status of ultimate truth but only conventional truth. In as much as it presents dharmas as representing the ultimate divisions in the analysis of experience, beyond which one cannot go, all Abhidharma tended to define dharmas as those things which exist in themselves (*svabhāva/sabhāva*). Nāgārjuna's point is that, on Buddhist principles, such ultimate divisions of analysis are always arbitrary and cannot be taken as referring to ultimate realities in themselves. Although he is not explicit, in presenting his critique of dharmas as 'self-existents', he seems to have in mind particularly the kind of ontology of a dharma we know from the works of the Sarvāstivāda-Vaibhāṣika Abhidharma.[32] This lays great stress on dharmas as the ultimate 'substantial bits' (*dravya*) of mentality or materiality out of which the world as a whole is constructed. For Nāgārjuna an account of the world in Abhidharma terms is perfectly legitimate, as long as we do not view it as an exact and final description of how things are; like the Buddha's teachings generally, Abhidharma must ultimately be seen as 'conventional', taught for the purpose of the abandoning of greed, hatred, and delusion.[33]

The Perfection of Wisdom literature is Mahāyānist in so far as it privileges the path of the bodhisattva; likewise, on the evidence of the other writings usually attributed to him, the author of the *Mūla-Madhyamaka-Kārikā* seems to have been a follower of the Mahāyāna. But if Nāgārjuna is a Mahāyānist, this fact is entirely incidental to the philosophy of the *Madhyamaka-Kārikā*. In seeking to establish his understanding of emptiness, he appeals not to the authority of the Perfection of Wisdom Sūtras, but to that of the discourses of the Buddha on dependent arising preserved in the ancient Saṃyukta division of the canon.[34] In fact neither the early Perfection of Wisdom sūtras nor Nāgārjuna seem to present their understanding of 'emptiness' as a teaching peculiar to the Mahāyāna; that is, the understanding of emptiness of all dharmas is not seen as exclusive to bodhisattvas and buddhas but as the wisdom common to *śrāvakas*, *pratyeka-buddhas* and buddhas. Certainly this is how Candrakīrti, Nāgārjuna's seventh-century commentator, understood the matter. Thus for the Perfection of Wisdom and for Nāgārjuna, 'the emptiness of dharmas' (*dharma-śūnyatā*) is not a further teaching, but something required by the logic of 'the emptiness of persons' (*pudgala-śūnyatā*). Self (*ātman*) and 'inherent existence' (*svabhāva*) are equivalents, only the scale is different: the doctrine that there is no substantial self underlying persons (*pudgala-nairātmya*) entails the doctrine that there is no substantial self underlying dharmas (*dharma-nairātmya*); just as there is no ultimate unchanging 'thing' behind the label 'person' or 'self', so there is no ultimate, unchanging thing behind the labels 'greed', 'hatred', or 'ignorance', behind the labels 'non-attachment', 'loving kindness', and 'wisdom'. And this is what arhats and buddhas have always seen. Some Mahāyāna writers, however, did want to claim the understanding of the emptiness of dharmas as the preserve of the bodhisattva: arhats understand the emptiness of persons and thereby remove the obstacles that consist in the defilements (*kleśa-āvaraṇa*), but only buddhas understand the emptiness of dharmas and remove all the obstacles to full knowledge (*jñeya-āvaraṇa*). Thus although they abandon the defilements, arhats are still subject to subtle traces left by the defilements (*kleśa-vāsana*), which can cause, for example, an arhat to skip like a monkey, echoing a previous life.[35]

Both the Perfection of Wisdom and Nāgārjuna understand themselves as explicating an understanding of the Buddha's teaching as originally taught by the Buddha, and in certain respects such a view of the matter may not be entirely unhistorical. The earliest Buddhist teachings place great emphasis on the wisdom of the arhat as transcending fixed views and opinions in a manner that is not dissimilar from the Perfection of Wisdom and Nāgārjuna. Moreover, non-Mahāyāna manuals that basically subscribe to the Abhidharma outlook share in significant respects a common understanding with the Perfection of Wisdom and

Nāgārjuna on these matters: certainly dharmas are ultimately ungraspable and evanescent; certainly the arhat's knowledge transcends all views, even right views.[36]

Of all Buddhist thinkers, it is Nāgārjuna who has repeatedly captured the modern imagination. Modern scholars have presented his thought as prefiguring Kant (Stcherbatsky), Wittgenstein (Gudmunsen), and, most recently, Rorty and Derrida (Huntington). Other scholars, such as Robinson and Hayes, have suggested that Nāgārjuna's arguments employ a kind of logical sleight of hand and in places are simply logically flawed.[37] Hayes has also questioned his influence on subsequent Indian Buddhist thought, yet he remains a towering and legendary figure for later Chinese and, especially, Tibetan Buddhist thought.

'Ideas-only' (*vijñapti-mātra*) and the Yogācāra

The basic understanding of this tradition is that the world we live in—the round of rebirth or saṃsāra—is to be explained in its entirety in terms of the workings of the mind: the threefold universe (see Chapter 5) is only 'ideas' (*vijñapti-mātra*).[38] The theories and teachings associated with this understanding are found in various sūtras, the most important being the *Saṃdhinirmocana* ('Unravelling the Mystery of Thought') and the *Laṅkāvatāra* ('Arrival in Laṅkā'); they receive their initial systematic exposition in the works of Asaṅga and Vasubandhu, such as Asaṅga's *Mahāyāna-Saṃgraha* ('Summary of the Great Vehicle') and Vasubandhu's *Viṃśatikā* ('Twenty Verses') and *Triṃśikā* ('Thirty Verses'), *Tri-Svabhāva-Nirdeśa* ('Exposition of the Three Natures'), and his commentary to the *Madhyānta-Vibhāga* ('Analysis of the Middle Path'), a work traditionally regarded as given, along with several others, to Asaṅga by the Bodhisattva Maitreya in the Tuṣita heaven. The work of these two thinkers was subsequently commented upon and elaborated in India by Sthiramati (sixth century) and Dharmapāla (seventh century), and in China by Paramārtha (sixth century) and Hsüan-tsang, who studied with Dharmapāla at Nālandā in the seventh century and later wrote the *Cheng-wei-shih lun* or

Vijñaptimātratāsiddhi, a commentary on Vasubandhu's *Triṃśikā* incorporating the views of various Indian teachers.

The teachings of this school in certain respects represent a reworking of particular Abhidharma themes in response to the Prajñāpāramitā and Madhyamaka teaching of emptiness. The *Saṃdhinirmocana Sūtra* thus presents its own teachings as a third and definitive 'turning of the wheel of the Dharma', following the Buddha's provisional teachings of the four truths in the deer park outside Benares, and of emptiness in the manner of the Prajñāpāramitā.[39] That is, for the *Saṃdhinirmocana*, the presentation of emptiness in the Prajñāpāramitā is too prone to the wrong sort of interpretation by the unwary and needs further explication.

The Prajñāpāramitā and Madhyamaka point out that the logic of 'dependent arising' demands that dharmas cannot be thought of as the absolute, ultimate existents of the universe. In peeling away the conventional truth of the existence of persons and selves and seeing the underlying dharmas, we do not arrive at ultimate existents, but only at another, perhaps deeper layer of conventional truth; the ultimate truth is that dharmas too are empty of their own existence. From the Yogācāra perspective, however, this is to tell us what things are ultimately not, but it is to tell us much too little about what things are and, crucially, how they come to appear other than the way they are. Thus while Madhyamaka was primarily concerned to critique a particular analysis of the ontology of a dharma, Yogācāra returns to giving a positive account of the workings of the mind in terms of dharmas in a new ontological framework. As the name of the school indicates—Yoga Practice—its approach is perhaps especially based in meditation, and the writings of Asaṅga and Vasubandhu show a special interest in calm meditation. There are two basic parts to the account of mind given in Yogācāra: the first concerns the eight types of consciousness (*vijñāna*) and the second the 'three natures' (*tri-svabhāva*). Let us turn to these in turn.

Early Buddhist thought analysed consciousness as consisting of six basic types corresponding to the five senses and the mind. Building on the traditions of the earlier Ābhidharmikas, Yogācārin thinkers give what amounts to a rather more complex account of the sixth, mind consciousness, focusing on what are in effect the deeper layers of the mind. The active or surface level of the mind continues to be seen as comprising six type of consciousness: our primary awareness of five types of sense data and our conscious thoughts, which for human beings are mostly related to the former in various ways. But underpinning these types of active consciousness are two further types of consciousness which are crucial in creating the world as we ordinarily experience it. The first is 'the defiled mind' (*kliṣṭa-manas*), so called because it is afflicted with four basic defilements: the view of individuality, the conceit 'I am', clinging to self and delusion.[40] The object of this defilement, what the defiled mind in some way takes as the self, is the eighth consciousness, 'the store consciousness' (*ālaya-vijñāna*).[41] Below the threshold of consciousness proper,[42] the store consciousness is the particular repository of all the seeds sown by the defilements of a being's active consciousness; it is the result of a being's past karma, the accumulation of all past tendencies, strong or weak, to greed, hatred, and delusion; as such the store consciousness is also the condition for the perpetuation of these defilements in present and future active consciousness; it thus continually interacts with active consciousness according to the principles of dependent arising.[43] Of course, the store consciousness is not a self, a thing in itself; what, in our subconscious, the defiled mind takes for a self is merely an underlying mass of ever changing causes and conditions, arising and falling, but which none the less, as it flows on, maintains a certain pattern which gives it the appearance of relative identity. The store consciousness is thus the underlying basis and support (*āśraya*) of our conscious lives: the largely hidden heart of our personalities.

The world of experience has three different natures (*trisvabhāva*). Clearly something is going on: we have experiences. The problem, according to the Yogācāra, is that what we experience is ourselves as conscious subjects enjoying a world of objects that exist 'out there', independently from us. This is experience in its 'imagined' (*parikalpita*) nature, for the world of experiencing subject or 'grasper' and experienced object or 'thing grasped' is in fact a world of unreal imaginings, of things that do not ultimately exist. Both the grasper and the things grasped are in fact ideas, pieces of information (*vijñapti*), thrown up by the traces and seeds deposited in the store consciousness. This is experience in its dependent (*para-tantra*) nature. The operation of the eight kinds of consciousness ultimately consists in nothing more than a flow of 'ideas' (*vijñapti-mātra*), arising in dependence upon each other.[44] By force of a long-standing habit —throughout beginningless saṃsāra—we have imagined in the dependent flow of 'pieces of information' a world of independent subjects and independent objects. But when, as buddhas, we understand the complete absence of the duality of subject and object in the 'dependent nature' of experience, then experience appears in its perfected (*niṣpanna*) nature. In crude summary, the imagined nature is the unawakened mind, the perfected nature is the awakened mind, while the dependent nature is the common basis.

As the realization of the Buddhist yogin at the culmination of the Buddhist path, the perfected nature consists in the non-conceptual knowledge (*nirvikalpaka-jñāna*) which is empty of any sense of experiencing subject and experienced object. Its attainment is marked by 'the turning around of the basis' (*āśraya-parāvṛtti*), a revolution at the very centre of one's being whereby all defilements are cut off, and the imagined nature is no longer imposed upon the dependent nature, which appears instead as the perfected nature. As a result of this 'turning around of the basis', the seeds in the store consciousness cease to function as the basis for the imagined nature.[45] What appears as the contradiction at the heart of reality is seen through: certainly the process of imagining the duality of subject and object exists, but since a subject and object are not in the end to be found, the process is empty (*śūnya*), and yet this 'emptiness' itself is something that is definitely found. The middle way is to be found in the way 'reality' is somehow existent, non-existent, and yet existent at the same time. Ultimately reality is thus characterized not as an absolute 'something' (either mind or matter), but simply as the way things are: 'thusness' (*tathatā*).[46]

Modern scholars have disagreed on the question of whether Yogācāra constitutes a true philosophical 'idealism', asserting that the mind only is real and that the external material world is unreal. The argument essentially turns, as Griffiths has neatly put it, on the question of whether Yogācāra is primarily making an epistemological point (that all we have access to is mental representation) or an ontological one (that mental representation is all that exists).[47] Certainly Yogācāra starts from the premiss that the world we know, the world we live in, is strictly a mental world: everything comes to us in the form of 'information' or 'ideas' (*vijñapti*). Apart from *vijñapti* there is no world, there is no experience. Equally certainly it is saying more than that simply in practice, *de facto*, we are trapped in our own private mental world unable to know whether or not there is in reality an external world that corresponds to our ideas about it, to our perceptions of it. Yogācāra is not a doctrine of solipsism. Vasubandhu's *Viṃśatikā* thus attempts to argue that, although objects do not exist out there apart from our perceptions of them, nevertheless similar past karma results in the sharing of common experiences in the present. But these experiences are simply the products of the workings of consciousness, amounting to the arising of similar pieces of information in different streams of consciousness. We are, as it were, dreaming similar dreams; and just as the pieces of information that come to us in a dream lack independent objects, so do the direct perceptions of our wakeful state:

> Thus people are hypnotized with a sleep arising from impressions left by the habit of false ways of thought, and, as in a dream, when they see things that are unreal, so long as they do not wake up they do not understand their non-existence. When, however, they wake up by acquiring the transcendent knowledge which is beyond thought and opposed to that same sleep, then, by the realization of the purified ordinary awareness that is gained as a consequence, they understand the non-existence of the objects of the senses.[48]

Yogācāra thus does not appear to be agnostic about the nature of the external world. Rather it claims to present an account of how we construct our world our of ideas, of how this causes us suffering, and of how we can turn this process around and escape from suffering. In other words, like all Buddhism it presents us with an account of the four truths. Yogācāra denies the ultimate independent existence of a separate experiencing subject on the one hand and another separate world 'out there' of experienced objects. That the world appears like this is an illusion constructed out of consciousness; or mind. But this is not to be taken as saying that I, the experiencing subject, somehow exist as my mind, my consciousness, while the external world of objects does not exist. It is precisely both that are ultimately fictions, illusions—'ideas' (*vijñapti*) fabricated by mind. True, Yogācāra privileges 'mind' or 'consciousness' in so far as it is the operation of the mind that brings about the illusion of the duality of subject and object. But 'mind' that is not an experiencer or enjoyer of external objects is not exactly mind as we ordinarily understand it. For Yogācāra, as for all Buddhist thought, it is the *way* things are rather than *what* actually is, that is crucial: the truth underlying reality is 'thusness' (*tathatā*).

In many ways Yogācāra represents the culmination of the north Indian Buddhist intellectual tradition. Its treatises set forth a full psychological theory (which represents a reworking of earlier Abhidharma systems), a complete map of the path (outlining in some detail the progress of calm and insight meditation), and a complex understanding of the nature of buddhahood. As with all Buddhist thought, one should not be misled by the philosophical sophistication of Madhyamaka and Yogācāra thought. Their teachings are not seen as mere intellectual abstraction which to all practical intents and purposes we can forget about. The theoretical content of these systems are as ever orientated towards releasing beings from suffering. For Madhyamaka, as long as we see a world of things that exist in themselves, we are trying, however subtly, to hold on to things that ultimately must slip from our grasp, and this can only cause ourselves and others suffering. Likewise, for Yogācāra, as long as we see the world in terms of really existent experiencing subjects and really existing experienced objects, we are trapped in a world of beings grasping at their experiences as objects of possession; once more this will only end in more suffering for all concerned. What both Madhyamaka and Yogācāra point towards is not simply a change of intellectual view, but a radical change of heart, deep within ourselves. While it is certainly the case that both Madhyamaka and Yogācāra are concerned with the highest understanding, the perfect wisdom that penetrates directly to the way things are, they also focus on the subtlest forms of greed—the subtlest tendencies of the mind to grasp, cling, and fix—as the root of all other forms of greed. In other words, the concern is with the greed and delusion as the principal causes of suffering, and a complete letting go as its cessation.

As I have already indicated, it is important to understand in what sense the Indian authors of the Madhyamaka and Yogācāra theoretical writings are 'Mahāyānists'. Essentially they are Mahāyānists in that they privilege the path of the Bodhisattva and recognize the authority of the Mahāyāna sūtras. But they do not reject the earlier tradition. These authors continued to operate within the existing ordination lineages of the Saṅgha, and when trying to justify their understanding of emptiness or the store consciousness they will as soon appeal to the generally accepted texts of the Nikāyas/Āgamas and Abhidharma as to the Mahāyāna sūtras. Much of Madhyamaka and Yogācāra theory represents a continuation of and development of particular lines of thought within the broad Abhidharma tradition. Abhidharma is not rejected or thrown out; rather a particular understanding of the ontology of a dharma is rejected. But, although dharmas may ultimately not exist in themselves, the broad Abhidharma framework remains as the theoretical basis for understanding the workings of consciousness, for analysing progress along the path, and for breaking down our basic attachment to self.

The Tathāgatagarbha

There is suffering, and the root defilements of greed, aversion, and delusion cause beings suffering in all its forms. The cessation of these defilements brings about the cessation of all that suffering. This is a statement of the first three of the four noble truths—a statement in primarily negative terms. But we can state the matter in more positive terms: it is not only the cessation of greed, aversion, and delusion that bring about the cessation of suffering but the positive cultivation of wisdom, loving kindness, and generosity. And this is the fourth noble truth: it is the development of such qualities that constitutes the path that leads to the cessation of suffering.

Another way of talking about the process of the arising of suffering and its cessation is in terms of the formula of dependent arising; again the usual statement is couched in negative terms: the progressive cessation of the various links in the chain ends in the cessation of suffering, but we saw too that this could be stated positively in terms of the progressive arising of various qualities beginning with faith and ending in knowledge and freedom. For the ordinary unawakened person the root causes of suffering, the defilements (*kleśa/kilesa*) of greed, aversion, and delusion, do battle with the root causes of awakening, the good qualities of wisdom, loving kindness, and generosity: we are internally in conflict. But this does not mean that we should conceive of ourselves as merely a battleground for a conflict that may go either way. For, although this may be how things appear in the short term, it is, according to the teaching of the Buddha as presented in the Nikāyas/Āgamas, our better nature that reflects our true nature: the mind is naturally radiant but becomes defiled by adventitious defilements (see p. 175). At heart we are not Māras but buddhas, and this is true of the being that is Māra himself. This way of thinking is part of the common heritage of all Buddhism, but in Mahāyāna sūtras it finds expression and is developed in the notion of the *tathāgata-garbha*: the 'womb' or 'embryo' (the Sanskrit *garbha* connotes both) of the Tathāgata. Thus in the Mahāyāna *Tathāgatagarbha Sūtra*, the Buddha observes:

> [W]hen I regard all beings with my buddha eye, I see that hidden within the kleśas of greed, desire, anger and stupidity there is seated augustly

> and unmovingly the tathāgata's wisdom, the tathāgata's vision, and the tathāgata's body . . . [A]ll beings, though they find themselves with all sorts of kleśas, have a tathāgatagarbha that is eternally unsullied, and that is replete with virtues no different from my own.[49]

The basic treatise of the *tathāgatagarbha* tradition of thought is the *Ratnagotravibhāga* (also known as the *Uttaratantra*) attributed to Maitreya/Asaṅga. The *tathāgatagarbha* is an element of Buddhahood (*buddha-dhātu*) at the heart of our being, our intrinsic 'buddha nature'. Although some Mahāyānist writings acknowledged the possibility of beings who are eternally cut off from the possibility of buddhahood, the prevailing tradition, particularly important in East Asian Buddhism and reaching its most developed statement in Dōgen's Zen, is that all beings are intrinsically Buddhas.

Talk of the *tathāgatagarbha* as our eternal and true nature in contrast to illusory and ultimately unreal defilements leads to a tendency to conceive of it as an ultimate absolutely existing thing. The Mahāyāna *Mahāparinirvāṇa Sūtra*, especially influential in East Asian Buddhist thought, goes so far as to speak of it as our true self (*ātman*). Its precise metaphysical and ontological status is, however, open to interpretation in the terms of different Mahāyāna philosophical schools; for the Mādhyamikas it must be empty of its own existence like everything else; for the Yogācārins, following the *Laṅkāvatāra*, it can be identified with store consciousness, as the receptacle of the seeds of awakening. Yet the problem of the metaphysics of the *tathāgatagarbha* persisted and is perhaps most clearly exemplified in the *rang-stong/gzhan-stong* debate in Tibet (see Chapter 10).

10

Evolving Traditions of Buddhism

South, East, North, and West

Theravāda Buddhism in Sri Lanka and South-East Asia: Southern Buddhism

Buddhism arrived in Sri Lanka in the third century BCE; for the next thousand years or so Sri Lanka was a great centre of Buddhist learning. The early spread and history of Buddhism in South-East Asia, on the other hand, is complex. While the Theravāda Buddhism of the Sri Lanka and South-East Asia should not be viewed as a uniform and monolithic whole, it does have a certain unity exemplified by the persistence of one main monastic Vinaya lineage and the authority of the Pali canon and its commentaries, inherited from the Mahāvihāra of ancient Anurādhapura. But this is no simple orthodoxy; a variety of interpretations and practices have probably always existed and persist down to modern times. Too often the models and norms for religious history employed by modern scholarship revolve around concepts of schism, heresy, orthodoxy, sect, and denomination, derived from the history of Christianity. These concepts are not always appropriate, and obscure the religious history of Buddhism rather than shed light upon it.

Sri Lanka

The initial formative phase of Theravāda Buddhism was completed by 1000 CE. This is not to say that there are no subsequent developments or changes, but that Theravāda Buddhism largely defines itself by reference to traditions and teachings that were established between the fifth and tenth centuries in Sri Lanka; the twelfth and thirteenth centuries should also be seen as a significant creative period.

Following the introduction of Buddhism to Sri Lanka by Mahinda in the third century BCE (see Chapter 2) there emerged three great divisions of the Saṅgha on the island, each centring on a monastery in the ancient capital of Anurādhapura. The oldest, the Mahāvihāra or 'great monastery', was established by Mahinda himself in the third century, the Abhayagiri-vihāra in the first century BCE, and the Jetavana in the third century CE. Famed as a centre of Buddhist learning, Anurādhapura attracted visiting monks from the Indian mainland—including one of Theravāda Buddhism's subsequently most celebrated commentators, Dhammapāla (seventh century?)—and also China (Fa-hsien in the early fifth century).

Beginning in the fifth century, a series of commentators (Buddhaghosa, Buddhadatta, Mahānāma, Upasena, Dhammapāla I, Dhammapāla II) drawing on the traditions and textual resources of the Mahāvihāra established the classical doctrinal form of the Theravāda, and it is their writings that have come down to us. The fifth century also saw the basic content and structure of the Pali canon finally established: (1) a Vinaya comprising two principal works; (2) a Sutta Piṭaka comprising the four primary Nikāyas and the fifteen works of the Khuddaka Nikāya; (3) an Abhidhamma Piṭaka comprising seven works.[1]

Since none of the writings of the monks of the Abhayagiri and Jetavana monasteries survive (with the possible exception of Upatissa's *Vimuttimagga*, which exists only in Chinese translation), it is not entirely clear in what manner their traditions differed from those of the Mahāvihāra.[2] The tendency to see the undoubted rivalry between them in terms of a Mahāvihāra opposition to their Mahāyāna sympathies is both simplistic and problematic. It is important to bear in mind, however, that the Abhayagiri and Jetavana monasteries continued to flourish and their monks were as much part of the Sri Lankan Buddhist scene as those of the Mahāvihāra.

Invasions of the island from south India resulted in the Sri Lankan court fleeing further south to Polonnaruva, which was established as the permanent capital of the island in the eleventh century after the defeat of the south Indian invaders by Vijaya

Bahu I. From the second century BCE south Indian kings had invaded and ruled on several occasions in Anurādhapura without causing any cultural discontinuity, but the wars of the tenth and eleventh centuries proved particularly destructive of ancient Sri Lankan culture; the extent to which the lineage of the Buddhist Saṅgha was disrupted is not entirely clear, but it appears that the order of nuns died out at this time and that contacts with Burma played some part in the re-establishment of the traditions of the three ancient lineages of the Mahāvihāra, Abhayagiri, and Jetavana.[3] In 1165, however, following a dispute between these three lineages, King Parākrama Bāhu I unified the Saṅgha according to the rule of the Mahāvihāra. But the Buddhism of Sri Lanka should not be regarded as a simple Mahāvihāra 'orthodoxy' at this period or earlier; indeed, it is doubtful that Buddhism anywhere has ever operated quite in the manner of an 'orthodoxy'. From early times continued contacts with south India (where it appears Theravāda traditions flourished until at least the fourteenth century) and the arrival of monks from outside the island meant that various Buddhist influences and practices, including those of the Mahāyāna and the Vajrayāna, were present on the island.

Invasion from south India led to the fall of Polonnaruva in 1215. The following centuries witnessed a relative decline in the institutions of Buddhism in Sri Lanka. From the sixteenth century the Portuguese (1505–1658), the Dutch (1658–1796), and finally the British controlled the coastal kingdom centred on Kōṭṭē and then Colombo, with only the central Kandyan kingdom retaining its independence. The state of monastic Buddhism reached a low ebb in the seventeenth and eighteenth centuries, resulting in the sending of missions to South East Asia in order to re-import the higher ordination lineage. This was successfully accomplished in 1753 during the reign of Kīrti Śrī Rājasiṃha (1747–81). In 1815 the British took control of the Kandyan kingdom, and their colonial rule of the whole island lasted until 1948. The nineteenth and twentieth centuries saw the emergence of new 'modernist' trends—sometimes referred to as 'Protestant Buddhism'—in response to Christian missionary activity, modernization, and increasing European interest in Buddhist thought and practice.'[4]

South-East Asia

Indian cultural influence began to extend into South-East Asia from the early centuries of the Christian era, and various forms of Hinduism and traditions of Buddhism had established themselves throughout the region by the end of the first millennium. Tradition has it that Buddhism first entered the area in the third century BCE with missions sent by Aśoka, and this is not impossible. Archaeological evidence confirms the existence of a form of Theravāda Buddhism in the Pyu and Mon kingdoms (in what is now Burma and Thailand) from the fifth century CE; this form of Theravāda may have been introduced from southern India rather than Sri Lanka.[5] Links between the capital of the Burmese kingdom at Pagan and Sri Lankan Theravāda in the eleventh century during the reign of King Anawratha (1044–77) indicate that by this period the Theravāda lineages of the Saṅgha were well established in the region.

The powerful kingdom of the Khmers (centred on Angkor) dominated much of the region to the south-east (parts of what is now Thailand and Cambodia) from the eighth to the fifteenth centuries and here different forms of both Hindu and Buddhist practice flourished. Inscriptional evidence from the eighth century suggests the presence of the Theravāda Saṅgha within the Khmer cultural sphere, and from the twelfth century Mon forms of Theravāda became increasingly influential both at court and among the population as a whole. The Thai kingdoms began to establish themselves from the thirteenth century, centring first on Sukhotai in the north (until the fifteenth century), then on Ayudhya (until the eighteenth century) and finally on Bangkok (until the present). State support for the Theravāda Saṅgha and links with Sri Lanka have been a feature of the kingdom.

While Cambodia and Burma became French and British colonies respectively, Thailand retained its independence throughout the colonial period. But modernizing influences were not absent from the country, and in the nineteenth century Rama IV (1851–68) instigated the establishment of the reformed Dhammayuttika lineage of the Saṅgha. The influence of this reform in Thailand and beyond has resulted in the gradual decline of many of the older esoteric traditions and practices of South-East Asian Theravāda associated with the Mahānikāya lineage and documented in the works of François Bizot.[6] These traditions flourished until most recently in Cambodia, but the fanatical activities of Pol Pot's Khmer Rouge between 1975 and 1978, when perhaps a million Cambodians died, involved the murder of many monks and the forced disrobing of the rest. This means that little is left on the ground.

China, Korea, and Japan: East Asian Buddhism

The Buddhism of China, Korea, and Japan constitutes a unity that can be referred to as East Asian or Eastern Buddhism because it shares a common basis in the scriptural resource of the Chinese Tripiṭaka and because Korean and Japanese forms and schools derive directly from Chinese forms and schools, although they subsequently developed distinctive local traditions. Buddhism began entering China during the Han dynasty (206 BCE–220 CE), probably in the first century BCE or CE, principally via the ancient silk routes through central Asia. From China Buddhism entered the Korean peninsula (fourth century) and thence Japan (sixth century).

Significant in the establishment of Buddhism as a part of Chinese life in the following centuries was the appeal of Buddhist ideas and meditation practices to the followers of neo-Taoism (*Hsüan Hsüeh*), although the growing popular acceptance of this 'foreign' doctrine also prompted periodic opposition from both Confucian and Taoist circles.[7] The T'ang dynasty (618–907) witnessed the greatest flourishing of Buddhism in China. Buddhism continued to flourish until the end of the thirteenth century under the Sung, but the period from the fifteenth century is generally regarded as one of relative decline. Yet in the first half of the twentieth century Buddhism was still the most significant religious force in China.[8] The Communist take-over of 1949 and especially the 'Cultural Revolution' of 1966–72 brought with them a widespread government suppression of Buddhism, which, in the more recent period, has given way to a more tolerant attitude.[9] The traditions of Chinese Buddhism also continue in Taiwan and Hong Kong.

The development of the Chinese canon

When Buddhism began entering China the Mahāyāna was still in its early stages of development; the writings of Nāgārjuna, Asaṅga, and Vasubandhu were still to come. The most important early centre of Buddhism in China seems to have been at Lo-yang and it is here, from the middle of the second century, that foreign monks such as An Shih-kao and Lokakṣema (Chih Lou-chia-ch'an) began the work of translating Indian Buddhist texts into Chinese; these first translations included texts on meditation (such as the non-Mahāyāna *Ānāpāna-smṛti Sūtra* or 'Discourse on Mindfulness of Breathing' and the proto-Mahāyāna *Pratyutpanna-buddha-saṃmukhâvasthita-samādhi Sūtra* or 'Discourse on the Samādhi of Direct Encounter with the Buddhas of the Present') and portions of the Perfection of Wisdom in 8,000 Lines (*Aṣṭa-sāhasrikā Prajñāpāramitā*).[10]

The manner of these early translations is characteristic of the whole process of translation of Indian Buddhist texts into Chinese. The Indian canonical collections were never translated into Chinese *en bloc*. The Chinese Tripiṭaka (*San-tsang*) or 'Great Treasury of Sūtras' (*Ta-tsang-ching*) evolved over a period of over a thousand years.[11] Rather than a strictly defined canon, the Chinese Tripiṭaka represents a library containing all the Chinese translations of Buddhist sūtras and śāstras made over the centuries, as well as a variety of indigenous Chinese treatises relating to Buddhism. The oldest surviving catalogue of Chinese Buddhist texts dates from the sixth century and details over 2,000 works; the first printed edition, produced from 130,000 wooden blocks and completed in 983, contained 1,076 works. Subsequent catalogues and editions, produced in Korea and Japan as well as China, show some divergence both in the arrangement of the canon and in its contents. The modern standard is the Taishō edition, produced in Japan between 1924 and 1932. Its fifty-five volumes, each some 1,000 pages in length, contain 2,184 works: volumes 1 to 32 consist of translations of ancient Indian works (1,692 texts); volumes 33 to 54 of works by Chinese monks (452 texts); volume 55 of ancient catalogues (40 texts). The whole is supplemented by a further 45 volumes containing works of Japanese origin, and other ancillary material.[12]

The Taishō edition groups texts on more or less historical principles. A more traditional arrangement is reflected by an important catalogue produced at the end of the nineteenth century by the Japanese scholar Bunyiu Nanjio.[13] This is basically a catalogue of an edition of the Chinese Tripiṭaka produced in the early seventeenth century at the end of the Ming dynasty which contains a total of 1,662 works and provides the easiest way for gaining an impression of the range and scope of the Chinese canon. The three traditional divisions of Sūtra (*ching*), Vinaya (*lü*), and Treatise (*lun*) are each subdivided according to the categories of 'Mahāyāna' and 'Hīnayāna', and finally supplemented by a fourth division. The Sūtra collection is the largest (1,081 texts); although largely taken up by the vast corpus of Mahāyāna sūtras, it also contains the Chinese Āgamas corresponding to the Pali Nikāyas. The Vinaya section (85 texts) contains translations of the Vinayas of various Indian schools and related works. The third division (154 texts) is devoted to treatises; this section includes the canonical Abhidharma texts of the Sarvāstivādins, as well as other Abhidharma, Madhyamaka, and Yogācāra treatises and commentaries. These three divisions of translations of Indian Buddhist materials are supplemented by a miscellaneous collection of writings (342 texts) by Indian and Chinese Buddhist masters.

The schools of East Asian Buddhism

The schools (*tsung*) of Chinese Buddhism divide into two main categories: those which have a more or less direct Indian counterpart and those which are native to China. The principal schools of the former category are the Vinaya, the Kośa, the Madhyamaka, the Yogācāra, and the Mantrayāna; of the latter category, Ch'an, Pure Land, T'ien-t'ai, and Hua-yen. In principle these are also the schools of Korean and Japanese Buddhism. In practice certain of the schools developed more significant local traditions than others. In Korea special mention should be made of the Sŏn (Ch'an) teaching of Chinul (1158–1210).[14] In Japan Tendai (T'ien-t'ai), Zen (Ch'an), Shingon (Mantrayāna), Pure Land, along with the distinctively Japanese tradition of Nichiren have been of special importance.

Chinese Buddhist monks eventually came to be ordained according to the Dharmaguptaka Vinaya, and Chinese Buddhist schools do not constitute separate ordination lineages, but focus on a lineage of teaching and interpretation of Buddhist thought and practice. Movement between the schools seems to have been normal. But early attempts to establish the norms of Buddhist monastic practice in China were felt to be hampered by a lack of knowledge of the Vinaya. It was this that prompted Fa-hsien, at the age of almost 60, to set out in 399 on a journey to India and Sri Lanka that was to last fourteen years. Subsequently the Vinaya School (Lü-tsung) of Chinese Buddhism was founded in the early seventh century by Tao-hsüan (596–667) as a focus for Chinese Vinaya studies.

The great translator Kumārajīva (344–413), a central Asian monk who had studied in Kashmir, arrived in China in 383; his translation of two works by Nāgārjuna and a third by Āryadeva marks the beginning of the Chinese Madhyamaka or 'Three Treatise School' (San-lun-tsung).[15] The development in China of the other great Indian Mahāyāna system, the Yogācāra, is associated with the work of the Indian monk Paramārtha, who arrived in Canton in 546, and Hsüan-tsang, who, as mentioned above, visited India in the seventh century and returned to China to found the 'Characteristics of Dharmas' (Fa-hsiang) school. Ancillary to this school was the Chu-she or (Abhidharma-)Kośa school.

The form of Mahāyāna Buddhist practice known as 'the vehicle of protective spells' (*mantra-yāna*) or tantra is most widespread within Tibetan Buddhism (see below), but a tradition of esoteric practice was introduced into China early in the eighth century by the Indians Śubhākarasiṃha (637–735) and Vajrabodhi

(671–741) and the Sri Lankan Amoghavajra (705–74). The principal text was the *Mahāvairocana* and *Vajraśekhara Sūtras*, associated with the practice of the *garbha-kośa-dhātu* and *vajra-dhātu maṇḍalas* respectively. A *maṇḍala* is a diagram (usually based on a square and/or circle orientated to the four directions) of the cosmos in the form of a vision of a set of buddhas and bodhisattvas which then acts as a basis for visualization and meditation for those who have been initiated into its practice by an accomplished master. Chinese Mantrayāna or 'True Word' (Chen Yen) flourished only briefly, although it enjoyed a limited revival in the twentieth century, partly because of Tibetan and Japanese influence. The school was, however, early on introduced to Japan by one of the great geniuses of Japanese culture, Kūkai or Kōbō Daishi (774–835), who in 804 travelled to China in search of instruction. Shingon remains a significant school of Japanese Buddhism today.[16]

Ch'an Buddhism

The term *ch'an* (Japanese *zen*) derives from the Sanskrit *dhyāna*, which, as we have seen, is used in Indian Buddhist theory to designate the attainment of a deep state of peace by the means of calm meditation. The term comes to refer to one of the important schools of East Asian Buddhism. Ch'an tradition looks to the legendary figure of the Indian monk Bodhidharma, who is said to have come east in the fifth or sixth century CE, as its first 'patriarch', but it is likely that the roots of Ch'an lie further back in Chinese Buddhist history with the interest shown in meditation practice by such figures as Tao-an (312–85), Hui-yüan (334–416), and Tao-sheng (360–434).

Ch'an tradition has it that, beginning with Bodhidharma, the lineage of teaching and the title of 'patriarch' passed from master to pupil. The transmission to the sixth patriarch, however, became the object of dispute. Originally it was assumed to have passed to Shen-hsiu (600–706), but in 734 this succession was challenged by a southern monk named Shen-hui (670–762), who claimed that in fact Hui-neng (638–713) had been the true sixth patriarch. Shen-hui and his 'southern' school of Ch'an were the effective winners of the dispute, with Hui-neng now looked upon as a second founder of Ch'an.

Shen-hui was an advocate of the doctrine of 'sudden awakening', and one of the things that he charged Shen-hsiu with was teaching a doctrine of 'gradual awakening'. This dispute over whether awakening should be regarded as a gradual process or a sudden event was not confined to Ch'an circles, but was a question that preoccupied Chinese Buddhism from an early date.[17] To some extent the problem reflects the old Abhidharma discussion over the question of whether, at the time of awakening, the four noble truths are seen gradually (as the Sarvāstivādins argued) or in a single instant (as the Theravādins, amongst others, argued): ultimate truth is not something one can see part of; one either sees it complete, or not at all. Yet the account of the bodhisattva path the Chinese inherited from India details various stages with definite attainments and points of no return. After Shen-hui, Ch'an became very much associated with a sudden awakening view.

Bodhidharma is said to have emphasized the teachings of the *Laṅkāvatāra Sūtra*, and the theoretical basis of Ch'an centres on the notions of the *tathāgatagarbha* and 'emptiness' as pointing beyond all conceptual forms of thought. Our innermost nature is simply the Buddha-nature (*fo-hsing*) which is to be realized in a direct and sudden experience of inner awakening (*wu/satori*). Ch'an tradition has a marked tendency to be critical of conventional theory and discursive philosophy, which it sees as cluttering the mind and creating obstacles to direct experience. Emphasis is put on just sitting in meditation (*tso ch'an/zazen*), the carrying out of ordinary routine tasks and the all-important instruction of the Ch'an master. Ch'an's own considerable literary and intellectual tradition centres on the stories of the sayings and deeds of these Ch'an masters, who may be portrayed as behaving in unexpected and spontaneous ways and responding to questions with apparent non-sequiturs and riddles (*kung-an/kōan*) in order to jolt their pupils from their habitual patterns of thought and prompt in them an awakening experience.

Question: 'If a man has his head shaved, wears a monk's robe, and takes the shelter Buddha gives, why then should he not be recognized as one who is aware of Buddha?' Master: 'It is not as good to have something as to have nothing.'[18]

Although as many as five different Ch'an schools had emerged by the ninth century, only two of these remained important after the government suppression of Buddhist monasticism in 842–5: the Lin Chi (Japanese Rinzai) and Ts'ao Tung (Japanese Sōtō). The former placed particular emphasis on the paradoxical riddle of the *kung-an*, and the master's bizarre behaviour; the latter placed more emphasis on formal sitting meditation; in Japan it is associated with the important figure of Dōgen (1200–53).

Pure Land Buddhism

As we saw in the opening chapter, the Buddha has always been seen as possessor of incomparable powers and as the incomparable teacher of the Dharma. For earliest Buddhism the actual person of the Buddha is no longer directly accessible after his final parinirvāṇa, and devotion to the Buddha centred on the worship of his relics, the recollection of his qualities (*buddhānusmṛti/buddhānussati*), and perhaps also visualization. Such practices clearly were felt to bring one in some sense closer to the presence of the Buddha. Early Buddhism also knew of Maitreya/Metteyya, the next buddha, who at present waits in the Tuṣita heaven; the aspiration to be reborn at the time when Maitreya will teach the Dharma may have become part of Buddhist practice early on. With the rise of the Mahāyāna came the idea that buddhas are at present teaching in other parts of the universe in their own special 'buddha fields' or 'pure lands' where the conditions for the practice of the Dharma are extremely favourable. With this came the aspiration to be reborn in these pure lands. The inspiration for Chinese and Japanese 'Pure Land' Buddhism is provided by three sūtras: the larger and the smaller *Sukhāvatī-vyūha* ('Vision of the Realm of Happiness') and the *Amitāyurdhyāna* ('Meditation on the Buddha of Boundless Life'). The two former are of Indian origin, while the last may have been composed in central Asia or China. These sūtras tell of the pure land of the Buddha Amitābha (Boundless Light) or Amitāyus, known in Japanese as Amida. The particular focus of East Asian Pure Land Buddhism became the vow of Amitābha in the *Sukhāvatī-vyūha* to bring to his pure land after death any one who sincerely calls on his name. The characteristic practice of Pure Land Buddhism, advocated in the writings of such masters as T'an-luan (476–542), Tao-cho (562–645), and Shan-tao (613–81), is known as *nien-fo* (Japanese *nembutsu*), calling on or uttering the name of the Buddha. Also associated with the school is a preoccupation with the old Indian idea that the practice of the Buddha's teaching must pass through successive periods of decline and eventually disappear.[19] This led to an emphasis on the futility of expecting to be able, by one's own efforts, to develop the good conduct and meditation necessary for awakening in the final days of the Dharma (*mo fa/mappō*); better to aspire to rebirth in Amitābha's pure land. The eventual development in Japan was a doctrine of grace associated above all with the figure of Shinran (1173–1262), founder of the 'True Pure Land School' (Jōdo Shinshū): it is not 'one's own power' (*jiriki*) but the 'power of the other' (*tariki*)—the grace of Amitābha—that is effective in bringing one to his pure land.[20]

Tien-t'ai and Hua-yen

By the middle of the sixth century Indian Buddhist texts of various sorts and from numerous schools all purporting to be the word of the Buddha had been translated into Chinese. Both Tien-t'ai and Hua-yen start from the premiss that the diverse and seemingly contradictory teachings represented by these texts must be ordered and arranged into a coherent whole. Both schools thus propose a system of division and classification of the Buddha's teachings (*p'an-chiao*). The theoretical basis for this is the concept of the Buddha's 'skill in means' (*upāya-kauśalya*): the notion that the Buddha adapted his teachings according to the ability of his hearers to understand.

For Chih-i (538–97), the founder of T'ien-t'ai, the Buddha's teaching should be arranged according to the 'five periods and eight teachings'. The final teaching of the Buddha is found in the

Lotus Sūtra. Chih-i expressed his understanding of Buddhist metaphysics and dependent arising in the form of a doctrine known as 'the threefold truth': phenomena are at once empty of existence, temporarily existing, and poised in the middle between existence and non-existence. Associated with the elaboration of this doctrine, which is seen as relating all things to each other and to the whole, is a theory of the 'interpenetration' of all phenomena: every individual thing in the universe contains and at the same time is contained in everything else, or, as Chih-i himself would put it, one thought is the 3,000 worlds.[21] While some of the writings of Chih-i represent sophisticated (and mind-boggling) intellectual meditations on the interdependence of all things, others also show a concern for the down-to-earth problems and practicalities of just sitting in meditation.[22]

The Hua-yen school was founded by Tu-shun (557–640) and its thought was developed especially in the writings of Fa-tsang (643–712). For Hua-yen the vast Avataṃsaka or 'Flower Garland' Sūtra collection represents the highest teaching. As with Tien-t'ai, great emphasis is put on an elaborate theory of the interpenetration of all phenomena.[23]

Nichiren

An important and distinctive form of Buddhism is associated with the name of the Japanese prophet Nichiren (1222–82). Nichiren's Buddhism springs from the view that Japanese Buddhism and Japanese society were, in the mid-thirteenth century, passing through a state of crisis. Although he criticized other forms of Buddhist practice as ineffective, his understanding of the Lotus Sūtra as the highest teaching of the Buddha derives from Tendai (T'ien-t'ai); his insistence on a single chant as the only effective form of practice in the days of *mappō* owes something to Japanese Pure Land traditions. Nichiren's Buddhism thus centres on the repeated chanting of the *daimoku*, homage to the sacred title of the Lotus Sūtra (*na-mu myō-hō-ren-ge-kyō*), backed up by a complex and sophisticated theory of the manner in which the syllables of the chant actualize Śākyamuni Buddha, transforming the individual and society. By all accounts Nichiren was an uncompromising and provocative teacher. In the centuries after his death Nichiren's message attracted a considerable following in Japan, and today the numerous sub-sects of Nichiren Buddhism together continue to constitute one of the significant schools of Buddhism in Japan. Among the important Nichiren sub-sects is the Nichiren Shōshū or Sōka Gakkai, which has been active in Japanese politics since the 1960s, and must also be reckoned a significant presence in the context of Buddhism in Europe and America.[24]

Tibet and Mongolia: Northern Buddhism

Tibetan tradition makes reference to a first and second diffusion of Buddhism in Tibet. Tradition links the introduction of Buddhism to Tibet with the two wives of King Srong-bsan-sgam-po (d. 649), one of whom came from Nepal and the other from China, who thus introduced both Indian and Chinese forms of Buddhism. But the Buddhist presence in Tibet remained superficial for another century. It was not until the latter half of the eighth century, during the reign of King Khri Srong-lde-brtsan (756–97?), that the Indian monk Śāntarakṣita was invited to establish the first monastery, bSam-yas. In order to accomplish his purpose, Śāntarakṣita is said to have had to call on an Indian yogin, Padmasambhava, to assist in the task of subduing the local demons hostile to Buddhism. Tradition records a dispute at bSam-yas or Lhasa in 792–4 between an Indian faction, headed by Śāntarakṣita's disciple Kamalaśīla, and a Chinese faction, headed by the teacher (*hva-shang*) Mahāyāna.[25] The dispute is characterized as centring on the question of gradual (the Indians) or sudden (the Chinese) awakening; the Indian opinion supporting gradual awakening is said to have prevailed, but all this is probably a simplification of a complex history, and we can assume some influence of Chinese forms of Buddhism on Tibetan Buddhism.

A 'second diffusion' of Buddhism in Tibet occurred after its suppression during the reign of gLang-dar-ma (838–42), and is associated especially with the activity of the Indian monk and yogin Atiśa (982–1054), which led to the founding of the monastery of Rva-spreng by his disciple 'Brom-ston in 1057, and the establishment of the bKa' gdams-pa school, which set the course for the future development of Buddhist monasticism in Tibet. Atiśa also wrote for his Tibetan pupils a short but extremely influential and much commented upon summary of Buddhist practice, the *Bodhi-patha-pradīpa* ('Lamp on the Path to Awakening').

The Kanjur and Tenjur

As with the Chinese translation of Buddhist texts, Indian canonical collections of Buddhist texts were not translated *en bloc*, rather individual texts were translated one by one over several centuries.[26] Tibetan Buddhist tradition divides its scriptures into two canonical collections: the Kanjur (*bKa' 'gyur*), or 'translated word of the Buddha', and the Tenjur (*bsTan 'gyur*), or 'translated treatises'.

The Kanjur came into existence at the beginning of the fourteenth century in response to a need to collect and arrange the enormous numbers of these texts that had been translated into Tibetan between the seventh and thirteenth centuries. The earliest woodblock printed edition was in fact produced in 1410 in Peking and not in Tibet. Like the Chinese Tripiṭaka, the Kanjur exists in several editions and recensions which diverge slightly in their arrangement and the number of texts they include, but it usually comprises 700–800 texts in just over 100 volumes. One of the most widely used and favoured editions today is a reproduction of the Derge (sDe dge) block-print edition of 1733.

The arrangement of the Kanjur does not follow the threefold division of the earlier Indian canonical collections; the following division into seven categories is typical: (1) Vinaya or monastic discipline (*'Dul-ba*), (2) Perfection of Wisdom (*Sher phyin*), which is often further divided, (3) the Buddhāvataṃsaka (*Phal-chen*), (4) Ratnakūṭa (*dKon-brtsegs*) (5) Sūtra (*mDo*), (6) the Mahāyāna Mahā-Parinirvāṇa (*Myang 'das*), and (7) tantra (*rGyud*). The huge Sūtra collection occupies a third of the Kanjur and is almost entirely devoted to Mahāyāna sūtras, although some material from the earlier Nikāyas/Āgamas is included. Next in size is the tantra collection which occupies about one-fifth of the Kanjur. At one-eighth of the whole, the Vinaya comes third in size.

The canonical Abhidharma texts, which constituted the third division of the older Indian canons, are not included in the Tibetan Kanjur. Tibetan study of the Abhidharma is based on Sarvāstivādin and Yogācārin treatises included in the other great canonical collection of Tibetan Buddhism, namely the Tenjur, which contains over 3,500 texts (mostly translations of Indian commentaries and treatises) in over 200 volumes.

Tantric Buddhism

The forms of Buddhist practice and teaching that were introduced to Tibet from the seventh to the twelfth centuries were fundamentally those current across northern and eastern India at the time. Tibetan Buddhist teaching and practice divides into two main types: (1) the conventional Mahāyāna 'gradual path' (*lam rim*) of the perfections and *bhūmis* as taught in the Mahāyāna sūtras and expounded by subsequent tradition; (2) the esoteric path of the *tantras* (Tibetan *rgyud*).

Tantra represents the final development of Indian Buddhism. It should not be regarded as a further development in Buddhist thought, but is rather a particular approach to the practice of the Buddhist path occurring within the general Mahāyāna philosophical framework, as set out by the Madhyamaka and Yogācāra, and giving special emphasis to the idea of the equivalence of nirvāṇa and saṃsāra. Tantra is also referred to as 'the vehicle of protective spells' (*mantra-yāna/sNgagstheg-pa*) or 'the vehicle of the diamond thunderbolt' (*vajra-yāna/rDo-rjetheg-pa*). Tibetan tradition links its practice in India and transmission to Tibet to a group of eighty-four *siddhas* (*grub-thob*) or 'accomplished ones', legendary for their extraordinary magical powers and their eccentric and unpredictable behaviour.[27]

Tantras are texts setting out certain esoteric meditation practices which present themselves as a secret teaching deriving directly from the Buddha himself. Modern scholarship, however, dates the production of these texts to a period over 1,000 years after the Buddha, and regards them as evolving as part of a wider Indian tantric movement. The Vajrayāna is seen as a powerful and extremely effective method of practice leading directly to the complete awakening of a buddha, but it requires absolute commitment and dedication. Tibetan Buddhist schools tend to follow their own particular lineages and versions of the gradual path and tantric teachings; in both instances, however, the teachings of different schools are broadly similar in outlook.

Tantras are generally classified according to a hierarchical scheme of four classes: action (*kriyā*), performance (*caryā*), yoga, and supreme yoga (*anuttara-yoga*).[28] Effective practice (*sādhana*) of any tantra depends on receiving the appropriate 'consecration' (*abhiṣeka/dBang*) and instruction directly from a teacher (*guru/ bLama*) who is a master of the tantra in question. The practice of the lowest tantras centres on external rituals and devotions directed towards the gods, goddesses, and buddhas of the tantra. At all stages of tantric practice a complex and elaborate symbolism links visualizations, liturgy, and ritual in order to fully engage and focus the activity of body, speech, and mind. The *caryā* and *yoga* tantras develop complex visualizations of and meditations on 'chosen deities' (*iṣṭa-devatā/yi-dam*) and buddhas of sublime realms; by a process of gradual identification, the practitioner actualizes their wisdom, compassion and other spiritual qualities. The higher tantras increasingly centre on an elaborate theory of yoga involving a complex physiology of the 'channels', 'centres', 'winds', and 'drops' of the subtle body which the practitioner learns to control and manipulate in order to transform his or her own body into the body of a buddha. One aspect of the theory of the subtle body involves an esoteric relationship between the experiences of bliss in sexual union and the primordial bliss of the mind. The initial consecration and practice associated with the supreme yoga tantras may thus involve sexual union with a consort, the underlying symbolism here being the union of wisdom (female) and compassion (male). Such a practice may also be performed as a visualization; in the case of ordained monks, whose vows prohibit any sexual activity, it can only be performed as such. The purpose here, as with all Buddhist practice, is not, of course, the feeding of desire but its final transformation and eradication: desire is employed at an advanced stage of practice in order finally to reveal its nature.

The schools of Tibetan Buddhism

The schools of Tibetan Buddhism focus on particular lineages of teachings passed from teacher to disciple, and not on different monastic ordination lineages. Four main schools of Tibetan Buddhism survive today, with, as one might expect, a number of sub-schools. The rNying-ma-pas trace their roots back to the first diffusion of Buddhism in Tibet and the legendary figure of Padmasambhava, many of whose teachings were considered to have been concealed as 'hidden treasures' (*gTer-ma*) to be subsequently found and taught by a series of 'treasure finders' (*gTer-stons*). The rNying-ma-pas preserve a distinctive classification of Buddhist teachings into nine 'vehicles'. The first three are the conventional vehicles of the disciple, solitary buddha, and bodhisattva; the middle three concern lower tantric practice, while the final three concern highest tantric practice, called by the rNying-ma-pas *rDzogs-chen* or 'great fulfilment', and understood as the realization of the primordial and spontaneous purity of mind. Characteristic of the rNying-ma school, although not confined to it, is a strong tradition of lay trantric teachers known as *sNgags-pa*-s.

The bKa'-brgyud-pas look back to the Indian yogin Nāropa (956–1040), and trace the lineage of their teachings through Mar-pa (1012–96), Mi-la Ras-pa (1040–1123), and sGam-po-pa (1079–1153). Their gradual path teachings derive from Atiśa's bKa'-gdams-pa tradition and were set out classically by sGam-po-pa in his *Jewel Ornament of Liberation*; their tantric teachings centre on the 'Great Seal' (*mahāmudrā/phyag-chen*). The bKa'-brgyud spawned various sub-schools. The Kar-ma bKa'-brgyud sub-school is headed by a teacher given the title Karma-pa; the first of these, Dus-gsum-mkhyen-pa (1110–93), is said to have prophesied the manner and circumstances of his future birth, so that his *spruls-skus* or 'creation body' (*nirmāṇa-kāya*) could be identified and installed as the next Karma-pa.[29] This custom whereby a teacher gives instructions for recognizing his reincarnated successor is now most famously associated with the office of the Dalai Lama of the dGe-lugs school.

Sa-skya-pa origins and history are intimately connected with the 'Khon family. 'Khon dKon-mchog rGyal-po founded the Sa-skya monastery in south-west Tibet in 1073. Characteristic of the Sa-skya school is a monastic tradition in association with a specifically 'Khon family lineage of married yogins passing the teaching from father to son or from uncle to nephew. From the beginning of the twelfth until the middle of the fourteenth century the Sa-skya-pas enjoyed considerable political influence in Tibet. Five 'great masters' are recognized, the most important of which is usually regarded as Sa-skya Paṇḍita (1182–1251). The Sa-skya-pa gradual-path 'sūtra' teachings, known as the 'Leaving behind the Four Desires' (*zhen-pa bzhi bral*), revolve around the exegesis of four lines said to have been uttered by the Bodhisattva of Wisdom, Mañjuśrī, to the 11-year-old Kun-dga' snying-po (1092–1158), the second of the five masters:

> If you desire this life, you are not a religious person.
> If you desire the round of existence, you have not turned around with conviction.
> If you desire benefit for yourself, you do not have the thought of awakening.
> If grasping ensues, you do not have the view.

The other main teaching of the school is a combined sūtra and tantra teaching called 'Path and Fruit' (*lam-'bras*), which is associated with the *Hevajra* tantra. This teaching is traced to the Indian tantric yogin Virūpa (*c.* ninth century), one of the eighty-four *siddhas*.

In more recent Tibetan history it is the powerful dGe-lugs-pa school that has been politically dominant. The dGe-lugs-pa school sees itself as the principal inheritor of the bKa' gdams-pa tradition. Founded in the fourteenth century by the scholar-monk Tsong kha pa (1357 1419), the school reaffirmed monasticism and is famed for its scholarship, particularly its exegesis of Madhyamaka thought. Its sūtra and tantra teachings are based on Tsong-kha-pa's two principal works: *The Great Gradual Path* (*Lam-rim chen-mo*), a commentary on Atiśa's *Lamp*, and *The*

Great Path of Mantra (*sngags-rim chen-mo*), which centres on the *Kālacakra* and *Guhya-samāja* tantras.

The head of the dGe-lugs was officially the abbot of Ganden (dGa'-ldan), the original dGe-lugs monastery founded by Tsong-kha-pa, but this position has been gradually overshadowed by the Dalai Lamas, chief incumbents of Drepung ('Bras-spungs) monastery. The title goes back to the sixteenth century and to dGe-lugs relations with the Mongols, whose ruler, Altan Khan, declared bSod-nams-rgya-mtsho, the third in a line of reincarnating dGe-lugs lamas, 'an ocean (Mongolian *dalai*) [of wisdom]'; bSod-nams-rgya-mtsho was thus subsequently regarded as the third *Dalai* Lama. From the time of the fifth Dalai Lama, bLo-bzang-rgya-mtsho (1612–82), the Dalai Lama has acted as Tibetan head of state. The Dalai Lama is thus neither the formal head of Tibetan Buddhism—a kind of Tibetan Buddhist equivalent to the Pope—nor strictly the head of the dGe-lugs-pa school. As the head of the Tibetan government in exile and as a teacher of great spiritual authority in his own right, the present Dalai Lama remains a focus for the Tibetan community's devotion and respect. Chinese troops invaded Tibet in 1950; by 1959 the Dalai Lama had little option but to flee to India. In Tibet first the People's Liberation Army and then the Red Guard continued the systematic destruction of Tibetan Buddhist culture involving the death of perhaps a million Tibetans and the destruction of over 6,000 monasteries.[30]

Buddhist thought in Tibet

Tibetan Buddhism has not developed distinctively Tibetan traditions of Buddhist philosophy quite in the manner of Chinese T'ien-t'ai and Hua-yen. Generally the Madhyamaka doctrine of emptiness is regarded as the highest and final philosophical statement of Buddhist teaching, though ideas and teachings associated with the Yogācāra remain influential, and the precise interpretation of Madhyamaka is nuanced in various ways. The most significant philosophical debate centred on the question of whether behind appearances there is some reality that can be characterized as ultimately existing or not, a true 'Absolute'. The view that there is such an ultimately existing reality is known as 'empty of what is other' (*gzhan stong*); that is to say, true reality is empty in so far as it is empty of everything other than itself. The view was expounded by Dol-po-pa Shes-rab rGyal-mtshan (1292–1361) and has found considerable support within Tibetan Buddhism. The more mainstream Madhyamaka view is known as 'empty of itself' (*rang stong*), emphasizing that ultimate truth about the nature of reality is that it is empty even of its own existence. This is a discussion that once more reflects the problems Buddhist thought has had in arriving at a proper statement of the middle between the two extremes of eternalism and annihilationism.[31]

A final note: Buddhism in the West

The earliest European contact with Buddhism is likely to have been around the beginning of the third century BCE, when Megasthenes, ambassador of Seleucus Nicator, Alexander the Great's successor in his eastern empire, was at the Mauryan court of Candragupta in Pāṭaliputra (modern Patna). Megasthenes' Greek account of Indian life does not survive in full, but it was the chief source of information about India in ancient Europe and is known from its frequent quotation by ancient authorities. Although there is clear evidence of trade between Alexandria and Rome, on the one hand, and south India and Sri Lanka, on the other, the extent of cultural exchange between the European classical world and India is unclear. For the fifteen hundred years from the time of Megasthenes down to the thirteenth century we have no real record of direct contact between Europeans and Asian Buddhists; knowledge of Indian and Chinese culture was to remain almost non-existent in Europe. But from the thirteenth century, with the gradually increasing trade and missionary activity which culminated in full-blown European colonialism in Asia, Europeans began travelling to Mongolia, China, India, and Tibet and writing accounts of their travels which included some reference to and information on Buddhism. One of the earliest and perhaps most celebrated accounts is that of Marco Polo, who was supposedly in China from 1275 to 1291. Yet these early European travellers' interest in and knowledge of Buddhism remained limited. Possibly the earliest sustained attempt to understand Buddhist thought by a European is represented by the Jesuit father Ippolito Desideri, who spent five years in the Tibetan capital, Lhasa, at the beginning of the eighteenth century, endeavouring to come to grips with Tsong kha pa's presentation of Madhyamaka Buddhist thought.[32]

A European tradition of oriental and Buddhist scholarship —associated with such names as William Jones (1746–94), Alexander Csoma de Körös (1798–1842), Eugène Burnouf (1801–52), Friedrich Max Müller (1823–1900), T. W. Rhys Davids (1843–1922), Hermann Oldenberg (1854–1920), Theodor Stcherbatsky (1866 1942), Louis de La Vallée Poussin (1869–1938), Giuseppe Tucci (1894–1984), and Étienne Lamotte (1903–83)—began to make available in Europe translations of Indian, Chinese, and Tibetan texts.[33] These fed the imaginations of the likes of Schopenhauer (1788–1860), Emerson (1803–82), Thoreau (1817–1862), W. B. Yeats (1865–1939), and T. S. Eliot (1888–1965).

Following this firing of the European imagination, the final years of the nineteenth century saw Europeans beginning to set off for Asia not just as civil servants or scholars, but in search of 'the wisdom of the east': in 1890 Madame Blavatsky and Colonel Olcott, who had founded the Theosophical Society in 1875 in New York, publicly took the refuges and precepts in Sri Lanka; in 1898 Allan Bennett, a former member of the esoteric Order of the Golden Dawn, left Britain, travelling to Sri Lanka and then on to Burma, where in 1901 he was ordained as the Buddhist monk Ānanda Metteyya; Anthon Gueth (1878–1956) made a similar trip from Germany to ordain as Nyanatiloka in 1904, returning to Sri Lanka to found the Dodanduwa 'Island Hermitage' in 1911; in 1912 the remarkable Frenchwoman Madame Alexandra David-Neel (1868–1969), had an audience with the thirteenth Dalai Lama in Kalimpong and subsequently spent many years in Sikkim and Tibet involved in Buddhist practice.

Back in Europe and America various Buddhist groups were established. East Asian immigration to the USA at the end of the nineteenth century was particularly significant in the early establishment of Zen traditions there. But it is the period since the Second World War that has witnessed the greatest growth in Western interest in Buddhism. A particular feature of this interest has been the increased contact with the living traditions of Asian Buddhist practice. This contact has resulted both from the movements of various Asian groups to all parts of the world in the period after the war and the growing numbers of Westerners travelling east since the late 1960s. Of particular significance in this context has been the presence since 1959 of the Tibetan refugee community in Dharmsala in north India; this has served as both a source of teachers coming to the West and a destination for Western travellers.

In the West today the various schools of Tibetan Buddhism are all represented in Europe, the USA, Australia and New Zealand. East Asian Buddhism is represented especially by Japanese Zen in the USA and also in Europe; the Nichiren subsect, Sōka Gakkai, is also a significant presence. The Theravada presence takes the form of the Saṅgha from Sri Lanka and South-East Asia and several *samatha* and *vipassanā* meditation schools and centres. There are also more eclectic groups, such as the Western Buddhist Order, founded in 1967 by the Englishman Sangharakshita (Dennis Lingwood, b. 1925) who, having been originally ordained as a Theravādin monk in India, came to regard traditional Asian forms of Buddhist practice as inappropriate to the West.

The number of Westerners ordaining into the Theravāda, Tibetan, and East Asian Saṅghas and living as monks both in Asia and the West has increased significantly in the last twenty-five years; in Buddhist circles in the West it is not uncommon to find Westerners with thirty or forty years of involvement with Buddhist practice behind them; some Westerners have gained an authority as teachers which is recognized by Asian Buddhists. The overall numbers of committed practitioners may still be relatively small, but the growth of interest among Westerners in Buddhism since the Second World War is a significant feature of religious practice in the West.

Nearly 2,500 years ago, 'out of compassion for the world, for the benefit and welfare of the many', Buddhist monks began their journey south to take the word of the Buddha across India. Several centuries later their successors began to follow the long trade routes east through central and South-East Asia into China. Several centuries later still, monks crossed the mountain passes to the north and entered Tibet. In India itself Buddhist monasteries were gradually deserted and all that remained were crumbling monuments to the past. The twentieth century has witnessed the establishment of the Buddha's word in the West and the return of the Buddhist Saṅgha to its homeland in India.[34] And despite 'the killing fields' of the Khmer Rouge and the ravages of the Red Guard, the richness and diversity of Buddhism remains: outside a cottage in the English countryside a small group of people places food in the bowls of European and American monks as they file past in silence; a hundred miles or so from the place of the Buddha's birth, pilgrims to the shrine of the primordial Buddha Svayambhunātha in Nepal turn the countless prayer wheels as they approach the great stūpa; in the hall of a monastery situated amidst the rice fields of Korea a group of monks sits silently in meditation; at Aukana in Sri Lanka a woman dressed in white carefully places an open lotus bud at the feet of the giant standing Buddha and raises her joined palms to her forehead.

Notes

References to Pali texts are normally to the volume and page number of the edition of the text published by the Pali Text Society (London and Oxford); these references can be used by the reader who knows no Pali since the pagination of the PTS editions is included in the translations cited in the bibliography below, either in the body of the text or at the head of the page; Buddhaghosa's *Visuddhimagga*, however, is cited by reference to the chapter and section of the translation (and the Harvard 1950 edition of the text). Other texts are cited in the notes by reference to the pagination of the cited translation (and of an edition of the text, where the latter is not included in the translation), or by reference to the chapter (in roman numerals) and verse/section (in arabic numerals) of the original.

Introduction

1. L. S. Cousins, 'Buddhism', in John R. Hinnells (ed.), *A Handbook of Living Religions* (Harmondsworth, 1984), 278–343 (278).
2. Cf. Richard H. Robinson and Willard L. Johnson, *The Buddhist Religion* (Belmont, Calif., 1982), 129–95; Cousins 'Buddhism', 279; Peter Harvey, *An Introduction to Buddhism* (Cambridge, 1990), 4.
3. This expression has been used by both Paul Harrison and Paul Williams; in an unpublished paper Williams has commented that he believes it to have been first used by Eric Cheetham in teaching materials used by the Buddhist Society, London.

Chapter 1. The Story of the Buddha

1. See Edward Thomas, *The Life of the Buddha* (London, 1949), 160–3; H. Härtel, 'Archaeological Research on Ancient Buddhist Sites', in Bechert, *The Dating of the Historical Buddha*, i. 61–89.
2. See Gregory Schopen, 'Burial "Ad Sanctos" and the Physical Presence of the Buddha in Early Indian Buddhism', *Religion*, 17 (1987), 193–225.
3. e.g. Dīgha Nikāya i. 49.
4. Padmanabh S. Jaini, *The Jaina Path of Purification* (Delhi, 1979), 10.

5. See Padmanabh S. Jaini, 'Śrāmaṇas: Their Conflict with Brāhmaṇical Society', in J. W. Elder (ed.), *Chapters in Indian Civilization* (Dubuque, 1970), i. 39–81.
6. See Dīgha Nikāya i. 161–77; Majjhima Nikāya i. 387–92.
7. For the list of six teachers see, e.g. Dīgha Nikāya i. 51–9; for the list of ten see Aṅguttara Nikāya iii. 276; cf. A. L. Basham, *History and Doctrines of the Ājīvikas* (London, 1951).
8. See Gavin Flood, *An Introduction to Hinduism* (Cambridge, 1996), 87–90.
9. This question has been discussed by Richard Gombrich; see his *Theravāda Buddhism: A Social History from Ancient Benares to Modern Colombo* (London, 1988), 60–86; 'Recovering the Buddha's Message', in Tadeusz Skorupski (ed.), *The Buddhist Forum*, 1 (1990), 5–20; 'The Buddha's Book of Genesis?', *Indo-Iranian Journal*, 35 (1992), 159–78; *How Buddhism Began: The Conditioned Genesis of the Early Teachings* (London, 1996).
10. Richard Gombrich, 'Dating the Buddha: A Red Herring Revealed', in Heinz Bechert (ed.), *The Dating of the Historical Buddha* (Göttingen, 1992), ii. 237–257.
11. Gananath Obeyesekere, 'Myth, History and Numerology in the Buddhist Chronicles', in Bechert, *The Dating of the Historical Buddha*, i. 152–82.
12. L. S. Cousins, 'The Dating of the Historical Buddha: A Review Article', *Journal of the Royal Asiatic Society*, 6 (1996), 57–63.
13. Étienne Lamotte, *History of Indian Buddhism from the Origins to the Śaka Era* (Louvain, 1988), 639.
14. For a discussion of changing attitudes towards the life of the Buddha in modern scholarship see Charles Hallisey, 'Roads Taken and Not Taken in the Study of Theravāda Buddhism', in Donald S. Lopez (ed.), *Curators of the Buddha: The Study of Buddhism under Colonialism* (Chicago, 1995), 31–61.
15. For the Nikāyas see especially the *Mahāpadāna* (Dīgha Nikāya ii. 1–54), *Mahāparinibbāna* (Dīgha Nikāya ii. 72–168), *Bhayabherava* (Majjhima Nikāya i. 16–24), *Ariyapariyesana* (Majjhima Nikāya i. 160–75) and *Mahāsaccaka* (Majjhima Nikāya i. 237–51) *Suttas*. For the parallel Chinese materials see Bareau, *Recherches sur la biographie du Buddha*. The materials in the Pali Nikāyas relevant to the life of the Buddha (excluding the *Mahāpadāna Sutta*) have been collated in Ñāṇamoli, *The Life of the Buddha* (Kandy, 1992). See also the *Catuṣpariṣat Sūtra* and items by Beal and Rockhill in the bibliography for this chapter.

16. For extracts from the *Mahavastu* and *Buddhacarita* see Edward Conze, *Buddhist Scriptures* (Harmondsworth, 1959), 19–66; for the *Nidānakathā* see Jayawickrama, *The Story of Gotama Buddha*.
17. e.g. Paul Bigandet, *The Life or Legend of Gaudama the Buddha of the Burmese* (London, 1911), a translation of an early modern Burmese text; Thich Nhat Hanh, *Old Paths, White Clouds* (London, 1992), a modern telling of the story drawing on a variety of ancient sources. See Frank Reynolds, 'The Many Lives of Buddha', in Donald Capps and Frank Reynolds (eds.), *The Biographical Process* (The Hague, 1976), 37–61 for further examples.
18. For Tibetan tradition, see Eugene Obermiller (trans.), *History of Buddhism (Chos-ḥbyung by Bu-ston)* (Heidelberg, 1931–2), ii. 7–72; for the Theravāda, see Buddhavaṃsa-aṭṭhakathā 298.
19. Adapted from Hultzshch's translation; see Thomas, *Life of the Buddha*, 18.
20. Bellanwila Wimalaratana, *Concept of Great Man (mahāpurisa) in Buddhist Literature and Iconography* (Singapore, n.d.).
21. Aṅguttara Nikāya i. 145–6.
22. Majjhima Nikāya i. 80, 245; cf. Lalitavistara ii. 387 (Lefmann ed. (Halle, 1902–8), 254).
23. Jātaka i. 71 (Jayawickrama, *The Story of Gotama Buddha*, 94).
24. Cf. Majjhima Nikāya i. 21–3 and Dīgha Nikāya ii. 30–35, Majjhima Nikāya i. 167, Saṃyutta Nikāya ii. 104–6; see Étienne Lamotte, 'Conditioned Co-production and Supreme Enlightenment', in Somaratna Balasooriya *et al.* (eds.), *Buddhist Studies in Honour of Walpola Rahula* (London, 1980), 118–32.
25. Lalitavistara ii. 490–97 (Lefmann ed. 325–31). This incident (Saṃyutta Nikāya i. 124, Suttanipāta v. 835) is placed in a different context in Pali sources, see Ñāṇamoli, *Life of the Buddha*, 60–4.
26. Majjhima Nikāya i. 167.
27. For example, the *Tevijja Sutta* explains the way to companionship with Brahmā as meditation on loving kindness, sympathetic joy, compassion, and equanimity (Dīgha Nikāya i. 235–53). See also Atthasālinī 129.
28. *Pāli Chanting with Translations* (Bangkok, 1974); cf. Majjhima Nikāya i. 168.
29. Buddhavaṃsa-aṭṭhakathā 3 does this for the first twenty years of the Buddha's teaching career.
30. Translation adapted from Rhys Davids, *Dialogues of the Buddha*, ii. 107 (Dīgha Nikāya ii. 100).
31. Dīgha Nikāya ii. 144.

32. Majjhima Nikāya i. 140.
33. e.g. Saṃyutta Nikāya iv. 380–4.
34. Sumaṅgala-Vilāsinī 59–67 gives an elaborate traditional explanation of *tathāgata*, see Bhikkhu Bodhi (trans.), *The Discourse on the All-Embracing Net of Views: The Brahmajāla Sutta and its Commentaries* (Kandy, 1978), 331–4.
35. Cf. David L. Snellgrove, *Indo-Tibetan Buddhism* (London, 1987), 5–11, 29–38.
36. Aṅguttara Nikāya ii. 37–9.
37. Cf. J. W. de Jong, 'The Study of Buddhism: Problems and Perspectives', in *Buddhist Studies by J. W. de Jong*, edited by G. Schopen (Berkeley, 1979), 15–26.
38. Dīgha Nikāya iii. 84.
39. Saṃyutta Nikāya iii. 120.
40. Dīgha Nikāya iii. 142–62; see also U. McNab *et al.* (trans.), *The Suttanta on the Marks* (Greenstreete, Wales, 1996).
41. See Visuddhimagga viii. 23; Frank Reynolds, 'The Several Bodies of the Buddha: Reflections on a Neglected Aspect of Theravāda Tradition', *History of Religions*, 16 (1977), 374–89; Paul Harrison, 'Is the *Dharma-kāya* the Real "Phantom Body" of the Buddha?', *Journal of the International Association of Buddhist Studies*, 15 (1992), 44–94.
42. Majjhima Nikāya iii. 8.

Chapter 2. The Word of the Buddha

1. Dīgha Nikāya ii. 119–20; Majjhima Nikāya i. 492–3.
2. e.g. Visuddhimagga xiv. 14; Abhidharmakośa vi. 5; Rupert Gethin, *The Buddhist Path to Awakening* (Leiden, 1992), 222–3.
3. Cf. Tilmann Vetter, *The Ideas and Meditative Practices of Early Buddhism* (Leiden, 1988), 10.
4. William Graham, *Beyond the Written Word* (Cambridge, 1987), 67–77. On the development of writing in India see Richard Salomon, 'On the Origin of the Early Indian Scripts: A Review Article', *Journal of the American Oriental Society*, 115 (1995), 271–9.
5. Walpola Rahula, *History of Buddhism in Ceylon* (Colombo, 1956), 158–61.
6. Verse attributed to Nan-chüan P'u-yüan (748–834); see Heinrich Dumoulin, *A History of Zen Buddhism* (London, 1963), 67.
7. John Ross Carter, *Dhamma: Western Academic and Sinhalese Buddhist Interpretations* (Tokyo, 1978), 131–5.

8. L. S. Cousins, 'Pāli Oral Literature', in Philip Denwood and Alexander Piatigorsky (eds.), *Buddhist Studies: Ancient and Modern* (London, 1983), 1–11; Rupert Gethin, 'The Mātikās: Memorization, Mindfulness and the List', in Janet Gyatso (ed.), *In The Mirror of Memory* (Albany, NY, 1992), 149–72.
9. Graham, *Beyond the Written Word*, and Wendy O'Flaherty, *Other Peoples' Myths* (New York, 1988), 56–64.
10. Vinaya ii. 139; see K. R. Norman, *Pāli Literature* (Wiesbaden, 1983), 3; Lamotte, *History of Indian Buddhism*, 549–93.
11. On the absence of evidence for the influence of Sinhalese Prakrit on the language of the Pali canon see K. R. Norman, 'Pāli and the Language of the Heretics' in his *Collected Papers*, i. (Oxford, 1990), 238–46.
12. Lamotte, *History of Indian Buddhism*, 156.
13. Ibid., 156–64.
14. Louis Renou and Jean Filliozat (ed.), *L'Inde classique*, 2 vols. (Paris, 1947–53), ii. 392 (§ 2037), 440 (§ 2124); Lamotte, *History of Indian Buddhism*, 165–79.
15. Richard Gombrich, '*How the Mahāyāna Began*' in *The Buddhist Forum*, 1 (1990), 21–30 (22).
16. Or alternatively: 'Thus have I heard at one time. The Lord . . .'—the Buddhist tradition recognizes two ways of punctuating this phrase. See Brian Galloway ' "Thus Have I Heard: At One Time . . ." ', *Indo-Iranian Journal*, 34 (1991), 87–104.
17. Vinaya ii. 289–90.
18. Dīgha Nikāya ii. 123–6.
19. See Gethin, 'The Mātikās'.
20. Manorathapūraṇī i. 123 (Cousins, 'Pāli Oral Literature'); cf. Vinaya iv. 15. See also Ronald Davidson, 'An Introduction to the Standards of Scriptural Authenticity in Indian Buddhism', in Robert E. Buswell (ed.), *Chinese Buddhist Apocrypha* (Honolulu, 1990), 291–325, and Étienne Lamotte, 'The Assessment of Textual Authenticity in Buddhism', *Buddhist Studies Review*, 1 (1984), 4–15.
21. Majjhima Nikāya i. 292–8.
22. J. McDermott, 'Scripture as Word of the Buddha', *Numen*, 31 (1984), 22–39; G. McQueen, 'Inspired Speech in Mahāyāna Buddhism', *Religion*, 11–12 (1981/2), 303–19, 49–65.
23. Cf. Gombrich, *Theravāda Buddhism*, 110–12.
24. Gombrich, *Theravāda Buddhism*, 104. The relevant rules are Pācittiya 68–9 of the Theravāda Vinaya (Vinaya iv. 134–5); see Mohan

Wijayaratna, *Buddhist Monastic Life* (Cambridge, 1990), 104–6. The rules are also found in other Vinayas; see Charles S. Prebish, *Buddhist Monastic Discipline: The Sanskrit Prātimokṣa Sūtras of the Mahāsāṃghikas and Mūlasarvāstivādins* (University Park, Pa., 1975), 104–6.

25. Janice Nattier and Charles Prebish, 'Mahāsāṃghika Origins', *History of Religions*, 16 (1976), 237–72; Lance Cousins, 'The "Five Points" and the Origins of the Buddhist Schools', *The Buddhist Forum*, 2 (1991), 27–60.
26. I am indebted to Ornan Rotem for this comparison.
27. See K. R. Norman, 'Aśoka's "Schism" Edict', *Collected Papers*, iii. (Oxford, 1992), 191–218.
28. Lamotte, *History of Indian Buddhism*, 279.
29. Cf. Obeyesekere, 'Myth, History and Numerology in the Buddhist Chronicles', in Bechert, *The Dating of the Historical Buddha*, i. 152–82.
30. Ñāṇamoli (trans.), *The Path of Purification* (Colombo, 1964).
31. Leo Pruden's translation in 4 vols. (Berkeley, 1988) from the French of Louis de La Vallée Poussin's translation in 6 vols. (Brussels, 1923–31) from the Chinese from the Sanskrit.
32. See Gregory Schopen, 'The Inscription on the Kuṣān Image of Amitābha and the Character of the Early Mahāyāna in India', *Journal of the International Association of Buddhist Studies*, 10 (1987), 99–137, and Paul Harrison, 'Who Gets to Ride in the Great Vehicle?', *Journal of the International Association of Buddhist Studies*, 10 (1987), 67–89.
33. Lamotte, *History of Indian Buddhism*, 544.

Chapter 3. Four Truths

1. Majjhima Nikāya i. 140.
2. Saṃyutta Nikāya v. 421–2.
3. See Gethin, 'The Mātikās'.
4. Visuddhimagga xvi. 34–5; Dīgha Nikāya iii. 216; Saṃyutta Nikāya iv. 259, v. 56; Nettippakaraṇa 12.
5. Gombrich, *Theravāda Buddhism*, 57–9.
6. *As You Like It*, ii. vii. 136–9.
7. *Story of Gotama*, 64–5 (Jātaka 48–9).
8. Lalitavistara ii. 525, 538–9 (Lefmann ed. 351, 358–9); Visuddhimagga xvi. 87. A. Wezler concludes that there is no evidence that the Buddha borrowed the schema of the four truths from Indian medical traditions; if anything, it is more likely that the latter indir-

ectly derive their fourfold schema from Buddhist texts: see 'On the Quadruple Division of the Yogaśāstra, the Caturvyūhatva of the Cikitsāśāstra and the "Four Noble Truths" of the Buddha', *Indologica Taurinensia*, 12 (1984), 291–337.

9. Harvey Aronson, 'Equanimity (Upekkhā) in Theravādin Buddhism', in A. K. Narain (ed.), *Studies in Pali and Buddhism: A Memorial Volume in Honor of Bhikkhu Jagdish Kashyap* (Delhi, 1979), 1–18, and *Love and Sympathy in Theravāda Buddhism* (Delhi, 1980), 3–18.
10. *Collins Dictionary of the English Language* (Glasgow, 1984).
11. Cf. Wilfred Cantwell Smith's *The Meaning and End of Religion* (New York, 1963), which attempts in part to trace the evolution of the contemporary concept of 'religion', and Ninian Smart's *The Phenomenon of Religion* (Oxford, 1978), which attempts to define religion as consisting in six basic dimensions.
12. Conze is referring to Christmas Humphreys, *Buddhism* (Harmondsworth, 1962), 71–6.
13. Majjhima Nikāya i. 426–437.
14. Ibid., 429.
15. Vetter's *The Ideas and Meditative Practices of Early Buddhism* is an example of a recent work that takes this view.
16. Saṃyutta Nikāya v. 437–8.
17. Steven Collins, *Selfless Persons* (Cambridge, 1982), 131–8. For an analyis of contemporary scholarly interpretations of the 'unanswered questions' see Richard Hayes, 'Nāgārjuna's Appeal', *Journal of Indian Philosophy*, 22 (1994), 299–378 (356–61).
18. Majjhima Nikāya i. 430.
19. Ibid., 169.
20. John R. Carter, *On Understanding Buddhists* (Albany, NY, 1993), 69.
21. Atthasālinī 24.
22. e.g. Dīgha Nikāya ii. 58; defined at Vibhaṅga 375; Visuddhimagga xvii. 239–46.
23. Majjhima Nikāya i. 134–5; see Edward Conze, *Buddhist Wisdom Books* (London, 1958), 34–5, for the parable of the raft in the Mahāyāna *Vajracchedikā Sūtra*.
24. Dhammapada aṭṭhakathā ii. 163; Vibhaṅga-aṭṭhakathā 433.
25. Ibid.
26. For a recent discussion see K. R. Norman, 'Mistaken ideas about *Nibbāna*', *The Buddhist Forum*, 3 (1994), 211–25; I follow Norman's interpretation of *upadhiśeṣa/upādisesa*.

27. Udāna 80.
28. L. S. Cousins, 'Nibbāna and Abhidhamma', *Buddhist Studies Review*, 1 (1984), 95–109.
29. Cf. bhāṣya to Abhidharmakośa ii. 55d; Visuddhimagga xvi. 62–74; Lamotte, *History of Indian Buddhism*, 609–11.
30. Guy Welbon, *The Buddhist Nirvāṇa and its Western Interpreters* (Chicago, 1968).
31. Étienne Lamotte (trans.), *The Teaching of Vimalakīrti (Vimalakīrtinirdeśa)*, trans. by Sara Boin (London, 1976), 203; Étienne Lamotte (trans.), *Le Traité de la grande vertu de sagesse de Nāgārjuna (Mahāprajñāpāramitāśāstra)*, 5 vols. (Louvain, 1944–80), i. 30 n. 2, iv. 2021–7.
32. François Bizot, *Le Figuier à cinq branches: Recherches sur le bouddhisme khmer* (Paris, 1976), 82; cf. Charles Hallisey, 'Nibbānasutta: An Allegedly Non-Canonical Sutta on Nibbāna as a Great City', *Journal of the Pali Text Society*, 18 (1993), 97–130.
33. Saṃyutta Nikāya ii. 105–6.
34. e.g. Dīgha Nikāya ii. 311, Majjhima Nikāya iii. 251, Saṃyutta Nikāya v. 8–10; see Gethin, *Buddhist Path to Awakening*, 190–7.
35. See especially the *Mahācattārīsaka Sutta* (Majjhima Nikāya iii. 71–8) and Gethin, *The Buddhist Path to Awakening*, 216–23.
36. e.g. Majjhima Nikāya i. 379–80.
37. See ibid. 301. Some sources classify items 1, 2, and 6 as to do with wisdom; see Śrāvakabhūmi 101; Satyasiddhiśāstra ii. 43, 448–9.

Chapter 4. The Buddhist Community

1. Milindapañha 264–7; cf. Kathāvatthu 267–8. See also George D. Bond, 'The Arahant: Sainthood in Theravāda Buddhism', in Richard Kieckhefer and George D. Bond (eds.), *Sainthood: Its Manifestations in World Religions* (Berkeley, 1988), 140–71 (144).
2. Vinaya i. 20–1.
3. Lamotte, *History of Indian Buddhism*, 169–70. The Mūlasarvāstivādin (along with the Mahāsāṃghika) *bhikṣu-prātimokṣa* can be found in Prebish, *Buddhist Monastic Discipline*, 42–113. For an analysis of the *skandhaka* portion of the Mūlasarvāstivādin Vinaya as preserved in Tibet see Anukul Banerjee, *Sarvāstivāda Literature* (Calcutta, 1979), 78–246.
4. Lamotte, *History of Indian Buddhism*, 165–6.
5. e.g. Vinaya i. 17.
6. Vinaya i. 56; see Wijayaratna, *Buddhist Monastic Life*, 117–21 on ordination.

7. Vinaya i. 79. Gombrich, *Theravada Buddhism*, 104.
8. Vinaya i. 82–4; cf. Sao Htun Hmat Win, *The Initiation of Novicehood and the Ordination of Monkhood in the Burmese Buddhist Culture* (Rangoon, 1986); François Bizot, *Les traditions de la pabbajjā en Asie du Sud-Est* (Göttingen, 1988).
9. Vinaya i. 78.
10. See e.g. Tambiah, *Buddhism and the Spirit Cults in North-East Thailand* (Cambridge, 1970), 97–115; Spiro, *Buddhism and Society*; Richard Gombrich, *Buddhist Precept and Practice* (Delhi, 1991); Karl Ludvig Reichelt, *Truth and Tradition in Chinese Buddhism* (Shanghai, 1934), 223–41; Holmes Welch, *The Practice of Chinese Buddhism 1900–1950* (Cambridge, Mass., 1967), 247–301; Christoph von Fürer-Haimendorf, *The Sherpas of Nepal* (London, 1964); Giuseppe Tucci, *The Religions of Tibet* (London, 1980).
11. Geoffrey Samuel, *Civilized Shamans; Buddhism in Tibetan Societies* (Washington, DC, 1993), 206; Kenneth Ch'en, *Buddhism in China* (Princeton, 1964), 246–7; in more recent times higher ordination has been the norm in China, see Welch, *The Practice of Chinese Buddhism*, 294.
12. Welch, *The Practice of Chinese Buddhism*, 105, 247, 275, 294.
13. This *pārājika* is often quoted by modern commentators as to do with laying false claim to 'miraculous' powers, but the Vinaya understands the term *uttari-manussa-dhamma* as applying to any spiritual attainment; see Gethin, *The Buddhist Path to Awakening*; 97–101.
14. Vinaya ii. 253–6.
15. Richard Gombrich, *Buddhist Studies Review*, 12 (1995), 95–6.
16. Majjhima Nikāya iii. 65.
17. Schopen, *Bones, Stones, and Buddhist Monks*, 248–50.
18. Tessa Bartholomeusz, *Women under the Bo Tree* (Cambridge, 1994); L. W. Bloss, 'The Female Renunciants of Sri Lanka', *Journal of the International Association of Buddhist Studies*, 10 (1978), 7–31; H. Kawanami, 'The Religious Standing of Burmese Buddhist Nuns (*thilá shin*)', *Journal of the International Association of Buddhist Studies*, 13 (1990), 17–39; P. Richman, 'Gender and Persuasion: The Portrayal of Beauty, Anguish, and Nurturance in an Account of a Tamil Nun', in José Cabezón (ed.), *Buddhism, Sexuality, and Gender* (Albany, NY, 1992), 111–36; Kathryn Tsai (trans.), *The Lives of the Nuns: Biographies of Chinese Buddhist Nuns from the Fourth to Sixth Centuries: A Translation of the Pi-ch'iu-ni chuan compiled by Shih Pao-ch'ang* (Honolulu, 1994); Hanna Havnevik, *Tibetan Buddhist Nuns: History, Cultural Norms and Social Reality* (Oslo, 1989).

19. Maha-Boowa Nyanasampanno, *The Venerable Phra Acharn Mun Bhuridatta Thera: Meditation Master* (Bangkok, 1982); Gombrich, *Buddhist Precept and Practice*, 333–4.
20. Niḥsargika-pāyantika/Nissaggiya-pācittiya 18, 19, 20; see Prebish, *Buddhist Monastic Discipline*, 70–1; Vinaya iii. 236–46.
21. Mūlasarvāstivādin Pāyantika 39 (Prebish, *Buddhist Monastic Discipline*, 81); Theravādin Pācittiya 40 (Vinaya iv. 90).
22. Mūlasarvāstivādin Pāyantika 73 (Prebish, *Buddhist Monastic Discipline*, 89); Theravādin Pācittiya 10 (Vinaya iv. 32–3).
23. Mūlasarvāstivādin Niḥsargika-Pāyantika 30, Pāyantika 38 (Prebish, *Buddhist Monastic Discipline*, 73–4, 81); Theravādin Nissaggiya-Pācittiya 23, Pācittiya 38 (Vinaya iii. 251, iv. 86–7).
24. See Wijayaratna, *Buddhist Monastic Life*, 65–6; Vinaya i. 210–12.
25. Gregory Schopen, 'The Ritual Obligations and Donor Roles of Monks in the Pāli Vinaya', *Journal of the Pali Text Society*, 16 (1992), 87–107.
26. Aṅguttara Nikāya i. 10; iv. 128–35; Harvey B. Aronson, *Love and Sympathy in Theravāda Buddhism* (Delhi, 1980), 24–8.
27. Mūlasarvāstivādin Pāyantika 28, 65 (Prebish, *Buddhist Monastic Discipline*, 79, 87); Theravādin Pācittiya 44, 45 (Vinaya iv. 96–7).
28. Suttanipata vv. 35–75.
29. This is the kind of view put forth in the works of Sukumar Dutt; see Steven Collins' introduction to Wijayaratna, *Buddhist Monastic Life*, pp. xii–xix.
30. Schopen in Lopez (ed.), *Buddhism in Practice*, 475.
31. For Fa-hsien see James Legge (trans.), *A Record of Buddhist Kingdoms* (Oxford, 1886); for Fa-hsien and Hsüan-tsang see Samuel Beal (trans.), *Si-yu-ki: Buddhist Records of the Western World* (1884), and *The Life of Hiuen-tsiang by the Shamans Hwai li and Yen-tsing* (1885); for I-tsing see J. Takakusu (trans.), *A Record of the Buddhist Religion as Practised in India and the Malay Archipelago (A.D. 671–695)* (Oxford, 1896).
32. While the shrine hall with its buddha-image has become a feature of Buddhist monasteries, this was not so true in the ancient period (cf. Rahula, *History of Buddhism in Ceylon*, 121–9).
33. Legge, *A Record of Buddhist Kingdoms*, 102; Takakusu, *A Record of the Buddhist Religion*, 65.
34. Vinaya i. 250; Lal Mani Joshi, *Studies in the Buddhistic Culture of India During the 7th and 8th Centuries A.D.* (Delhi, 1977), 65–73; Rahula, *History of Buddhism in Ceylon*, 135–52; R. A. L. H.

Gunawardana, *Robe and Plough: Monasticism and Economic Interest in Early Medieval Sri Lanka* (Tucson, Ariz., 1979), 53–136.

35. Rahula, *History of Buddhism in Ceylon*, 146–7; Gunawardana, *Robe and Plough*, 97–100.
36. Gunawardana, *Robe and Plough*, 80–6, 147–53; Gombrich, *Theravāda Buddhism*, 165–6; Gregory Schopen, 'Deaths, Funerals, and the Division of Property in a Monastic Code', in Lopez (ed.), *Buddhism in Practice*, 473–502, and 'Monastic Law Meets the Real World: A Monk's Continuing Right to Inherit Family Property in Classical India', *History of Religions*, 35 (1995), 101–23.
37. Visuddhimagga ii.; Vimuttimagga 27–38; Reginald Ray, *Buddhist Saints in India* (New York, 1994), 293–323.
38. Gunawardana, *Robe and Plough*, 41–7.
39. Cf. Gombrich, *Theravāda Buddhism*, 156–7.
40. Visuddhimagga iii. 31–4.
41. John Strong (trans.), *The Legend of King Aśoka* (Princeton, 1983); Romila Thapar, *Aśoka and the Decline of the Mauryas* (Delhi, 1973), 184–202 (for a translation of Aśoka's edicts); Anuradha Seneviratna (ed.), *King Aśoka and Buddhism: Historical and Literary Studies* (Kandy, 1994).
42. Mahāvaṃsa xxv. 98–116; Gananath Obeyesekere *et al.* (eds.), *The Two Wheels of Dhamma: Essays on the Theravāda Tradition in India and Ceylon* (Chambersburg, Pa., 1972); Daigan Matsunaga and Alicia Matsunaga, *Foundation of Japanese Buddhism*, 2 vols. (Tokyo, 1974–6), ii. 284–8; John Powers, *Introduction to Tibetan Buddhism* (Ithaca, NY, 1995), 139; Bardwell L. Smith (ed.), *Religion and Legitimation of Power in Thailand Laos and Burma* (Chambersburg, Pa., 1978).
43. L. S. Cousins, 'Good or Skilful? *Kusala* In Canon and Commentary', *Journal of Buddhist Ethics*, 3 (1996), 136–64 (electronic journal: *http://www.gold.ac.uk/jbe* (UK address); *http://jbe.la.psu.edu* (USA address)).
44. Wijayaratna, *Buddhist Monastic Life*, 132.
45. From the *Saddharmalaṅkāraya*; quoted by Rahula, *History of Buddhism in Ceylon*, 194.
46. Schopen, 'The Ritual Obligations and Donor Roles of Monks'; Richard Gombrich, 'The Monk in the Pali Vinaya: Priest or Wedding Guest?', *Journal of the Pali Text Society*, 21 (1995), 193–7.
47. Rahula, *History of Buddhism in Ceylon*, 112–14; Gunawardana, *Robe and Plough*, 143–4; cf. Welch, *The Practice of Chinese Buddhism*, 14, 128.

48. E. W. Adikaram, *Early History of Buddhism in Ceylon* (Migoda, 1946), 135–42; Gombrich, *Buddhist Precept and Practice*, 123–4).
49. Rahula, *History of Buddhism in Ceylon*, 163–5; Gregory Schopen, 'Filial Piety and the Monk in the Practice of Indian Buddhism', *T'oung Pao*, 70 (1984), 110–26.
50. Rahula, *History of Buddhism in Ceylon*, 158–63.
51. Sukumar Dutt, *Buddhist Monks and Monasteries of India* (London, 1962), 319–66; Joshi, *Studies in the Buddhistic Culture of India*, 121–41.
52. See Donald S. Lopez (ed.), *Buddhism in Practice* (Princeton, 1995), 475.
53. Cf. Ray, *Buddhist Saints in Ancient India*, 447. Other studies of the 'forest tradition' are Stanley Tambiah, *The Buddhist Saints of the Forest and the Cult of Amulets* (Cambridge, 1984); J. L. Taylor, *Forest Monks and Nation-State: An Anthropological and Historical Study in Northeastern Thailand* (Singapore, 1993); Michael Carrithers, *The Forest Monks of Sri Lanka* (Delhi, 1983); Kamala Tiyavanich, *Forest Recollections: Wandering Monks in Twentieth Century Thailand* (Honolulu, 1997).
54. See Gombrich, *Precept and Practice*; Richard Gombrich and Gananath Obeyesekere, *Buddhism Transformed: Religious Change in Sri Lanka* (Princeton, 1988); Spiro, *Buddhism and Society*; Stanley Tambiah, *World Conqueror and World Renouncer* (Cambridge, 1976); Tambiah, *The Buddhist Saints of the Forest*.
55. Ray, *Buddhist Saints in India*; Reichelt, *Truth and Tradition in Chinese Buddhism*; Tucci, *The Religions of Tibet*, 110–62; Welch, *The Practice of Chinese Buddhism*.
56. Welch, *The Practice of Chinese Buddhism*, 70.
57. Ch'en, *Buddhism in China*, 363; Welch, *The Practice of Chinese Buddhism*, 104.
58. Welch, *The Practice of Chinese Buddhism*, 207–8.
59. Robinson and Johnson, *The Buddhist Religion*, 181.
60. Gombrich, *Theravāda Buddhism*, 74–6; Schopen, *Bones, Stones, and Buddhist Monks*, 80.
61. Vinaya i. 236–8; Majjhima Nikāya i. 379–80.
62. Conze, *Buddhist Scriptures*, 24–6.
63. Margaret Cone and Richard Gombrich, *The Perfect Generosity of Prince Vessantara* (Oxford, 1977).
64. Spiro, *Buddhism and Society*, 11–14; Samuel, *Civilized Shamans*, 24–7, discusses the relevance of such a schema to Tibetan Buddhist society.

Chapter 5. The Buddhist Cosmos

1. Saṃyutta Nikāya ii. 180–1.
2. Ibid., 181–2.
3. Dīgha Nikāya i. 215–23.
4. Dīgha Nikāya i. 223. This interpretation is in keeping with the commentary (Sumaṅgalavilāsinī 393–4), but the precise interpretation of this passage is problematic.
5. e.g. Dīgha Nikāya i. 62.
6. Dīgha Nikāya i. 17–9; Majjhima Nikāya i. 326–31; cf. Saṃyutta Nikāya i. 142–4.
7. Aṅguttara Nikāya i. 227–8; Abhidharmakośa iii. 73–4; Manorathapūraṇī ii. 340–1.
8. Atthasālinī 160–1.
9. Aṅguttara Nikāya iii. 415; cf. Atthasālinī 88–9.
10. Dīgha Nikāya iii. 269.
11. Atthasālinī 95–104; Conze, *Buddhist Scriptures*, 70–3 (= Papañcasūdanī i. 198–200, 203–4); Bhikkhu Bodhi (trans.), *The Discourse on the All-Embracing Net of Views*, 118–25 (= Sumaṅgalavilāsinī 69–76; Dīgha-nikāya-aṭṭhakathā-ṭīkā i. 143–54).
12. Atthasālinī 128.
13. Aṅguttara Nikāya ii. 126, 230; iv. 39, 241; see Marasinghe, *Gods in Early Buddhism*, 244–68.
14. Abhidhammāvatāra 182–289.
15. Visuddhimagga xiii. 31–62; Abhidharmakośa iii. 89–90, 100–2.
16. Dīgha Nikāya iii. 84–5.
17. Saṃyutta Nikāya i. 61–2 = Aṅguttara Nikāya ii. 47–9.
18. Simon Weightman, *Hinduism in the Village Setting* (Milton Keynes, 1978).
19. Giuseppe Tucci, *The Religions of Tibet* (London, 1980), 163–90; John Powers, *Introduction to Tibetan Buddhism* (Ithaca, NY), 431–47.
20. Spiro, *Burmese Supernaturalism* (Englewood Cliffs, NJ, 1967), 253–7; Richard Gombrich, 'Buddhism and Society', *Modern Asian Studies*, 6 (1972), 483–94 (490).
21. Visuddhimagga vii. 115.
22. F. Capra, *The Tao of Physics* (London, 1976).
23. Basham, *The Wonder That Was India*, 490.

Chapter 6. No Self

1. Bṛhadāraṇyaka Upaniṣad 3. 7. 23; 3. 8. 11; 4. 4. 25.
2. Ibid., 3. 9. 26; 4. 2. 4; 4. 4. 22; 4. 5. 15; cf. 4. 5. 14.

3. Ibid., 4. 4. 5; Chāndogya Upaniṣad 3. 14. 4.
4. 1. 4–5; cf. M. Hulin, *Sāṃkhya Literature* (Wiesbaden, 1978), 130–1.
5. Cf. David Hume, *A Treatise of Human Nature* (Oxford, 1978), i. 4. 6; A. H. Lesser, 'Eastern and Western Empiricism and the "No Self" Theory', *Religious Studies*, 15 (1979), 55–64.
6. For *saṃjñā* as recognition see Nyanaponika, *Abhidhamma Studies* (Kandy, 1976), 72; Gethin, *Buddhist Path to Awakening*, 41.
7. Collins, *Selfless Persons*, 97–103.
8. Saṃyutta Nikāya iii. 66–7.
9. Majjhima Nikāya i. 138–9, 232–3; Saṃyutta Nikāya ii. 125, 249; iii. 67–8, 88–9, 104, 105, 187–8. See Rupert Gethin, 'The Five Khandhas', *Journal of Indian Philosophy*, 14 (1986), 35–53 (43–4).
10. Chāndogya Upaniṣad 6. 8–16; cf. K. R. Norman, 'A Note on *attā* in the *Alagaddūpama-sutta*' in *Collected Papers*, ii. (Oxford, 1991), 200–9.
11. Dīgha Nikāya ii. 66–8.
12. Saṃyutta Nikāya i. 135; Milindapañha 25–8.
13. Majjhima Nikāya i. 140.
14. Gethin, 'The Five Khandhas', 48–9.
15. Vinaya i. 39–44; Majjhima Nikāya i. 497–502; *Catuṣpariṣatsūtra* 93; Mahāvastu iii. 62.
16. Lamotte, *History of Indian Buddhism*, 495; Daniel Boucher, 'The *Pratītyasamutpādagāthā* and its Role in The Medieval Cult of the Relics', *Journal of the International Association of Buddhist Studies*, 14 (1991), 1–27.
17. Majjhima Nikāya iii. 63; Saṃyutta Nikāya v. 387; etc.
18. e.g. *Kindred Sayings* ii. 16 (Saṃyutta Nikāya ii. 20).
19. Majjhima Nikāya i. 190–1; Boucher, 'The *Pratītyasamutpādagāthā* and its Role in the Medieval Cult of the Relics', 2.
20. Visuddhimagga xvii. 166–7.
21. Milindapañha 46.
22. Saṃyutta Nikāya ii. 20.
23. Dīgha Nikāya i. 202.
24. Ibid., ii. 68.
25. Saṃyutta Nikāya iii. 137.
26. Norman, 'A Note on *attā* in the *Alagaddūpama-sutta*'; cf. Bṛhadāraṇyaka Upaniṣad 4. 4–5, Chāndogya Upaniṣad 3. 14.
27. Views 1–8, 17–62 (Dīgha Nikāya i. 13–22, 28–38).
28. e.g. Majjhima Nikāya i. 300; Atthasālinī 353–4; Conze, *Buddhist Thought in India*, 38; Alex Wayman, 'The Twenty Reifying Views' in A. K. Narain (ed.), *Studies in Pali and Buddhism: A Memorial Volume in Honor of Bhikkhu Jagdish Kashyap* (Delhi, 1979), 375–80.

29. Majjhima Nikāya i. 8.
30. Visuddhimagga xvii. (cf. Vibhaṅga-aṭṭhakathā 130–213); Abhidharmakośa iii. 21–36. For some account of Asaṅga's interpretation see Jeffrey Hopkins, *Meditation on Emptiness* (London, 1983), 707–11.
31. Vibhaṅga-aṭṭhakathā 150.
32. For *avidyā* as not the mere absence of knowledge, see B. K. Matilal, 'Ignorance or Misconception? A Note on Avidyā in Buddhism', in S. Balasooriya *et al.* (eds.), *Buddhist Studies in Honour of Walpola Rahula* (London, 1980), 154–64.
33. For *upādāna* as purposeful and goal-orientated see Vibhaṅga-aṭṭhakathā 185–7, 192.
34. Vibhaṅga-aṭṭhakathā 196.
35. Visuddhimagga xvii. 66–100; the 24 types of conditional relation (*paccaya*) are the subject of the *Paṭṭhāna*, the seventh book of the Abhidharma Piṭaka.
36. Visuddhimagga xvii. 105–7; Vibhaṅga-aṭṭhakathā 147–8. For the Sarvāstivādin understanding of types of condition, see Abhidharmakośa ii. 60–73.
37. Dīgha Nikāya ii. 55; Saṃyutta Nikāya ii. 92.
38. Cf. Vibhaṅga-aṭṭhakathā 192.
39. Visuddhimagga viii. 39.
40. Vibhaṅga-aṭṭhakathā 198–9.
41. Saṃyutta Nikāya ii. 29–32; cf. Bhikkhu Bodhi, 'Transcendental Dependent Arising', *The Wheel* (1980), 277/8; Vimuttimagga, 267.
42. Saṃyutta Nikāya ii. 25.
43. The oldest surviving painting appears to be in the Ajantā caves (sixth century) in India: see J. Przyluski, 'La Roue de la vie à Ajaṇṭā', *Journal Asiatique* (1920), 313–31. Cf. Visuddhimagga vii. 7–8 for the image of the wheel.
44. See David Snellgrove, *Buddhist Himālaya* (Oxford , 1957), 14–15.
45. See Collins, *Selfless Persons*, 7–10.
46. Saṃyutta Nikāya iv. 400–1.
47. Ibid., iii. 46–7.
48. Ibid., 126–32.

Chapter 7. The Buddhist Path

1. Visuddhimagga xiv. 32.
2. e.g. Dīgha Nikāya i. 63; Majjhima Nikāya i. 179.
3. Aṅguttara Nikāya i. 189.
4. Conze, *Buddhist Thought in India*, 48.

5. John Ross Carter (ed.), *The Threefold Refuge in Theravāda Buddhist Tradition* (Chambersburg, Pa., 1982).
6. Dīgha Nikāya ii. 140–1.
7. On six recollections (*anusmṛti/anussati*) see Aṅguttara Nikāya iii. 284–8, 312–17.
8. Peter Skilling, 'The Rakṣā Literature of the Śrāvakayāna', *Journal of the Pali Text Society*, 16 (1992), 109–82; Gombrich, *Buddhist Precept and Practice*, 236–46.
9. Vinaya ii. 194.
10. Dīgha Nikāya iii. 194–206.
11. Milindapañha 150–4.
12. Dīgha Nikāya ii. 74–5.
13. Milindapañha 34–5.
14. Dīgha Nikāya iii. 133, 235.
15. Majjhima Nikāya i. 368–71.
16. *Laṅkāvatāra Sūtra* 211–22 (244–59).
17. e.g. Dīgha Nikāya i.; Majjhima Nikāya i. 180. Cf. Visuddhimagga i. 23, Aṅguttara Nikāya v. 1, Dīgha Nikāya ii. 86; Bhikkhu Bodhi, *The All-Embracing Net of Views*, 276–8.
18. Abhidhammatthasaṅgaha-ṭīkā 54.
19. Aṅguttara Nikāya i. 10.
20. Visuddhimagga iii. 104–33; Vimuttimagga 63–70.
21. e.g. Richard Gombrich, 'From Monastery to Meditation Centre: Lay Meditation in Modern Sri Lanka' in Denwood and Piatigorsky (eds.), *Buddhist Studies Ancient and Modern* (London, 1983), 20–34.
22. Visuddhimagga vii. 101–2 on the practice of *sīlānussati* by lay followers.
23. The Theravādin term is *upacāra*, the Sarvāstivādin *anāgamya* or *samantaka*.
24. Madhyāntavibhāga-śāstra vi. 3–4; Mahāyānasūtrālaṃkāra xvi. 11–14; Śrāvakabhūmi 108–10; Beyer, *The Buddhist Experience*, 107 (Kamalaśīla's *Bhāvanākrama i.*); Alex Wayman (trans.), *Calming the Mind and Discerning the Real* (New York, 1978), 141–3 (Tsong-kha-pa's *Lam-rim chen-mo*); Jeffrey Hopkins, *Meditation on Emptiness* (London, 1983), 67–90.
25. Donald Swearer, 'The Way of Meditation', in Donald Lopez (ed.), *Buddhism in Practice*, (Princeton, 1995), 207–15, (212).
26. Cf. L. S. Cousins, 'Buddhist *Jhāna*', *Religion*, 3 (1973), 115–31 (121), Spiro, *Buddhism and Society*, 56.

27. Phra Mahā Boowa Ñāṇasampanno, *Forest Dhamma: A Selection of Talks on Buddhist Practice* (Bangkok, 1973), 16–22; Geshe Gedün Lodrö, *Walking through Walls: A Presentation of Tibetan Meditation* (Ithaca, NY, 1992), 222–9, 252–4.
28. e.g. Majjhima Nikāya i. 276.
29. e.g. in Visuddhimagga presentation of forty *kammaṭṭhāna.*
30. Dīgha Nikāya i. 77–83; Visuddhimagga xii–xiii (see Conze, *Buddhist Scriptures*, 121–33).
31. Gethin, *The Buddhist Path to Awakening*, 97–101.
32. e.g Patrick Pranke, 'On Becoming a Buddhist Wizard', in Lopez, *Buddhism in Practice*, 343–58, a Burmese text; Tambiah, *The Buddhist Saints of the Forest*, 272.
33. On the four *brahma-vihāras* as leading to awakening see Richard Gombrich, *How Buddhism Began* (London, 1996), 57–64.
34. Visuddhimagga ix. 108–9.
35. Ibid., 8–11, 103; Harvey B. Aronson, *Love and Sympathy in Theravāda Buddhism* (Delhi, 1980).
36. Visuddhimagga xx. 104.
37. Ibid., xxi. 43.
38. Ibid., xxi. 49.
39. Abhidharma-samuccaya 104. Louis de La Vallée Poussin, 'A Summary Note on the Path', *Abhidharmakośabhāṣyam*, trans. by Pruden, iii. pp. xiv–xxii.
40. See *Satipaṭṭhāna Sutta*, Dīgha Nikāya ii. 290–315, Majjhima Nikāya i. 55–63.
41. Saṃyutta Nikāya iii. 155; Aṅguttara Nikāya iv. 127.
42. Winston King, *Theravāda Meditation* (University Park, Pa., 1980).
43. Johannes Bronkhorst, *The Two Traditions of Meditation in Ancient India* (Delhi, 1993).
44. Louis de La Vallée Poussin, 'Musīla et Nārada', *Mélanges chinois et bouddhiques*, 5 (1937), 189–222; Lambert Schmithausen, 'On Some Aspects of Descriptions or Theories of "Liberating Insight" and "Enlightenment" in Early Buddhism', in Klaus Bruhn and Albrecht Wezler (ed.), *Studien zum Jainismus und Buddhismus: Gedenkschrift für Ludwig Alsdorf* (Wiesbaden, 1981), 199–250; Paul Griffiths, 'Concentration or Insight: The Problematic of Theravāda Buddhist Meditation-Theory', *Journal of the American Academy of Religion*, 59 (1981), 605–24; Vetter, *The Ideas and Meditative Practices of Early Buddhism*; Gombrich, *How Buddhism Began*, 96–134.

45. L. S. Cousins, 'Samatha-Yāna and Vipassanā-Yāna', in G. Dhammapala *et al.* (eds.), *Buddhist Studies in Honour of Hammalava Saddhātissa* (Nugegoda, 1984), 56–68. For a clear statement from Kamalaśīla's Bhāvanākrama I see Beyer, *The Buddhist Experience*, 109.

Chapter 8. The Abhidharma

1. Atthasālinī 12–17; E. W. Burlingame (trans.), *Buddhist Legends Translated from the Original Pali Text of the Dhammapada Commentary*, 3 vols. (London, 1969), iii. 35–6.
2. On the Sarvāstivādin legend of the preaching of the Abhidharma, see Lamotte, *History of Indian Buddhism*, 186.
3. An asterisk before a title indicates a reconstructed Sanskrit or Pali title from an ancient Chinese translation in the case of texts whose Sanskrit or Pali original is lost.
4. Erich Frauwallner, *On the Date of the Buddhist Master of the Law, Vasubandhu* (Rome, 1951); Padmanabh S. Jaini, 'On the Theory of Two Vasubandhus', *Bulletin of the School of Oriental and African Studies*, 22 (1958), 48–53.
5. Warder, *Indian Buddhism*, 309.
6. For the Yogācārin list see Walpola Rahula (trans.), *Le Compendium de la super-doctrine (philosophie) (Abhidharmasamuccaya) d'Asaṅga*, (Paris, 1971), 6–18; Louis de La Vallée Poussin (trans.), *Vijñaptimātratāsiddhi: Le Siddhi de Hiuan-Tsang* (Paris, 1928–9), i. 296–395; Junjiro Takakusu, *The Essentials of Indian Philosophy* (Bombay, 1956), 96.
7. Atthasālinī 64.
8. Milindapañha 87; Atthasālinī 142.
9. Saṃyutta Nikāya ii. 95.
10. Dhammasaṅgaṇi 36–7.
11. Atthasālinī 279.
12. Shwe Zan Aung (trans.), *Compendium of Philosophy*, (London, 1910), 30–2; Lama Anagarika Govinda, *The Psychological Attitude of Early Buddhist Philosophy* (London, 1969), 134–42.
13. Rupert Gethin, '*Bhavaṅga* and Rebirth according to the Abhidhamma', *The Buddhist Forum*, 3 (1994), 11–35.
14. Gombrich, *Buddhist Precept and Practice* (New Delhi, 1991), 256–7, 271–2.
15. Kathāvatthu 361–6; Abhidharmakośa iii. 10–19; Alex Wayman, 'The Intermediate-State Dispute in Buddhism' in L. S. Cousins

et al. (eds.), *Buddhist Studies in Honour of I. B. Horner* (Dordrecht, 1974), 227–39; W. Y. Evans-Wentz (trans.), *The Tibetan Book of the Dead* (London, 1957).

16. Saṃyutta Nikāya iii. 154.
17. Paul Williams, 'Buddhadeva and Temporality', *Journal of Indian Philosophy*, 4 (1977), 279–94.
18. Conze, *Buddhist Thought in India*, 282; Abhidharmakośa iii. 85–90.
19. Lamotte, *History of Indian Buddhism*, 603; Abhidharmakośa iv. 2–3.
20. Padmanabh Jaini, 'The Sautrāntika Theory of *Bīja*', *Bulletin of the School of Oriental Studies*, 22 (1959), 237–49; Conze, *Buddhist Thought in India*, 141–3; Abhidharmakośa ii. 36.
21. Gethin, '*Bhavaṅga* and Rebirth according to the Abhidhamma'.
22. L. S. Cousins, 'Person and Self', in *Buddhism into the Year 2000: International Conference Proceedings* (Bangkok and Los Angeles, 1994), 15–32.
23. K. Venkataramanan, 'Sāmmitīyanikāya Śāstra', *Visva-Bharati Annals*, 5 (1953), 154–243; Kathāvatthu 1–69; Satyasiddhiśāstra ii. 69–74; Abhidharmakośa ix.

Chapter 9. The Mahāyāna

1. Charles Hallisey, 'Tuṇḍilovādasutta: An Allegedly Non-Canonical Sutta', *Journal of the Pali Text Society*, 15 (1990), 154–95 and 'Nibbānasutta: An Allegedly Non-Canonical Sutta on Nibbāna as a Great City', *Journal of the Pali Text Society*, 18 (1993), 97–130; Padmanabh Jaini, 'Ākāravattārasutta: An 'Apocryphal' Sutta from Thailand', *Indo-Iranian Journal*, 35 (1992), 193–223.
2. Paul Harrison, 'Searching for the Origins of the Mahāyāna', *Eastern Buddhist*, 28 (1995), 48–69.
3. Gregory Schopen, 'The Phrase "*sa pṛthivīpradeśaś caityabhūto bhavet*" in the *Vajracchedikā*: Notes on the Cult of the Book in Mahāyāna', *Indo-Iranian Journal*, 17 (1975), 147–81, and 'Two Problems in the History of Indian Buddhism: The Layman/Monk Distinction and the Doctrines of the Transference of Merit', *Studien zur Indologie und Iranistik*, 10 (1985), 9–47; Richard Gombrich, 'How the Mahāyāna Began', *The Buddhist Forum*, 1 (1990), 21–30.
4. Cf. Conze, *Buddhist Scriptures*, 23, 30–3, 164, for extracts from the Mahāvastu, *Mahāprajñāpāramitā Śāstra and Vajracchedikā.
5. Mahāvastu i. 124–40; Paul, Harrison, 'Sanskrit Fragments of a Lokottaravādin Tradition', in L. A. Hercus *et al.* (eds.), *Indological and Buddhist Studies* (Canberra, 1982), 211–34.

6. For the Theravāda account of the Bodhisattva path see Bhikkhu Bodhi (trans.), 'A Treatise on the Pāramīs', in *The Discourse on the All-Embracing Net of Views*, 254–330 (= Cp-a 276–332); H. Saddhatissa (trans.), *The Birth Stories of the Ten Bodhisattas* (London, 1975).
7. Louis de La Vallée Poussin (trans.), *Vijñaptimātratāsiddhi: La Siddhi de Hiuan-Tsang*, 2 vols. (Paris, 1928–9), 676–7, 721–5.
8. Also Śrīmālādevī 78–94; and Laṅkāvatāra Sūtra 63; cf. Herbert V. Guenther (trans.), *The Jewel Ornament of Liberation* (London, 1970), 4–6.
9. On the notion of 'skill in means' see Michael Pye, *Skilful Means* (London, 1978); Williams, *Mahāyāna Buddhism*, 143–50.
10. Oral teachings from His Holiness Sakya Trinzin on the *Zhen pa bzhi bral* or 'Leaving behind the four desires', Tibet House, New Delhi, 11–15 Jan. 1982. (Cf. Williams, *Mahāyāna Buddhism*, 199.)
11. Lodrö, *Walking through Walls*, 367–75.
12. Kamalaśīla's Bhāvanākrama 1; see Beyer, *The Buddhist Experience*, 111.
13. Guenther, *Jewel Ornament of Liberation*, 112, 232–56.
14. Conze, *Large Sūtra on Perfect Wisdom*, 163–78; Guenther, *Jewel Ornament of Liberation*, 239–56.
15. Daśabhūmikasūtra (Rahder ed., Leuven 1926), 91; Cleary, *The Flower Ornament Scripture* ii. 108.
16. La Vallée Poussin, *La Siddhi*, 671; Williams, *Mahāyāna Buddhism*, 181–3; Nagao, 'The Bodhisattva Returns to this World', in Leslie Kawamura (ed.), *The Bodhisattva Doctrine in Buddhism* (Waterloo, Ontario, 1981), 61–79.
17. Paul Harrison, 'Is the *Dharma-kāya* the Real "Phantom Body" of the Buddha?', *Journal of the International Association of Buddhist Studies*, 15 (1992), 44–94.
18. Richard Gombrich, 'The Significance of Former Buddhas in Theravādin Tradition', in Somaratna Balasooriya *et al.* (eds.), *Buddhist Studies in Honour of Walpola Rahula* (London, 1980), 62–72.
19. Conze, *Buddhist Scriptures*, 211–14 (= Milindapañha 237–9; Mahāprajñāpāramitā-śāstra 93b–c).
20. R. Birnbaum, *The Healing Buddha* (London, 1980); Paul Harrison (trans.), *The Samādhi of Direct Encounter with the Buddhas of the Present* (Tokyo, 1990); Alan Sponberg and Helen Hardacre (eds.), *Maitreya: The Future Buddha* (Cambridge, 1988); Stephan Beyer, *The Cult of Tārā: Magic and Ritual in Tibet* (Berkeley, 1973). For

material on Amitābha, see section on 'Pure Land Buddhism' in Chapter 10.

21. Vibhaṅga-aṭṭhakathā 433; Gombrich, *Buddhist Precept and Practice*, 341; Reynolds, 'The Many Lives of the Buddha', 53.
22. Lamotte, *History of Indian Buddhism*, 690–9; John Strong, *The Legend of Upagupta* (Princeton, 1991); Ray, *Buddhist Saints in India*, 178–212, 358–95; Maha-Boowa Nyanasampanno, *The Venerable Phra Acharn Mun Bhuridatta Thera*, 190–2.
23. Williams, *Mahāyāna Buddhism*, 41–2; Jan Nattier, 'The *Heart Sūtra*: A Chinese Apocryphal Text?', *Journal of the International Association of Buddhist Studies*, 15 (1992), 192–223.
24. Pañcaviṃśatisahasrikā 61.
25. On these similes see Conze, *Buddhist Thought in India*, 222; *Buddhist Wisdom Books*, 68–71; Lamotte, *Le Traité* i. 357–87.
26. Visuddhimagga xx. 104 gives a number of similes, most of which are traceable to earlier Nikāya sources, see p. 140 above.
27. Étienne Lamotte, 'Three Sūtras from the Saṃyuktāgama Concerning Emptiness', *Buddhist Studies Review*, 10 (1993), 1–23; Majjhima Nikāya iii. 104–18; Dhammasaṅgaṇi 25–6 ('the section on emptiness); Paṭisambhidāmagga i. 177–84 ('the discussion of emptiness').
28. Mūla-Madhyamaka-Kārikā xxiv. 11.
29. Ibid., 8–10.
30. Ibid., xxv. 19–20.
31. Ibid., xiii. 8.
32. Paul Williams, 'On the Abhidharma Ontology', *Journal of Indian Philosophy*, 9 (1981), 227–57.
33. Cf. Śūnyatāsaptati-kārikā 69.
34. A. K. Warder, 'Is Nāgārjuna a Mahāyānist?' in M. Sprung (ed.), *The Problem of Two Truths in Buddhism and Vedānta*, (Dordrecht, 1973), 78–88.
35. Cf. Williams, *Mahāyāna Buddhism*, 46–7; Hopkins, *Meditation on Emptiness*, 29–30; Donald Lopez, 'Do *Śrāvakas* Understand Emptiness', *Journal of Indian Philosophy*, 16 (1988), 65–105. Étienne Lamotte, 'Passions and Impregnations of the Passions in Buddhism', in L. S. Cousins *et al.* (eds.), *Buddhist Studies in Honour of I. B. Horner* (Dordrecht, 1974), 94–104.
36. Bhikkhu Ñāṇananda, *Concept and Reality in Early Buddhist Thought* (Kandy, 1976); Luis O. Gómez, 'Proto-Mādhyamika in the Pāli Canon', *Philosophy East and West*, 26 (1976), 137–65; Collins, *Selfless Persons*, 117–31; Padmanabh Jaini, '*Prajñā* and *dṛṣṭi* in the

Vaibhāṣika Abhidharma', in Lancaster, Lewis (ed.), *Prajñāpāramitā and Related Systems: Studies in Honor of Edward Conze*, (Berkeley, 1977), 403–15. And see nn. 21–2 above.

37. Th. Stcherbatsky, *The Conception of Buddhist Nirvāṇa* (Leningrad, 1927); C. Gudmunsen, *Wittgenstein and Buddhism* (London, 1977); C. W. Huntington, *The Emptiness of Emptiness: An Introduction to Early Indian Mādhyamika* (Honolulu, 1989); Andrew Tuck, *Comparative Philosophy and the Philosophy of Scholarship: On the Western Interpretation of Nāgārjuna* (Oxford, 1990); Paul Williams, 'On the Interpretation of Madhyamaka Thought', *Journal of Indian Philosophy*, 19 (1991), 191–218; Richard Hayes, 'Nāgārjuna's Appeal', *Journal of Indian Philosophy*, 22 (1994), 299–378, for a useful and provocative discussion and bibliography.
38. Viṃśatikā 1 (Anacker, *Seven Works of Vasubandhu*, 161).
39. Lamotte, *Saṃdhinirmocana*, 206–7; Powers, *Wisdom of the Buddha*, 139–41.
40. *Mahāyāna-Saṃgraha* i. 6 (Lamotte, *La Somme*, 16).
41. Triṃśikā 5–6; La Vallée Poussin, *La Siddhi*, 250–3.
42. Triṃśikā 3.
43. Mahāyāna-Saṃgraha i. 19–20.
44. Ibid., ii. 15.
45. Laṅkāvatāra Sūtra 55; La Vallée Poussin, *La Siddhi*, 607–12; Triṃśikā 26–30; Conze, *Buddhist Thought in India*, 257; Lambert Schmithausen, *Ālayavijñāna* (Tokyo, 1987), 198; Williams, *Mahāyāna Buddhism*, 92–3.
46. Madhyānta-Vibhāga-bhāṣya i. 1–3, 13–14.
47. Griffiths, *On Being Mindless*, 82–3.
48. Viṃśatikā-vṛtti to 17c.
49. Tathāgatagarbha Sūtra 96.

Chapter 10. Evolving Traditions

1. Atthasālinī 18; Steven Collins, 'On The Very Idea of the Pāli Canon', *Journal of the Pali Text Society*, 15 (1990), 89–126.
2. K. R. Norman, 'The Literary Works of the Abhayagirivihārins', *Collected Papers*, iv (Oxford, 1993), 202–17; Peter Skilling, 'A Citation from the *Buddhavaṃsa of the Abhayagiri School', *Journal of the Pali Text Society*, 18 (1993), 165–75; and '*Vimuttimagga* and Abhayagiri: the Form-Aggregate according to the *Saṃskṛtāsaṃskṛta-Viniścaya*', *Journal of the Pali Text Society*, 20 (1994), 171–210.

3. Gunawardana, *Robe and Plough*, 271–7.
4. Gombrich and Obeyesekere, *Buddhism Transformed*.
5. Janice Stargardt, 'The Oldest Known Pali Texts, 5th–6th Century: Results of the Cambridge Symposium on the Pyu Golden Pali Text from Śrī Kṣetra', *Journal of the Pali Text Society*, 21 (1995), 199–213; Peter Skilling, 'The Advent of Theravāda Buddhism to Mainland South-east Asia', *Journal of the International Association of Buddhist Studies*, 20 (1997), 93–107.
6. L. S. Cousins, 'Aspects of Esoteric Southern Buddhism', in Peter Connolly and Sue Hamilton (eds.), *Indian Insights: Buddhism, Brahmanism and Bhakti* (London, 1997), 185–207; F. Bizot, *Le Figuier à cinq branches* (Paris, 1976); F. Bizot, *Le Chemin de Laṅkā* (Paris, 1992).
7. Ch'en, *Buddhism in China*, 61–9, 135–44; Erik Zürcher, *The Buddhist Conquest of China*, 2 vols. (Leiden, 1959).
8. Holmes Welch, *The Practice of Chinese Buddhism; The Buddhist Revival in China* (Cambridge, Mass., 1968); *Buddhism under Mao* (Cambridge, Mass, 1972).
9. Alan Sponberg, 'A Report on Buddhism in the People's Republic of China', *Journal of the International Association of Buddhist Studies*, 5 (1982), 109–17.
10. Paul Harrison, 'The Earliest Chinese Translations of Mahāyāna Buddhist Sūtras: Some Notes on the Works of Lokakṣema', *Buddhist Studies Review*, 10 (1993), 135–77.
11. On the Chinese Tripiṭaka see Renou and Filliozat, *L'Inde classique*, ii. 398–461; Ch'en, *Buddhism in China*, 365–86; J. W. de Jong, 'Buddha's Word in China', in Gregory Schopen (ed.), *Buddhist Studies by J. W. de Jong* (Berkeley, 1979), 77–101.
12. For a detailed analysis of the Taishō edition see Renou and Filliozat, *L'Inde classique*, ii. 431–61.
13. Bunyiu Nanjio, *A Catalogue of the Chinese Translation of the Buddhist Tripiṭaka* (Oxford, 1883).
14. Robert Buswell, 'Buddhism in Korea' in *Buddhism and Asian History*, 151–8; *Tracing Back the Radiance: Chinul's Korean Way of Zen* (Honolulu, 1991).
15. Ch'en, *Buddhism in China*, 81.
16. Ibid., 325–37; Welch, *The Buddhist Revival in China*, 196–9; Matsunaga, *Foundation of Japanese Buddhism*, i. 171–201.
17. Ch'en, *Buddhism in China*, 119–20.
18. Chang, *Original Teachings of Ch'an Buddhism*, 276.

19. Lamotte, *History of Indian Buddhism*, 191–202; Ch'en, *Buddhism in China*, 297–300; Jan Nattier, *Once Upon a Future Time: Studies in a Buddhist Prophecy of Decline* (Berkeley, 1991).
20. Daniel Stevenson, 'Pure Land Buddhist Worship and Meditation in China' and 'Death-Bed Testimonials of the Pure Land Faithful', in Lopez, *Buddhism in Practice*, 359–79, 592–602; Matsunaga, *Foundation of Japanese Buddhism*, ii. 85–127.
21. Paul L. Swanson, *Foundations of T'ien T'ai Philosophy: The Flowering of the Two Truths Theory in Chinese Buddhism* (Berkeley, 1989).
22. See Chih-i's *Hsiu-hsi chih-kuan tso-ch'an fa yao*, Dwight Goddard (ed.), *A Buddhist Bible* (Boston, 1970), 437–96.
23. Garma Chang, *The Buddhist Teaching of Totality* (London, 1972); Francis Cook, *Hua-yen Buddhism* (University Park, Pa., 1977).
24. Matsunaga, *Foundation of Japanese Buddhism* ii. 147–181.
25. Snellgrove, *Indo-Tibetan Buddhism*, 426–50; David Seyfort Ruegg, *Buddha-nature, Mind and the Problem of Gradualism in a Comparative Perspective* (London, 1989).
26. Kenneth Ch'en, 'The Tibetan Tripiṭaka', *Harvard Journal of Asian Studies*, 9 (1945–7), 53–62; Renou and Filliozat (ed.), *L'Inde classique*, ii. 388–97; Tadeusz Skorupski, *A Catalogue of the sTog Palace Kanjur* (Tokyo, 1985); Paul Harrison, 'A Brief History of the Tibetan bKa' 'gyur', in José Ignacio Cabezón and Roger R. Jackson (eds.), *Tibetan Literature: Studies in Genre* (Ithaca, NY, 1996), 70–94.
27. James B. Robinson (trans.), *Buddha's Lions: The Lives of the Eighty-Four Siddhas* (Berkeley, 1979); Keith Dowman (trans.), *Masters of Mahamudra: Songs and Histories of the Eighty-Four Buddhist Siddhas*, (Albany, NY, 1985).
28. Snellgrove, *Indo-Tibetan Buddhism*, 119–21; Tadeusz Skorupski, 'The Canonical *Tantras* of the New Schools', in Cabezón and Jackson, *Tibetan Literature*, 95–110. See Tucci, *The Religions of Tibet*, 76–87 for the slightly different rNying-ma-pa scheme.
29. Tucci, *The Religions of Tibet*, 41, 134–5; Snellgrove, *Indo-Tibetan Buddhism*, 498–99.
30. Powers, *Introduction to Tibetan Buddhism*, 169–87; Donald S. Lopez and Cyrus Stearns, 'A Report on Religious Activity in Central Tibet', *Journal of the International Association of Buddhist Studies*, 9 (1986), 101–7.
31. Williams, *Mahāyāna Buddhism*, 105–9; Shenpen Hookham, *The Buddha Within: The Tathāgatagarbha Doctrine according to the*

Shentong Interpretation of the Ratnagotravibhāga (Albany, NY, 1991).

32. Donald S. Lopez, *Curators of the Buddha* (Chicago, 1995), 253–7.
33. J. W. de Jong, *A Brief History of Buddhist Studies in Europe and America* (Varanasi, 1976).
34. Trevor O. Ling, *Buddhist Revival in India: Aspects of the Sociology of Buddhism* (London, 1980).

Select Bibliography

Texts (Pali, Sanskrit, Chinese, and Tibetan)

Only texts which have been translated into a modern European language are listed here. A translation into French has been cited where no English translation is available or where the translation constitutes an important scholarly work of reference in its own right. An asterisk before a title indicates a reconstructed Sanskrit or Pali title from an ancient Chinese translation in the case of texts whose Sanskrit or Pali original is lost.

Abhidhammattha-saṃgaha (Anuruddha). Bhikkhu Bodhi (trans.), *A Comprehensive Manual of Abhidhamma* (Kandy, 1993).

**Abhidharma-hṛdaya* (Dharmaśrī). C. Willemen (trans.), *The Essence of Metaphysics* (Brussels, 1975).

Abhidharmakośa-bhāṣya (Vasubandhu). Louis de La Vallée Poussin (trans.), *L'Abhidharmakośa de Vasubandhu: traduction et annotations*, 6 vols. (Brussels, 1971), trans. by Leo M. Pruden, 4 vols. (Berkeley, 1988).

Abhidharmasamuccaya (Asaṅga). Walpola Rahula (trans.), *Le Compendium de la super-doctrine (philosophie) (Abhidharmasamuccaya) d'Asaṅga* (Paris, 1971).

Amitāyurdhyāna Sūtra. Max Müller (ed.), *Sacred Books of the East*, XLIX. 161–201.

**Amṛtarasa* (Ghoṣaka). José Van Den Broeck (trans.), *Le saveur de l'immortel* (Louvain-la-Neuve, 1977).

Aṅguttara Nikāya. E. M. Hare and F. L. Woodward (trans.), *The Book of the Gradual Sayings*, 5 vols. (London, 1923–6).

Atthasālinī [of Buddhaghosa?]. Maung Tin (trans.), *The Expositor* (London, 1920).

Avataṃsaka Sūtra. Thomas Cleary (trans.), *The Flower Ornament Scripture*, 3 vols. (Boston, 1984–7).

Bhāvanākrama 1 (Kamalaśīla). Stephan Beyer, *The Buddhist Experience: Sources and Interpretation*, 99–115.

Bodhipathapradīpa (Atiśa). Ronald Davidson, 'Atiśa's *A Lamp for the Path to Awakening*', in Lopez (ed.), *Buddhism in Practice* (Princeton, 1995), 290–301; Richard Sherburne (trans.), *A Lamp for the Path and Commentary*, (London, 1983).

Buddhacarita (Aśvaghoṣa). E. H. Johnston (trans.), *The Buddhacarita or Acts of the Buddha*, 2 vols. (Calcutta, 1936).
Buddhavaṃsa-aṭṭhakathā (Madhuratthavilāsinī) (Buddhadatta). I. B. Horner (trans.), *The Clarifier of the Sweet Meaning* (London, 1978).
Catuṣpariṣat Sūtra. Ria Kloppenborg (trans.), *The Catuṣpariṣatsūtra: The Sūtra on the Foundation of the Buddhist Order: Relating to the Events from the Bodhisattva's Enlightenment up to the Conversion of Upatiṣya and Kolita*, (Leiden, 1979).
Ch'eng wei-shih lun (Hsüan-tsang). (1) Louis de La Vallée Poussin (trans.), *Vijñaptimātratāsiddhi: La Siddhi de Hiuan-Tsang*, 2 vols. (Paris, 1928–9). (2) Wei Tat (trans.), *Ch'eng Wei-Shih Lun: The Doctrine of Mere Consciousness by Hsüan Tsang* (Hong Kong, 1973).
Daśabhūmika Sūtra. Thomas Cleary (trans.), *The Flower Ornament Scripture*, ii (Boston, 1986).
Dhammapada-aṭṭhakathā (Buddhaghosa). Eugene Watson Burlingame (trans.), *Buddhist Legends Translated from the Original Pali Text of the Dhammapada Commentary*, 3 vols. (London, 1969).
Dhammasaṅgaṇi. C. A. F. Rhys Davids (trans.), *Buddhist Psychological Ethics* (London, 1900).
Dīgha Nikāya. Maurice Walshe, *The Long Discourses of the Buddha* (London, 1987).
Hsiu-hsi chih-kuan tso-ch'an fa-yao (Chih-i). Dwight Goddard (ed.), *A Buddhist Bible* (Boston, 1970), 437–96.
Jātaka. E. B. Cowell and *et al.* (trans.), *The Jātaka or the Stories of the Buddha's Former Births*, 6 vols. (London, 1895–1907).
Jātakamāla (Ārya Śūra). Peter Khoroche (trans.), *Once the Buddha Was a Monkey* (Chicago, 1989).
Kathāvatthu. C. A. F. Rhys Davids (trans.), *Points of Controversy* (London, 1915).
Lalitavistara Sūtra. Gwendolyn Bays (trans.), *The Lalitavistara Sūtra*, 2 vols. (Berkeley, 1983).
Lam rim chen mo (Tsong-kha-pa). Alex Wayman (trans.), *Calming the Mind and Discerning the Real: Buddhist Meditation and the Middle View* (New York, 1978).
Laṅkāvatāra Sūtra. D. T. Suzuki (trans.), *The Laṅkāvatārasūtra* (London, 1932).
Madhyāntavibhāga Śāstra (Vasubandhu). Stefan Anacker (trans.), *Seven Works of Vasubandhu*, (Delhi, 1984), 191–286.
**Mahāprajñāpāramitāśāstra* [Nāgārjuna?]. Étienne Lamotte (trans.), *Le Traité de la grande vertu de sagesse de Nāgārjuna*, 5 vols. (Louvain, 1944–80).

Mahāvaṃsa. Wilhelm Geiger (trans.), *Mahāvaṃsa: The Great Chronicle of Ceylon* (London, 1912).

Mahāvastu. John James Jones (trans.), *The Mahāvastu*, 3 vols. (London, 1949–56).

Mahāyānasaṅgraha (Asaṅga). (1) Étienne Lamotte (trans.), *La Somme du Grand Véhicule d'Asaṅga*, 2 vols. (Louvain, 1938–9). (2) John P. Keenan (trans.), *The Summary of the Great Vehicle by Bodhisattva Asaṅga* (Berkeley, 1992).

Mahāyānasūtrālaṃkāra (Asaṅga). Sylvain Lévi (trans.), *Exposé de la doctrine du Grand Véhicule selon le système Yogācāra*, 2 vols. (Paris, 1907–11).

Majjhima Nikāya. Bhikkhu Nāṇamoli and Bhikkhu Bodhi (trans.), *The Middle Length Discourses of the Buddha* (London, 1995).

Milindapañha. Isaline B. Horner (trans.), *Milinda's Questions* 2 vols. (London, 1963 4).

Mo-ho chih-kuan (Chih-i). Neal Donner and Daniel Stevenson (trans.), *The Great Calming and Contemplation: A Study and Annotated Translation of the First Chapter of Chih-i's Mo-ho Chih-kuan* (Honolulu, 1993).

Mūla-Madhyamaka-kārikā (Nāgārjuna). Kenneth K. Inada (trans.), *Nāgārjuna: A Translation of his Mūlamadhyamakakārikā* (Tokyo, 1970).

Nettippakaraṇa (Kaccāna). Bhikkhu Ñāṇamoli (trans.), *The Guide According to Kaccāna Thera* (London, 1962).

Nidānakathā. N. A. Jayawickrama (trans.), *The Story of Gotama Buddha: The Nidāna-Kathā of the Jātakaṭṭhakathā*, (Oxford, 1990).

Pañcaviṃśatisāhasrikā Prajñāpāramitā. Edward Conze (trans.), *The Large Sūtra on Perfect Wisdom with the Divisions of the Abhisamayālaṃkāra* (Delhi, 1979).

Paṭisambhidāmagga. Bhikkhu Ñāṇamoli (trans.), *The Path of Discrimination* (London, 1982).

Paṭṭhāna. U Nārada (trans.), *Conditional Relations*, 2 vols. (London, 1969–81).

Prajñāpāramitā-Hṛdaya Sūtra. Edward Conze, *Buddhist Wisdom Books: Containing* The Diamond Sūtra *and* The Heart Sūtra (London, 1958), 77–107; Conze, *Buddhist Scriptures*, 162–4.

Ṛg Veda. Wendy Doniger O'Flaherty, *The Rig Veda: An Anthology* (Harmondsworth, 1981).

Saṃdhinirmocana Sūtra. John Powers (trans.), *Wisdom of the Buddha: The Saṃdhinirmocana Mahāyāna Sūtra* (Berkeley, 1995).

**Satya-siddhi-śastra* (Harivarman). Aiyaswami Sastri, *Satyasiddhiśāstra of Harivarman* 2 vols (Baroda, 1975–8)
Śrāvakabhūmi [Asaṅga?]. Alex Wayman, *Analysis of the Śrāvakabhūmi Manuscript* (Berkeley, 1961).
Śrīmālādevī-siṃhanāda Sūtra. Alex Wayman and Hideko Wayman (trans.), *The Lion's Roar of Queen Śrīmālā: A Buddhist Scripture on the Tathāgatagarbha Theory* (New York, 1974).
Sukhāvatīvyūha Sūtras. Luis Gómez (trans.), *The Land of Bliss: The Paradise of the Buddha of Measureless Light: Sanskrit and Chinese Versions of the Sukhāvatīvyūha Sūtras* (Honolulu and Kyoto, 1996).
Sutta-Nipāta. H. Saddhatissa (trans.), *The Sutta-Nipata* (London, 1985).
Tathāgatagarbha Sūtra. William Grosnick, 'The *Tathāgatagarbha Sūtra*', in Donald Lopez (ed.), *Buddhism in Practice* (Princeton, 1995), 92–106.
Thar-pa rin-po-che'i rgyan (sGam-po-pa). Herbert Guenther (trans.), *The Jewel Ornament of Liberation* (London, 1970).
Theragāthā and Therīgāthā. K. R. Norman (trans.), *Elders' Verses*, 2 vols. (London, 1969–71).
Triṃśikā (Vasubandhu). Stefan Anacker (trans.), *Seven Works of Vasubandhu* (Delhi, 1984), 181–90.
Tri-Svabhāva-Nirdeśa (Vasubandhu). Stefan Anacker (trans.), *Seven Works of Vasubandhu* (Delhi, 1984), 287–97.
Udāna. Peter Masefield (trans.), *The Udāna* (Oxford, 1994).
Upaniṣads. Patrick Olivelle, *Upaniṣads* (Oxford, 1996).
Vajracchedikā Sūtra. Edward Conze, *Buddhist Wisdom Books: Containing* The Diamond Sūtra *and* The Heart Sūtra (London, 1958), 21–74.
Vibhaṅga. U Thiṭṭila (trans.), *The Book of Analysis* (London, 1969).
Vibhaṅga-aṭṭhakathā (Sammohavinodanī) [Buddhaghosa?]. Ñāṇamoli (trans.), *The Dispeller of Delusion*, 2 vols. (London, 1987–90).
Vimalakīrti-nirdeśa Sūtra. Étienne Lamotte (trans.), *The Teaching of Vimalakīrti* (London, 1976).
Viṃśatikā (Vasubandhu). Stefan Anacker (trans.), *Seven Works of Vasubandhu* (Delhi, 1984), 157–79.
**Vimuttimagga* (Upatissa). N. R. M. Ehara *et al.* (trans.), *The Path of Freedom* (Kandy, 1977).
Vinaya-Piṭaka. I. B. Horner (trans.), *The Book of the Discipline*, 6 vols. (Oxford, 1938–66).
Visuddhimagga (Buddhaghosa). Ñāṇamoli (trans.), *The Path of Purification* (Colombo, 1964).

General, introductory, and background

Basham, A. L., *The Wonder that Was India: A Survey of the History and Culture of the Indian Sub-continent before the Coming of the Muslims* (London, 1967).

Bechert, Heinz, and Gombrich, Richard (eds.), *The World of Buddhism: Buddhist Monks and Nuns in Society and Culture* (London, 1984).

Beyer, Stephan, *The Buddhist Experience: Sources and Interpretations* (Encino, Calif., 1974).

Conze, Edward, *Buddhist Scriptures* (Harmondsworth, 1959).

—— *Buddhist Thought in India* (London, 1962).

Cousins, L. S., 'Buddhism', in John R. Hinnells (ed.), *A Handbook of Living Religions* (Harmondsworth, 1984), 278–343.

Dundas, Paul, *The Jains* (London, 1992).

Gombrich, Richard, *Theravāda Buddhism: A Social History from Ancient Benares to Modern Colombo* (London, 1988).

Harvey, Peter, *An Introduction to Buddhism: Teachings, History and Practices* (Cambridge, 1990).

Kitagawa, Joseph M., and Cummings, Mark D. (eds.), *Buddhism and Asian History* (New York, 1989).

Lamotte, Étienne, *History of Indian Buddhism from the Origins to the Śaka Era* (Louvain, 1988).

Lopez, Donald S. (ed.), *Buddhism in Practice* (Princeton, 1995).

Nakamura, Hajime, *Indian Buddhism: A Survey with Bibliographical Notes* (Hirakata, 1980).

Norman, K. R., *Pāli Literature: Including the Canonical Literature in Prakrit and Sanskrit of all the Hīnayāna Schools of Buddhism* (Wiesbaden, 1983).

Prebish, Charles S. (ed.), *Buddhism: A Modern Perspective* (University Park, Pa., 1975).

Rahula, Walpola, *What the Buddha Taught* (London, 1967).

Renou, Louis and Jean Filliozat (ed.), *L'Inde classique: manuel des études indiennes* (Paris, 1947–53).

Robinson, Richard H., and Johnson, Willard L. *The Buddhist Religion: A Historical Introduction* (Belmont, Calif., 1982).

Saddhatissa, H., *The Buddha's Way* (London, 1971).

Warder, A. K., *Indian Buddhism* (Delhi, 1980).

Zwalf, W. (ed.), *Buddhism: Art and Faith* (London, 1985).

Chapter 1: The Story of the Buddha

Bareau, André, *Recherches sur la biographie du Buddha dans les Sūtrapiṭaka et les Vinayapiṭaka anciens* (Paris, 1963–71).

Beal, Samuel (trans.), *The Romantic Legend of Śākya Buddha: A Translation of the Chinese Version of the Abhiniṣkramaṇasūtra* (London, 1875).

Bechert, Heinz (ed.), *The Dating of the Historical Buddha/Die Datierung des historischen Buddha, Parts 1–2* (Göttingen, 1991–2).

Carrithers, M., *The Buddha* (Oxford, 1983).

Cousins, L. S., 'The Dating of the Historical Buddha: A Review Article', *Journal of the Royal Asiatic Society*, 6 (1996), 57–63.

Dallapiccola, Anne Libera (ed.), *The Stūpa: Its Religious, Historical and Architectural Significance* (Wiesbaden, 1980).

Herbert, Patricia, *The Life of the Buddha* (London, 1993).

Jayawickrama, N. A. (trans.), *The Story of Gotama Buddha: The Nidāna-Kathā of the Jātakaṭṭhakathā* (Oxford, 1990).

Nagao, Gadjin, 'The Life of the Buddha: An Interpretation', *The Eastern Buddhist*, 20 (1987), 1–31.

—— 'The Buddha's Life as Parable for Later Buddhist Thought', *The Eastern Buddhist*, 24 (1991), 1–32.

Ñāṇamoli, *The Life of the Buddha* (Kandy, 1992).

Pye, Michael, *The Buddha* (London, 1979).

Reynolds, Frank E., 'The Many Lives of Buddha: A Study of Sacred Biography and Theravāda Tradition', in Donald Capps and Frank E. Reynolds (eds.), *The Biographical Process: Studies in the History and Psychology of Religion* (The Hague, 1976), 37–61.

—— 'The Several Bodies of the Buddha: Reflections on a Neglected Aspect of Theravāda Tradition', *History of Religions*, 16 (1977), 374–89.

Rockhill, W. W., *The Life of the Buddha and the Early History of his Order Derived from Tibetan Works of the Bkah-hgyur and Bstan-Hgyur* (London, 1907).

Thich Nhat Hanh, *Old Paths, White Clouds: The Life Story of the Buddha* (London, 1992).

Thomas, Edward J., *The Life of the Buddha: As Legend and History* (London, 1949).

Chapter 2: The Word of the Buddha

Bareau, André, *Les sectes bouddhiques du petit véhicule* (Saigon, 1955).

Bechert, Heinz, 'The Importance of Aśoka's so-called Schism Edict', in L. A. Hercus *et al.* (eds.), *Indological and Buddhist Studies: Volume in Honour of Professor J. W. de Jong on his Sixtieth Birthday* (Canberra, 1982), 61–8.

Carter, John R., *Dhamma: Western Academic and Sinhalese Buddhist Interpretations: A Study of a Religious Concept* (Tokyo, 1978).

Collins, Steven, 'On The Very Idea of the Pāli Canon', *Journal of the Pali Text Society*, 15 (1990), 89–126.

—— 'Notes on Some Oral Aspects of Pali Literature', *Indo-Iranian Journal*, 35 (1992), 121–35.

Cousins, L. S., 'Pāli Oral Literature', in P. Denwood and A. Piatigorsky (eds.), *Buddhist Studies: Ancient and Modern* (London, 1983), 1–11.

—— 'The "Five Points" and the Origins of the Buddhist Schools', *The Buddhist Forum*, 2 (1991), 27–60.

Davidson, R. E., 'An Introduction to the Standards of Scriptural Authenticity in Indian Buddhism', in Robert E. Buswell (ed.), *Chinese Buddhist Apocrypha* (Honolulu, 1990), 291–325.

Galloway, Brian, ' "Thus Have I Heard: At One Time . . ." ', *Indo-Iranian Journal*, 34 (1991), 87–104.

Gethin, Rupert, 'The Mātikās: Memorization, Mindfulness and the List', in J. Gyatso (ed.), *In The Mirror of Memory: Reflections on Mindfulness and Remembrance in Indian and Tibetan Buddhism* (Albany, NY, 1992), 149–72.

Graham, William A., *Beyond the Written Word: Oral Aspects of Scripture in the History of Religion* (Cambridge, 1987).

Hallisey, Charles, 'Councils as Ideas and Events in the Theravāda', *The Buddhist Forum*, 3 (1991), 133–48.

Harrison, Paul, 'Who Gets to Ride in the Great Vehicle? Self-Image and Identity among the Followers of the Early Mahāyāna', *Journal of the International Association of Buddhist Studies*, 10 (1987), 67–89.

Hinüber, Oskar von, *A Handbook of Pāli Literature* (Berlin, 1996).

Lamotte, Étienne, 'The Assessment of Textual Authenticity in Buddhism', *Buddhist Studies Review*, 1 (1984), 4–15.

Lopez, Donald S. (ed.), *Buddhist Hermeneutics* (Honolulu, 1988).

McDermott, J. P., 'Scripture as Word of the Buddha', *Numen*, 31 (1984), 22–39.

McQueen, G., 'Inspired Speech in Mahāyāna Buddhism', *Religion*, 11–12 (1981–2), 303–19, 49–65.

Nattier, Janice J., and Prebish, Charles S., 'Mahāsāṃghika Origins: The Beginnings of Buddhist Sectarianism', *History of Religions*, 16 (1976), 237–72.

Norman, K. R., 'Aśoka's "Schism" Edict', *Collected Papers* III (Oxford, 1992), 191–218.

Prebish, Charles S., 'A Review of Scholarship on the Buddhist Councils', *Journal of Asian Studies*, 33 (1974), 239–54.

Schopen, Gregory, 'The Inscription on the Kuṣān Image of Amitābha and the Character of the Early Mahāyāna in India', *Journal of the International Association of Buddhist Studies*, 10 (1987), 99–137.

Chapter 3: Four Truths

Cousins, L. S., 'Nibbāna and Abhidhamma', *Buddhist Studies Review*, 1 (1984), 95–109.

Hallisey, Charles, 'Nibbānasutta: An Allegedly Non-Canonical Sutta on Nibbāna as a Great City', *Journal of the Pali Text Society*, 18 (1993), 97–130.

Norman, K. R., 'The Four Noble Truths: A Problem of Pāli Syntax', in L. A. Hercus *et al.* (eds.), *Indological and Buddhist Studies: Volume in Honour of Professor J. W. de Jong on his Sixtieth Birthday* (Canberra, 1982), 377–91.

—— 'Mistaken Ideas about Nibbāna', *The Buddhist Forum*, 3 (1994), 211–25.

Saddhatissa, Hammalawa, *Buddhist Ethics: Essence of Buddhism* (London, 1970).

Welbon, Guy, *The Buddhist Nirvāṇa and its Western Interpreters* (Chicago, 1968).

Wezler, A., 'On the Quadruple Division of the Yogaśāstra, the Caturvyūhatva of the Cikitsāśāstra and the "Four Noble Truths" of the Buddha', *Indologica Taurinensia*, 12 (1984), 291–337.

Chapter 4: The Buddhist Community

Banerjee, Anukul Chandra, *Sarvāstivāda Literature* (Calcutta, 1979).

Bartholomeusz, Tessa, *Women under the Bo Tree* (Cambridge, 1994).

Beal, Samuel (trans.), *The Life of Hiuen-tsiang by the Shamans Hwai li and Yen-tsing*, 1885).

Buswell, Robert E., *The Zen Monastic Experience: Buddhist Practice in Contemporary Korea* (Princeton, 1992).

Carrithers, Michael, *The Forest Monks of Sri Lanka: An Anthropological and Historical Study* (Delhi, 1983).

Dutt, Sukumar, *Buddhist Monks and Monasteries of India* (London, 1962).

Evers, H., *Monks, Priests and Peasants: A Study of Buddhism and Social Structure in Central Ceylon* (Leiden, 1972).

Foulk, T. Griffith, 'Daily Life in the Assembly', in Donald S. Lopez (ed.), *Buddhism in Practice* (Princeton, 1995), 455–72.

Gombrich, Richard, *Precept and Practice: Traditional Buddhism in the Rural Highlands of Ceylon* (Oxford, 1971).

Gombrich, Richard, 'The Monk in the Pāli Vinaya: Priest or Wedding Guest?', *Journal of the Pali Text Society*, 21 (1995), 193–7.

Gunawardana, R. A. L. H., *Robe and Plough: Monasticism and Economic Interest in Early Medieval Sri Lanka* (Tucson, Ariz., 1979).

Havnevik, Hanna, *Tibetan Buddhist Nuns: History, Cultural Norms and Social Reality* (Oslo, 1989).

Holt, John C., *Discipline: The Canonical Buddhism of the Vinayapiṭaka* (Delhi, 1981).

Huxley, Andrew S., 'The Vinaya: Legal System or Performance Enhancing Drug', *The Buddhist Forum*, 4 (1996), 141–63.

Hyer, Paul, and Jagchid, Sechin, *A Mongolian Living Buddha: Biography of the Kanjurwa Khutughtu* (Albany, NY, 1983).

Joshi, Lal Mani, *Studies in the Buddhistic Culture of India During the 7th and 8th Centuries* A.D. (Delhi, 1977).

Kamala Tiyavanich, *Forest Recollections: Wandering Monks in Twentieth Century Thailand* (Honolulu, 1997).

Legge, James (trans.), *A Record of Buddhist Kingdoms* (Oxford, 1886).

Miller, Robert James, *Monasteries and Culture Change in Inner Mongolia* (Wiesbaden, 1959).

Prebish, Charles S., *Buddhist Monastic Discipline: The Sanskrit Prātimokṣa Sūtras of the Mahāsāṃghikas and Mūlasarvāstivādins* (University Park, Pa., and London, 1975).

Rabten, Geshe, *The Life and Teaching of Geshe Rabten: A Tibetan Lama's Search for Truth* (London, 1980).

Rahula, Walpola, *History of Buddhism in Ceylon: The Anurādhapura Period* (Colombo, 1956).

Ray, Reginald, *Buddhist Saints in India: A Study in Buddhist Values and Orientations* (New York, 1994).

Schopen, Gregory, 'Deaths, Funerals, and the Division of Property in a Monastic Code', in Donald S. Lopez (ed.), *Buddhism in Practice* (Princeton, 1995), 473–502.

—— *Bones, Stones, and Buddhist Monks: Collected Papers on the Archaeology, Epigraphy, and Texts of Monastic Buddhism in India* (Honolulu, 1997).

Seneviratna, Anuradha (ed.), *King Aśoka and Buddhism: Historical and Literary Studies* (Kandy, 1994).

Spiro, Melford E., *Buddhism and Society: A Great Tradition and its Burmese Vicissitudes* (Berkeley, 1982).

Takakusu, J. (trans.), *A Record of the Buddhist Religion as Practised in India and the Malay Archipelago (*A.D. *671–695)* (Oxford, 1896).

Tambiah, Stanley J., *World Conqueror and World Renouncer* (Cambridge, 1976).
—— *The Buddhist Saints of the Forest and the Cult of Amulets* (Cambridge, 1984).
Tsai, Kathryn Ann (trans.), *The Lives of the Nuns: Biographies of Chinese Buddhist Nuns from the Fourth to Sixth Centuries: A Translation of the Pi-ch'iu-ni chuan compiled by Shih Pao-ch'ang* (Honolulu, 1994).
Welch, Holmes, *The Practice of Chinese Buddhism 1900–1950* (Cambridge, Mass., 1967).
Wijayaratna, Mohan, *Buddhist Monastic Life: According to the Texts of the Theravāda Tradition* (Cambridge, 1990).

Chapter 5: The Buddhist Cosmos

Boyd, J. W., *Satan and Māra: Christian and Buddhist Symbols of Evil* (Leiden, 1975).
Fuller, Christopher John, *The Camphor Flame: Popular Hinduism and Society in India* (Princeton, 1992).
Gethin, Rupert, 'Meditation and Cosmology: From the Aggañña Sutta to the Mahāyāna' *History of Religions*, 36 (1997), 183–219.
Gombrich, Richard, *Precept and Practice: Traditional Buddhism in the Rural Highlands of Ceylon* (Oxford, 1971).
—— 'Buddhism and Society', *Modern Asian Studies*, 6 (1972), 483–94.
—— 'Ancient Indian Cosmology', in C. Blacker and M. Loewe (eds.), *Ancient Cosmologies* (London, 1975), 110–42.
Kirfel, W., *Die Kosmographie der Inder* (Bonn and Leipzig, 1920).
Kloetzli, R., *Buddhist Cosmology: From Single World System to Pure Land* (Delhi, 1983).
Kongtrul, Jamgön (Lödrö Tayé), *Myriad Worlds: Buddhist Cosmology in Abhidharma, Kālacakra and Dzog-chen* (Ithaca, NY, 1995).
Ling, T. O., *Buddhism and the Mythology of Evil: A Study in Theravāda Buddhism* (London, 1962).
Marasinghe, M. M. J., *Gods in Early Buddhism: A Study in Their Social and Mythological Milieu as Depicted in the Nikāyas of the Pāli Canon* (Vidyalankara, 1974).
Masson, Joseph, *La Religion populaire dans le canon bouddhique pāli* (Louvain, 1942).
Reynolds, F. E., and Reynolds, M. B. (trans.), *Three Worlds according to King Ruang: A Thai Buddhist Cosmology*, (Berkeley, 1982).

Sadakata, Akira, *Buddhist Cosmology: Philosophy and Origins* (Tokyo, 1997).

Spiro, Melford E., *Burmese Supernaturalism: A Study in the Explanation and Reduction of Suffering* (Englewood Cliffs, NJ, 1967).

Tambiah, Stanley J., *Buddhism and the Spirit Cults in North-East Thailand* (Cambridge, 1970).

Chapter 6: No Self

Bodhi, Bhikkhu, 'Transcendental Dependent Arising', *The Wheel*, 277/8 (Kandy, 1980).

Collins, S., *Selfless Persons: Imagery and Thought in Theravāda Buddhism* (Cambridge, 1982).

Cox, Collet, 'Dependent Origination: Its Elaboration in Early Sarvāstivādin Abhidharma Texts', in Ram Karan Sharma (ed.), *Researches in Indian Philosophy: Essays in Honour of Professor Alex Wayman* (Delhi, 1993), 119–41.

Gethin, R. M. L., 'The Five Khandhas: Their Treatment in the Nikāyas and Early Abhidhamma', *Journal of Indian Philosophy*, 14 (1986), 35–53.

Hamilton, Sue, *Identity and Experience: The Constitution of the Human Being According to Early Buddhism* (London, 1996).

Lesser, A. H., 'Eastern and Western Empiricism and the "No Self" Theory', *Religious Studies*, 15 (1979), 55–64.

Norman, K. R., 'A Note on *attā* in the *Alagaddūpama-sutta*' in *Collected Papers*, ii (Oxford, 1991), 200–9.

Nyanatiloka, 'The Significance of Dependent Origination in Theravāda Buddhism', *The Wheel*, 140 (Kandy, 1969).

Wayman, Alex, 'The Twenty Reifying Views (sakkāyadiṭṭhi)', in Narain A. K. (ed.), *Studies in Pali and Buddhism: A Memorial Volume in Honor of Bhikkhu Jagdish Kashyap* (Delhi, 1979), 375–80.

Chapter 7: The Buddhist Path

Aronson, Harvey B., *Love and Sympathy in Theravāda Buddhism* (Delhi, 1980).

Bronkhorst, Johannes, *The Two Traditions of Meditation in Ancient India* (New Delhi, 1993).

Buswell, Robert E., and Gimello, Robert M. (eds.), *Paths to Liberation: The Mārga and its Transformation in Buddhist Thought* (Honolulu, 1992).

Cousins, L. S., 'Buddhist *Jhāna*: Its Nature and Attainment according to the Pāli Sources', *Religion*, 3 (1973), 115–31.

—— 'Samatha-Yāna and Vipassanā-Yāna', in G. Dhammapala *et al.* (eds.), *Buddhist Studies in Honour of Hammalava Saddhātissa* (Nugegoda, 1984), 56–68.

—— 'Vitakka/Vitarka and Vicāra: Stages of Samādhi in Buddhism and Yoga', *Indo-Iranian Journal*, 35 (1992), 137–57.

—— 'The Origins of Insight Meditation', *The Buddhist Forum*, 4 (1996), 35–58.

Endo, Toshiichi, *Dāna: The Development of its Concepts and Practice* (Colombo, 1987).

Gethin, Rupert, *The Buddhist Path to Awakening: A Study of the Bodhi-Pakkhiyā Dhammā* (Leiden, 1992).

Gombrich, Richard F., 'From Monastery to Meditation Centre: Lay Meditation in Modern Sri Lanka', in Philip Denwood and Alexander Piatigorsky (eds.), *Buddhist Studies Ancient and Modern* (London, 1983), 20–34.

Gómez, Luis O., 'The Bodhisattva as Wonder Worker', in Lewis Lancaster (ed.), *Prajnaparamita and Related Systems: Studies in Honor of Edward Conze* (Berkeley, 1977), 221–61.

Griffiths, Paul, 'Concentration or Insight: The Problematic of Theravāda Buddhist Meditation-Theory', *Journal of the American Academy of Religion*, 49 (1981), 605–24.

King, W. L., *Theravāda Meditation: The Buddhist Transformation of Yoga* (University Park, Pa., 1980).

La Vallée Poussin, Louis de, 'A Summary Note on the Path', in *Abhidharmakośabhāṣyam*, translated from the French by Leo M. Pruden (Berkeley, 1989), III, pp. xiv–xxii.

Lati Rinbochay, *et al.*, *Meditative States in Tibetan Buddhism* (London, 1983).

Lodrö, Geshe Gedün, *Walking through Walls: A Presentation of Tibetan Meditation* (Ithaca, NY, 1992).

Pranke, Patrick, 'On Becoming a Buddhist Wizard', in Donald S. Lopez (ed.), *Buddhism in Practice* (Princeton, 1995), 343–58.

Ruegg, David Seyfort, 'Ahimsā and Vegetarianism in the History of Buddhism', in Somaratna Balasooriya *et al.* (eds.), *Buddhist Studies in Honour of Walpola Rahula* (London, 1980), 234–41.

Skilling, Peter, 'The Rakṣā Literature of the Śrāvakayāna', *Journal of the Pali Text Society*, 16 (1992), 109–82.

Swearer, Donald K., 'The Way of Meditation', in Donald S. Lopez (ed.), *Buddhism in Practice* (Princeton, 1995), 207–15.

Vetter, Tilmann, *The Ideas and Meditative Practices of Early Buddhism* (Leiden, 1988).

Chapter 8: The Abhidharma

Cousins, L. S., 'The Paṭṭhāna and the Development of the Theravādin Abhidhamma', *Journal of the Pali Text Society*, (1981), 22–46.

—— 'Person and Self', in *Buddhism into the Year 2000: International Conference Proceedings* (Bangkok and Los Angeles, 1994), 15–32.

Cox, Collett, *Disputed Dharmas: Early Buddhist Theories on Existence: An Annotated Translation of the Section on Factors Dissociated from Thought from Saṅghabhadra's Nyāyānusāra* (Tokyo, 1995).

Frauwallner, Erich, *Studies in Abhidharma Literature and the Origins of Buddhist Philosophical Systems* (Albany, NY, 1995).

Gethin, Rupert, '*Bhavaṅga* and Rebirth according to the Abhidhamma', *The Buddhist Forum*, 3 (1994), 11–35.

Gorkom, Nina van, *Abhidhamma in Daily Life* (London, 1990).

Govinda, Lama Anagarika, *The Psychological Attitude of Early Buddhist Philosophy and its Systematic Representation according to Abhidhamma Tradition* (London, 1969).

Guenther, Herbert V., *Philosophy and Psychology in the Abhidharma* (Berkeley, 1976).

Jaini, Padmanabh S., 'The Sautrāntika Theory of *Bīja*', *Bulletin of the School of Oriental Studies*, 22 (1959), 237–49.

—— 'The Development of the Theory of the *Viprayukta-Saṃskāras*', *Bulletin of the School of Oriental and African Studies*, 22 (1959), 531–47.

—— 'The Vaibhāṣika Theory of Words and Meanings', *Bulletin of the School of Oriental and African Studies*, 22 (1959), 95–107.

—— '*Prajñā* and *dṛṣṭi* in the Vaibhāṣika Abhidharma', in Lewis Lancaster (ed.), *Prajñāpāramitā and Related Systems: Studies in Honor of Edward Conze* (Berkeley, 1977), 403–15.

Jayasuriya, W. F., *The Psychology and Philosophy of Buddhism: An Introduction to the Abhidhamma* (Kuala Lumpur, 1976).

Karunadasa, Y., *The Buddhist Analysis of Matter* (Colombo, 1967).

Nyanaponika Thera, *Abhidhamma Studies: Researches in Buddhist Psychology* (Kandy, 1976).

Nyanatiloka Mahāthera, *Guide through the Abhidhamma Piṭaka* (Kandy, 1971).

Potter, Karl H. (ed.), *Abhidharma Buddhism to 150 A.D.* (Delhi, 1996).

Rowlands, Mark (ed.), *Abhidhamma Papers* (Manchester, 1982).

Takakusu, Junjiro, 'The Abhidharma Literature of the Sarvāstivādins', *Journal of the Pali Text Society*, 5 (1905), 67–146.

Wayman, Alex, 'The Intermediate-State Dispute in Buddhism', in L. S. Cousins *et al.* (eds.), *Buddhist Studies in Honour of I. B. Horner* (Dordrecht, 1974), 227–39.

Williams, Paul, 'Buddhadeva and Temporality', *Journal of Indian Philosophy*, 4 (1977), 279–94.

—— 'On the Abhidharma Ontology', *Journal of Indian Philosophy*, 9 (1981), 227–57.

Chapter 9: The Mahāyāna

Dayal, Har, *The Bodhisattva Doctrine in Buddhist Sanskrit Literature* (London, 1932).

Gombrich, Richard F., 'How the Mahāyāna Began', *The Buddhist Forum*, 1 (London, 1990), 21–30.

Griffiths, Paul J., *On Being Mindless: Buddhist Meditation and the Mind–Body Problem* (La Salle, Ill. 1986).

—— *On Being Buddha: The Classical Doctrine of Buddhahood* (Albany, NY, 1994).

Harrison, Paul, 'Who Gets to Ride in the Great Vehicle? Self-Image and Identity among the Followers of the Early Mahāyāna', *Journal of the International Association of Buddhist Studies*, 10 (1987), 67–89.

—— 'Searching for the Origins of the Mahāyāna: What are we Looking for?', *Eastern Buddhist*, 28 (1995), 48–69.

Hayes, Richard, 'Nāgārjuna's Appeal', *Journal of Indian Philosophy*, 22 (1994), 299–378.

Hopkins, Jeffrey, *Meditation on Emptiness* (London, 1983).

Huntington, C. W., *The Emptiness of Emptiness: An Introduction to Early Indian Mādhyamika* (Honolulu, 1989).

Lancaster, Lewis, 'The Oldest Mahāyāna Sūtra: Its Significance for the Study of Buddhist Development', *Eastern Buddhist*, 8 (1975), 30–41.

Lopez, Donald S., 'Do *Śrāvakas* Understand Emptiness?', *Journal of Indian Philosophy*, 16 (1988), 65–105.

—— 'Sanctification on the Bodhisattva Path', in Richard Kieckhefer and George D. Bond (eds.), *Sainthood: Its Manifestations in World Religions* (Berkeley, 1988), 172–217.

Matilal, Bimal Krishna, 'A Critique of Indian Idealism', in L. S. Cousins *et al.* (eds.), *Buddhist Studies in Honour of I. B. Horner* (Dordrecht, 1974), 139–58.

Napper, Elizabeth, *Dependent-Arising and Emptiness: A Tibetan Buddhist Interpretation of Mādhyamika Philosophy Emphasizing the Compatibility of Emptiness and Conventional Phenomena* (London, 1989).
Pagel, Ulrich, *The Bodhisattvapiṭaka: Its Doctrines and their Position in Mahāyāna Literature* (Tring, Herts. 1995).
Pye, Michael, *Skilful Means* (London, 1978).
Ruegg, David Seyfort, *La Théorie du tathāgatgarbha et du gotra: études sur la sotériologie et du gnoséologie du bouddhisme* (Paris, 1969).
—— *The Literature of the Madhyamaka School of Philosophy in India* (Wiesbaden, 1981).
—— *Buddha-nature, Mind and the Problem of Gradualism in a Comparative Perspective* (London, 1989).
Schopen, Gregory, 'The Phrase "*sa pṛthivīpradeśaś caityabhūto bhavet*" in the *Vajracchedikā*: Notes on the Cult of the Book in Mahāyāna', *Indo-Iranian Journal*, 17 (1975), 147–81.
—— 'Mahāyāna in Indian Inscriptions', *Indo-Iranian Journal*, 21 (1979), 1–19.
Sponberg, Alan, and Hardacre, Helen (eds.), *Maitreya: The Future Buddha* (Cambridge, 1988).
Streng, Frederick J., *Emptiness: A Study in Religious Meaning* (New York, 1967).
Tuck, Andrew P., *Comparative Philosophy and the Philosophy of Scholarship: On the Western Interpretation of Nāgārjuna* (Oxford, 1990).
Williams, Paul M., *Mahāyāna Buddhism: The Doctrinal Foundations* (London, 1989).

Chapter 10: Evolving Traditions

Almond, P., *The British Discovery of Buddhism* (Cambridge, 1988).
Batchelor, Stephen, *The Awakening of the West: The Encounter of Buddhism and Western Culture* (London, 1994).
Baumann, Martin, 'The Dharma has Come West: A Survey of Recent Studies and Sources', *Journal of Buddhist Ethics*, 4 (1997), 194–211. Electronic journal: *http://www.gold.ac.uk* (UK address); *http://jbe.la.psu.edu* (USA address).
Chang Chung-yuan, *Original Teachings of Ch'an Buddhism* (New York, 1971).
Chang, Garma C. C., *The Buddhist Teaching of Totality: The Philosophy of Hwa-yen Buddhism* (London, 1972).

Ch'en, Kenneth, 'The Tibetan Tripiṭaka', *Harvard Journal of Asian Studies*, 9 (1945–7), 53–62.

—— *Buddism in China: A Historical Survey* (Princeton, 1964).

Cook, Francis H., *Hua-yen Buddhism: The Jewel Net of Indra* (University Park, Pa., 1977).

Cousins, L. S., 'Aspects of Esoteric Southern Buddhism', in Peter Connolly and Sue Hamilton (eds.), *Indian Insights: Buddhism, Brahmanism and Bhakti* (London, 1997), 185–207.

De Silva, Lynn, *Buddhism: Beliefs and Practices in Sri Lanka* (Colombo, 1980).

Dumoulin, Heinrich, *A History of Zen Buddhism* (London, 1963).

Gombrich, Richard F., and Obeyesekere, Gananath, *Buddhism Transformed: Religious Change in Sri Lanka* (Princeton, 1988).

Hakeda, Yoshito S., *Kūkai: Major Works: Translated with an Account of his Life and a Study of his Thought* (New York, 1972).

Hurvitz, Leon, 'Chin-i (538–597): An Introduction to the Life and Ideas of a Chinese Buddhist Monk', *Mélanges Chinois et Bouddhiques*, 12 (1963), 1–372.

de Jong, J. W., *A Brief History of Buddhist Studies in Europe and America* (Varanasi, 1976).

Lancaster, Lewis R. (ed.), *Introduction of Buddhism to Korea: New Cultural Perspectives* (Berkeley, 1989).

—— (ed.), *Assimilation of Buddhism in Korea: Religious Maturity and Innovation in the Silla Dynasty* (Berkely, 1991).

Ling, Trevor O., *Buddhist Revival in India: Aspects of the Sociology of Buddhism* (London, 1980).

Lopez, Donald S., *Curators of the Buddha: The Study of Buddhism under Colonialism* (Chicago, 1995).

Matsunaga, Daigan, and Matsunaga, Alicia, *Foundation of Japanese Buddhism*, 2 vols. (Tokyo, 1974–6).

Mellor, Philip A., 'Protestant Buddhism? The Cultural Translation of Buddhism in England', *Religion*, 21 (1991), 73–92.

Nanjio, Bunyiu, *A Catalogue of the Chinese Translation of the Buddhist Tripiṭaka: The Sacred Canon of the Buddhists in China and Japan* (Oxford, 1883).

Nattier, Jan, *Once Upon a Future Time: Studies in a Buddhist Prophecy of Decline* (Berkeley, 1991).

Powers, John, *Introduction to Tibetan Buddhism* (Ithaca, NY, 1995).

Samuel, Geoffrey, *Civilized Shamans: Buddhism in Tibetan Societies* (Washington, DC, 1993).

Snellgrove, David L., *Indo-Tibetan Buddhism: Indian Buddhists and their Tibetan Successors* (London, 1987).
Swanson, Paul L., *Foundations of T'ien T'ai Philosophy: The Flowering of the Two Truths Theory in Chinese Buddhism* (Berkeley, 1989).
Tucci, Giuseppe, *The Religions of Tibet* (London, 1980).
Welch, Holmes, *The Buddhist Revival in China* (Cambridge, Mass., 1968).
—— *Buddhism under Mao* (Cambridge, Mass., 1972).

Glossary of Technical Terms and Names

Abhidharma/Abhidhamma 'higher teaching'; one of the three main divisions of the ancient Buddhist canon

Ābhidharmika/Ābhidhammika a specialist in Abhidharma

Āgama a division of the Sūtra Piṭaka section of the ancient Buddhist canon (= Nikāya)

aggregate (*skandha/khandha*) the five aggregates (physical form, feeling, recognition, other mental forces, consciousness) that together constitute a living being

akuśala/akusala bad, unskilful, unwholesome

Ānanda one of the Buddha's principal disciples; his attendant

anātman/anattā 'not self'; the Buddhist denial of a permanent and substantial self

arhat/arahat an awakened Buddhist saint; cf. *śrāvaka*

Asaṅga *c.*4th-century CE Indian Buddhist thinker associated with the Yogācāra school of thought

Aśoka/Asoka Indian emperor who reigned *c.*268–232 BCE and was a patron of Buddhism

ātman/attā 'self'

aṭṭhakathā a primary Pali commentary to a text of the Buddhist canon

Bhagavat 'the Blessed One', 'the Lord'; an epithet of the Buddha

bhāṣya an exegetical commentary

bhāvanā '(mental/spiritual) development'; Buddhist meditation

bhikṣu/bhikkhu a Buddhist monk

bhikṣuṇī/bhikkhunī a Buddhist nun

bodhisattva/bodhisatta one on the path to Buddhahood

Brahmā a class of high gods

Buddhaghosa 5th-century CE compiler and author of Pali commentarial and exegetical works associated with the Theravāda school

dependent arising (*pratītyasamutpāda/paṭiccasamuppāda*) the Buddhist doctrine of causality

deva a god

Dharma/Dhamma the underlying law of reality; the teaching of the Buddha

dharmas/dhammas the mental and physical phenomena, or the teachings, that constitute Dharma

dhyāna/jhāna a meditation attainment

duḥkha/dukkha 'pain'; the unease or unsatisfactoriness which characterizes existence

karma/kamma good and bad actions of body, speech, and mind whose pleasant and unpleasant results are experienced in this and subsequent lives

kuśala/kusala good, skilful, wholesome

Madhyamaka 'the middle'; alongside Yogācāra, one of the two principal schools of Mahāyāna Buddhist thought

Mādhyamika a follower of Madhyamaka (q.v.)

Mahāsāṃghika 'a follower of the great community', an ancient Buddhist school

Mahāyāna 'great vehicle'; a broad school of Buddhism

Mantrayāna 'the secret spell vehicle', commonly referred to as Tantric Buddhism

Māra the tempter figure in Buddhist mythology

Maudgalyāyana/Moggallāna the disciple of the Buddha regarded as chief in meditational powers

Nāgārjuna *c.*2nd-century CE Buddhist thinker associated with the Madhyamaka school of thought

never-returner (*sakṛd-/sakad-āgāmin*) one who has attained the third of the four noble paths culminating in arhatship

Nikāya a division of the Sūtra Piṭaka section of the ancient Buddhist canon (= Āgama)

nirvāṇa/nibbāna the 'blowing out' of the fires of greed, hatred, and delusion; the ultimate goal of Buddhist practice; the unconditioned

once returner (*anāgāmin*) one who has attained the second of the four noble paths culminating in arhatship

parinirvāṇa/parinibbāna the final death of a buddha or arhat; or another term for nirvāṇa (q.v.)

prajñā/paññā 'wisdom', 'understanding' (Buddhist meditation), cf. *Śamatha*

Prajñāpāramitā 'perfection of wisdom'; a class of Mahāyāna Buddhist literature

prātimokṣa/pāṭimokkha the Buddhist monastic rule contained in the Vinaya

pratyeka-buddha/pacceka-buddha a solitary buddha (as distinct from a *samyak-sambuddha*)

Pudgalavādin a follower of the Pudgalavāda or 'teaching that the person exists'; an ancient Buddhist school

puṇya/puñña 'merit'; auspicious and fortunate karma
samādhi 'concentration', cf. *dhyāna*
śamatha/samatha 'calm' (one of two main types of Buddhist meditation); cf. *vipaśyana*
saṃsāra the round of rebirth
samyak-sambuddha/sammā-sambuddha a perfectly awakened one as distinct from a *śrāvaka* or *pratyeka-buddha*
Saṅgha the Buddhist monastic order of monks and nuns
Śāriputra/Sāriputta the disciple of the Buddha regarded as chief in wisdom
Sarvāstivādin a follower of the Sarvāstivāda or 'teaching that all exists'; a Buddhist school
śāstra a commentarial or exegetical manual as distinct from the 'word of the Buddha' contained in the sūtras
Sautrāntika 'a follower of the Sūtras'; a school of thought which denied the authority of the Sarvāstivādin Abhidharma
śīla/sīla ethics, good conduct
śrāvaka/sāvaka 'hearer'; a disciple of the Buddha as distinct from one following the bodhisattva path to full buddhahood of the *samyak-sambuddha*
stream-attainer (*srotāpanna/sotāpanna*) one who has attained the first of the four noble paths culminating in arhatship
śūnyatā/suññatā 'emptiness'; a Buddhist spiritual term used to characterize the ultimate nature of things
sūtra/sutta a discourse attributed to the Buddha; one of the three main divisions of the ancient Buddhist canon
tantra a class of esoteric ritual and meditational Buddhist texts used in Vajrayāna/Mantrayāna Buddhism
Tathāgata 'the thus gone/come'; an epithet of the Buddha
Theravādin a follower of the Theravāda or 'teaching of the elders'; a Buddhist school
ṭīkā a subcommentary
Tripiṭaka/Tipiṭaka 'three baskets' (= the three basic divisions of the ancient Buddhist canon)
Tuṣita/Tusita the heaven of 'the Contented' where the bodhisattva awaits the appropriate time to take birth as a human being before finally becoming a buddha
Upaniṣads a set of sacred brahmanical texts included in the Veda
upāsaka male lay follower
upāsikā female lay follower

Vaibhāṣika a follower of the teaching of the *Mahāvibhāṣā*, a commentary on the Sarvāstivādin Abhidharma

Vajrayāna 'the diamond/thunderbolt vehicle', commonly referred to as tantric Buddhism

Vasubandhu (the Elder) *c.*4th-century CE Indian Buddhist thinker associated with the Yogācāra school of thought; by tradition the same as Vasubandhu the Younger

Vasubandhu (the Younger) *c.*5th-century CE Indian Buddhist thinker, author of the *Abhidharmakośa*, a compendium of Vaibhāṣika/Sautrāntika thought; by tradition the same as Vasubandhu the Elder

Veda the corpus of sacred brahmanical texts

vijñapti-mātra the idealist doctrine of 'ideas only'

Vinaya '(monastic) discipline'; one of the three main divisions of the ancient Buddhist canon

vipaśyanā/vipassanā 'insight' (one of two main types of Buddhist meditation); cf. *śamatha*

Yogācāra 'yoga practice'; alongside Madhyamaka, one of the two principal schools of Mahāyāna Buddhist thought; also known as *citta-mātra/vijñapti-mātra*

Index